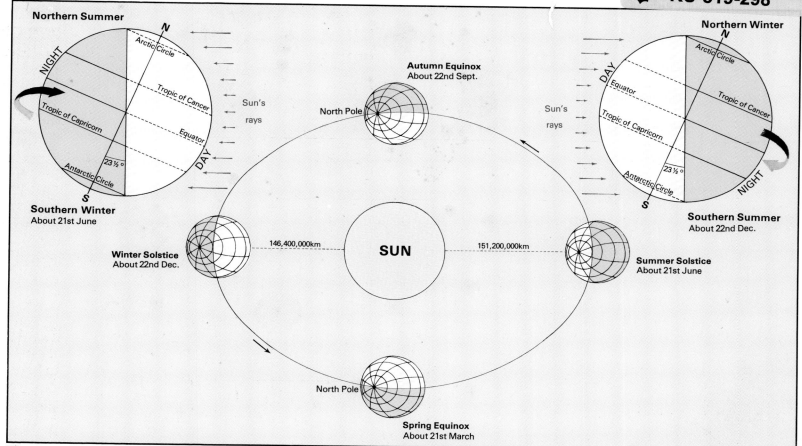

Northern Summer

NIGHT — DAY
Arctic Circle
Tropic of Cancer
Tropic of Capricorn
Equator
23½°
Antarctic Circle
N
S

Southern Winter
About 21st June

Northern Winter

DAY
Arctic Circle
Equator
Tropic of Capricorn
Tropic of Cancer
23½°
Antarctic Circle
NIGHT
N
S

Southern Summer
About 22nd Dec.

Sun's rays

Autumn Equinox
About 22nd Sept.

North Pole

SUN

146,400,000km   151,200,000km

Winter Solstice
About 22nd Dec.

Summer Solstice
About 21st June

North Pole

Spring Equinox
About 21st March

4 THE ATTITUDE OF THE EARTH TO THE SUN – SUMMER AND WINTER

Not to scale

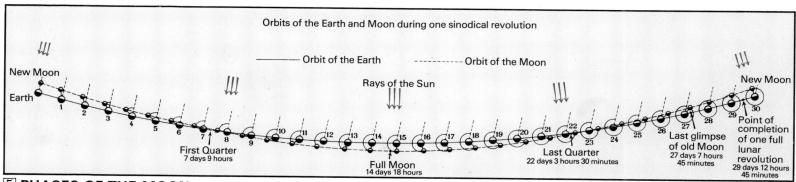

Orbits of the Earth and Moon during one sinodical revolution

—— Orbit of the Earth   - - - Orbit of the Moon

Rays of the Sun

New Moon
Earth

1 2 3 4 5 6 7 8 9 10 11 12 13 14 15 16 17 18 19 20 21 22 23 24 25 26 27 28 29 30

New Moon

First Quarter
7 days 9 hours

Full Moon
14 days 18 hours

Last Quarter
22 days 3 hours 30 minutes

Last glimpse of old Moon
27 days 7 hours 45 minutes

Point of completion of one full lunar revolution
29 days 12 hours 45 minutes

5 PHASES OF THE MOON

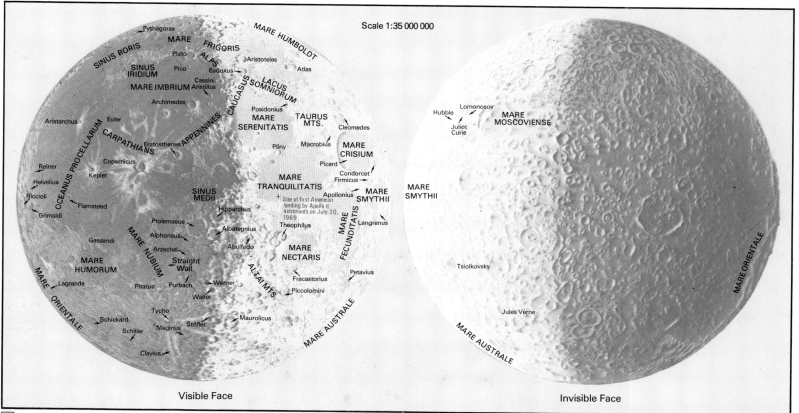

Scale 1:35 000 000

Pythagoras
SINUS RORIS
MARE FRIGORIS
Plato
ALPS
Pico
SINUS IRIDIUM
Cassini
Aristillus
MARE IMBRIUM
Archimedes
Aristarchus
Euler
OCEANUS PROCELLARUM
CARPATHIANS
Eratosthenes
APPENNINES
Reiner
Copernicus
Kepler
Helvelius
Riccioli
Flamsteed
Grimaldi
SINUS MEDII
Ptolemaeus
Hipparchus
Alphonsus
Arzachel
SINUS NUBIUM
MARE NUBIUM
Straight Wall
Gassendi
MARE HUMORUM
Lagrande
Pitatus
Purbach
Werner
Walter
MARE ORIENTALE
Schickard
Schiller
Tycho
Maginus
Stöfler
Clavius

MARE HUMBOLDT
Aristoteles
Atlas
Eudoxus
LACUS SOMNIORUM
CAUCASUS
Posidonius
MARE SERENITATIS
TAURUS MTS.
Pliny
Macrobius
Cleomedes
MARE CRISIUM
Picard
Condorcet
Firmicus
MARE TRANQUILITATIS
+ Site of first American landing by Apollo 11 astronauts on July 20, 1969
Apollonius
MARE SMYTHII
Albategnius
Theophilus
Abulfedo
MARE FECUNDITATIS
Langrenus
MARE NECTARIS
ALTAI MTS.
Fracastorius
Piccolomini
Petavius
Maurolicus
MARE AUSTRALE

Hubble
Lomonosov
Juliot Curie
MARE MOSCOVIENSE
MARE SMYTHII
MARE ORIENTALE
Tsiolkovsky
Jules Verne
MARE AUSTRALE

Visible Face   Invisible Face

6 THE MOON

Graphic Atlas
of the World

Graphic Atlas
of the World

NATIONWIDE BOOK SERVICE

⊕ BARTHOLOMEW

ISBN 0 7028 0267 0

7815x
Printed and published in Scotland by
John Bartholomew & Son Limited, Edinburgh

John Bartholomew & Son Ltd.,
Duncan Street,
Edinburgh,
EH9 1TA
Scotland

This edition published 1980 by Nationwide Book Service
by arrangement with John Bartholomew & Son Ltd

BARTHOLOMEW ✪ ESSELTE MAP SERVICE

Contents

THE SOLAR SYSTEM

1 The Sun's family
2 Relative sizes of the Sun and the planets
3 Important facts about the Sun and the planets
4 The attitude of the Earth to the Sun—summer and winter
5 Phases of the Moon
6 The Moon

THE WORLD

Page

2-3   ENVIRONMENT
Geographical environment

4-5   CLIMATE
1 Precipitation, pressure, winds—January
2 Precipitation, pressure, winds—July
3 Annual precipitation
4 Temperature, ocean currents—January
5 Temperature, ocean currents—July
6 Climate in relation to plant growth

6-7   GEOLOGY
Solid geology and timescale
Inset maps:
1 Continental drift
2 Plate tectonics
3 Mountain building
4 Earthquakes and volcanoes

8-9   THE OCEANS
Ocean basins and their structure
Inset maps:
1 Fishing
2 Major storm areas

10-11   POPULATION
Population distribution, population increase
Inset cartograms:
1 Population increase
2 Calorie consumption
3 Animal protein consumption
4 Literacy

12-13   POLITICAL
Countries of the World
Inset maps:
1 Military politics
2 Trade politics

14-15   ENERGY
Distribution of fuel and energy sources
Inset maps:
1 Oil production, consumption, sea transport
2 Coal production, consumption
3 Production of energy
4 Consumption of energy

16-17   ECONOMY
Principal products
THE WORLD IN DIFFERENT MAP
PROJECTIONS: see back end-papers

EUROPE

18-19   EUROPE, environment, political divisions, population
Main map—environment
Inset maps:
1 Political divisions
2 Population

20-21   EUROPE, physical, economic
1 Organic production
2 Inorganic production
3 Relief
4 Annual rainfall, ocean currents
5 Temperature, winds—January
6 Temperature, winds—July
7 Climate in relation to plant growth
8 Soils

BRITISH ISLES

22-23 SCOTLAND, environment
24-25 CENTRAL UNITED KINGDOM, environment
26-27 SOUTHERN UNITED KINGDOM, environment
28-29 BRITISH ISLES, geology, soils, physical regions
  1 Solid Geology
  2 Pleistocene drift, and ice limits
  3 Soils
  4 Physical regions
  5 Profiles of three common soils
30-31 BRITISH ISLES, climate, relief
  1 Temperature—January
  2 Temperature—July
  3 Temperature regions
  4 Prevailing winds
  5 Snow cover
  6 Mean annual rainfall
  7 Relief
32-33 BRITISH ISLES, agriculture, livestock, fishing
  1 Land use
  2 Land cover categories
  3 Growing season
  4 Crops
  5 Food markets and processing centres
  6 Livestock
  7 Fishing
  8 Weather forecast areas
34-35 BRITISH ISLES, population, journey to work, administrative areas
  1 Population
  2 Resident population of the London area
  3 Journey to work
  4 Administrative areas
36-37 BRITISH ISLES, industry, energy
  1 Industrial products
  2 Engineering and heavy industry
  3 Chemicals and plastics
  4 Imports
  5 Energy
38 BRITISH ISLES, communications, recreation
  1 Road network
  2 Rail network
  3 Air network
  4 Outdoor recreation

CONTINENTAL EUROPE

39-51 39 THE BENELUX, environment
      40-41 BRITISH ISLES
            AND CENTRAL EUROPE, environment
      42-43 SCANDINAVIA, environment
      44-45 SOUTH WEST EUROPE, environment
      46 THE BALKANS, environment
      47 WESTERN TURKEY, environment
      48-49 THE MEDITERRANEAN REGION, environment
      50-51 WESTERN U.S.S.R., environment

ASIA

52-53 NORTHERN ASIA, environment
54-55 SOUTHERN ASIA, environment
56-57 CHINA AND JAPAN, environment
58-59 ASIA, physical, economic
  1 Climate in relation to plant growth
  2 Soils
  3 Organic production
  4 Inorganic production
60-61 ASIA, physical, population, political divisions
  1 Relief
  2 Annual rainfall, ocean currents
  3 Temperature, winds—January
  4 Temperature, winds—July
  5 Population
  6 Political divisions

AUSTRALASIA

62-63 AUSTRALASIA, environment, political divisions, population
      Main map—environment
      Inset maps:
  1 Political divisions
  2 Population
64-65 AUSTRALASIA, physical, economic
  1 Relief
  2 Annual rainfall, ocean currents
  3 Temperature, winds— January
  4 Temperature, winds—July
  5 Climate in relation to plant growth
  6 Soils
  7 Organic production
  8 Inorganic production

AFRICA

SOUTH AMERICA

NORTH AMERICA

THE POLAR REGIONS

DIFFERENT MAP PROJECTIONS

MAP SYMBOLS

Maps show a great variety of information. This consists of many kinds of colours, lines, and writing, each carefully selected to distinguish different items clearly. For example, some names are written in upright letters and others in sloping *(italic)* letters. Upright letters are used only for labelling features associated with Man.

Names of countries (e.g., **JAPAN**) and administrative areas (e.g., K E N T) use capital (UPPER CASE) letters, while those of towns (e.g., Calais) and cities (e.g., Sydney) use "small" (lower case) letters. The more important towns use larger sized letters (e.g., Wolverhampton), and capital cities (e.g., Berlin) are distinguished by their names being shown underlined. Explorers' routes (e.g. Scott) and the names of historical sites (e.g. Stonehenge and Troy) are also written in upright letters.

Names written in *italic* letters refer to natural features (e.g., lakes, rivers, islands, deserts, mountains, and seas). Sometimes the dates are given when explorers followed particular routes (e.g., Amundsen 1903-06).

Table of Symbols
(Environmental maps only)
NATURAL GEOGRAPHY

Mountain	*Mt. Everest* ·8848 (height in metres)		Pack Ice		e.g., *Ross Ice Shelf*
Pass	*Brenner* ⇌ *1372* (altitude in metres)		Coral Reefs		e.g., *Great Barrier Reef*
Submarine depth	*Challenger Deep* ▾*11034* (depth in metres)		Lake		e.g., *Lake Geneva*
Major river		e.g., *Hwang Ho*	Seasonal Lake		e.g., *L.Tuz*
Minor river		e.g., *R. Cherwell*	Salt Pan		e.g., *Makarikari Pan*
Seasonal river		e.g., *R. Sarysu*	Marsh or Swamp		e.g., *The Everglades*
Waterfall or cascade		e.g., *Angel Falls*			

HUMAN GEOGRAPHY

Geographical region	*Siberia*
Administrative area	F I F E
Federated state	A L A S K A
Dependent state	**HONG KONG** (U.K.)
Independent state	**B O L I V I A**

International boundary	———		International boundary in dispute	- - - - - - -
National boundary	———		Regional, and county boundary	—·—·—·—
Provincial or State boundary	———		Limit of National Park	- - - - - - - - - e.g., SERENGETI NATIONAL PARK
Towns with over 5 000 000 inhabitants			e.g., Moscow	
Towns with 1 000 000 – 5 000 000 inhabitants	■		e.g., Hamburg	
Towns with 250 000 – 1 000 000 inhabitants	●		e.g., Cincinnati	
Towns with 50 000 – 250 000 inhabitants	·		e.g., Hargeisa	
Towns with less than 50 000 inhabitants	○		e.g., Dubrovnik	

NB: See page 26 for classification of towns in British Isles

Ruins	∴ e.g., Carthage		Aqueduct	e.g., Los Angeles
	∿∿∿∿∿ e.g., Hadrian's Wall		Tunnel aqueduct	e.g., *Loch Ericht*
Motorways Major roads Other roads			Canal	e.g., *Lenin Canal*
Principal railways	+–+–+–+ + + + + (under construction)		Dam	e.g., *Kariba*
Train ferries	- - - - - - e.g., Dover–Dunkirk		Reservoir	e.g., *Volgograd Reservoir*
Car ferries	- - - - - - - - - e.g., Fishguard–Rosslare		Tunnels	→)- -(← e.g., *Simplon*
Airport	⊕			

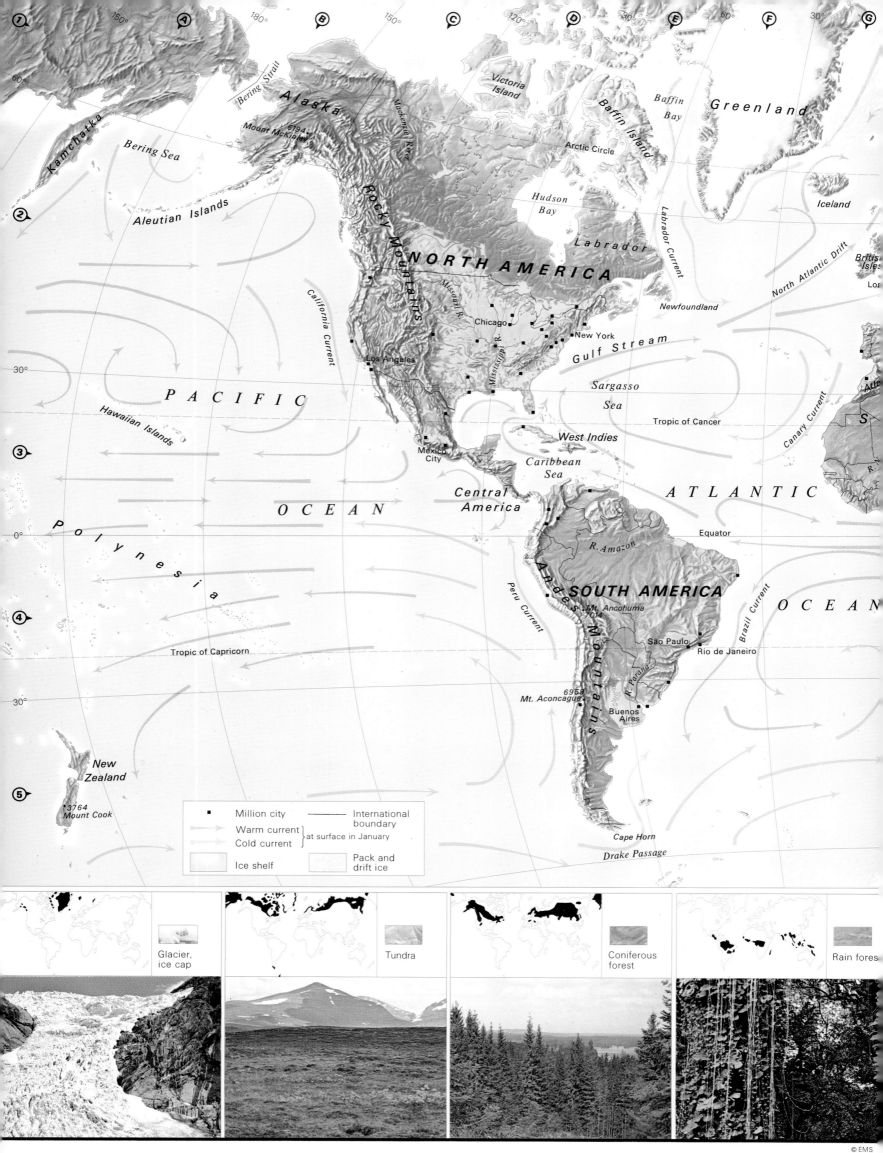

Map labels

Top row markers: Ⓐ Ⓑ Ⓒ Ⓓ Ⓔ Ⓕ Ⓖ

150° 180° 150° 120° 90° 60° 30°

60°

① ② ③ ④ ⑤

Kamchatka

Alaska

Bering Strait

Mount McKinley 6194

Mackenzie River

Victoria Island

Baffin Island

Baffin Bay

Greenland

Arctic Circle

Bering Sea

Aleutian Islands

Iceland

ROCKY MOUNTAINS

NORTH AMERICA

Hudson Bay

Labrador

Labrador Current

North Atlantic Drift

British Isles

California Current

Missouri R.

Chicago

New York

Newfoundland

Gulf Stream

PACIFIC

Mississippi R.

Los Angeles

Sargasso Sea

Tropic of Cancer

Canary Current

Hawaiian Islands

30°

Mexico City

West Indies

Caribbean Sea

ATLANTIC

OCEAN

Central America

Equator

R. Amazon

0°

Polynesia

SOUTH AMERICA

Andes Mountains

Peru Current

Mt. Ancohuma 7014

São Paulo

Rio de Janeiro

Brazil Current

OCEAN

Tropic of Capricorn

Mt. Aconcagua 6958

R. Paraná

Buenos Aires

30°

New Zealand

Mount Cook 3764

Cape Horn

Drake Passage

Legend

■ Million city
→ Warm current } at surface in January
→ Cold current
 Ice shelf
 Pack and drift ice
━━━ International boundary

Lower panels

Glacier, ice cap

Tundra

Coniferous forest

Rain forest

2 **THE WORLD,** geographical environment

© EMS

ARCTIC OCEAN

Svalbard

North Cape

Norwegian Sea

Barents Sea

Novaya Zemlya

Taymyr Peninsula

R. Ob

R. Lena

Arctic Circle

Bering Strait

Alaska

6194 Mount McKinley

Scandinavia

Ural Mountains

S i b e r i a

Kamchatka

Bering Sea

Moscow

R. Volga

R. Yenisei

R. Ob

Altai

Sea of Okhotsk

Sakhalin

Aleutian Islands

EUROPE

The Alps

ASIA

Kirghiz Steppe

Gobi

Manchuria

Honshu

Oya Siwo

Black Sea

Caucasus Mts.

Caspian Sea

Tien Shan

Takla Makan

Kunlun Shan

Peking

Seoul

Tokyo

Kuro Siwo

PACIFIC

Mediterranean Sea

R. Euphrates

Tibet

Himalayas

Ho

Shanghai

Yangtze Kiang

OCEAN

ara

AFRICA

R. Nile

Red Sea

Khuas

Mt. Everest 8848

R. Ganges

Calcutta

Tropic of Cancer

Sahara

Rub al Khali

Bombay

R. Mekong

South China Sea

Philippine Islands

Micronesia

uinea

Arabian Sea

Ceylon

Equator

Sumatra

Borneo

Melanesia

R. Congo

R. Zaire

5895 Mt. Kilimanjaro

Sunda Islands

Djakarta

Java

New Guinea

R. Zambezi

Madagascar

INDIAN

Benguela Current

Kalahari Desert

OCEAN

Coral Sea

Cape Town

Cape of Good Hope

AUSTRALIA

Tropic of Capricorn

Westralian Current

Darling River

Sydney

Tasman Sea

West Wind Drift

Tasmania

Mount Cook 3764

New Zealand

Cultivated land

Savanna

Steppe

Desert

0 400 800 km
30°
60°
200 600 1000 km

0 200 400 600 miles
30°
60°
100 300 500 miles

PRECIPITATION PRESSURE WINDS

January
Northern winter, southern summer

Precipitation in mm

- 400
- 100
- 25
- 0

L   Low pressure

H   High pressure

→   Prevailing wind direction

Short arrows = less constant winds
Long arrows = more constant winds
Thin arrows = light winds
Thick arrows = strong winds
∘ ∘ ∘ ∘   Doldrums

• Place names see map 3

Map 1 labels: North West Monsoon, North East Trades, North East Trades, North East Monsoon, South East Trades, South East Trades, South East Trades, Westerlies, Westerlies

PRECIPITATION PRESSURE WINDS

July
Northern summer, southern winter

Precipitation in mm

- 400
- 100
- 25
- 0

L   Low pressure

H   High pressure

→   Prevailing wind direction

Short arrows = less constant winds
Long arrows = more constant winds
Thin arrows = light winds
Thick arrows = strong winds
∘ ∘ ∘ ∘   Doldrums

• Place names see map 3

Map 2 labels: North East Trades, North East Trades, South East Trades, South West Monsoon, South West Monsoon, South East Monsoon, South East Trades, South East Trades, Westerlies, Westerlies

ANNUAL PRECIPITATION

Precipitation in mm

- 2000
- 1000
- 500
- 100
- 0

Mean annual precipitation for the following places in mm

Cherrapunji	11 437	Rio de Janeiro	1
Douala	4 109	Perth	
Cayenne	3 744	Chicago	
Tamatave	3 530	Lisbon	
Valdivia	2 396	Dakar	
Bombay	2 078	Moscow	
Bergen	1 958	Verkhoyansk	
San José	1 944	Barrow	
Djakarta	1 755	Las Vegas	
Tokyo	1 563	Kashgar	
Juneau	1 387	Walvis Bay	
New York	1 123	Aswân	
Brisbane	1 092	Arica	

compare: London 610

Map 3 labels: Arctic Circle, Barrow, Juneau, Bergen, Moscow, Verkhoyansk, Chicago, New York, Lisbon, Kashgar, Tokyo, Las Vegas, Cherrapunji, Tropic of Cancer, Aswân, Bombay, Dakar, San José, Cayenne, Douala, Djakarta, Equator, Arica, Walvis Bay, Tamatave, Rio de Janeiro, Valdivia, Tropic of Capricorn, Perth, Brisbane

© EMS

4   **THE WORLD,** climate

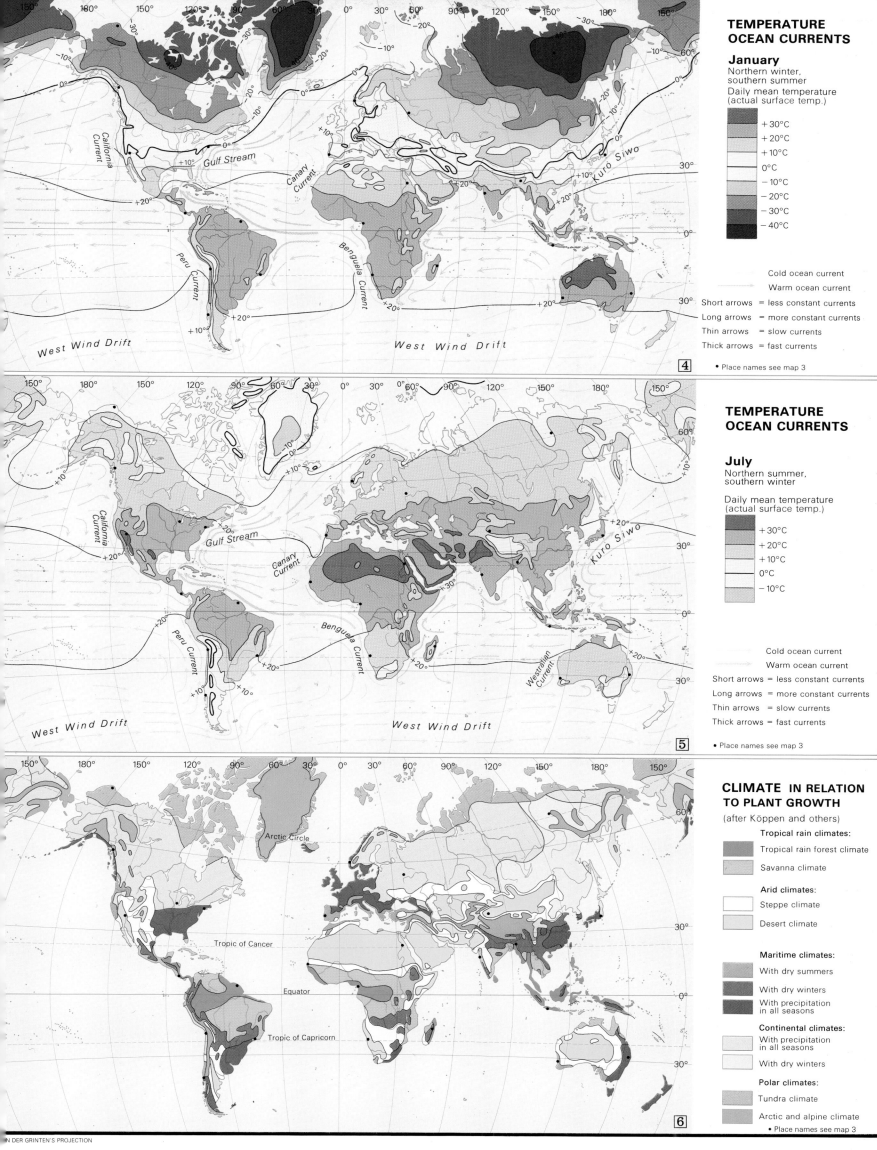

TEMPERATURE OCEAN CURRENTS

January
Northern winter,
southern summer

Daily mean temperature
(actual surface temp.)

- +30°C
- +20°C
- +10°C
- 0°C
- −10°C
- −20°C
- −30°C
- −40°C

Cold ocean current
Warm ocean current

Short arrows = less constant currents
Long arrows = more constant currents
Thin arrows = slow currents
Thick arrows = fast currents

4

• Place names see map 3

TEMPERATURE OCEAN CURRENTS

July
Northern summer,
southern winter

Daily mean temperature
(actual surface temp.)

- +30°C
- +20°C
- +10°C
- 0°C
- −10°C

Cold ocean current
Warm ocean current

Short arrows = less constant currents
Long arrows = more constant currents
Thin arrows = slow currents
Thick arrows = fast currents

5

• Place names see map 3

CLIMATE IN RELATION TO PLANT GROWTH
(after Köppen and others)

Tropical rain climates:
- Tropical rain forest climate
- Savanna climate

Arid climates:
- Steppe climate
- Desert climate

Maritime climates:
- With dry summers
- With dry winters
- With precipitation in all seasons

Continental climates:
- With precipitation in all seasons
- With dry winters

Polar climates:
- Tundra climate
- Arctic and alpine climate

• Place names see map 3

6

Labels on maps: California Current, Gulf Stream, Canary Current, Kuro Siwo, Peru Current, Benguela Current, West Wind Drift, Westralian Current, Arctic Circle, Tropic of Cancer, Equator, Tropic of Capricorn

PROTEROZOIC

PRE-CAMBRIAN

The oldest rocks known
date back 3.9 billion years

CAMBRIAN

Life in sea o
Trilobites
Worms
Jellyfish

5000–4000 mill.years ago
Pre-Cambrian folding

600

Great extent of shallo

The earth was formed several billion
years ago — equivalent to more than
four feet on the scale used here to show
the last 600 million years.

CONTINENTAL DRIFT

PERMIAN/TRIASSIC
200 million years ago

PANGAEA

JURASSIC/CRETACEOUS
135 million years ago

LAURASIA

Tethys Sea

GONDWANALAND

TERTIARY
65 million years ago

QUATERNARY
Present day

NORTH
AMERICA

EURASIA

SOUTH
AMERICA

AFRICA

AUSTRALIA

ANTARCTICA

Boundary between plates

1

PLATE TECTONICS

Canadian
Shield

PACIFIC
PLATE

AMERICAN PLATE

NAZCA
PLATE

Baltic
Shield

EURASIAN PLATE

AFRICAN PLATE

INDIAN PLATE

ANTARCTIC
PLATE

2

Active ocean ridge   Fracture zone
Ocean trench   Direction of movement

Pre-Cambrian folding
(later partly overlaid
through sedimentation
and younger folding)

©EMS

6   THE WORLD, geology

FISHING

Density of animal plankton

Over 500 milligrams per cubic metre wa...

200–500 " " "

50–200 " " "

under 50 " " "

Important catch of:

whale

herring, cod and similar fish

tuna

crab, prawn and other shellfish

8 THE OCEANS

©EMS

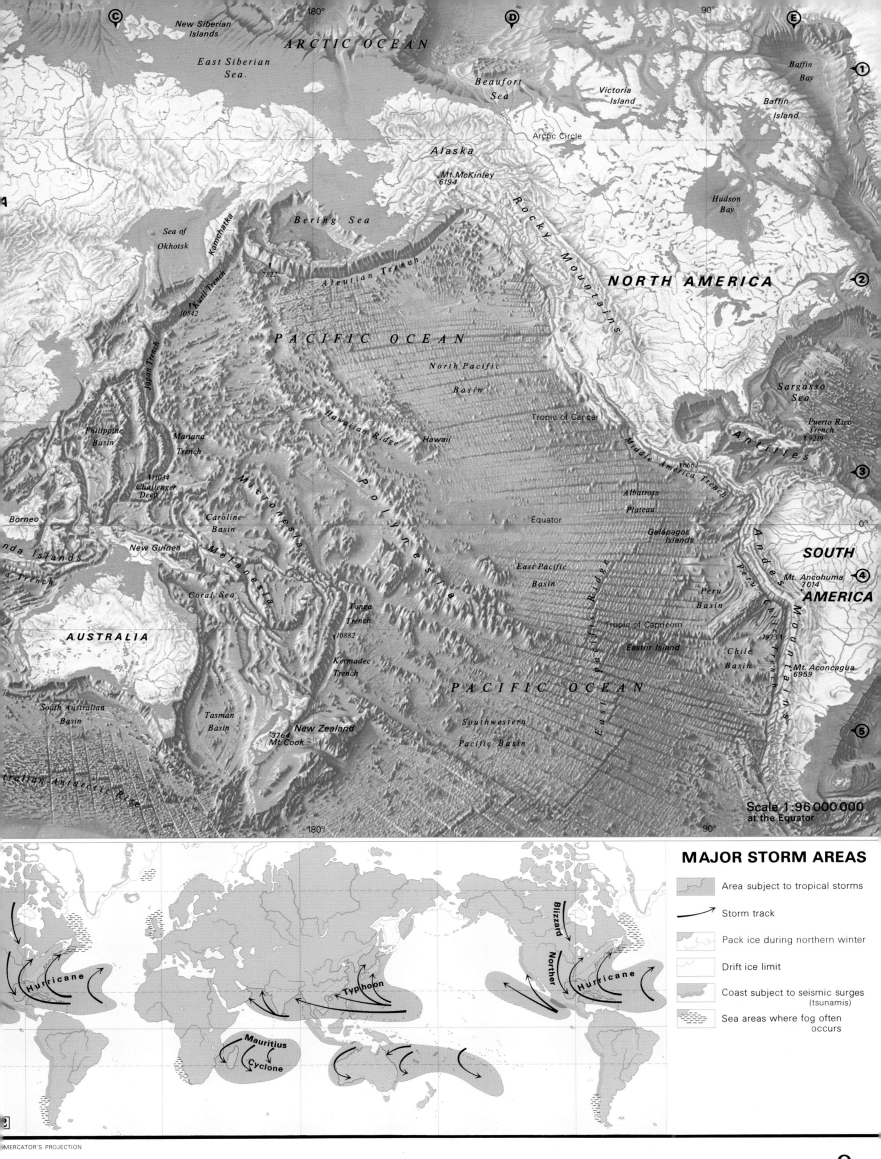

ARCTIC OCEAN

New Siberian
Islands

East Siberian
Sea.

Beaufort
Sea

Baffin
Bay

Victoria
Island

Baffin
Island

Arctic Circle

Alaska

Mt.McKinley
6194

Hudson
Bay

Sea of
Okhotsk

Bering Sea

Kamchatka

NORTH AMERICA

7822

Aleutian Trench

Kuril Trench

10542

Japan Trench

Rocky Mountains

PACIFIC OCEAN

North Pacific
Basin

Sargasso
Sea

Hawaiian Ridge

Tropic of Cancer

Puerto Rico
Trench
9219

Philippine
Basin

Hawaii

Middle America Trench

Antilles

Mariana
Trench

Micronesia

10662

11034
Challenger
Deep

Caroline
Basin

Polynesia

Albatross
Plateau

Borneo

Equator

Galápagos
Islands

0°

nda Islands

New Guinea

Melanesia

East Pacific
Basin

SOUTH

a Trench

Mt. Ancohuma
7014

Coral Sea

Peru
Basin

AMERICA

Tonga
Trench

10882

East Pacific Ridge

Tropic of Capricorn

Peru-Chile Trench

AUSTRALIA

Easter Island

Andes Mountains

Chile
Basin

9973

Mt. Aconcagua
6959

Kermadec
Trench

South Australian
Basin

Tasman
Basin

3764
Mt Cook

New Zealand

PACIFIC OCEAN

Southwestern
Pacific Basin

stralian-Antarctic Ridge

Scale 1:96 000 000
at the Equator

180°

90°

MAJOR STORM AREAS

MAJOR STORM AREAS

Blizzard

Norther

Typhoon

Hurricane

Hurricane

Mauritius
Cyclone

Area subject to tropical storms

Storm track

Pack ice during northern winter

Drift ice limit

Coast subject to seismic surges
(tsunamis)

Sea areas where fog often
occurs

MERCATOR'S PROJECTION

9

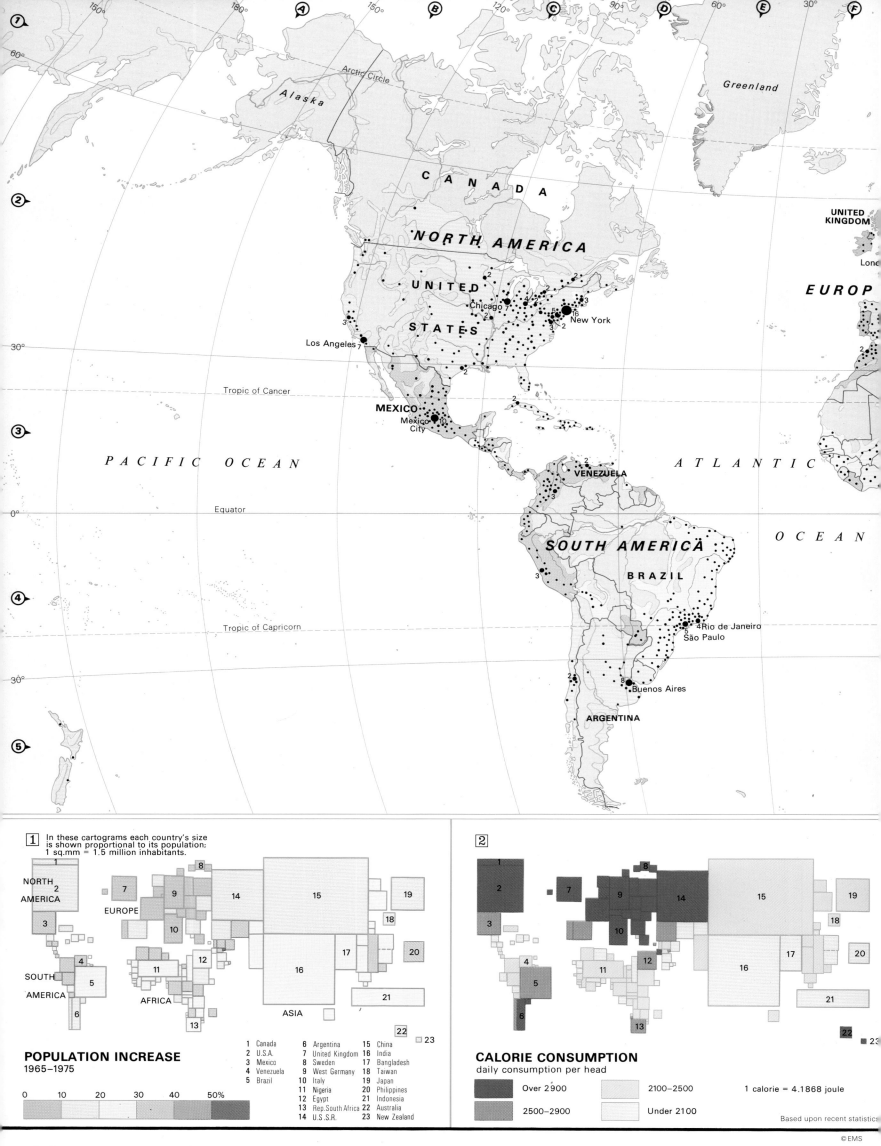

Map labels (top map):

Arctic Circle
Alaska
Greenland
CANADA
NORTH AMERICA
UNITED STATES
UNITED KINGDOM
EUROP
Lond
2
Chicago 7
4
5 16 New York
3
2
2
2
2
Los Angeles 7
3
Tropic of Cancer
MEXICO
Mexico City ●10
2
VENEZUELA 2
3
PACIFIC OCEAN
ATLANTIC
Equator
SOUTH AMERICA
BRAZIL
OCEAN
3
2
Tropic of Capricorn
4 Rio de Janeiro
5 São Paulo
2
8 Buenos Aires
ARGENTINA
30°

Grid references: 150° 180° 150° A 120° B C 90° D 60° E 30° F
60° 30° 0° Equator 30°
① ② ③ ④ ⑤

© EMS
Based upon recent statistics

1 POPULATION INCREASE
1965–1975

In these cartograms each country's size is shown proportional to its population; 1 sq.mm = 1.5 million inhabitants.

NORTH AMERICA
EUROPE
SOUTH AMERICA
AFRICA
ASIA

0   10   20   30   40   50%

1 Canada	6 Argentina	15 China
2 U.S.A.	7 United Kingdom	16 India
3 Mexico	8 Sweden	17 Bangladesh
4 Venezuela	9 West Germany	18 Taiwan
5 Brazil	10 Italy	19 Japan
	11 Nigeria	20 Philippines
	12 Egypt	21 Indonesia
	13 Rep.South Africa	22 Australia
	14 U.S.S.R.	23 New Zealand

2 CALORIE CONSUMPTION
daily consumption per head

Over 2900
2500–2900
2100–2500
Under 2100

1 calorie = 4.1868 joule

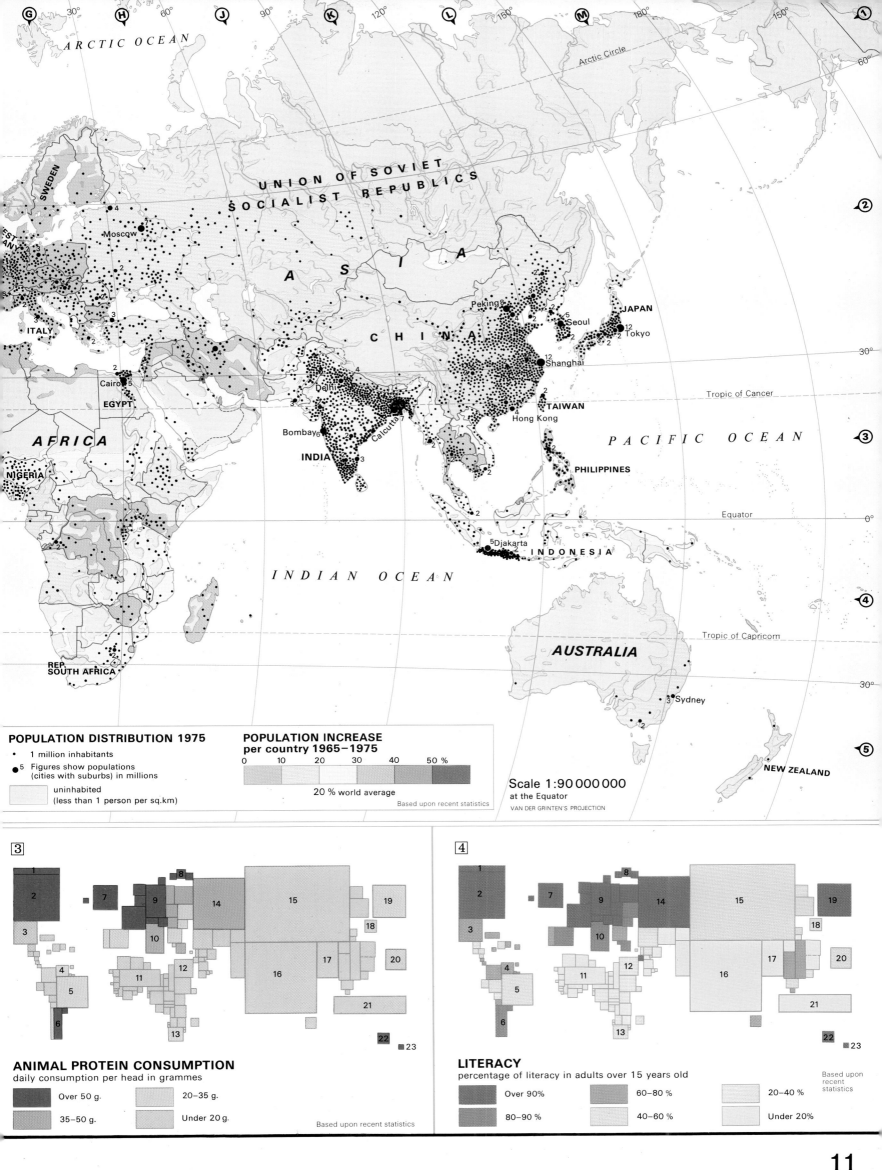

POPULATION DISTRIBUTION 1975

- • 1 million inhabitants
- •5 Figures show populations (cities with suburbs) in millions

uninhabited (less than 1 person per sq.km)

POPULATION INCREASE
per country 1965–1975

0	10	20	30	40	50 %

20 % world average

Based upon recent statistics

Scale 1:90 000 000
at the Equator

VAN DER GRINTEN'S PROJECTION

ANIMAL PROTEIN CONSUMPTION
daily consumption per head in grammes

Over 50 g.		20–35 g.
35–50 g.		Under 20 g.

Based upon recent statistics

LITERACY
percentage of literacy in adults over 15 years old

Over 90%	60–80 %	20–40 %
80–90 %	40–60 %	Under 20%

Based upon recent statistics

MILITARY POLITICS

| N.A.T.O., C.E.N.T.O., A.N.Z.U.S. | Other 'western' allies | Warsaw Pact | Other communist states | Arab League | Other states |

AMERICAN ASPECT

centre Chicago

EUROPEAN ASPECT

centre London

EAST ASIATIC ASPECT

centre Peking

W. William-Ols projection

© EMS

U.S.S.R.

Arctic Circle

Kamchatka

Bering Strait

Bering Sea

ALASKA (U.S.A.)

Aleutian Islands

International Date Line

Monday
Sunday

Beaufort
Sea

Victoria Island

Baffin
Bay

Baffin Island

GREENLAND (DENMARK)

Jan Mayen I. (NORWAY)

Reykjavik ICELAND

Faeroe Islands (DENMARK)

Mackenzie River

CANADA

NORTH AMERICA

Labrador

Hudson
Bay

UNITED
KINGDOM

REP. OF
IRELAND Dublin

EUROPE

FRA

Newfoundland

St. Pierre &
Miquelon (FR.)

UNITED STATES

Ottawa

Washington

SP

PORTUGAL
Lisbon

Madr

Midway I. (U.S.A.)

Hawaiian Islands

Tropic of Cancer

HAWAII (U.S.A.)

PACIFIC

OCEAN

Bermuda (U.K.)

Gulf of
Mexico

Florida

Nassau

Havana

MEXICO

Mexico City
Belmopan BELIZE

THE BAHAMAS

CUBA
Kingston

HAITI
Port-
au-Prince Santo Domingo

DOMINICAN REP.
Puerto Rico (U.S.A.)

ATLANTIC

Canary Islands (SP.)

Madeira (PORT.)

GIBRALTAR
Rabat
MOROCCO

MAURITANIA
Nouakchott

AZORES (PORT.)

Marshall
Islands
(U.S. TRUST
/U.N.)

Palmyra I. (U.S.A.)

Christmas Island (U.K.)

Equator

Gilbert
Islands
(U.K.)

(U.S.A.)

Phoenix Islands
(U.K.)

Tuvalu
(Ellice Is.)

Marquesas
Islands

Wallis &
Futuna Is.
(FR.)

Tokelau
Islands (N.Z.)

WESTERN
SAMOA
Apia Samoa
(U.S.A.)

FRENCH POLYNESIA

Tahiti

Tuamotu
Archipelago

FIJI
Suva

Cook
Islands
(N.Z.)

Society
Islands

TONGA
Nukualofa

Mururoa Is.

Tubuai
Islands

Tropic of Capricorn

Pitcairn I. (U.K.)

Easter Island (CHILE)

Kermadec
Islands
(N.Z.)

Wellington

NEW ZEALAND

JAMAICA

Guatemala
GUATEMALA
EL SALVADOR
San Salvador

HONDURAS
Tegucigalpa
Managua
NICARAGUA

San José
COSTA
RICA

PANAMA
CANAL ZONE
(PAN.-U.S.A.)

Clipperton I. (FR.)

BARBADOS
GRENADA
TRINIDAD & TOBAGO
Port of Spain

Caracas

Panamá

VENEZUELA
Bogotá
COLOMBIA

GUYANA
Georgetown
SURINAM
Paramaribo FRENCH GUIANA

CAPE VERDE
ISLANDS Praia

SENEGAL
Dakar
THE GAMBIA
Banjul Bamako
GUINEA-BISSAU GUINEA
Conakry
SIERRA LEONE
Freetown
Monrovia
LIBERIA

Nouakchott

VO
Ouagad

IVORY COAST
Abidjan

OCEAN

Galápagos Islands (ECU.)

Quito
ECUADOR

R. Amazon

BRAZIL

SOUTH AMERICA

Ascension I. (U.K.)

PERU Lima

La Paz
BOLIVIA
Sucré

Brasília

Trindade I. (BRAZ.)

St. Helena (U.K.)

PARAGUAY

Asunción

CHILE

R. Paraná

Santiago

Buenos Aires

URUGUAY
Montevideo

Tristan da Cunha

ARGENTINA

Falkland Islands (U.K.)

South Georgia (U.K.)

Tierra del Fuego

Scale 1:90 000 000

- • National capital
- —— International boundary
- --- Disputed boundary

VAN DER GRINTEN'S PROJECTION

AMERICAN ASPECT

EUROPEAN ASPECT

EAST ASIATIC ASPECT

centre Chicago

centre London

centre Peking

TRADE POLITICS

| E.E.C. | E.E.C. associated, Commonwealth | E.F.T.A. | L.A.F.T.A. | Comecon | Other countries | ° O.P.E.C. |

Map labels (North and South America — geographic features and place names):

Kamchatka · Bering Sea · Aleutian Islands · Bering Strait · Alaska · Beaufort Sea · Prudhoe Bay · Mackenzie River · Greenland · Baffin Bay · Baffin Island · Arctic Circle · Godthåb · Iceland · British Isles · Midla... · Kemano · Alberta · NORTH AMERICA · Saskatchewan · Labrador · Hudson Bay · Beaverlodge · Grand Coulee · Elliott Lake · Montreal · Columbia River · Wyoming · North Dakota · Great Lakes · St. Lawrence R. · Newfoundland · Fremont Co. · Pennsylvania · Utah · Kansas · Illinois · West Virginia · California · Hoover · Kentucky · Panhandle · Tennessee · Valencia · Texas · Mississippi R. · Louisiana · Gulf of Mexico · Tampico · West Indies · Tropic of Cancer · Caribbean Sea · Maracaibo · PACIFIC OCEAN · Hawaiian Islands · ATLANTIC OCEAN · Orito · Equator · R. Amazon · SOUTH AMERICA · OCEAN · Santa Cruz · Minas Gerais · Tropic of Capricorn · Don Otto · R. Paraná · Malargüe · New Zealand · Comodoro Rivadavia · Tierra del Fuego

Inset map 1 — OIL: production, consumption, sea transport (metric tons):

CANADA 80 · 89 · 532 · U.S.A. 776 · WESTERN EUROPE 704 · 443 · 22 · COMMUNIST COUNTRIES INC. CHINA 396 · JAPAN 237 · 1 · MEXICO 25 · 29 · NORTH AFRICA 180 · 13 · 59 · REST OF ASIA 29 · 14 · NORTHERN SOUTH AMERICA 190 · 59 · WEST AFRICA 102 · 8 · 895 · MIDDLE EAST 26 · 71 · SOUTH EAST ASIA 64 · SOUTHERN SOUTH AMERICA 42 · 72 · 12 · OCEANIA 31

Based upon recent statistics

Inset map 2 — COAL: production, consumption (metric tons):

NORTH AMERICA 554 · 501 · WESTERN EUROPE 338 · 1271 · COMMUNIST COUNTRIES INC. CHINA 1240 · JAPAN 32 · 91 · 376 · 97 · 85 · SOUTHERN ASIA · LATIN AMERICA 10 · 14 · AFRICA 64 · 63 · OCEA... 64 · 37

Based upon recent statistics

OIL: production, consumption, sea transport (metric tons)

190 production (million tons/year) · 59 consumption (million tons/year) · transport of crude oil (million tons/year)

less than 20
20–100
100–200
200–400
400–800
over 800

COAL: production, consumption (metric tons)

338 production (million tons/year) · 376 consumption (million tons/year) · lignite counted as its equivalent in coal

© EMS

14 THE WORLD, energy

LAND

deposits of:
- uranium
- crude oil
- tar sands or oil shales
- natural gas
- coal
- lignite

sedimentary basin (partly oil-bearing)
bedrock without thick sediment cover
hydro-electric power > 500 MW

SEA

sedimentary basin (partly oil-bearing)
shallow seabed without thick sediment cover

shallow sea (continental shelf)
200 m
2000 m
deep sea

Scale 1:90 000 000 at the Equator

THE WORLD'S SOURCES OF ENERGY
Based upon recent statistics

- Hydro-electric & nuclear power 2.2%
- Natural gas 18%
- Coal, lignite 32.5%
- Crude oil 47.3%

PRODUCTION OF ENERGY
Total annual production of primary energy (crude oil, natural gas, coal, lignite, peat, hydro-electric and nuclear power)

primary energy expressed in million metric tons coal

441 ← 1972
99 ← 1962
AFRICA

Based upon recent statistics

CONSUMPTION OF ENERGY
Total annual consumption of primary energy per person by country (expressed in kilograms of coal)

100   1000   3000   6000   kilograms per person

VAN DER GRINTEN'S PROJECTION

15

PRINCIPAL MINERAL PRODUCTS

20%	5%	2.5% of world production		20%	5%	2.5%		20%	5%	2.5%		20%	5%	2.5%	
▲	▲	▴ Petroleum		Fe	Fe	Fe Iron		Al	Al	Al Bauxite		P	P	P Phosphates
△	△	△ Natural gas		Co	Co	Co Cobalt (China excluded)		Cu	Cu	Cu Copper (Czechoslovakia excluded)		S	S	S Sulphur
■	■	▪ Coal		Mn	Mn	Mn Manganese		Pb	Pb	Pb Lead		Ti	Ti	Ti Titanium (USSR & China excluded)
▢	▢	▫ Lignite		Ni	Ni	Ni Nickel		Sn	Sn	Sn Tin (USSR & China excluded)		Pt	Pt	Pt Platinum
Ⓤ	Ⓤ	ⓤ Uranium		W	W	W Tungsten		Zn	Zn	Zn Zinc		Ag	Ag	Ag Silver (China, Czechoslovakia & Romaexcluded)
⬡	⬡	⬡ Diamonds		◆	◆	◆ Other Ferrous metals (including antimony, chromite, magnesite and molybdenum)		Hg	Hg	Hg Mercury		Au	Au	Au Gold (China exclude

© EMS/BARTHOLOME

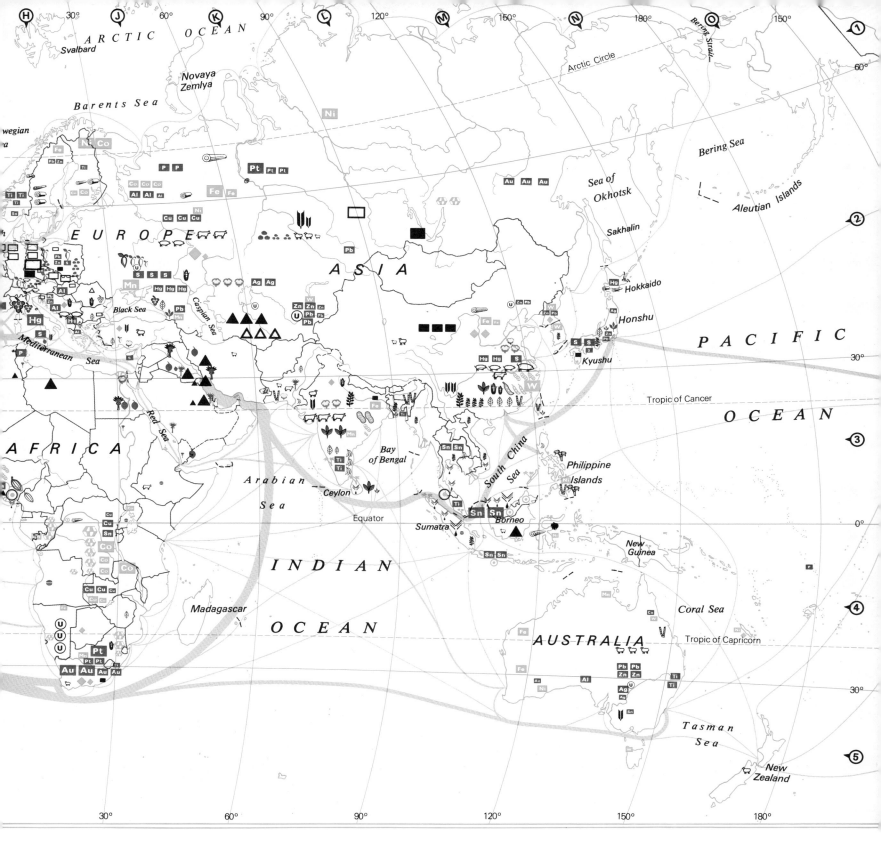

PRINCIPAL VEGETABLE AND ANIMAL PRODUCTS

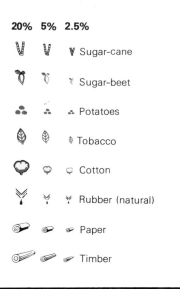

20%	5%	2.5% of world production	20%	5%	2.5%		20%	5%	2.5%
		Wheat			Citrus fruits				Sugar-cane
		Maize			Grapes				Sugar-beet
		Rice			Dates				Potatoes
		Copra			Bananas				Tobacco
		Palm-oil			Coffee				Cotton
		Ground-nuts			Cocoa				Rubber (natural)
		Soya-beans			Tea				Paper
									Timber

20%	5%	2.5%
		Cattle
		Sheep
		Pigs

PRINCIPAL SHIPPING ROUTES

Widths of routes are proportional to the volume of maritime traffic and tonnage carried relative to total world trade.

Based upon recent statistics (1973-5 average)

VAN DER GRINTEN'S PROJECTION

Scale 1:90 000 000
at the Equator

17

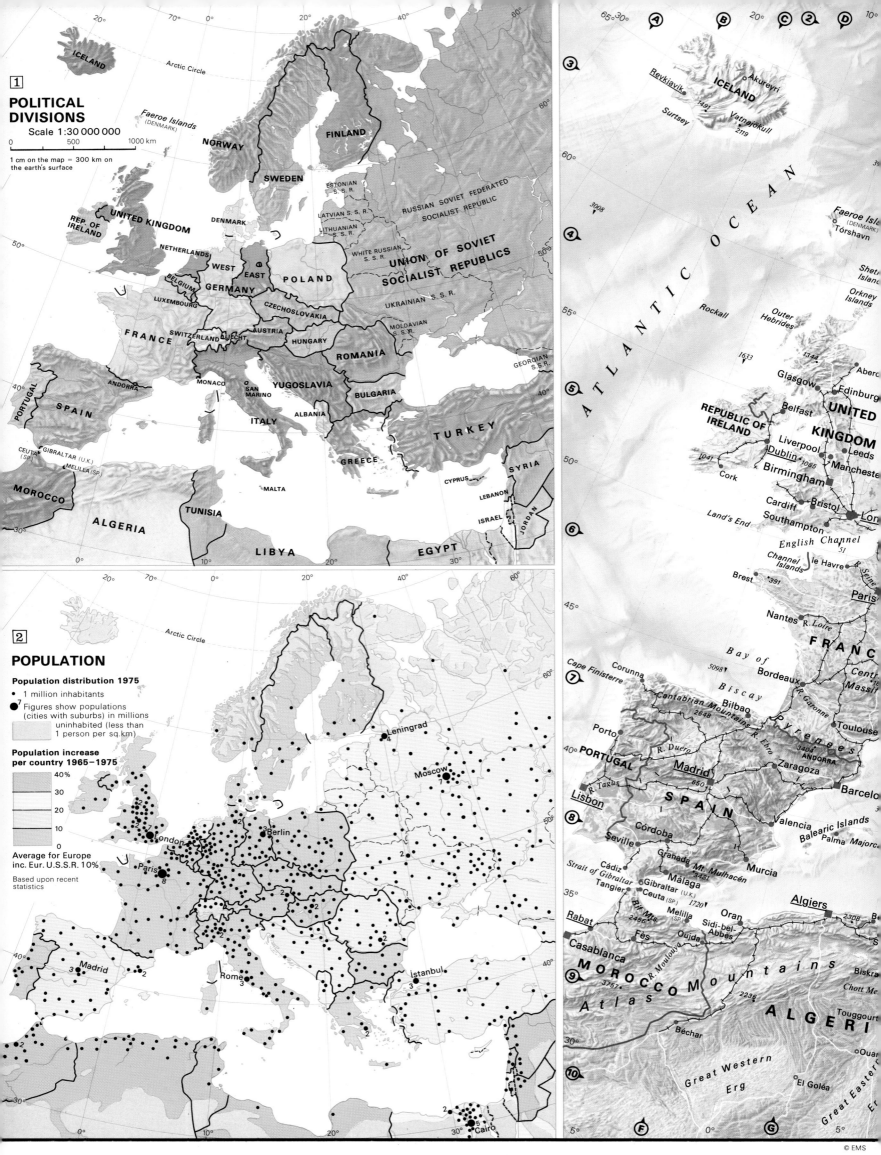

1 POLITICAL DIVISIONS

Scale 1:30 000 000

0 — 500 — 1000 km

1 cm on the map = 300 km on the earth's surface

ICELAND

Faeroe Islands (DENMARK)

NORWAY
SWEDEN
FINLAND

REP. OF IRELAND
UNITED KINGDOM
DENMARK

ESTONIAN S.S.R.
LATVIAN S.S.R.
LITHUANIAN S.S.R.
RUSSIAN SOVIET FEDERATED SOCIALIST REPUBLIC

NETHERLANDS
WEST GERMANY
EAST GERMANY
BELGIUM
LUXEMBOURG
POLAND
WHITE RUSSIAN S.S.R.
UNION OF SOVIET SOCIALIST REPUBLICS

FRANCE
SWITZERLAND
LIECHT.
AUSTRIA
CZECHOSLOVAKIA
HUNGARY
UKRAINIAN S.S.R.
MOLDAVIAN S.S.R.
ROMANIA
GEORGIAN S.S.R.

ANDORRA
MONACO
SAN MARINO
YUGOSLAVIA
BULGARIA
ITALY
ALBANIA
GREECE
TURKEY

PORTUGAL
SPAIN
CEUTA (SP)
GIBRALTAR (U.K.)
MELILLA (SP)
MALTA
CYPRUS
SYRIA
LEBANON
ISRAEL
JORDAN

MOROCCO
ALGERIA
TUNISIA
LIBYA
EGYPT

2 POPULATION

Population distribution 1975

- 1 million inhabitants
- ● Figures show populations (cities with suburbs) in millions
  uninhabited (less than 1 person per sq. km)

Population increase per country 1965–1975

40%
30
20
10

Average for Europe inc. Eur. U.S.S.R. 10%

Based upon recent statistics

Leningrad 4
Moscow
Berlin 3
London 7
Paris 8
Madrid 3
Rome
Istanbul 3
Cairo 5

ATLANTIC OCEAN

ICELAND
Reykjavik 1491
Akureyri
Surtsey
Vatnajökull 2119

Faeroe Isles (DENMARK)
Tórshavn

Rockall
Outer Hebrides
Shetland Islands
Orkney Islands

Glasgow
Edinburgh
Belfast
Aberdeen

REPUBLIC OF IRELAND
UNITED KINGDOM
Dublin
Liverpool
Leeds
Manchester
Cork
Birmingham
Cardiff
Bristol
Land's End
Southampton
London

English Channel 51
Channel Islands
le Havre
Brest 391
Seine
Paris

Nantes
R. Loire
FRANCE
Central Massif

Bay of Biscay
Bordeaux
R. Garonne

Cape Finisterre
Corunna
Cantabrian Mountains 2648
Bilbao
Pyrenees 3404
ANDORRA
Toulouse

Porto
R. Duero
PORTUGAL
Zaragoza
Barcelona

Lisbon
R. Tagus
Madrid 650
SPAIN
Valencia
Balearic Islands
Palma Majorca

Córdoba
Seville
Granada
Mt. Mulhacén 3481
Murcia

Cádiz
Málaga
Gibraltar (SP.) 1720
Strait of Gibraltar
Tangier
Ceuta (SP.)
Melilla (SP.)
Oran
Algiers

Rabat
Rif Mts. 2456
Sidi-bel-Abbès

Casablanca
Fès
Oujda
MOROCCO
R. Moulouya
Atlas Mountains 2238
ALGERIA
Biskra

Béchar
Great Western Erg
El Goléa
Touggourt

18 **EUROPE,** environment, political divisions, population

© EMS

BERT'S CONFORMAL CONIC PROJECTION

Scale 1:15 000 000

| 0 | 200 | 400 | 600 km |

1 cm on the map = 150 km on the earth's surface

| 0 | 100 | 200 | 300 | 400 miles |

1 inch on the map = 240 miles on the earth's surface

Legend:

🦫 Moscow
More than 5 000 000 inhabitants

■ Naples
1 000 000–5 000 000 inhabitants

● Catania
250 000–1 000 000 inhabitants

• Sevastopol
50 000 – 250 000 inhabitants

○ Misurata
Less than 50 000 inhabitants

Valletta Capital cities underlined

————— International boundary

- - - - - Disputed intl. boundary

————— Other boundary

+—+—+ Main railway

————— Main road

————— Canal

⊥ Dam

3086 · Height in metres

▼4791 Depth in metres

Tundra

Glacier

Coniferous forest

Deciduous and mixed forest

Marshland

Arable land

Grassland, pasture

Steppe, semi-desert

Sand desert

Other Desert

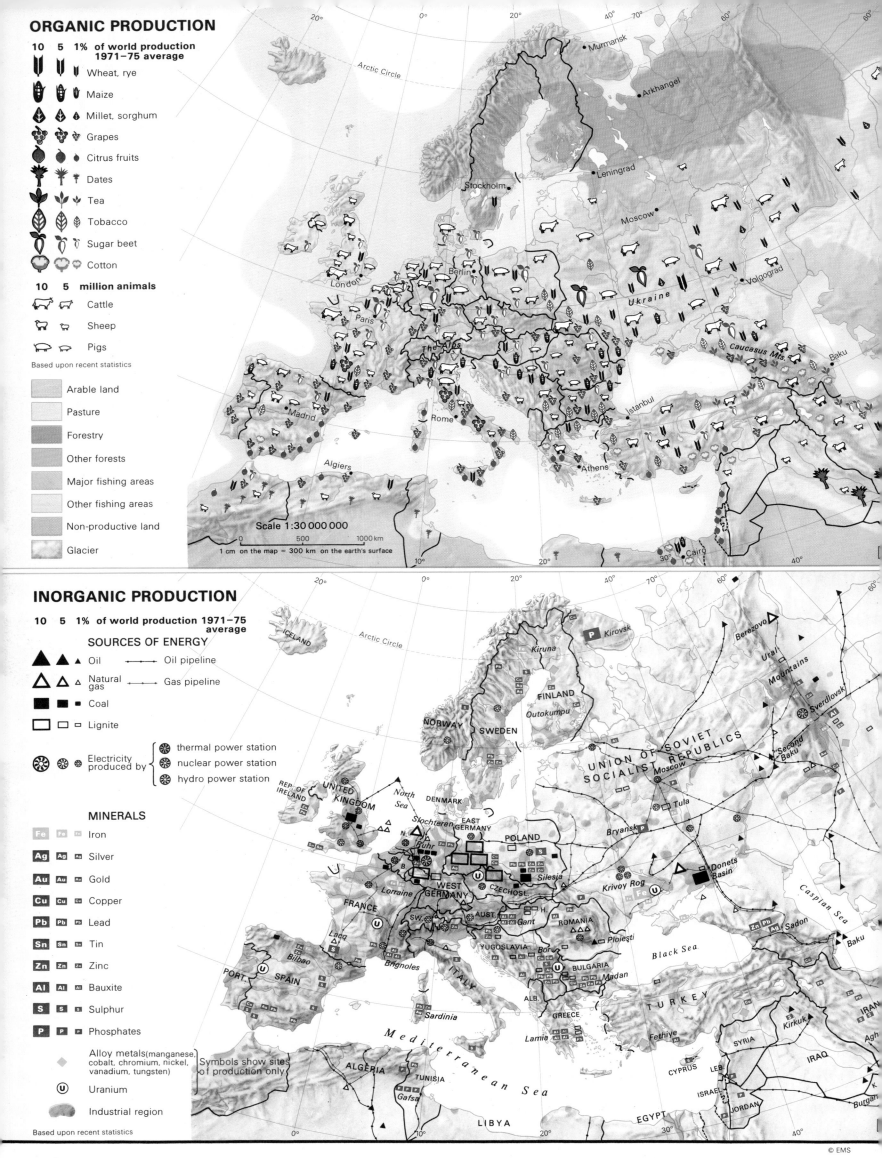

ORGANIC PRODUCTION

10 5 1% of world production
1971–75 average

- Wheat, rye
- Maize
- Millet, sorghum
- Grapes
- Citrus fruits
- Dates
- Tea
- Tobacco
- Sugar beet
- Cotton

10 5 million animals

- Cattle
- Sheep
- Pigs

Based upon recent statistics

- Arable land
- Pasture
- Forestry
- Other forests
- Major fishing areas
- Other fishing areas
- Non-productive land
- Glacier

Scale 1:30 000 000

0   500   1000 km

1 cm on the map = 300 km on the earth's surface

INORGANIC PRODUCTION

10 5 1% of world production 1971–75
average

SOURCES OF ENERGY

- ▲ ▲ ▲ Oil   •——•——• Oil pipeline
- △ △ △ Natural   •——•——• Gas pipeline
  gas
- ■ ■ ▪ Coal
- ▭ ▭ ▫ Lignite

- Electricity
  produced by
  {
    thermal power station
    nuclear power station
    hydro power station
  }

MINERALS

- Fe Fe Fe Iron
- Ag Ag Ag Silver
- Au Au Au Gold
- Cu Cu Cu Copper
- Pb Pb Pb Lead
- Sn Sn Sn Tin
- Zn Zn Zn Zinc
- Al Al Al Bauxite
- S S S Sulphur
- P P P Phosphates

- ◆ Alloy metals (manganese,
  cobalt, chromium, nickel,
  vanadium, tungsten)

  Symbols show sites
  of production only

- Ⓤ Uranium
- Industrial region

Based upon recent statistics

© EMS

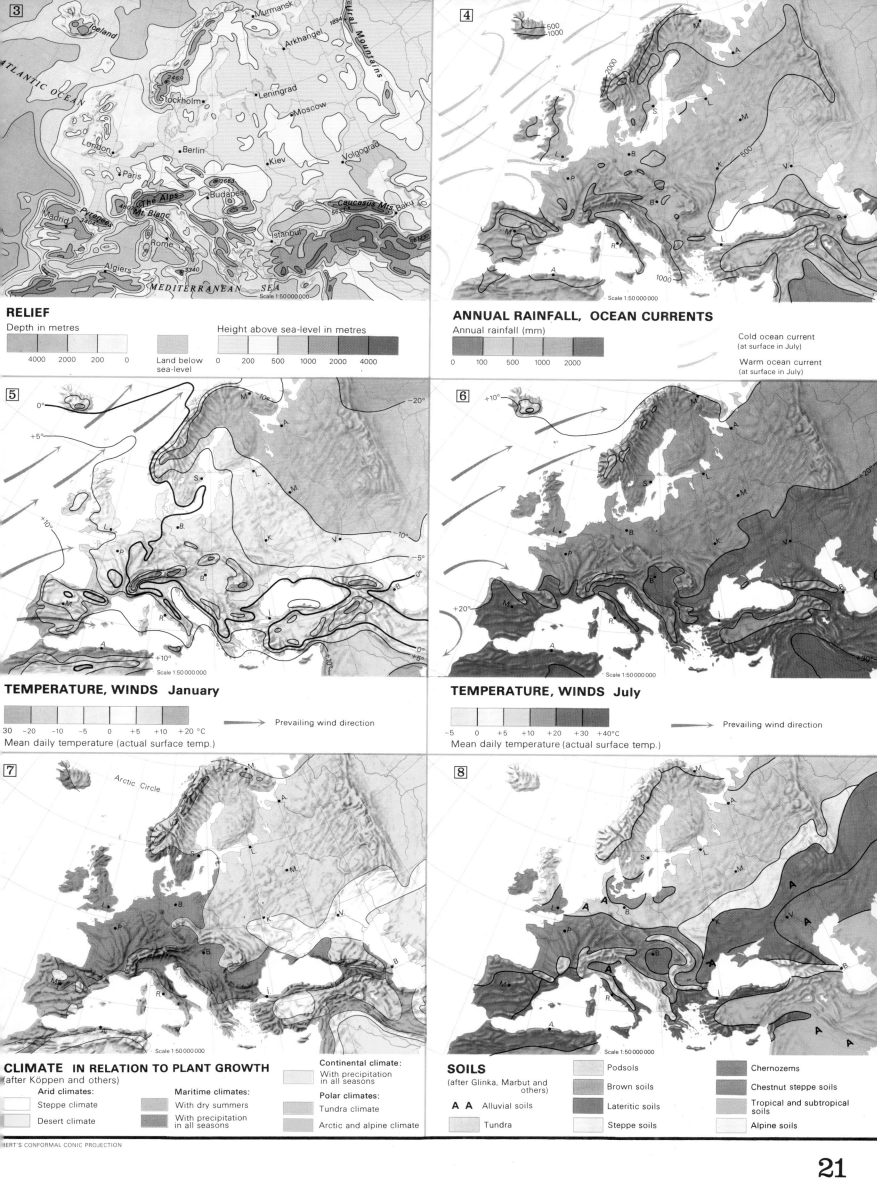

RELIEF

Depth in metres

4000   2000   200   0

Land below sea-level

Height above sea-level in metres

0   200   500   1000   2000   4000

ANNUAL RAINFALL, OCEAN CURRENTS

Annual rainfall (mm)

0   100   500   1000   2000

Cold ocean current
(at surface in July)

Warm ocean current
(at surface in July)

TEMPERATURE, WINDS   January

30   -20   -10   -5   0   +5   +10   +20 °C

Mean daily temperature (actual surface temp.)

→ Prevailing wind direction

TEMPERATURE, WINDS   July

-5   0   +5   +10   +20   +30   +40°C

Mean daily temperature (actual surface temp.)

→ Prevailing wind direction

CLIMATE IN RELATION TO PLANT GROWTH
(after Köppen and others)

Arid climates:

Steppe climate

Desert climate

Maritime climates:

With dry summers

With precipitation
in all seasons

Continental climate:

With precipitation
in all seasons

Polar climates:

Tundra climate

Arctic and alpine climate

SOILS
(after Glinka, Marbut and others)

A A   Alluvial soils

Tundra

Podsols

Brown soils

Lateritic soils

Steppe soils

Chernozems

Chestnut steppe soils

Tropical and subtropical
soils

Alpine soils

ERT'S CONFORMAL CONIC PROJECTION

21

Legend

Mountain

Moorland, unimproved grassland

Improved grassland

Arable land

Woodland

▼119 Depth in metres

Edinburgh — More than 250 000 inhabitants

Carlisle — 50 000 – 250 000 inhabitants

Ballymena — 10 000 – 50 000 inhabitants

Stornoway — Less than 10 000 inhabitants

International boundary

National boundary

County/region boundary

Main railway

✈ Airport ✕ Pass

Canal ⟋ Dam

Tunnel aqueduct

Motorway

Main road

Other road

Car ferry

•1343 Height in metres

Prehistoric remains

∴Jarlshof

NORTH SEA

to Lerwick

to Aberdeen

© EMS/BARTHOLOMEW

22 SCOTLAND, environment

0   10   20   30   40   50 km

1 cm on the map = 12.5 km on the earth's surface

0   10   20   30 miles

1 inch on the map = 20 miles on the earth's surface

Scale 1:1 250 000

| | 0 | 10 | 20 | 30 | 40 | 50 km |
1 cm on the map = 12.5 km on the earth's surface

| | 0 | 10 | 20 | 30 miles |
1 inch on the map = 20 miles on the earth's surface

Legend

Edinburgh — More than 250 000 inhabitants
Carlisle — 50 000 – 250 000 inhabitants
Ballymena — 10 000 – 50 000 inhabitants
Ffestiniog — Less than 10 000 inhabitants
Dublin — Capital city underlined
∴ Castlerigg
International boundary
National boundary
County/region boundary
Motorway
Main road
Other road
Car ferry
Main railway
Airport
Canal
Tunnel aqueduct
Mountain
•1085 Height in metres
▼219 Depth in metres
Moorland, unimproved grassland
Improved grassland
Arable land
Woodland
Prehistoric remains

Legend

Birmingham — More than 1 000 000 inhabitants
Nottingham — 250 000 – 1 000 000 inhabitants
Southend-on-Sea — 50 000 – 250 000 inhabitants
Aberystwyth — 10 000 – 50 000 inhabitants
Okehampton — Less than 10 000 inhabitants

London — Capital city underlined
International boundary
National boundary
County boundary
Main railway
Train ferry
Motorway
Main road
Other road
Car ferry
Canal
Stonehenge — Prehistoric remains
⊕ Airport
Dam
•1085 Height in metres
▼ 170 Depth in metres

Mountain
Moorland, unimproved grassland
Improved grassland
Arable land
Woodland

26

0 10 20 30 40 50 km
1 cm on the map = 12.5 km on the earth's surface

Scale 1:1 250 000

© EMS/BARTHOLOMEW

CONIC PROJECTION

0   10   20   30 miles

1 inch on the map = 20 miles on the earth's surface

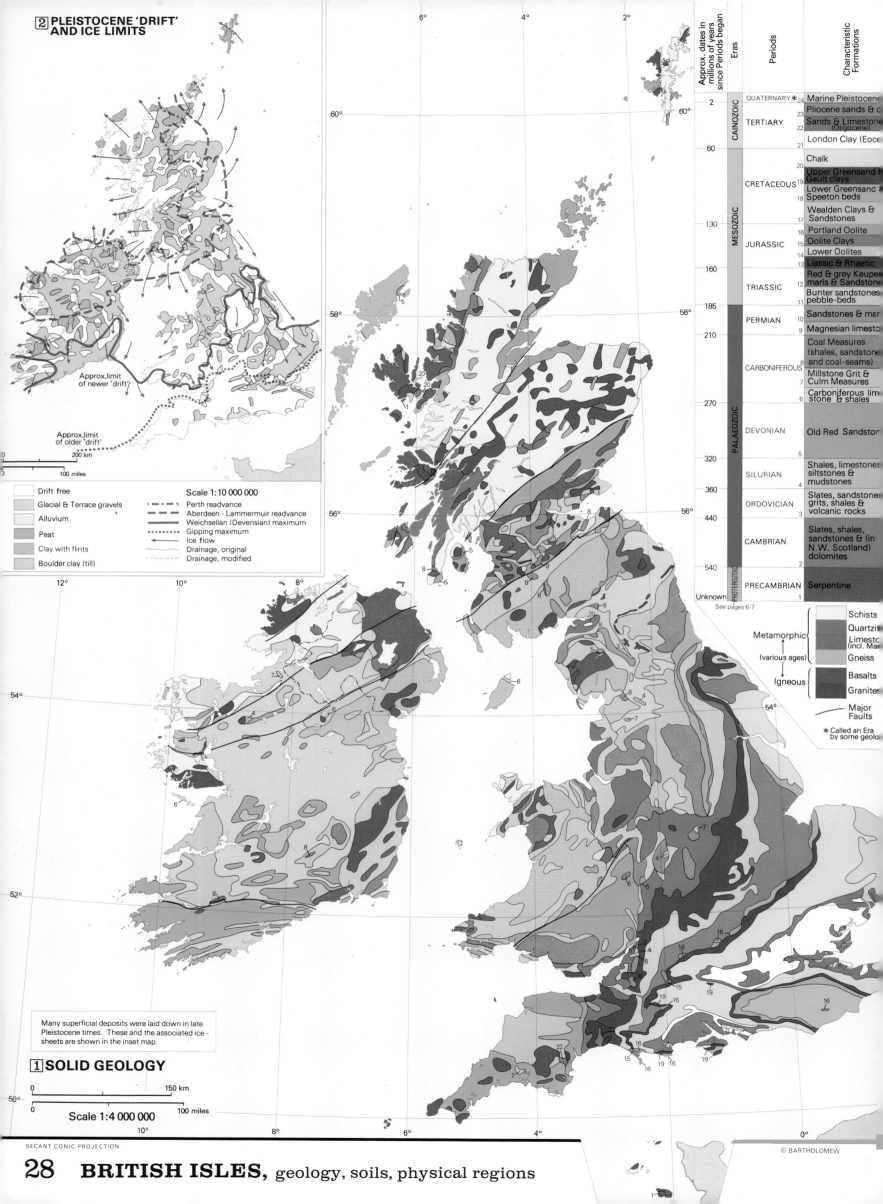

Approx. limit of newer 'drift'

Approx. limit of older 'drift'

200 km

100 miles

Drift free	Scale 1:10 000 000
Glacial & Terrace gravels	—·—·— Perth readvance
Alluvium	——— Aberdeen - Lammermuir readvance
Peat	——— Weichselian (Devensian) maximum
Clay with flints	········ Gipping maximum
Boulder clay (till)	←— Ice flow
	←— Drainage, original
	←-- Drainage, modified

Approx. dates in millions of years since Periods began	Eras	Periods	Characteristic Formations
2	CAINOZOIC	QUATERNARY * 24	Marine Pleistocene
		TERTIARY 23	Pliocene sands & c
		22	Sands & Limestone (Oligocene)
60		21	London Clay (Eoce
	MESOZOIC	CRETACEOUS 20	Chalk
		19	Upper Greensand & Gault clays
		18	Lower Greensand & Speeton beds
130		17	Wealden Clays & Sandstones
		JURASSIC 16	Portland Oolite
		15	Oolite Clays
		14	Lower Oolites
160		13	Liassic & Rhaetic
		TRIASSIC 12	Red & grey Keuper marls & Sandstone
185		11	Bunter sandstones pebble-beds
	PALAEOZOIC	PERMIAN 10	Sandstones & mar
210		9	Magnesian limesto
		CARBONIFEROUS 8	Coal Measures (shales, sandstone and coal-seams)
270		7	Millstone Grit & Culm Measures
		6	Carboniferous lime stone & shales
320		DEVONIAN 5	Old Red Sandstor
		SILURIAN 4	Shales, limestones siltstones & mudstones
360		ORDOVICIAN 3	Slates, sandstones grits, shales & volcanic rocks
440		CAMBRIAN 2	Slates, shales, sandstones & (in N.W. Scotland) dolomites
540	PROTEROZOIC	PRECAMBRIAN 1	Serpentine
Unknown			

See pages 6-7

Metamorphic (various ages)	Schists
	Quartzit
	Limesto (incl. Ma
	Gneiss
Igneous	Basalts
	Granites

— Major Faults

* Called an Era by some geolo

Many superficial deposits were laid down in late Pleistocene times. These and the associated ice-sheets are shown in the inset map.

① SOLID GEOLOGY

150 km

100 miles

Scale 1:4 000 000

Highlands
Monadhliath Mts.
Grampians
The Trossachs
Sidlaw Hills
Ochil Hills
Carrick Hills
Lammermuir Hills
Cheviots

Mts. of Donegal
Mts. of Mourne
Mts. of Mayo
Slieve Aughty Mts.
Wicklow Mts.
Mts. of Munster
Cambrian Mts.

10 The Pennines
11 Cumbrian Hills
12 Cleveland Hills
13 Yorkshire Wolds
14 Lincoln Wolds
15 Lincoln Edge
16 Northampton Uplds.
17 Chilterns
18 North Downs
19 South Downs
20 N. Berks Downs
21 N. Hants Downs
22 Purbeck Hills
23 Mendips
24 Cotswolds
25 Malvern Hills

PHYSICAL REGIONS

Scale: 1:10 000 000

Antrim Plateau	Fenlands
Mts. of Donegal	East Anglia
Mts. of Mayo	London Basin
Central Plain	The Weald
Mts. of Munster	Hampshire Basin
Wicklow Mts.	S.W. Peninsula
Mts. of Mourne	Welsh Uplands
Scottish Highlands	
Scottish Lowlands	
Southern Uplands	
Lake District	
The Pennines	
English Lowlands	

5 PROFILES OF THREE COMMON SOILS
after Kubiena

Brown earth   Gley   Podsol

Depth of profile — 1 metre

A
B
C

Typical of fertile arable land

Typical of wet pasture land

Typical of sandy heaths and uplands

Soils are naturally divided into different layers or horizons. These, called A, B, and C, lie on unweathered rock known as horizon D.

3 SOILS (mainly after Cruikshank)

Calcareous brown earth	Basin peat and alluvial gleys
Brown earth	Peaty gley and blanket peat
Acid brown earth	Peaty podsol
Gley	Podsol

SECANT CONIC PROJECTION

0 — 150 km   0 — 100 miles   Scale 1:4 000 000

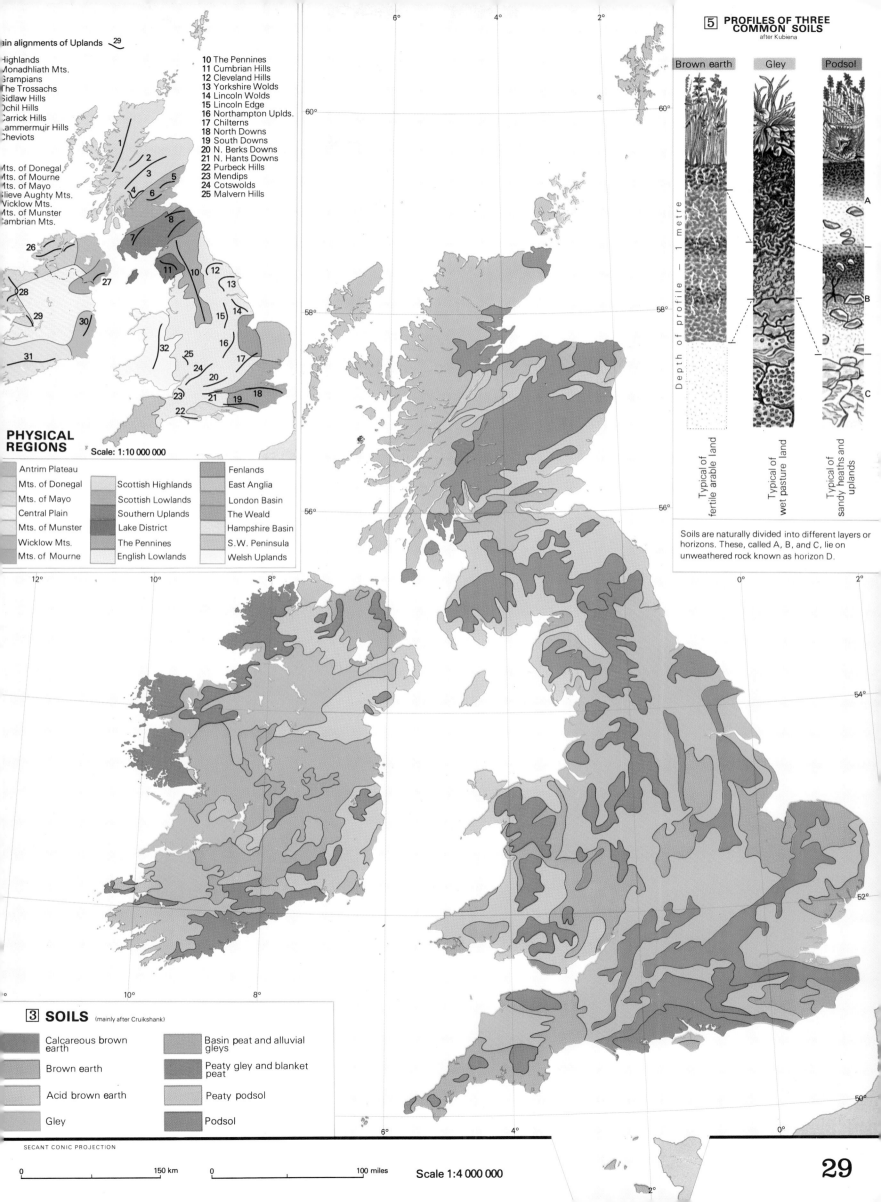

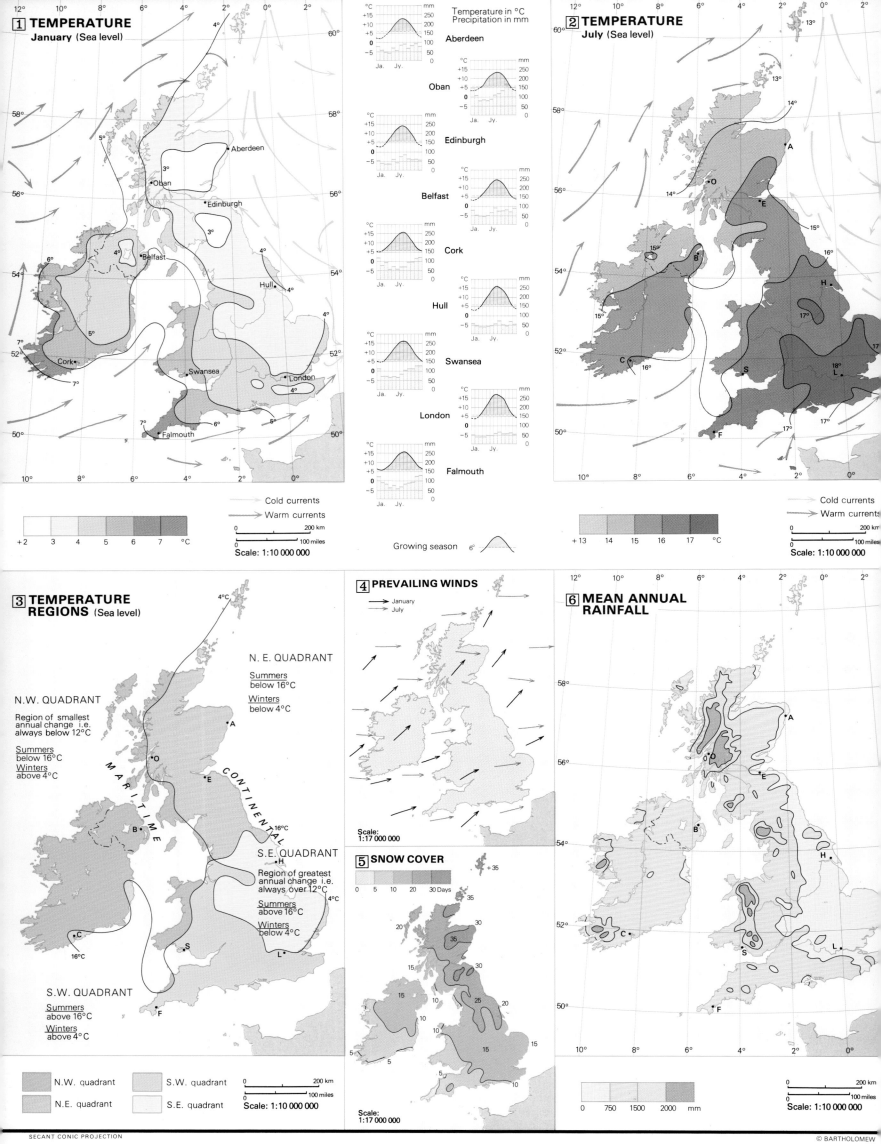

1 TEMPERATURE
January (Sea level)

Temperature in °C
Precipitation in mm

Aberdeen
Oban
Edinburgh
Belfast
Cork
Hull
Swansea
London
Falmouth

Cold currents
Warm currents

Growing season

+2 3 4 5 6 7 °C

0   200 km
0   100 miles
Scale: 1:10 000 000

2 TEMPERATURE
July (Sea level)

Cold currents
Warm currents

+13 14 15 16 17 °C

0   200 km
0   100 miles
Scale: 1:10 000 000

3 TEMPERATURE REGIONS (Sea level)

N.E. QUADRANT

Summers
below 16°C

Winters
below 4°C

N.W. QUADRANT

Region of smallest
annual change i.e.
always below 12°C

Summers
below 16°C
Winters
above 4°C

MARITIME

CONTINENTAL

S.E. QUADRANT

Region of greatest
annual change i.e.
always over 12°C

Summers
above 16°C
Winters
below 4°C

S.W. QUADRANT

Summers
above 16°C
Winters
above 4°C

N.W. quadrant   S.W. quadrant
N.E. quadrant   S.E. quadrant

0   200 km
0   100 miles
Scale: 1:10 000 000

4 PREVAILING WINDS

January
July

Scale:
1:17 000 000

5 SNOW COVER

0   5   10   20   30 Days

Scale:
1:17 000 000

6 MEAN ANNUAL RAINFALL

0   750   1500   2000   mm

0   200 km
0   100 miles
Scale: 1:10 000 000

1 RELIEF

Heights in metres

	1000
	500
	200
	100
	0

Land below sea level

	0
	100
	200
	500
	1000

Depths in metres

SECANT CONIC PROJECTION

0   50   100   150 km
0   50   100 miles

Scale 1:4 000 000

31

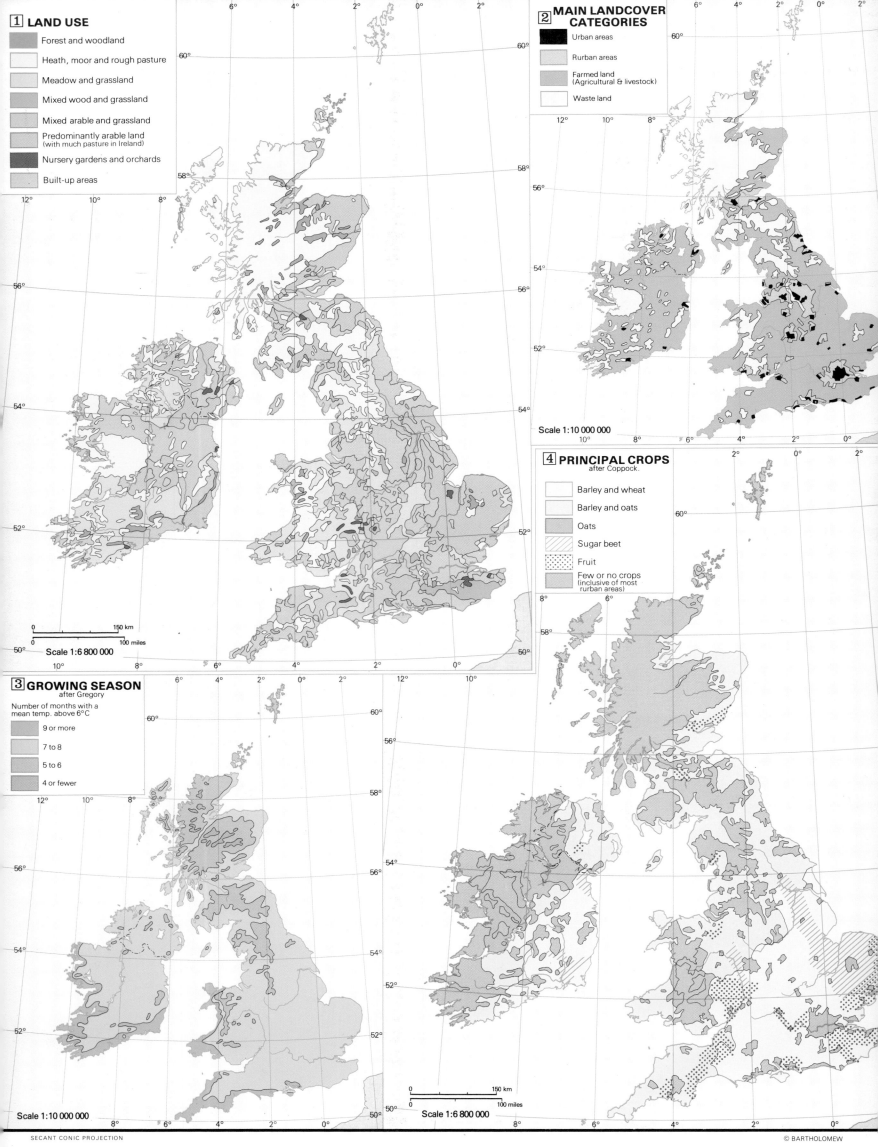

1 LAND USE

- Forest and woodland
- Heath, moor and rough pasture
- Meadow and grassland
- Mixed wood and grassland
- Mixed arable and grassland
- Predominantly arable land (with much pasture in Ireland)
- Nursery gardens and orchards
- Built-up areas

0   150 km
0   100 miles
Scale 1:6 800 000

2 MAIN LANDCOVER CATEGORIES

- Urban areas
- Rurban areas
- Farmed land (Agricultural & livestock)
- Waste land

Scale 1:10 000 000

4 PRINCIPAL CROPS after Coppock.

- Barley and wheat
- Barley and oats
- Oats
- Sugar beet
- Fruit
- Few or no crops (inclusive of most rurban areas)

3 GROWING SEASON after Gregory

Number of months with a mean temp. above 6°C

- 9 or more
- 7 to 8
- 5 to 6
- 4 or fewer

Scale 1:10 000 000

0   150 km
0   100 miles
Scale 1:6 800 000

SECANT CONIC PROJECTION

© BARTHOLOMEW

32   BRITISH ISLES, agriculture, livestock, fishing

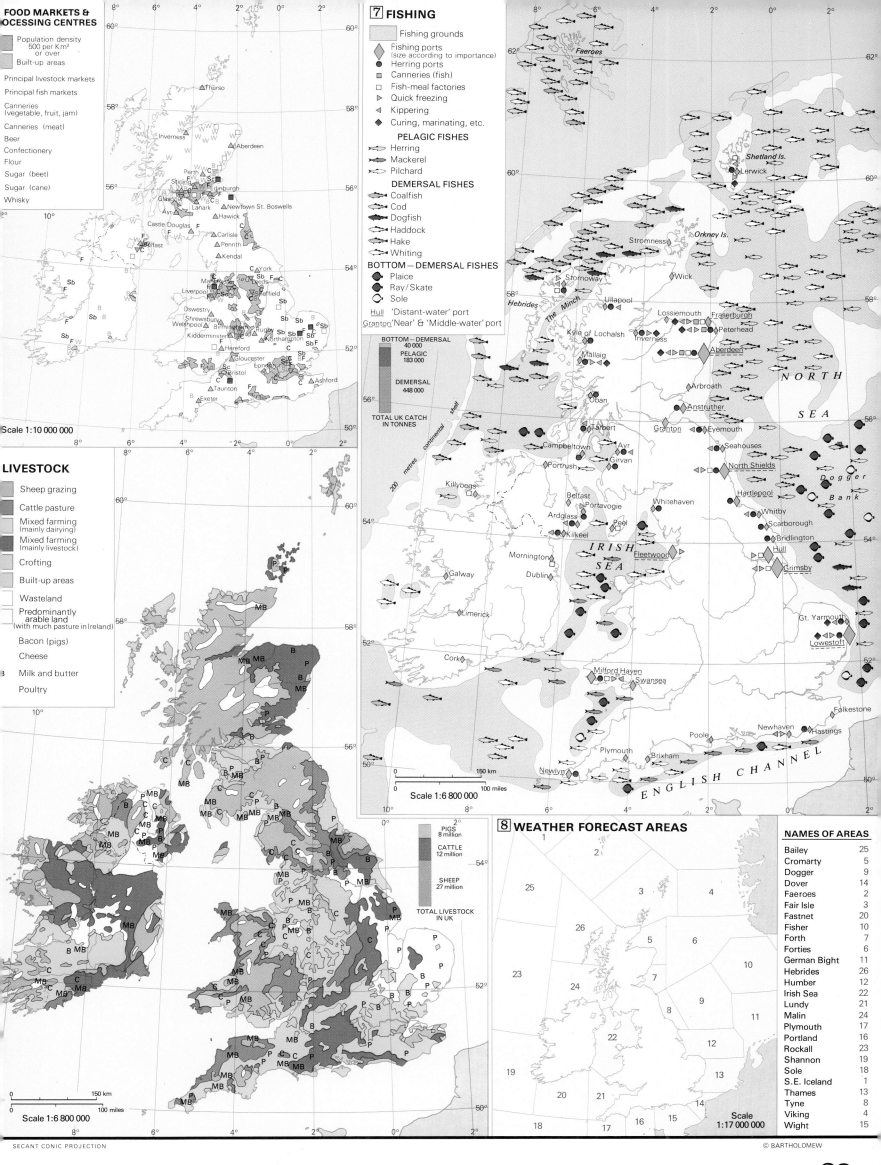

Areas with more than
1 person per km²

Areas with less than
1 person per km²

■ Over 2 000 000 inhabitants

■ 1 000 000 - 2 000 000

■ 500 000 - 1 000 000

■ 250 000 - 500 000

■ 100 000 - 250 000

■ 50 000 - 100 000

▪ 25 000 - 50 000

· 10 000 - 25 000

· 1 000 - 10 000

Based on the most recent census returns. The latest
comprehensive census made for the British Isles (N.
Ireland excepted) occurred in 1971. The most recent
N. Ireland census occurred in 1961.

0 ————————— 150 km
0 ————————— 100 miles

Scale 1:4 000 000

SECANT CONIC PROJECTION

© BARTHOLO

34   BRITISH ISLES, population

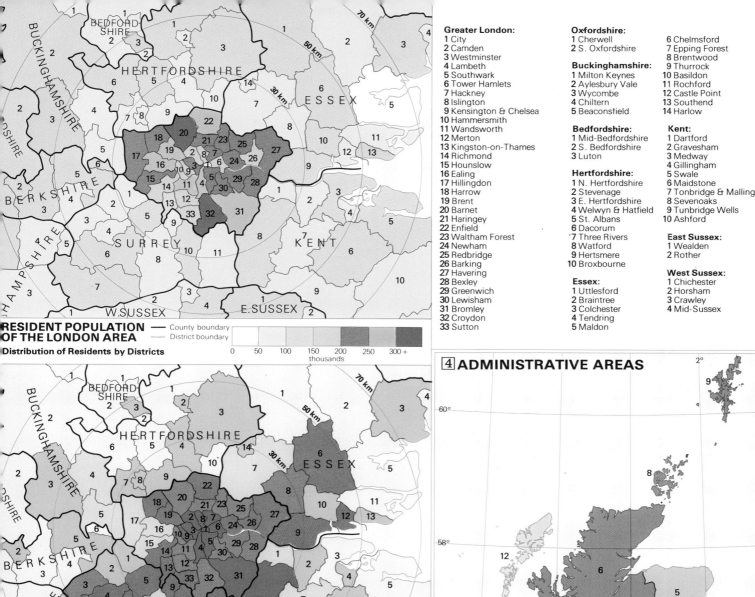

RESIDENT POPULATION OF THE LONDON AREA
Distribution of Residents by Districts

— County boundary
— District boundary

| 0 | 50 | 100 | 150 | 200 | 250 | 300 + |
thousands

Greater London:
1 City
2 Camden
3 Westminster
4 Lambeth
5 Southwark
6 Tower Hamlets
7 Hackney
8 Islington
9 Kensington & Chelsea
10 Hammersmith
11 Wandsworth
12 Merton
13 Kingston-on-Thames
14 Richmond
15 Hounslow
16 Ealing
17 Hillingdon
18 Harrow
19 Brent
20 Barnet
21 Haringey
22 Enfield
23 Waltham Forest
24 Newham
25 Redbridge
26 Barking
27 Havering
28 Bexley
29 Greenwich
30 Lewisham
31 Bromley
32 Croydon
33 Sutton

Oxfordshire:
1 Cherwell
2 S. Oxfordshire

Buckinghamshire:
1 Milton Keynes
2 Aylesbury Vale
3 Wycombe
4 Chiltern
5 Beaconsfield

Bedfordshire:
1 Mid-Bedfordshire
2 S. Bedfordshire
3 Luton

Hertfordshire:
1 N. Hertfordshire
2 Stevenage
3 E. Hertfordshire
4 Welwyn & Hatfield
5 St. Albans
6 Dacorum
7 Three Rivers
8 Watford
9 Hertsmere
10 Broxbourne

Essex:
1 Uttlesford
2 Braintree
3 Colchester
4 Tendring
5 Maldon

6 Chelmsford
7 Epping Forest
8 Brentwood
9 Thurrock
10 Basildon
11 Rochford
12 Castle Point
13 Southend
14 Harlow

Kent:
1 Dartford
2 Gravesham
3 Medway
4 Gillingham
5 Swale
6 Maidstone
7 Tonbridge & Malling
8 Sevenoaks
9 Tunbridge Wells
10 Ashford

East Sussex:
1 Wealden
2 Rother

West Sussex:
1 Chichester
2 Horsham
3 Crawley
4 Mid-Sussex

Hampshire:
1 Basingstoke & Deane
2 Winchester
3 East Hampshire
4 Hart
5 Rushmoor

Surrey:
1 Spelthorne
2 Runnymede
3 Surrey Heath
4 Woking
5 Elmbridge
6 Guildford
7 Waverley
8 Mole Valley
9 Epsom & Ewell
10 Reigate & Banstead
11 Tandridge

Berkshire:
1 Newbury
2 Reading
3 Wokingham
4 Bracknell
5 Windsor & Maidenhead
6 Slough

JOURNEY TO WORK
Commuters to Central London
(St. Paul's Cathedral taken as centre of map)

— County boundary
— District boundary

| 0 | 10 | 20 | 30 | 40 | 50 + |
percentage of residents

Scotland:
1 Borders
2 Central
3 Dumfries & Galloway
4 Fife
5 Grampian
6 Highland
7 Lothian
8 Orkney
9 Shetland
10 Strathclyde
11 Tayside
12 Western Isles

England:
1 Avon
2 Bedfordshire
3 Berkshire
4 Buckinghamshire
5 Cambridgeshire
6 Cheshire
7 Cleveland
8 Cornwall
9 Cumbria
10 Derbyshire
11 Devon
12 Dorset
13 Durham
14 East Sussex
15 Essex
16 Gloucestershire
17 Greater London
18 Greater Manchester
19 Hampshire
20 Hereford & Worcester
21 Hertfordshire
22 Humberside
23 Isle of Wight
24 Isles of Scilly
25 Kent
26 Lancashire
27 Leicestershire
28 Lincolnshire
29 Merseyside
30 Norfolk
31 Northampton
32 Northumberland
33 North Yorkshire
34 Nottinghamshire
35 Oxfordshire
36 Salop (Shropshire)
37 Somerset
38 South Yorkshire
39 Staffordshire
40 Suffolk
41 Surrey
42 Tyne & Wear
43 Warwickshire
44 West Midlands
45 West Sussex
46 West Yorkshire
47 Wiltshire

Wales:
1 Clwyd
2 Dyfed
3 Gwent
4 Gwynedd
5 Mid Glamorgan
6 Powys
7 South Glamorgan
8 West Glamorgan

N. Ireland:
a Antrim
b Armagh
c Down
d Fermanagh
e Londonderry
f Tyrone
(formerly N. Ireland counties)

Eire:
1 Carlow
2 Cavan
3 Clare
4 Cork
5 Donegal
6 Dublin
7 Galway
8 Kerry
9 Kildare
10 Kilkenny
11 Laoighis (Laois)
12 Leitrim
13 Limerick
14 Longford
15 Louth
16 Mayo
17 Meath
18 Monaghan
19 Offaly
20 Roscommon
21 Sligo
22 Tipperary
23 Waterford
24 Westmeath
25 Wexford
26 Wicklow

SECANT CONIC PROJECTION

4 ADMINISTRATIVE AREAS

Isle of Man

Scale 1:6 000 000

| 0 | 200 km |
| 0 | 120 miles |

Channel Islands

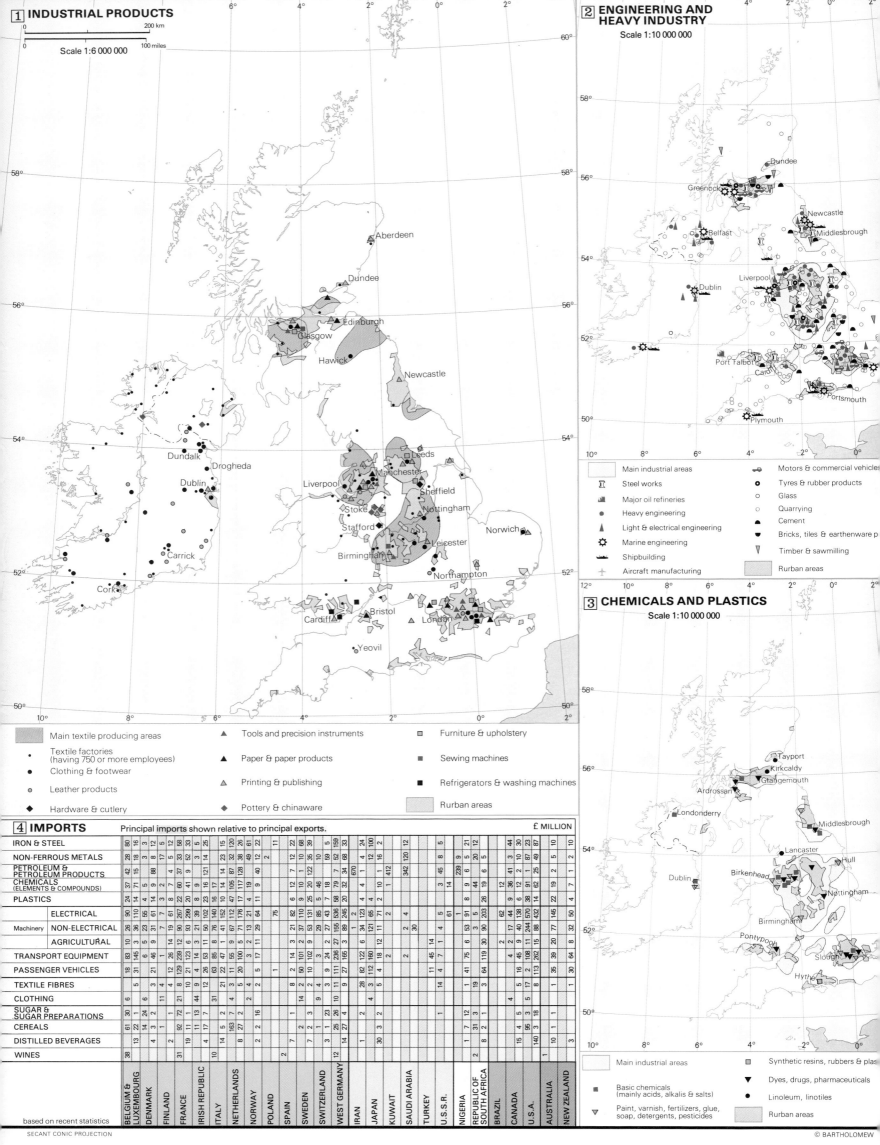

1 INDUSTRIAL PRODUCTS

Scale 1:6 000 000

0 — 200 km
0 — 100 miles

2 ENGINEERING AND HEAVY INDUSTRY

Scale 1:10 000 000

Legend (Map 2)

	Main industrial areas
	Steel works
	Major oil refineries
	Heavy engineering
	Light & electrical engineering
	Marine engineering
	Shipbuilding
	Aircraft manufacturing
	Motors & commercial vehicles
	Tyres & rubber products
	Glass
	Quarrying
	Cement
	Bricks, tiles & earthenware products
	Timber & sawmilling
	Rurban areas

3 CHEMICALS AND PLASTICS

Scale 1:10 000 000

Legend (Map 3)

	Main industrial areas
	Basic chemicals (mainly acids, alkalis & salts)
	Paint, varnish, fertilizers, glue, soap, detergents, pesticides
	Synthetic resins, rubbers & plastics
	Dyes, drugs, pharmaceuticals
	Linoleum, linotiles
	Rurban areas

Legend (Map 1)

	Main textile producing areas
	Textile factories (having 750 or more employees)
	Clothing & footwear
	Leather products
	Hardware & cutlery
	Tools and precision instruments
	Paper & paper products
	Printing & publishing
	Pottery & chinaware
	Furniture & upholstery
	Sewing machines
	Refrigerators & washing machines
	Rurban areas

4 IMPORTS

Principal imports shown relative to principal exports.

£ MILLION

	BELGIUM & LUXEMBOURG	DENMARK	FINLAND	FRANCE	IRISH REPUBLIC	ITALY	NETHERLANDS	NORWAY	POLAND	SPAIN	SWEDEN	SWITZERLAND	WEST GERMANY	IRAN	JAPAN	KUWAIT	SAUDI ARABIA	TURKEY	U.S.S.R.	NIGERIA	REP. OF SOUTH AFRICA	BRAZIL	CANADA	U.S.A.	AUSTRALIA	NEW ZEALAND
IRON & STEEL	80	16	3	12	12	58	5	25		15	120	26	61		11		22	68	39		5	159	33		24	100		12			5			21	12		44	30	87		10	10
NON-FERROUS METALS	28	18	3	12	17	33	3	14		12	120	38	12		12		12	10	10	59	52	68	5		4	22	16	120		8		9	25	20	5		3	21	49		5	10
PETROLEUM & PETROLEUM PRODUCTS	42	15		88		4	37	9		4	87	128		40			7	1	122		34	670			412		342	107	239	6	6		45	30			41	1	9			
CHEMICALS (ELEMENTS & COMPOUNDS)	37	71	4	6	29	7	60	9		17	105	117	9	9		4		12	10	5	7	58	79	32	4		10	1	4		3	14		9	49	19		12	36	91	62		19	7
PLASTICS	24	14	4	14	8	22	20	8		16	47	17	11			6	9	9	5	7	58	20	4	4	2			8		9	26		9	38	14		22	4
Machinery — ELECTRICAL	90	110	5	61	61	267	39	140		112	176	64		75		82	110	85	45	536	245		4		123	71		4		5	61		91	6	203	62	44	570	432		145	50
Machinery — NON-ELECTRICAL	26	36	3	31	31	19	90	21		50	102	67	71		29		21	37	53	29	155	89		34		12	11	7	30	4		53	29	90		17	244	88		77	32
Machinery — AGRICULTURAL	10	3	2	9	14	12	4	1		1	26	27	3			3	2	4			14	1		6		2	30	10	14		6	8		2	9	11		20	7
TRANSPORT EQUIPMENT	83	145	6	46	1	26	239	14		85	123	55	1		17		14	101	2	24	236	165		122	60	18	2		45	7	1		75		4	45	108	262		39	64
PASSENGER VEHICLES	18	31	2	21		12	129	4		63	123	11	20	1		2	50	10	4	82	112	4		1		11	4		41	64		16	2	1	113	262		35	30
TEXTILE FIBRES		5	3	4	8	10	13	4		3	3	2	1		8	2	5	2	4	3			28			1	14		1	19	3		5	12	8		1	
CLOTHING	6		8	11		4	21	44		31		4	5			14	5	3	10		2	4				4	1	5					
SUGAR & SUGAR PREPARATIONS	5	30	1	24	2	1	72	13		7		1	16			1	3	23	26	4		2	2			5	7	12	1		5	3	18			
CEREALS	61	14	22	11	3	1	92	11	11	5	163		27	2		2		1	25	27			3		1		4	95	3	1			
DISTILLED BEVERAGES		13		4		4	2		19	11	4	14	1		5	2		7	1	3		30		14		1			15	4	8	8		10	3
WINES	38			4	31		10					2											2		1				

based on recent statistics

SECANT CONIC PROJECTION

© BARTHOLOMEW

36 BRITISH ISLES, industry, energy

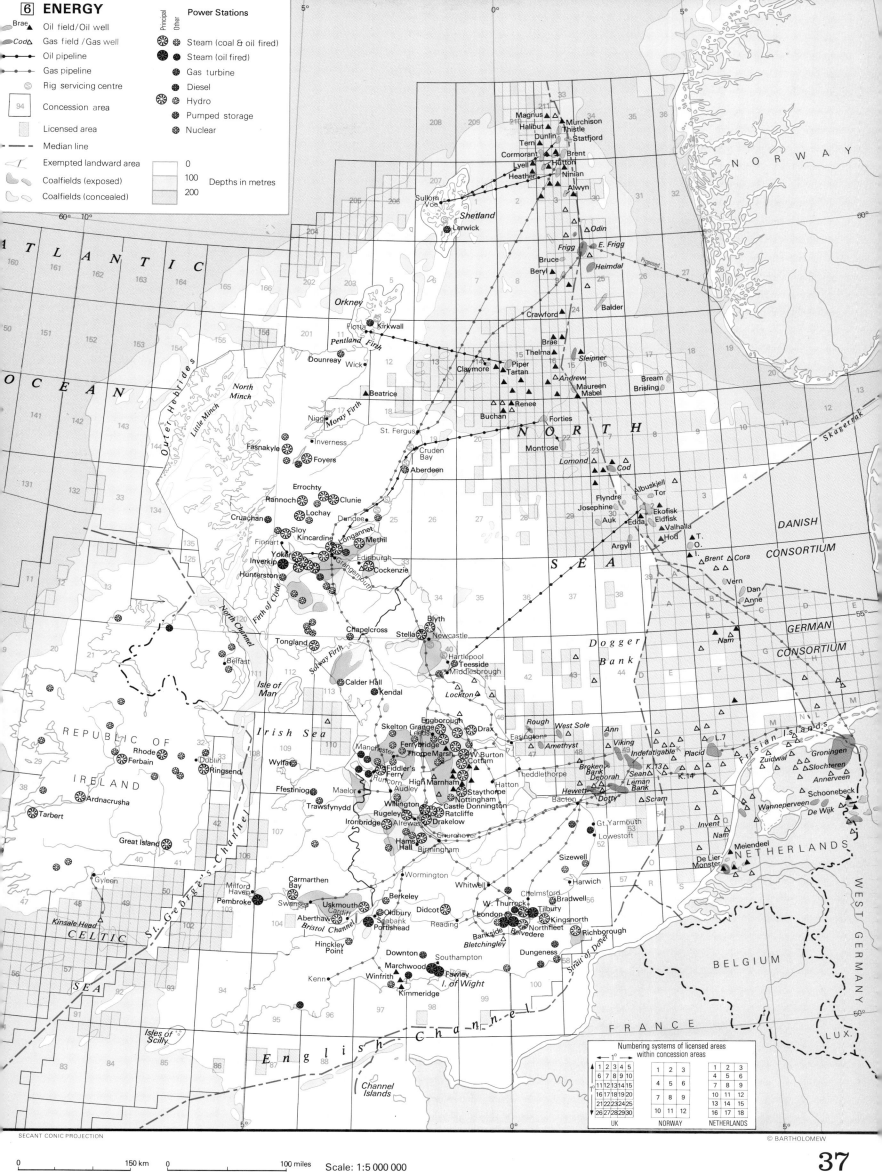

Power Stations

Principal Other

Brae ▲	Oil field/Oil well	
Cod △	Gas field/Gas well	

Oil pipeline
Gas pipeline
Ⓢ Rig servicing centre
94 Concession area
Licensed area
Median line
Exempted landward area
Coalfields (exposed)
Coalfields (concealed)

Steam (coal & oil fired)
Steam (oil fired)
Gas turbine
Diesel
Hydro
Pumped storage
Nuclear

0
100
200
Depths in metres

ATLANTIC OCEAN

NORWAY

NORTH SEA

DANISH CONSORTIUM

GERMAN CONSORTIUM

Dogger Bank

REPUBLIC OF IRELAND

Irish Sea

St. George's Channel

CELTIC SEA

English Channel

Channel Islands

Isles of Scilly

NETHERLANDS

BELGIUM

WEST GERMANY

LUX.

FRANCE

SECANT CONIC PROJECTION

Numbering systems of licensed areas
within concession areas

1	2	3	4	5
6	7	8	9	10
11	12	13	14	15
16	17	18	19	20
21	22	23	24	25
26	27	28	29	30

UK

1	2	3
4	5	6
7	8	9
10	11	12

NORWAY

1	2	3
4	5	6
7	8	9
10	11	12
13	14	15
16	17	18

NETHERLANDS

© BARTHOLOMEW

0   150 km   0   100 miles   Scale: 1:5 000 000

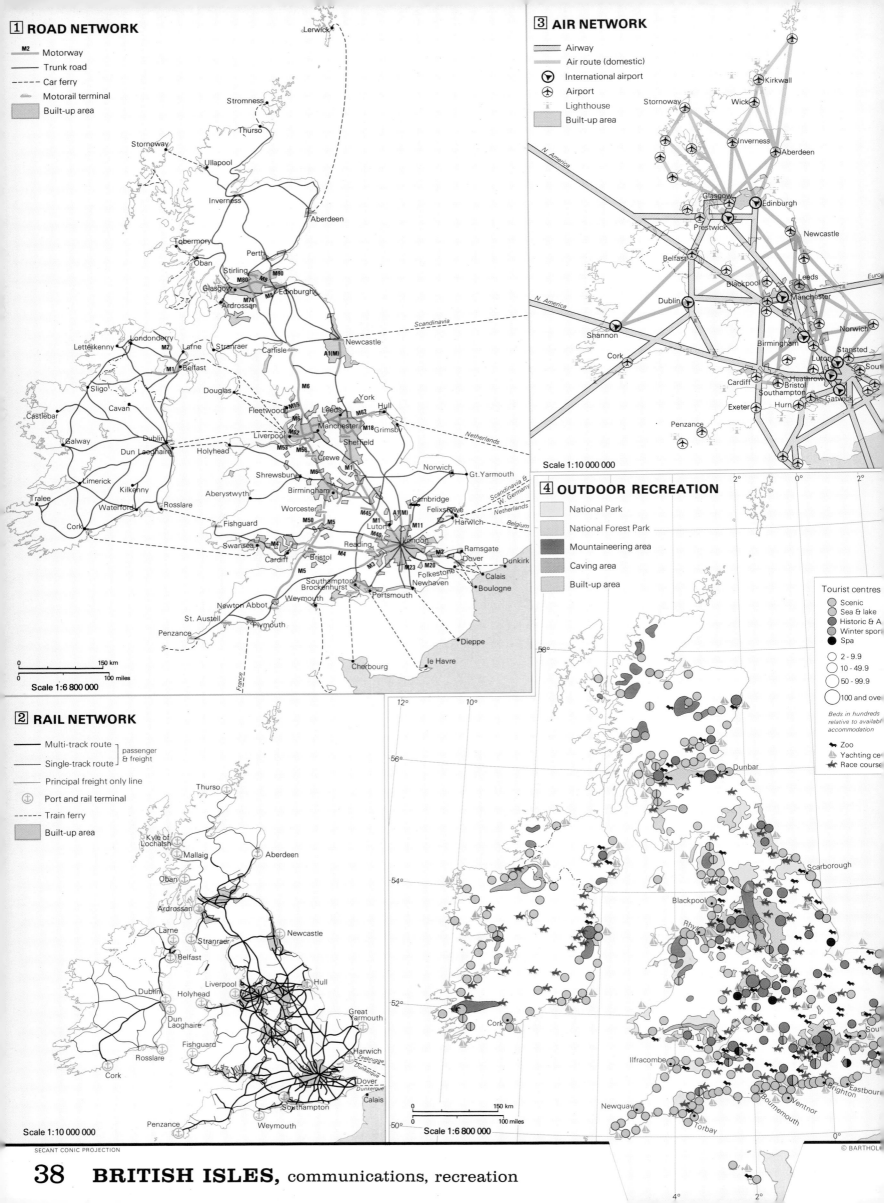

1 ROAD NETWORK

M2	Motorway
	Trunk road
- - -	Car ferry
	Motorail terminal
	Built-up area

Scale 1:6 800 000

2 RAIL NETWORK

	Multi-track route
	Single-track route
	Principal freight only line
⊕	Port and rail terminal
- - -	Train ferry
	Built-up area

passenger & freight

Scale 1:10 000 000

SECANT CONIC PROJECTION

3 AIR NETWORK

	Airway
	Air route (domestic)
▼	International airport
✈	Airport
	Lighthouse
	Built-up area

Scale 1:10 000 000

4 OUTDOOR RECREATION

	National Park
	National Forest Park
	Mountaineering area
	Caving area
	Built-up area

Tourist centres
- Scenic
- Sea & lake
- Historic & A
- Winter spor
- Spa

2 - 9.9
10 - 49.9
50 - 99.9
100 and ove

Beds in hundreds relative to availabl accommodation

Zoo
Yachting ce
Race course

Scale 1:6 800 000

© BARTHOL

THE BENELUX, environment

39

Scale 1:5 000 00

MBERT'S CONFORMAL CONIC PROJECTION

| | 50 | | 100 | 150 | 200 km |

| 0 | 50 | 100 | 150 miles |

on the map = 50 km on the earth's surface

1 inch on the map = 80 miles on the earth's surface

Scale 1:5 000 000

© EMS

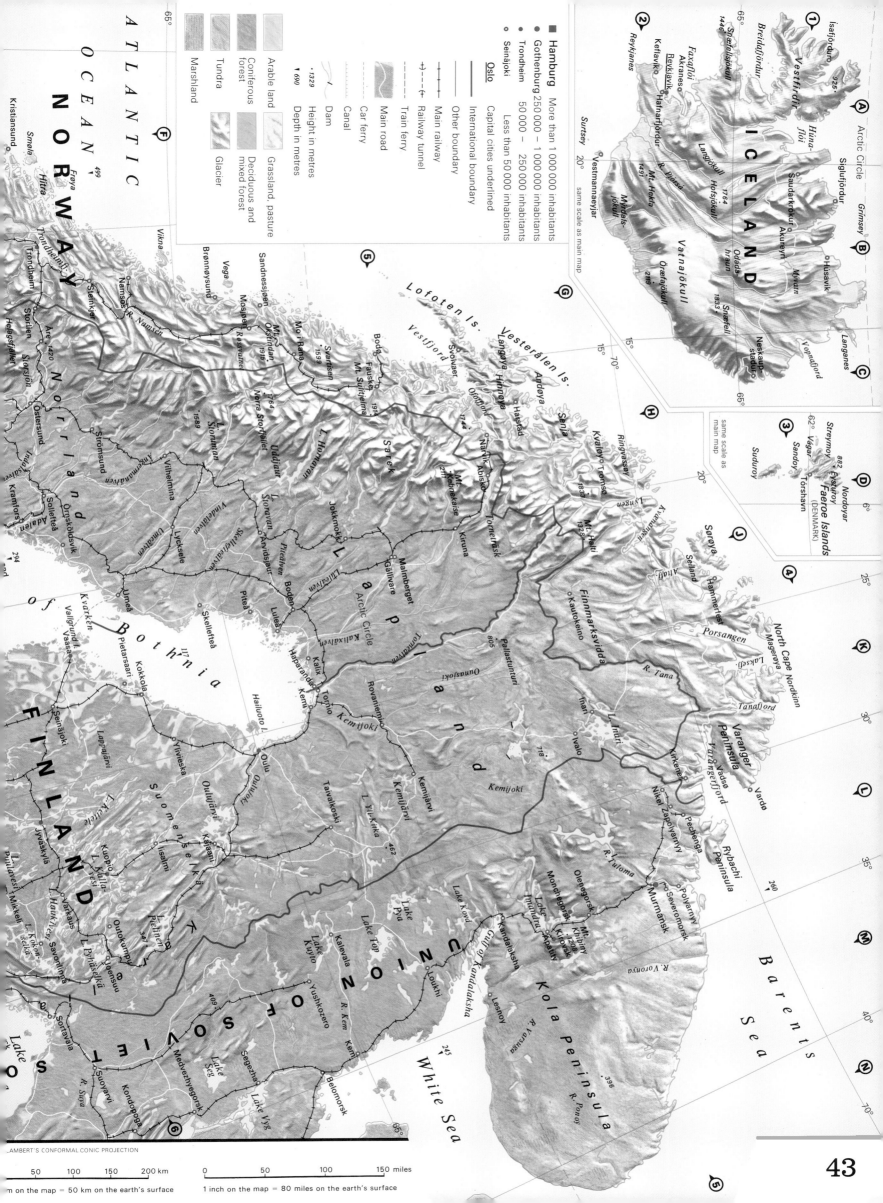

SOUTH WEST EUROPE, environment 45

50   100   150   200 km   0   50   100   150 miles

n the map = 50 km on the earth's surface   1 inch on the map = 80 miles on the earth's surface

Scale 1:5 000 00

© EMS

30°

Mogilev
Podolskiy · E · Dneprodzerzhinsk · F · Thorez Krasnyy · G · Volgodonsk 40°
Uman Kirovograd Dnepropetrovsk Sinelnikovo Donetsk Makeyevka Luch Shakhty
Beltsy Rybnitsa Krivoy Rog Zaporozhye Novoshakhtinsk Novocherkassk
Pervomaysk Nikopol Taganrog Rostov na Donu R. Don Salsk
Kishinev Marganets Zhdanov Bataysk
Kotovsk UKRAINIAN S.S.R. ·324 Azov
Tiraspol NIKOLAYEV U. S. S. Berdyansk Yeysk RUSSIAN S.F.S.R.
Bendery Kherson Melitopol Primorsko Tikhoretsk Kropotkin 45°
R. Dniester Kakhovka Akhtarsk Armavir Stavropol
Odessa Novaja Kakhovka Reservoir Slavyansk Ust Labinsk
Belgorod Sea of na Kubani Labinsk Nevinnomyssk
Galati Dnestrovsky Genichesk Azov R. Kuban Maykop Cherkessk
R. Dnieper 14 Kerch Krasnodar Apsheronsk
Izmail L. Sivash Feodosiya Krymsk Caucasus
Danube Dzhankoy Novorossiysk Mts.
Bolgrad Delta Crimea Tuapse 2867 Mt. Elbrus
Tulcea 5633
Yevpatoriya GEORGIAN S.S.R.
Danube Simferopol 2
Constanta Sevastopol 1545 Alushta 1768 Sukhumi
Dobrogea Yalta Sochi
R. Danube 2050
Tolbukhin

Black Sea

Varna 2244

Burgas 2045
Rize
3937
Sinop Pontine Bafra Samsun Ordu Trabzon R. Çoruh
Kastamonu Mountains
Zonguldak R. Yesil 3305 40°
Karabük 2600 Amasya R. Kelkit
Bosporus Çankırı Çorum
Istanbul Bolu Kızıl Irmak R. Tokat Sivas
(Constantinople) Üsküdar İzmit Adapazarı 2378
1350 Sea of Marmara Ankara Yozgat
Bursa Eskişehir R. Sakarya 870 Kırıkkale Kızıl Irmak R.
İnegöl Gordium
Bandırma Kütahya Polatlı Kırşehir
Balıkesir TURKEY Kayseri
L. Tuz Nevşehir 3916
Uşak Afyonkarahisar Anatolia 3090
Pergamum Akşehir Niğde Maraş
gama Salihli 2591 L. Eğridir L. 3734 R. Seyhan 3
Akhisar R. Simav 2157 Beyşehir Cilician R. Ceyhan
zmir Isparta Konya Ereğli Gates Gaziantep
yrna Nazilli Denizli 3585 Ceyhan
Aydın Burdur Karaman Taurus Adana Osmaniye Kilis
iletus Mountains Mersin Tarsus
Halicarnassus 3086 Antalya 2374 İskenderun Aleppo
Rhodes Antakya (Halab)
3864 Idlib
Rhodes Megista I. 2538 SYRIA
Kárpathos Latakia 1562 Hama
CYPRUS Kyrenia 35°
Nicosia Famagusta Baniyâs
1952 Larnaca 1463 Homs
D · E · Tripoli
Limassol LEBANON
30° 35°

BERT'S CONFORMAL CONIC PROJECTION

50 100 150 200 km
on the map = 50 km on the earth's surface

0 50 100 150 miles
1 inch on the map = 80 miles on the earth's surface

WESTERN TURKEY, environment **47**

■ İstanbul
More than 1 000 000 inhabitants

● Catania
250 000 – 1 000 000 inhabitants

• Novi Sad
50 000 – 250 000 inhabitants

○ Famagusta
Less than 50 000 inhabitants

Valletta Capital cities underlined

International boundary

Other boundary

Main railway

Railway tunnel

Train ferry

Main road

Car ferry = Pass

Canal ∴ Historical site

Dam

2591· Height in metres

▾2538 Depth in metres

Arable land

Grassland, pasture

Coniferous forest

Deciduous and mixed forest

Steppe, semi-desert

Desert

Marshland

Legend

♜	Cairo	More than 5 000 000 inhabitants
■	Milan	1 000 000 – 5 000 000 inhabitants
●	Bordeaux	250 000 – 1 000 000 inhabitants
●	Cagliari	50 000 – 250 000 inhabitants
○	Touggourt	Less than 50 000 inhabitants
	Cairo	Capital cities underlined

————	International bdy.
– – – –	Disputed intl. bdy.
————	Other boundary
┿┿┿┿	Main railway
– · – · –	Train ferry
	Main road
·········	Canal
	Dam
	Wadi
∴	Historical site
·1277	Height in metres
▽3068	Depth in metres

Arable land

Steppe, semi-desert

Grassland, pasture

Sand desert

Coniferous forest

Other desert

Deciduous and mixed forest

Salt pan

Marshland, swamp

© EMS

Scale 1:10 000 000

| 0 | 100 | 200 | 300 | 400 km |

1 cm on the map = 100 km on the earth's surface

| 0 | 100 | 200 miles |

1 inch on the map = 160 miles on the earth's surface

Scale 1:10 000 000

0   100   200   300   400 km

1 cm on the map = 100 km on the earth's surface

© EMS

R. Ob
65°
70°
R. Ob
60°
Varodnaya
Berezovo
Khanty Mansysk
Serginol
Mezhdurechenskiy
R. Irtysh
Tobolsk
Omsk   55°
R. Irtysh
Pavlodar
Semipalatinsk
80°
Lake Zaysan
50°
R. Pechora
R. Kama
Konzhakovsky Kamen 1569
Krasnoturinsk
Ivdel
Serov
Krasnoturinsk
R. Tavda
Tavda
Tyumen
Ishim
R. Ishim
Petropavlovsk
Kokchetav
R. Ishim
Tselinograd
Temirtau
Karaganda
1565
Avaguz
Solikamsk
Berezniki
Kizel
Votkinsk
Nizhniy Tagil
Alapayevsk
Irbit
Kungur
Kamensk Uralskiy
Shadrinsk
Kurgan
R. Tobol
Kustanay
45°
342   Balkhash
Lake Balkhash
Kudymkar
Chusovoy
Perm
Lysva
Sverdlovsk
Asbest
Polevskoy
Chelyabinsk
Kopeysk
Korkino
Miass
Troitsk
Rudnyy
L. Tenghiz
R. Ili
Glazov
Krasnokamsk
SOCIALIST REPUBLIC
Reyda
Pervouralsk
Zlatoust
Satka
Kartaly
R. Sarysu
1565
Izhevsk
Mozhga
Sarapul
Neftekamsk
Birsk
R. Ufa
1638
Magnitogorsk
Karsakpay
Dzhezkazgan
1565
KAZAKH S.S.R.
Kazan
R. Kama
Nizhnekamsk
R. Belaya
Beloretsk
Baykonur
2176
Chistopol
Almetyevsk
Oktyabrskiy
R. Ural
Kirghiz   Steppe
West Turkistan
Dzhambul
Ala Tau Range
4484
Kuybyshev Reservoir
Melekess
Bugulma
Sterlitamak
Salavat
Ishimbay
Orsk
Karsakpay
Togliatti
Bugurustan
Kumertauo
Aralsk
Chimkent
Namangan
40°
Kuybyshev
Novokuybyshevsk
Orenburg
Novotroitsk
Mednogorsk
Syr Darya
Kzyl Orda
Tashkent
Almalyk
Kokand
Zhigulevsk
Buzuluk
SOCIALIST   REPUBLICS
Aktyubinsk
Kyzyl-Kum
UZBEKISTAN   S.S.R.
Chirchik
Gulistan
Syzran
Chapayevsk
Uralsk
R. Emba
Aral Sea
Samarkand
5494
Volsk
Balakovo
Engels
R. Ural
Ust-Urt
Nukus
Urgench
Bukhara
Karshi
Kamyshin
Volgograd Reservoir
Guryev
Kungrado
Tashauz
Amu Darya
Chardzhou
35°
ASIA
EUROPE
R. Volga
Astrakhan
Volzhskiy
Akhtubinsk
TURKMENISTAN S.S.R.
Mary
Kushka
R. Kuma
Elista
Caspian Sea
Kara-Bogaz-Gol
Kara-Kum
Ashkhabad
Kopet Dagh
Mashhad
3594
Volgodonsk
Shevchenko
-28
-132
Kara-Kum
Bujnurd
Neishabur
Khurasan
AFGHANISTAN
65°
oretsk
ropotkin
Stavropol
Nevinnomyssk
Mineralnye Vody
Georgievsk
Makhachkala
1880
2340
Sabzwar
Herat
R. Kuban
Labinsk
Cherkessk
Yessentuki
Pyatigorsk
Kislovodsk
Nalchik
Grozny
Orazhonikidze
Derbent
Krasnovodsk
Sumgait
935
Neishabur
Mashhad
IRAN (PERSIA)
35°
Mt. Elbrus 5638
Caucasus Mts.
3047
4480
Baku
R. Atrek
Gurgan
Sabzwar
3341
Bujnurd
60°
Sukhumi
Kutaisi
Tskhinvali
GEORGIAN S.S.R.
Tbilisi
AZERBAYDZHAN S.S.R.
Krasnovodsk
995
Gurgan
Sari
Babul
Resht
Pahlevi
Batumi
Akhaltsikhe
Kirovabad
Kirovakan
Stepanakert
Ardebil
Elburz Mountains
TURKEY
1042
ARMENIAN S.S.R.
Yerevan
L. Sevan
Nakhichevan
Kars
Mt. Ararat 5165
4811
Trabzon
Ardebil
Resht

Legend

Shanghai More than 5 000 000 inhabitants
Nagoya 1 000 000 – 5 000 000 inhabitants
Mandalay 250 000 – 1 000 000 inhabitants
Manipur 50 000 – 250 000 inhabitants
Krasnovodsk Less than 50 000 inhabitants
<u>Katmandu</u> Capital cities underlined

Internatl. bdy. —— Disputed international boundary
Other boundary —— Historical site
Canal —— Dam
Main railway —— Main road
Railway under construction

3772 Height in metres 7222 Depth in metres

Tundra
Coniferous forest
Arable land
Grassland, pasture
Deciduous and mixed forest
Rain forest
Steppe, semi-desert
Salt desert
Sand desert
Other desert
Glacier Swamp

ARCTIC OCEAN

North Pole

Severnaya Zemlya

C. Chelyuskin

Taymyr Peninsula

Laptev Sea

East Siberian Sea

Wrangel I.

New Siberian Islands

Bering Strait

Chukotsk Peninsula Provideniya

Saint Lawrence I.

Anadyr

Pevek

Bering Sea

Khatanga

Central Siberian Plateau

Tura

Mirnyy

R. Lena

R. Vilyuy

Yakutsk

R. Aldan

Tiksi

R. Indigirka

R. Kolyma

Cherskiy Range

Verkhoyansk

Verkhoyansk Range

Ambarchik

Kamchatka

Ust Kamchatsk

Mt. Klyuchevskaya Sopka

Magadan

Okhotsk

Sea of Okhotsk

Petropavlovsk Kamchatskiy

Kuril Trench

S i b e r i a

Lower Tunguska R.

Stony Tunguska R.

Yeniseysk R. Angara

Kansk

Krasnoyarsk

Kyzyl

Abakan

Sayan Ranges

Irkutsk

L. Baykal

Cheremkhovo Angarsk

Ulan Ude

Kyakhta

Sukhe Bator

R. Selenga

Ulan Bator (Urga)

M O N G O L I A

Saynshand

Dalandzadgad

G o b i

Hovd

Hami

Nan Shan

Tsaidam

Koko Nor

Golmo

Sining

Lanchow

Hwang Ho

S O C I A L I S T   R E P U B L I C

Ust Kut

Bratsk

Kirensk

Chita

Borzya

Hailar

Choybalsan

R. Kerulen

Yablonovyy Range

Great Khingan Mts

Stanovoy Range

Skovorodino

R. Amur

Blagoveshchensk

Svobodnyy

Komsomolsk na Amure

Belogorsk

Nikolayevsk na Amure

Heilung Kiang

Nunkiang

Birobidzhan

Khabarovsk

Tsitsihar

Hokang

Kiamusze

Sungari R.

Sovetskaya Gavan

Yuzhno Sakhalinsk

Sakhalin

Aleksandrovsk

Okha

Severo Kurilsk

Kuril Islands

Soya Strait

Wakkanai

Asahigawa

Sapporo

Hokkaido

Hakodate

Harbin

Kirin

Changchun

Szeping

Fushun

Shenyang (Mukden)

Penki

Anshan

Antung

Manchuria

Sikhote Alin Ra.

L. Khanka

Vladivostok

Nakhodka

Chongjin

NORTH KOREA

Pyongyang

Sea of Japan

Aomori

Akita

Sendai

Niigata

Honshu

JAPAN

Utsunomiya

Tokyo

Yokohama

Japan Trench

INNER MONGOLIA (AUTONOMOUS REGION)

Huhehot

Paotow

Ordos Plateau

Changkiakow

Chinchow

Peking

Tatung

Tangshan

Tientsin

Luta (Dairen)

Yellow Sea

Seoul

Inchon

SOUTH KOREA

Taejon

Taegu

Pusan

Kwangju

Fukuoka

Kitakyushu

Kyoto

Kobe Osaka

Hiroshima

Matsuyama

Shikoku

Kyushu

Nagasaki

Kagoshima

Kyoto Nagoya

Fujiyama

NINGSIA HUI (AUTONOMOUS REGION)

Yinchwan

Taiyuan

Shihkiachwang

Tsingtao

Tsinan

Sinhailien

Kaifeng

Suchow

Yenan

Hantan

Sinsiang

Changyeh

Yumenshih

Changyeh

Koko Nor

Sienyang

Loyang

Chinkiang

Wusih

Shanghai

Hangchow

Ningpo

East China Sea

Sian

Paoki

Hwainan

Nanking

Wuhan

C H I N A

Chengtu

Red Basin

Chungking

Ichang

Yangtze Kiang

Changsha

Nanchang

Wenchow

Foochow

Ryukyu Islands

Naha

Kunming

Liuchow

KWANGSI CHUANG (AUTONOMOUS REGION)

Nanning

Kweilin

Nan Ling

Hengyang

Canton

Swatow

Amoy

HONG KONG (U.K.)

MACAO (PORT.)

Taipei

TAIWAN (FORMOSA)

Tainan

Kaosiung

Formosa Strait

Luzon Strait

Bonin Is. (JAPAN)

Kazan Is. (JAPAN)

Iwo Jima

Ramapo Deep 10374

P A C I F I C   O C E A N

Mariana Islands (U.S.A.)

Guam I. (U.S.A.)

Mariana Trench 11034 Challenger Deep

Tropic of Cancer

BURMA

Mandalay

Myitkyina

Chittagong

Manipur

Dacca

VIETNAM

Hanoi

Haiphong

Tsamkong

LAOS

Laoag

PHILIPPINES

AMBERT'S AZIMUTHAL EQUAL-AREA PROJECTION

Scale 1:25 000 000

1 cm on the map = 250 km on the earth's surface

1 inch on the map = 400 miles on the earth's surface

0 250 500 750 1000 km

0 200 400 600 miles

53

© EMS

Scale 1:25 000 000

| 0 | 250 | 500 | 750 | 1000 km |

1 cm on the map = 250 km on the earth's surface

| 0 | 200 | 400 | 600 miles |

1 inch on the map = 400 miles on the earth's surface

AMBERT'S AZIMUTHAL EQUAL-AREA PROJECTION

CHINA AND JAPAN, environment **57**

Legend:

Shanghai — More than 5 000 000 inhabitants
Nagoya — 1 000 000 – 5 000 000 inhabitants
Fukuoka — 250 000 – 1 000 000 inhabitants
Tsanghsien — 50 000 – 250 000 inhabitants
Saynshand — Less than 50 000 inhabitants
Seoul — Capital cities underlined

International boundary
Disputed intl. boundary
Other boundary
Main railway
Main road
Pass
Canal
Dam
Marshland, swamp
4107 · Height in metres
▼ 5415 Depth in metres

Grassland, pasture
Arable land
Coniferous forest
Deciduous and mixed forest
Rain forest
Semi-desert, steppe
Sand desert
Salt desert
Other desert

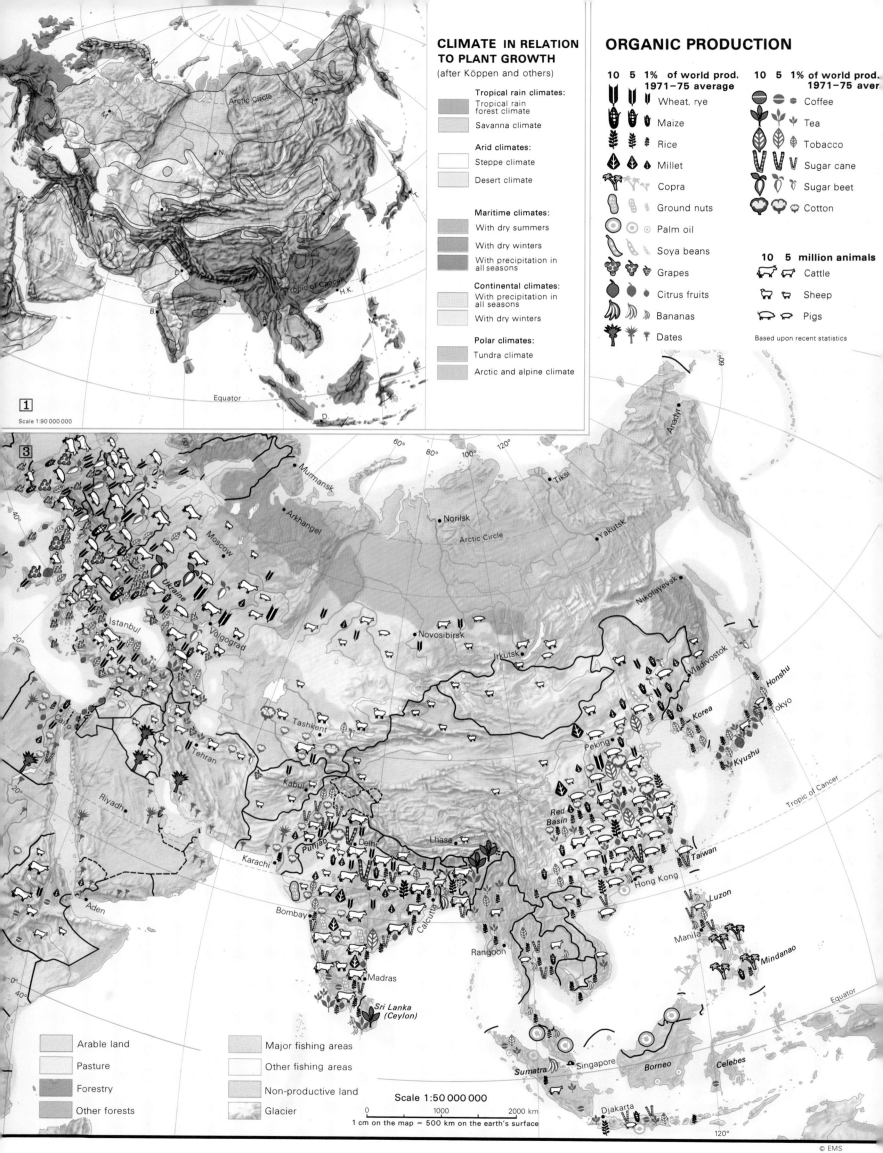

CLIMATE IN RELATION TO PLANT GROWTH
(after Köppen and others)

Tropical rain climates:
- Tropical rain forest climate
- Savanna climate

Arid climates:
- Steppe climate
- Desert climate

Maritime climates:
- With dry summers
- With dry winters
- With precipitation in all seasons

Continental climates:
- With precipitation in all seasons
- With dry winters

Polar climates:
- Tundra climate
- Arctic and alpine climate

1
Scale 1:90 000 000

ORGANIC PRODUCTION

10	5	1% of world prod. 1971−75 average		10	5	1% of world prod. 1971−75 aver
		Wheat, rye				Coffee
		Maize				Tea
		Rice				Tobacco
		Millet				Sugar cane
		Copra				Sugar beet
		Ground nuts				Cotton
		Palm oil				
		Soya beans		10	5	million animals
		Grapes				Cattle
		Citrus fruits				Sheep
		Bananas				Pigs
		Dates				Based upon recent statistics

3

- Arable land
- Pasture
- Forestry
- Other forests

- Major fishing areas
- Other fishing areas
- Non-productive land
- Glacier

Scale 1:50 000 000
0   1000   2000 km
1 cm on the map = 500 km on the earth's surface

© EMS

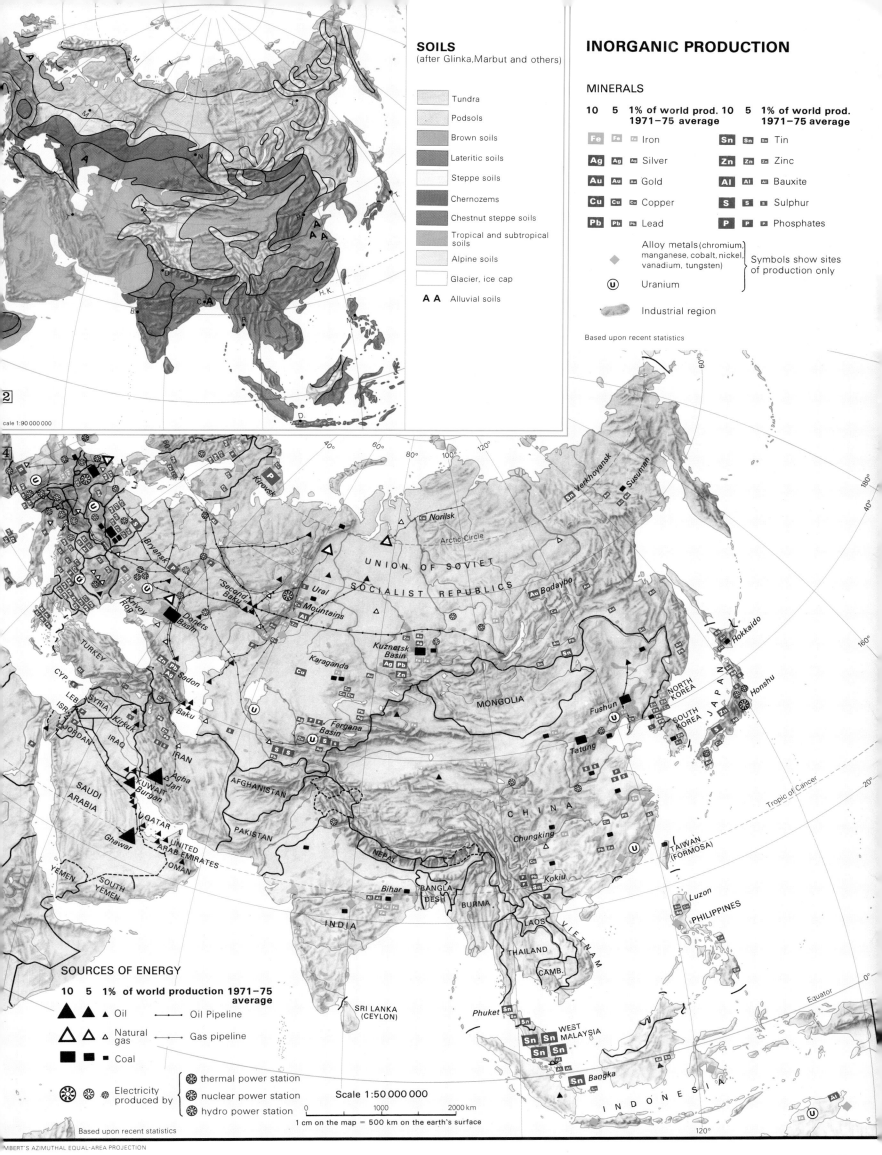

SOILS
(after Glinka, Marbut and others)

Tundra

Podsols

Brown soils

Lateritic soils

Steppe soils

Chernozems

Chestnut steppe soils

Tropical and subtropical soils

Alpine soils

Glacier, ice cap

A A Alluvial soils

INORGANIC PRODUCTION

MINERALS

10	5	1% of world prod. 1971–75 average		10	5	1% of world prod. 1971–75 average
Fe	Fe	Fe Iron		Sn	Sn	Sn Tin
Ag	Ag	Ag Silver		Zn	Zn	Zn Zinc
Au	Au	Au Gold		Al	Al	Al Bauxite
Cu	Cu	Cu Copper		S	S	S Sulphur
Pb	Pb	Pb Lead		P	P	P Phosphates

◆ Alloy metals (chromium, manganese, cobalt, nickel, vanadium, tungsten) } Symbols show sites of production only

Ⓤ Uranium

Industrial region

Based upon recent statistics

cale 1:90 000 000

SOURCES OF ENERGY

10 5 1% of world production 1971–75 average

▲ ▲ ▲ Oil   ⊷ Oil Pipeline

△ △ △ Natural gas   ⊷ Gas pipeline

■ ■ ■ Coal

Electricity produced by { ✳ thermal power station
✳ nuclear power station
✳ hydro power station }

Scale 1:50 000 000

0   1000   2000 km

1 cm on the map = 500 km on the earth's surface

Based upon recent statistics

MBERT'S AZIMUTHAL EQUAL-AREA PROJECTION

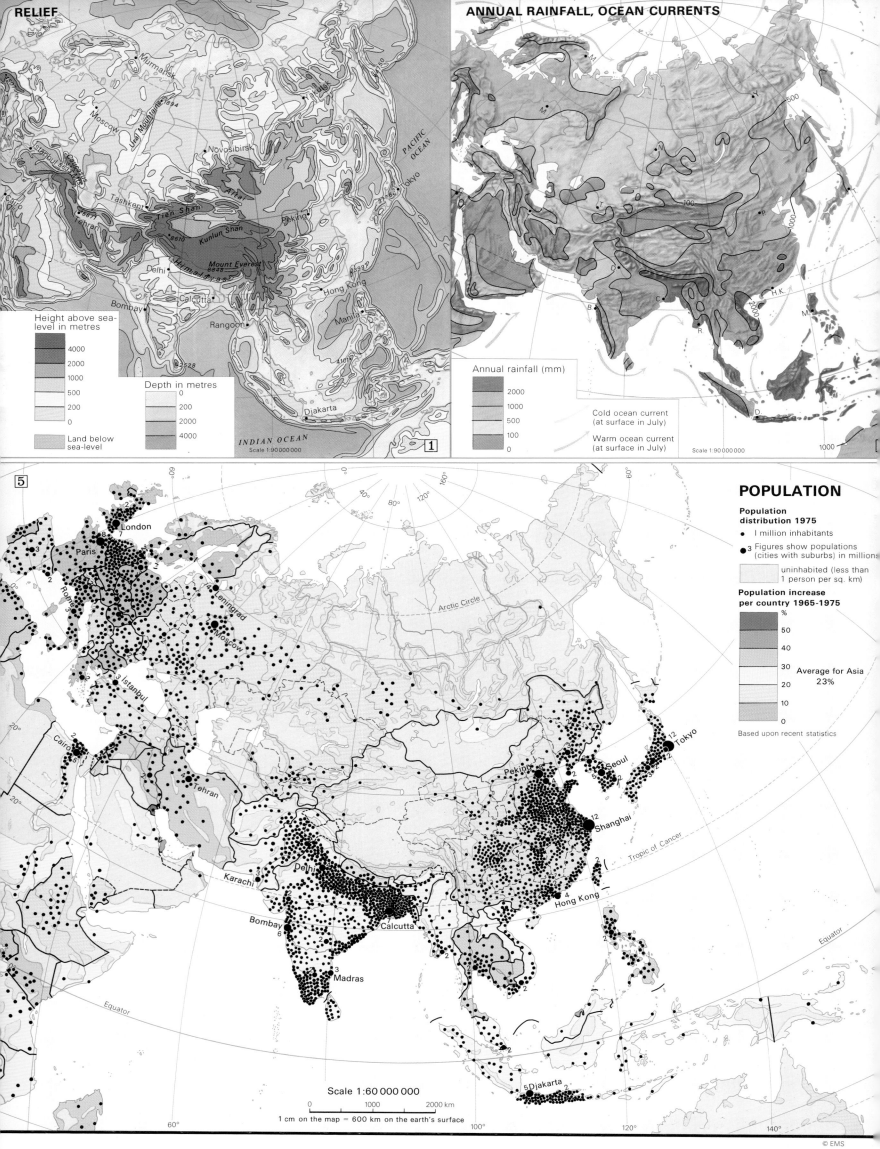

RELIEF

Murmansk

Moscow

Ural Mountains 1894

Novosibirsk

Yakutsk

PACIFIC OCEAN

Istanbul

Caucasus 5633

Cairo

Tashkent

Tien Shan

Altai

Tehran

5671

Tokyo

Kunlun Shan

8610

Peking

Delhi

Himalayas

Mount Everest 8848

Hong Kong

Bombay

Calcutta

Manila

Rangoon

8392

4101

Djakarta

Height above sea-level in metres

4000
2000
1000
500
200
0

Depth in metres

0
200
2000
4000

Land below sea-level

2528

INDIAN OCEAN
Scale 1:90 000 000

1

ANNUAL RAINFALL, OCEAN CURRENTS

M

M

Y

500

M

O

100

T

P.

H.K.

B

2000

M

R

Annual rainfall (mm)

2000
1000
500
100
0

Cold ocean current (at surface in July)

Warm ocean current (at surface in July)

D

1000

Scale 1:90 000 000

5

60° 40° 80° 120° 60°

London
8 7
Paris
Roma 3
2 3 3

Leningrad

Arctic Circle

Moscow

Istanbul 2

Cairo 5

Tehran 4

Karachi 3

Delhi

Bombay 6

Calcutta

Madras 3

Peking

Seoul 6 2

Tokyo 12 2

Shanghai 12

Hong Kong 4

2

2

Djakarta 5

Tropic of Cancer

Equator

Equator

POPULATION

Population distribution 1975

• I million inhabitants

●3 Figures show populations (cities with suburbs) in millions

uninhabited (less than 1 person per sq. km)

Population increase per country 1965-1975

%
50
40
30
20
10
0

Average for Asia 23%

Based upon recent statistics

Scale 1:60 000 000

0   1000   2000 km

1 cm on the map = 600 km on the earth's surface

60° 100° 120° 140°

© EMS

60   **ASIA,** physical, population, political divisions

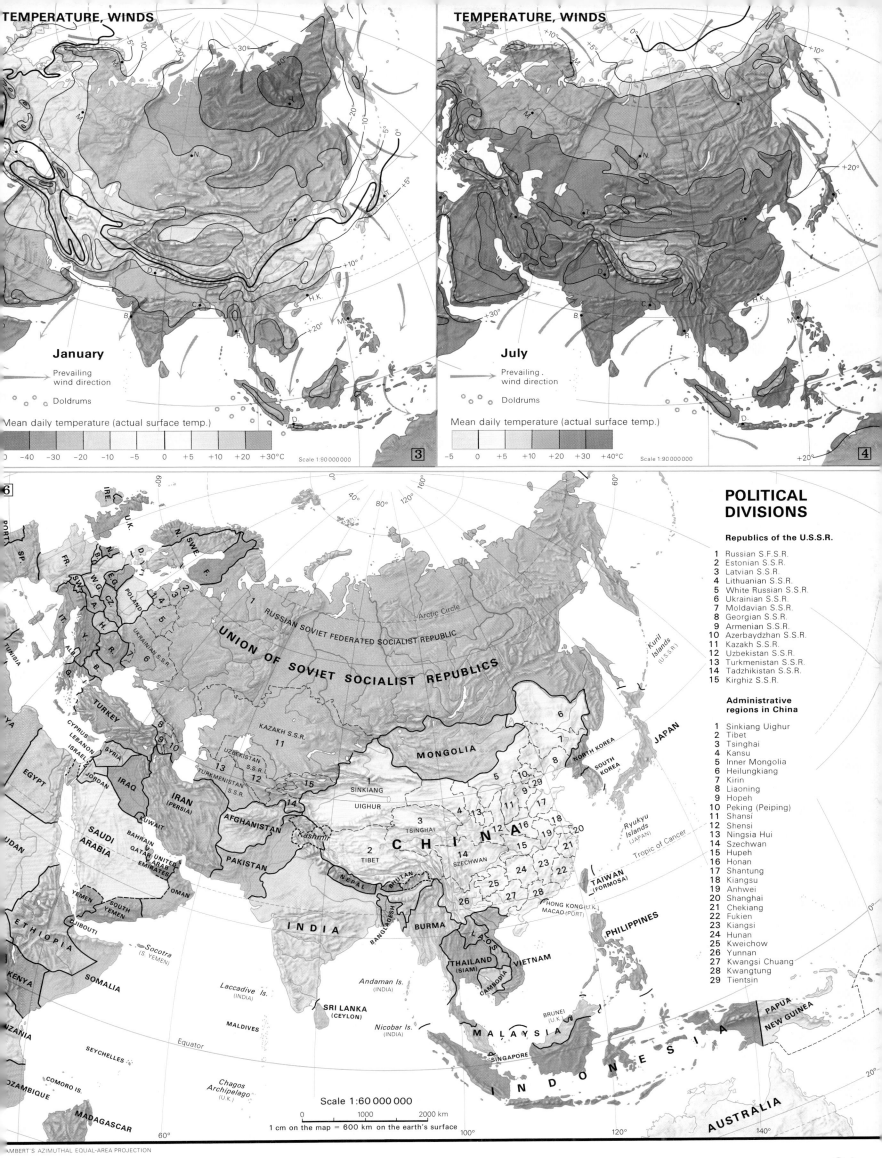

TEMPERATURE, WINDS

January
→ Prevailing wind direction
○ Doldrums

Mean daily temperature (actual surface temp.)

−40 −30 −20 −10 −5 0 +5 +10 +20 +30°C   Scale 1:90 000 000

TEMPERATURE, WINDS

July
→ Prevailing wind direction
○ Doldrums

Mean daily temperature (actual surface temp.)

−5 0 +5 +10 +20 +30 +40°C   Scale 1:90 000 000

POLITICAL DIVISIONS

Republics of the U.S.S.R.

1 Russian S.F.S.R.
2 Estonian S.S.R.
3 Latvian S.S.R.
4 Lithuanian S.S.R.
5 White Russian S.S.R.
6 Ukrainian S.S.R.
7 Moldavian S.S.R.
8 Georgian S.S.R.
9 Armenian S.S.R.
10 Azerbaydzhan S.S.R.
11 Kazakh S.S.R.
12 Uzbekistan S.S.R.
13 Turkmenistan S.S.R.
14 Tadzhikistan S.S.R.
15 Kirghiz S.S.R.

Administrative regions in China

1 Sinkiang Uighur
2 Tibet
3 Tsinghai
4 Kansu
5 Inner Mongolia
6 Heilungkiang
7 Kirin
8 Liaoning
9 Hopeh
10 Peking (Peiping)
11 Shansi
12 Shensi
13 Ningsia Hui
14 Szechwan
15 Hupeh
16 Honan
17 Shantung
18 Kiangsu
19 Anhwei
20 Shanghai
21 Chekiang
22 Fukien
23 Kiangsi
24 Hunan
25 Kweichow
26 Yunnan
27 Kwangsi Chuang
28 Kwangtung
29 Tientsin

Scale 1:60 000 000

0   1000   2000 km

1 cm on the map = 600 km on the earth's surface

LAMBERT'S AZIMUTHAL EQUAL-AREA PROJECTION

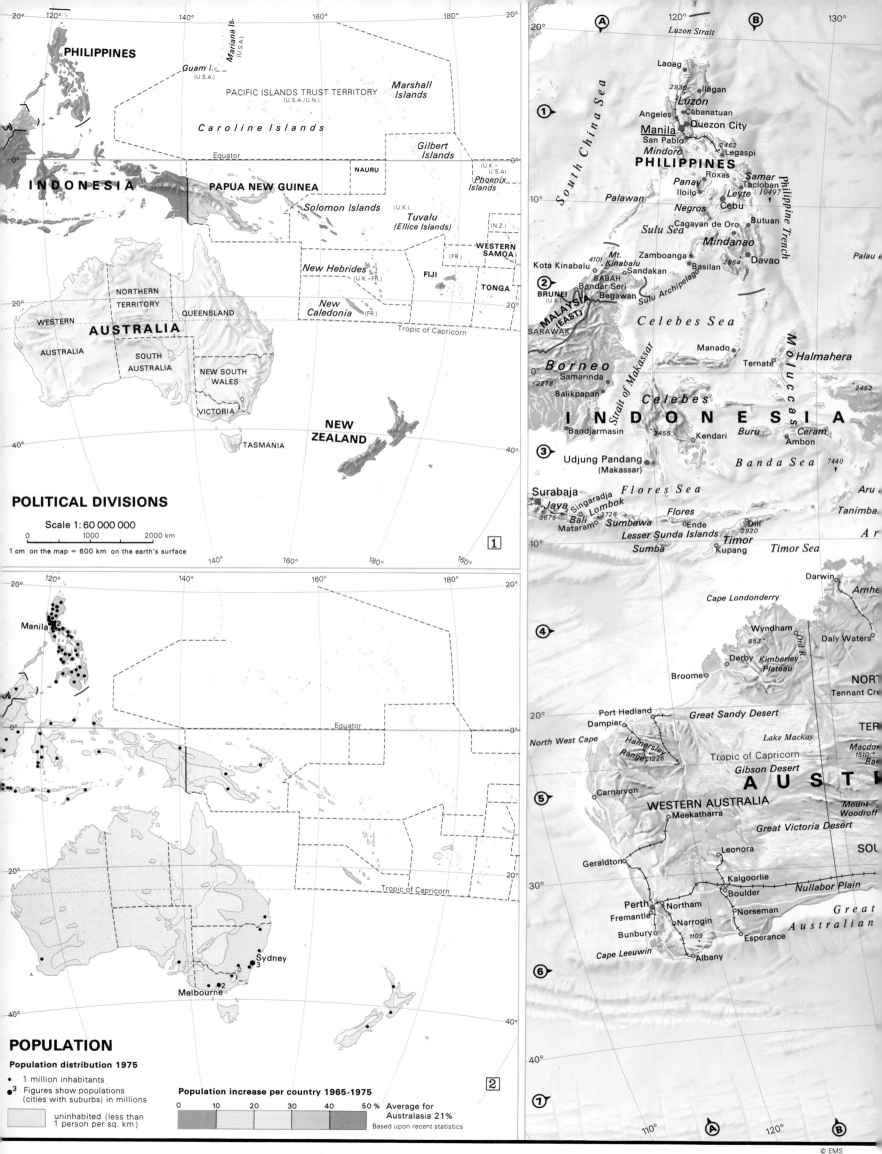

Ⓓ

International boundary — Main railway
Other boundary — Main road

• 3764 Height in metres
6920↓ Depth in metres

Arable land

Grassland, pasture

Rain forest

Other forest

Savanna

Steppe, semi-desert

Sand desert

Other desert

Saltpan   Marsh, swamp

Mariana Islands (U.S.A.)

Saipan I.
Tinian I.
Rota I.
Guam I. (U.S.A.)

11034 Challenger Deep
Mariana Trench

Ulithi

Yap Is. 8527

Fais

Sorol Faraulep

Pulap

Lamotrek Truk Is.

M i c r o n e s i a

Eniwetok Bikini Marshall Islands (U.S.A./U.N.)

Kwajalein Wotje

Ralik Chain Ratak Chain Maloelap

Ponape Majuro

Senjavin Group Jaluit Mili

Caroline Islands (U.S.A./U.N.)

Makin

②

170°

10°

Gilbert Islands 180°

Howland I. (U.S.A.)
Baker I.

Kapingamaringi Equator 0°

6920↓

NAURU Ocean Island Kingsmill Group 6478

Djajapura Manus I. Kavieng M e l   PACIFIC OCEAN (U.K.–U.S.A.)

Bismarck Archipelago New Ireland

Wewak Rabaul Phoenix Islands (U.K.)

New Guinea PAPUA NEW GUINEA Madang New Britain

4508 Lae Planet Deep 9140 2743 Bougainville I. Nanumea ③

Solomon Islands Choiseul I. Tuvalu (Ellice Islands) Nukufetau

Owen Stanley Range Santa Isabel I. Funafuti

Port Moresby Solomon Sea Malaita I. Nukulaelae Tokelau Islands (N.Z.)

Torres Strait Honiara San Cristobal I. 10°

Cape York Guadalcanal I. Santa Cruz Islands

Cape Arnhem Rennell I. Rotuma I. Wallis Is. (FR.) WESTERN SAMOA

Cape York Peninsula 20 Futuna Is. (FR.) Apia

Gulf of Carpentaria Coral Sea Espíritu Santo I. 1880 New Hebrides (U.K.–FR.) Vanua Levu Niuafou ④

Malekula I. Vila Viti Levu 1324

Cairns Vanua Levu Niuafou

1611 Efate I. FIJI Suva

Forsayth Charters Towers Chesterfield Is. Vila Kandavu Niue I. (N.Z.)

Townsville Ayr Bowen TONGA ⑤

Mount Isa Hughenden Mackay Loyalty Is. 7660 Nukualofa

kly Tableland New Caledonia (FR.) Tropic of Capricorn Tongatapu

QUEENSLAND Longreach Rockhampton Nouméa 10882

Gladstone Horizon Depth

Springs Bundaberg

IA Maryborough Gympie

mpson Desert Charleville Dalby Toowoomba Norfolk I. (AUSTR.)

Quilpie Roma Brisbane ⑥

Cunnamulla Ipswich

Lake Eyre Walgett Grafton Kermadec Islands (N.Z.)

Bourke Armidale Lord Howe I. (AUSTR.) 30°

Woomera Broken Hill Cobar Tamworth Galathea Depth 9994

t Augusta Knob Port Pirie Dubbo Maitland North Cape

Whyalla Mildura Parkes Newcastle Whangarei

coln Adelaide Orange Wollongong Auckland North Island

148 Spencer Gulf Wagga Wagga Bathurst Goulburn Hamilton Rotorua

Murray Bridge Bendigo Albury Canberra NEW New Plymouth Gisborne

Horsham Murray R. Mount Kosciusko 2231 ZEALAND Wanganui Napier

Ballarat VICTORIA Australian Alps Cape Howe Nelson Cook Strait Palmerston North

Mount Gambier Melbourne Tasman Sea Westport Wellington 2103 ⑦

Warrnambool Geelong Yallourn South Island

Devonport Launceston 1617 Mount Cook 3764 Christchurch

Burnie Southern Alps Timaru

TASMANIA Hobart Chatham Islands (N.Z.)

South East Cape 5604 Invercargill Dunedin

ERT'S AZIMUTHAL EQUAL-AREA PROJECTION

63

0 250 500 750 1000 km
0 200 400 600 miles

cale 1:25 000 000 1 cm on the map = 250 km on the earth's surface 1 inch on the map = 400 miles on the earth's surface

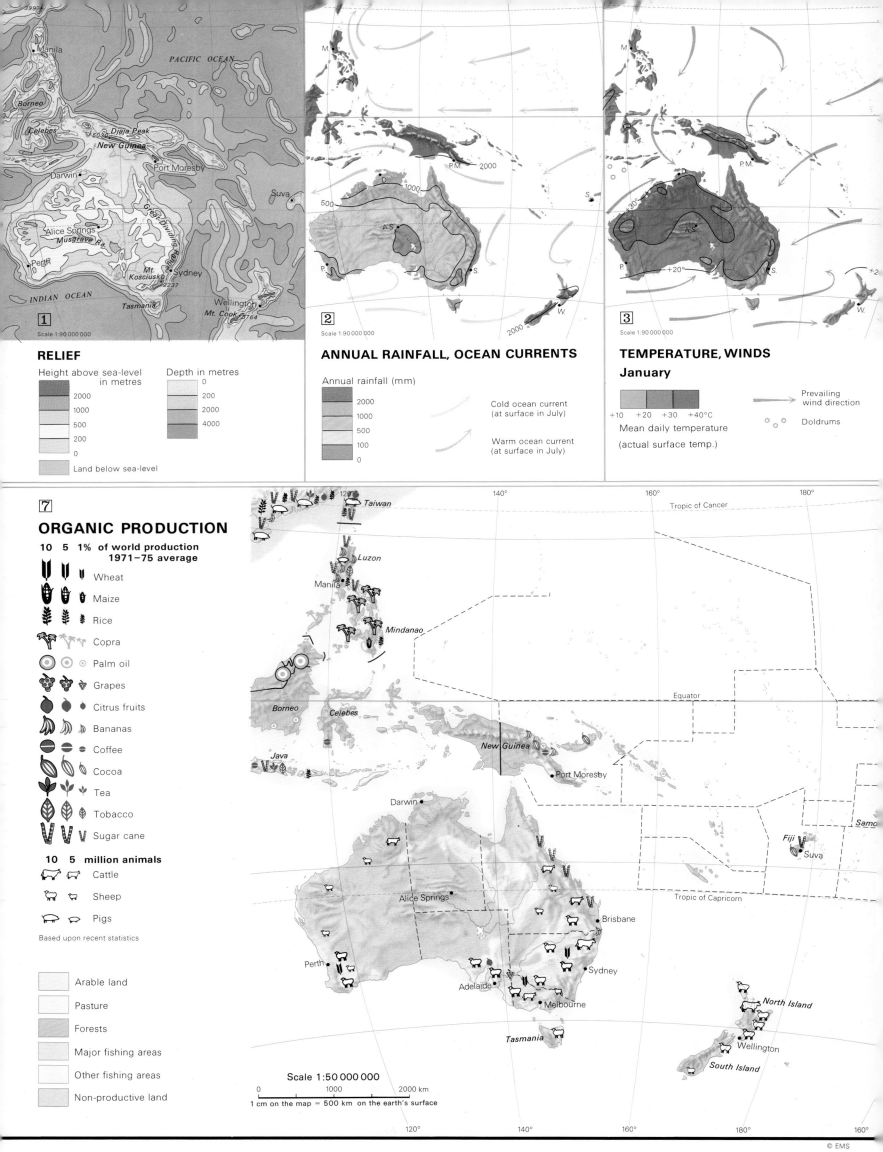

1 RELIEF

Height above sea-level in metres
- 2000
- 1000
- 500
- 200
- 0

Land below sea-level

Depth in metres
- 0
- 200
- 2000
- 4000

Scale 1:90 000 000

2 ANNUAL RAINFALL, OCEAN CURRENTS

Annual rainfall (mm)
- 2000
- 1000
- 500
- 100
- 0

Cold ocean current (at surface in July)

Warm ocean current (at surface in July)

Scale 1:90 000 000

3 TEMPERATURE, WINDS
January

Mean daily temperature (actual surface temp.)
- +10 +20 +30 +40°C

Prevailing wind direction

Doldrums

Scale 1:90 000 000

7 ORGANIC PRODUCTION

10 5 1% of world production 1971–75 average

- Wheat
- Maize
- Rice
- Copra
- Palm oil
- Grapes
- Citrus fruits
- Bananas
- Coffee
- Cocoa
- Tea
- Tobacco
- Sugar cane

10 5 million animals

- Cattle
- Sheep
- Pigs

Based upon recent statistics

- Arable land
- Pasture
- Forests
- Major fishing areas
- Other fishing areas
- Non-productive land

Scale 1:50 000 000

0   1000   2000 km

1 cm on the map = 500 km on the earth's surface

© EMS

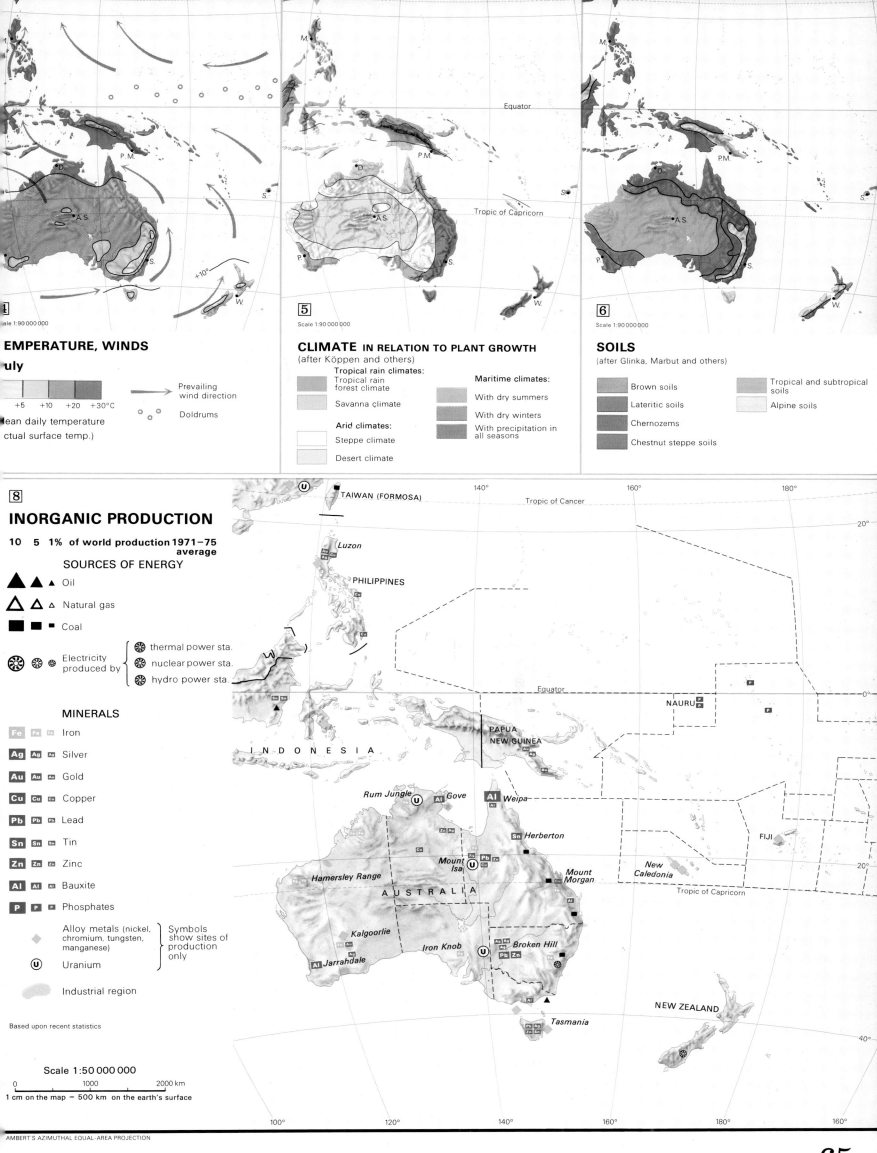

4

Scale 1:90 000 000

TEMPERATURE, WINDS

July

+5	+10	+20	+30°C

Mean daily temperature
(actual surface temp.)

→ Prevailing wind direction

○ Doldrums

5

Scale 1:90 000 000

CLIMATE IN RELATION TO PLANT GROWTH
(after Köppen and others)

Tropical rain climates:
- Tropical rain forest climate
- Savanna climate

Arid climates:
- Steppe climate
- Desert climate

Maritime climates:
- With dry summers
- With dry winters
- With precipitation in all seasons

6

Scale 1:90 000 000

SOILS
(after Glinka, Marbut and others)

- Brown soils
- Lateritic soils
- Chernozems
- Chestnut steppe soils
- Tropical and subtropical soils
- Alpine soils

8

INORGANIC PRODUCTION

10 5 1% of world production 1971–75 average

SOURCES OF ENERGY

- ▲ Oil
- △ Natural gas
- ■ Coal
- ⊛ Electricity produced by
  - ⊛ thermal power sta.
  - ⊛ nuclear power sta.
  - ⊛ hydro power sta.

MINERALS

- Fe Iron
- Ag Silver
- Au Gold
- Cu Copper
- Pb Lead
- Sn Tin
- Zn Zinc
- Al Bauxite
- P Phosphates
- ◆ Alloy metals (nickel, chromium, tungsten, manganese) — Symbols show sites of production only
- Ⓤ Uranium
- Industrial region

Based upon recent statistics

Scale 1:50 000 000

0	1000	2000 km

1 cm on the map = 500 km on the earth's surface

LAMBERT'S AZIMUTHAL EQUAL-AREA PROJECTION

TAIWAN (FORMOSA)

Tropic of Cancer

Luzon

PHILIPPINES

Equator

NAURU

INDONESIA

PAPUA NEW GUINEA

FIJI

Rum Jungle

Gove

Weipa

Herberton

Mount Isa

New Caledonia

Mount Morgan

Tropic of Capricorn

Hamersley Range

AUSTRALIA

Kalgoorlie

Iron Knob

Broken Hill

Jarrahdale

NEW ZEALAND

Tasmania

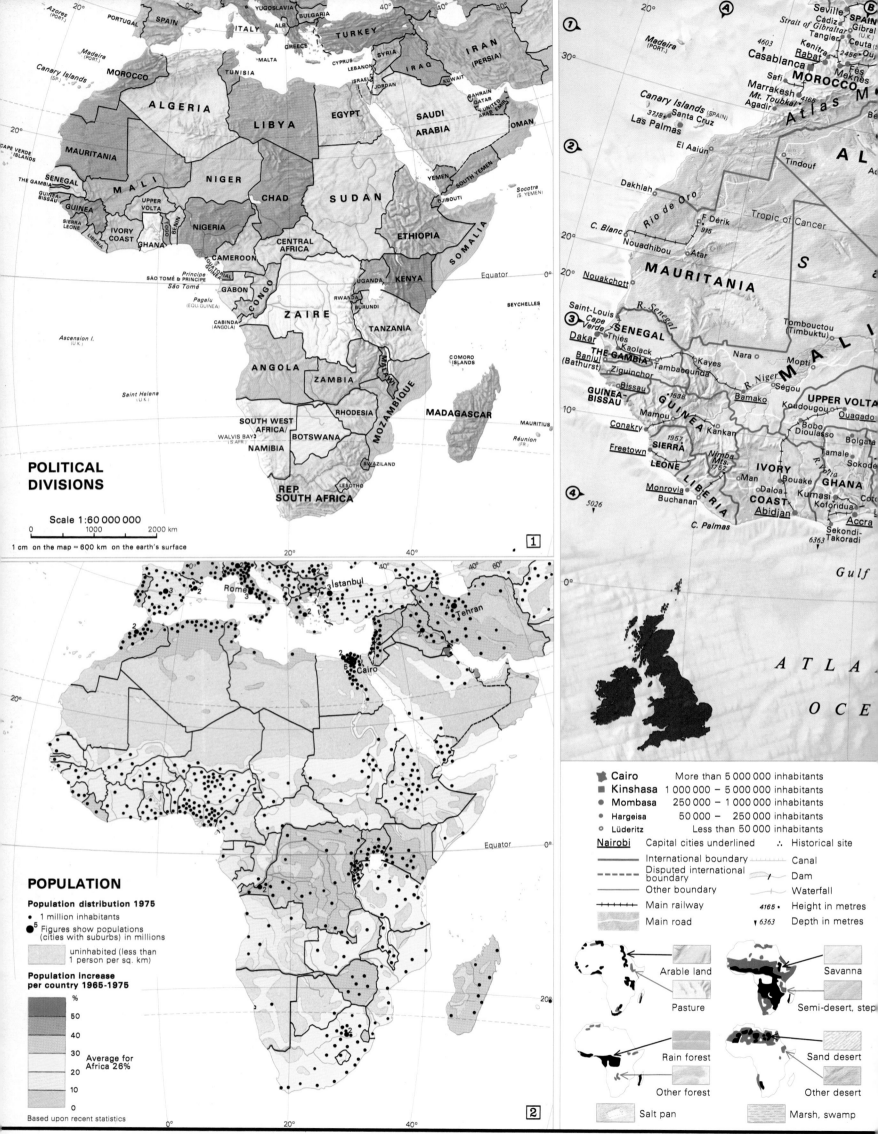

POLITICAL DIVISIONS

Scale 1:60 000 000

0   1000   2000 km

1 cm on the map = 600 km on the earth's surface

1

POPULATION

Population distribution 1975

• 1 million inhabitants

●5 Figures show populations (cities with suburbs) in millions

uninhabited (less than 1 person per sq. km)

Population increase per country 1965-1975

%
50
40
30   Average for
20   Africa 26%
10
0

Based upon recent statistics

2

Cairo   More than 5 000 000 inhabitants
Kinshasa   1 000 000 – 5 000 000 inhabitants
Mombasa   250 000 – 1 000 000 inhabitants
Hargeisa   50 000 – 250 000 inhabitants
Lüderitz   Less than 50 000 inhabitants
Nairobi   Capital cities underlined   ∴ Historical site

International boundary   Canal
Disputed international boundary   Dam
Other boundary   Waterfall
Main railway   4165• Height in metres
Main road   ▼6363 Depth in metres

Arable land   Savanna
Pasture   Semi-desert, step
Rain forest   Sand desert
Other forest   Other desert
Salt pan   Marsh, swamp

© EMS

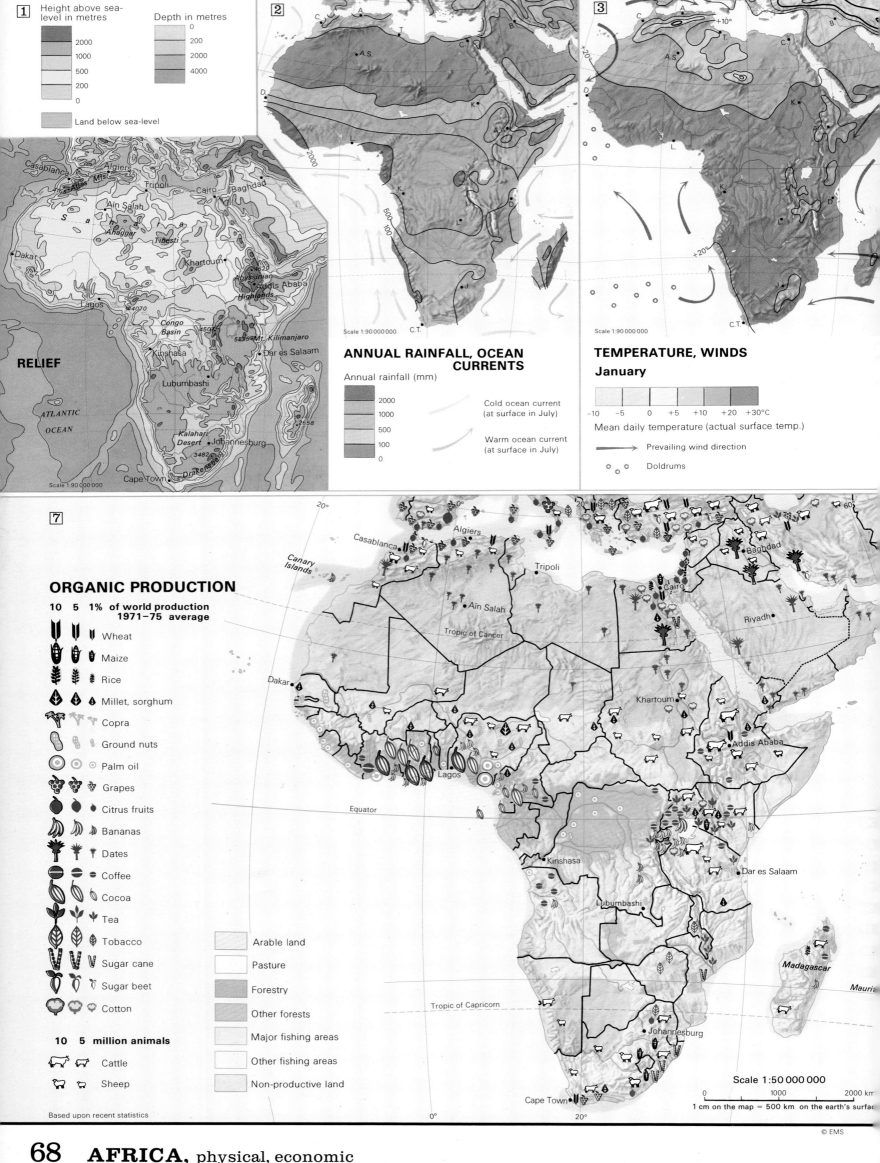

1 Height above sea-level in metres

	2000
	1000
	500
	200
	0

Depth in metres

	0
	200
	2000
	4000

Land below sea-level

Casablanca · Algiers
Atlas Mts.
Tripoli
Cairo · Baghdad
Dakar
S a h a r a
Aïn Salah
Ahaggar
Tibesti
Khartoum
·4620
Abyssinian Addis Ababa
Highlands
Lagos
·4070
Congo
Basin ·4507
·5895 Mt. Kilimanjaro
Kinshasa
Dar es Salaam
Lubumbashi

RELIEF

ATLANTIC
OCEAN

Kalahari
Desert · Johannesburg
·2658
·3482
Drakensberg
Cape Town

Scale 1:90 000 000

2

Scale 1:90 000 000 C.T.

ANNUAL RAINFALL, OCEAN CURRENTS

Annual rainfall (mm)

	2000
	1000
	500
	100
	0

Cold ocean current (at surface in July)

Warm ocean current (at surface in July)

3

Scale 1:90 000 000 C.T.

TEMPERATURE, WINDS

January

-10 -5 0 +5 +10 +20 +30°C

Mean daily temperature (actual surface temp.)

Prevailing wind direction

o o o Doldrums

7

ORGANIC PRODUCTION

10 5 1% of world production
1971–75 average

		Wheat
		Maize
		Rice
		Millet, sorghum
		Copra
		Ground nuts
		Palm oil
		Grapes
		Citrus fruits
		Bananas
		Dates
		Coffee
		Cocoa
		Tea
		Tobacco
		Sugar cane
		Sugar beet
		Cotton

10 5 million animals

		Cattle
		Sheep

	Arable land
	Pasture
	Forestry
	Other forests
	Major fishing areas
	Other fishing areas
	Non-productive land

Based upon recent statistics

Casablanca
Algiers
Canary
Islands
Tripoli
Baghdad
Cairo
Aïn Salah
Tropic of Cancer
Riyadh
Dakar
Khartoum
Addis Ababa
Lagos
Equator
Kinshasa
Dar es Salaam
Lubumbashi
Tropic of Capricorn
Madagascar
Mauri
Johannesburg
Cape Town

Scale 1:50 000 000

0 1000 2000 km

1 cm on the map = 500 km on the earth's surface

© EMS

68 AFRICA, physical, economic

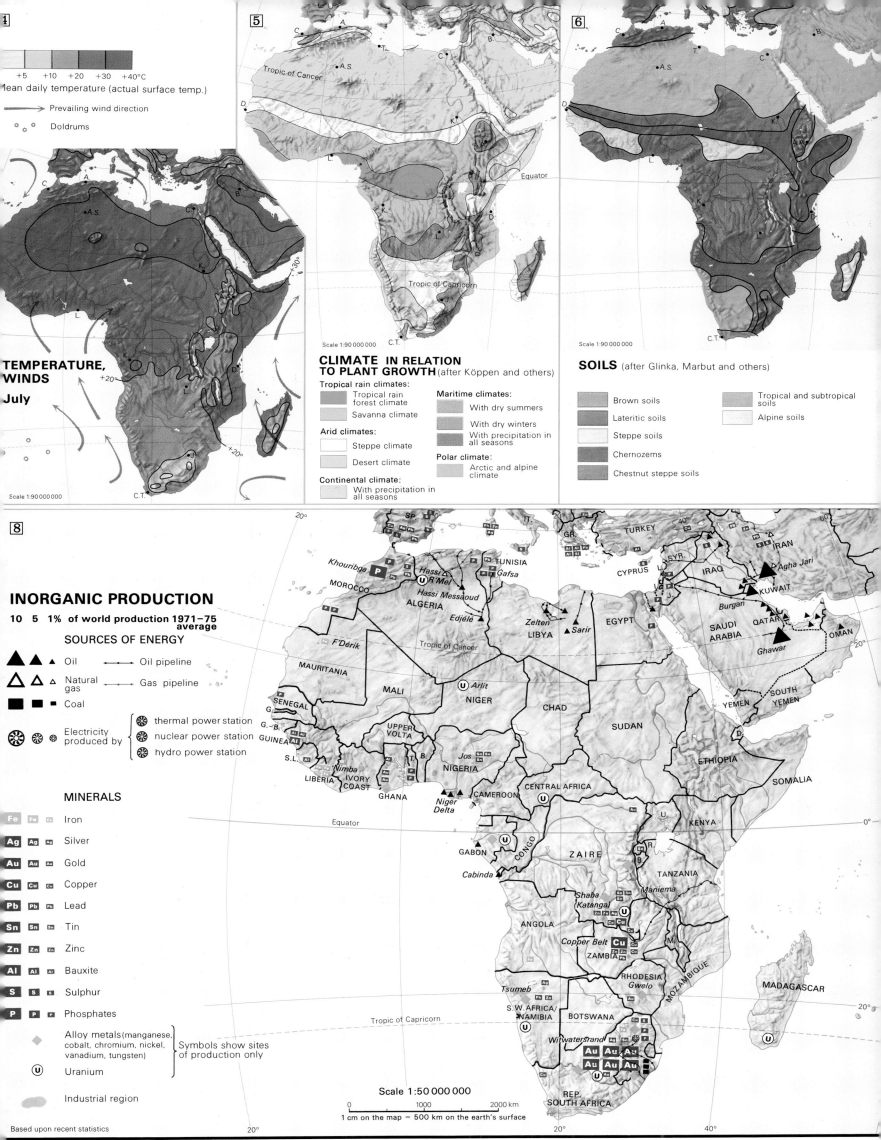

1

+5 +10 +20 +30 +40°C

Mean daily temperature (actual surface temp.)

→ Prevailing wind direction

○ ○ ○ Doldrums

TEMPERATURE, WINDS

July

Scale 1:90 000 000

5

Tropic of Cancer

·A.S.

Equator

·K

·L

·D

Tropic of Capricorn

C.T.

Scale 1:90 000 000

CLIMATE IN RELATION TO PLANT GROWTH (after Köppen and others)

Tropical rain climates:

Tropical rain forest climate

Savanna climate

Arid climates:

Steppe climate

Desert climate

Continental climate:

With precipitation in all seasons

Maritime climates:

With dry summers

With dry winters

With precipitation in all seasons

Polar climate:

Arctic and alpine climate

6

·A.S.

·D

·K

·L

C.T.

Scale 1:90 000 000

SOILS (after Glinka, Marbut and others)

Brown soils

Lateritic soils

Steppe soils

Chernozems

Chestnut steppe soils

Tropical and subtropical soils

Alpine soils

8

INORGANIC PRODUCTION

10 5 1% of world production 1971−75 average

SOURCES OF ENERGY

▲ ▲ ▲ Oil   •—•—• Oil pipeline

△ △ △ Natural gas   ◦—◦—◦ Gas pipeline

■ ■ ▪ Coal

⊛ ⊛ ⊛ Electricity produced by { thermal power station / nuclear power station / hydro power station }

MINERALS

Fe Fe ᶠᵉ   Iron

Ag Ag ᵃᵍ   Silver

Au Au ᵃᵘ   Gold

Cu Cu ᶜᵘ   Copper

Pb Pb ᵖᵇ   Lead

Sn Sn ˢⁿ   Tin

Zn Zn ᶻⁿ   Zinc

Al Al ᵃˡ   Bauxite

S S ˢ   Sulphur

P P ᵖ   Phosphates

◆ Alloy metals (manganese, cobalt, chromium, nickel, vanadium, tungsten) } Symbols show sites of production only

Ⓤ Uranium

Industrial region

Based upon recent statistics

MILLER'S STEREOGRAPHIC PROJECTION

Scale 1:50 000 000

0   1000   2000 km

1 cm on the map = 500 km on the earth's surface

POLITICAL DIVISIONS

Names of the American states, with their standard abbreviations

Ala.	Alabama
	Alaska
Ariz.	Arizona
Ark.	Arkansas
Calif.	California
Colo.	Colorado
Conn.	Connecticut
Del.	Delaware
Fla.	Florida
Ga.	Georgia
	Hawaii
	Idaho
Ill.	Illinois
Ind.	Indiana
	Iowa
Kans.	Kansas
Ky.	Kentucky
La.	Louisiana
Me.	Maine
Md.	Maryland
Mass.	Massachusetts
Mich.	Michigan
Minn.	Minnesota
Miss.	Mississippi
Mo.	Missouri
Mont.	Montana
Nebr.	Nebraska
Nev.	Nevada
N.H.	New Hampshire
N.J.	New Jersey
N.Mex.	New Mexico
N.Y.	New York
N.C.	North Carolina
N.Dak.	North Dakota
	Ohio
Okla.	Oklahoma
Oreg.	Oregon

Pa.	Pennsylvania
R.I.	Rhode Island
S.C.	South Carolina
S.Dak.	South Dakota
Tenn.	Tennessee
Tex.	Texas
	Utah
Vt.	Vermont
Va.	Virginia
Wash.	Washington
W.Va.	West Virginia
Wis.	Wisconsin
Wyo.	Wyoming

POPULATION

Population distribution 1975

• 1 million inhabitants

•³ Figures show populations (cities with suburbs) in millions

uninhabited (less than 1 person per sq.km)

Population increase per country 1965-1975

	50%
	40
	30
	20
	10
	0

Average for North and Central America 19%

Based upon recent statistics

Scale 1:60 000 000

| 0 | 1000 | 2000 km |

1 cm on the map = 600 km on the earth's surface

New York — More than 5 000 000 inhabitants
Chicago — 1 000 000 − 5 000 000 inhabitants
Cincinnati — 250 000 − 1 000 000 inhabitants
Little Rock — 50 000 − 250 000 inhabitants
Cheyenne — Less than 50 000 inhabitants

Ottawa Capital cities underlined · Historical Site

International bdy.   Canal
Other boundary   Dam
Main railway   Waterfall
Main road   4335• Height in metres
   ▼6700 Depth in metres

Arable land   Tundra
Prairie, pasture   Coniferous forest
Desert   Deciduous forest
Semi-desert, steppe   Rain forest

Salt desert   Marsh, swamp   Ice cap, glacier

© EMS

A	Strait of Juan de Fuca	120°
B	Vancouver	
C	BRITISH COLUMBIA	115°
D	1	110°
E	Moose Jaw	
F	105°	
G	100°	MANITOBA

CANADA

ALBERTA · Medicine Hat · Swift Current · Moose Jaw · Regina · Brandon · Winnipeg
SASKATCHEWAN · Lethbridge · Estevan · Portage la Prairie · Winnipeg

Place names (map labels)

Victoria · Bellingham · Penticton · Kimberley · South Saskatchewan · Lethbridge · Medicine Hat · Swift Current · Moose Jaw · Regina · Brandon · Winnipeg · Manitoba

Seattle · Tacoma · Olympia · Everett · Columbia River · Grand Coulee Dam · Spokane · Coeur d'Alene · Kalispell · GLACIER NATIONAL PARK 3194 · Great Falls · Milk River · Fort Peck Dam · Minot · Grand Forks

WASHINGTON · Mount Rainier 4392 · Astoria · Portland · Walla Walla · Lewiston · Helena · Butte · MONTANA · Billings · Miles City · Garrison Dam · NORTH DAKOTA · Bismarck · Fargo

OREGON · Salem · Albany · Eugene · Medford · Harney Basin · Boise · Nampa · Snake River Plain · YELLOWSTONE NATIONAL PARK · Yellowstone Falls 3859 · Yellowstone River · Sheridan · Aberdeen · SOUTH DAKOTA · Pierre · Sioux Falls

Mount Shasta 4317 · Eureka · Cape Mendocino · Redding · Lassen Peak 3187 · Reno · Carson City · Ely · Wheeler Peak 3982 · Great Salt Lake 1300 · Ogden · Logan · Grand Teton 4196 · WYOMING · Casper · Longs Peak 4345 · Black Hills 2207 · Rapid City · Sioux City

Santa Rosa · Sacramento · Berkeley · Oakland · San Francisco · San Jose · Stockton · Modesto · Fresno · Salinas · Monterey · San Luis Obispo · CALIFORNIA · Sierra Nevada · Mount Whitney 4418 · Death Valley −86 · Las Vegas · UTAH · Salt Lake City · Provo · Bingham Canyon · Uinta Mts. 4123 · Wasatch Range · Green River · Colorado R. · COLORADO · Mount Elbert 4399 · Boulder · Denver 1600 · Greeley · Rock Springs · Cheyenne · Laramie · NEBRASKA · Grand Island · Lincoln · North Platte R. · South Platte R. · Platte River · Hastings · Republican River

GREAT NEVADA BASIN · Humboldt River · Elko · Great Salt Lake Desert · San Joaquin Valley · Bakersfield · Santa Barbara · Santa Monica · Mojave Desert · Glendale · Pasadena · Los Angeles · Torrance · Long Beach · Santa Catalina · Anaheim · Riverside · San Bernardino · Palomar Mountain 1871 · Salton Sea · Imperial Valley · Colorado River · ARIZONA · Phoenix · Mesa · Globe · Gila River · Tucson · Bisbee · Nogales · Yuma · Mexicali · Ensenada · Tijuana · San Diego

Grand Canyon · GRAND CANYON NATIONAL PARK 3851 · Painted Desert · Colorado Plateau · Lake Powell · San Juan River · San Juan Mountains · Flagstaff · Gallup · Albuquerque · Santa Fe · Rio Grande 4011 · Grand Junction · Mount Wilson 4342 · Colorado Springs · Pueblo · Trinidad · Dodge City · Hutchinson · Salina · KANSAS · Wichita

NEW MEXICO · Las Cruces · El Paso 2667 · Ciudad Juárez · Roswell · Llano Estacado · Lubbock 3659 · Midland · Odessa · San Angelo · Sweetwater · Abilene · Fort Worth · Arlington · Wichita Falls · Red River · Lawton · Oklahoma City · OKLAHOMA · Enid · Canadian River · Panhandle · Amarillo · Cimarron River · Arkansas River

TEXAS · Edwards Plateau · San Antonio · Pecos River · Colorado River · Rio Grande

MEXICO · Hermosillo · Guaymas · Ciudad Obregón · Navojoa · Los Mochis · Guasave · Culiacán · La Paz · C. San Lucas 2406 · Mazatlán · Durango · Chihuahua · Delicias · Hidalgo del Parral · R. Conchos · Bolsón de Mapimí · Gómez Palacio · Torreón · Saltillo · Monterrey · Linares · Ciudad Victoria · Matehuala · Fresnillo · Piedras Negras · Nueva Rosita · Monclova · Nuevo Laredo · Laredo · Reynosa · Matamoros · Corpus Christi · Brownsville · Sierra Madre · Western Sierra Madre · Eastern Sierra Madre · Bolsón de Mapimí · Rio Bravo del Norte · Rio Grande · R. Nazas · R. Yaqui

PACIFIC OCEAN 4389 · Channel Islands · Gulf of California · Lower California · Tropic of Cancer

Legend

New York More than 5 000 000 inhabitants
■ **Chicago** 1 000 000 – 5 000 000 inhabitants
● **Cincinnati** 250 000 – 1 000 000 inhabitants
• **Little Rock** 50 000 – 250 000 inhabitants
○ **Cheyenne** Less than 50 000 inhabitants

<u>Ottawa</u> Capital cities underlined

International boundary
Other boundary
+—+—+ Main railway

Coniferous forest
Deciduous and mixed forest — Main road
Arable land — Canal
Prairie, pasture — Aqueduct — Dam
4418 · Height in metres
▼ 4389 Depth in metres
Semi-desert, steppe — Marsh, swamp
Desert — Savanna

© EMS

ALBER'S EQUAL-AREA PROJECTION

Scale 1:10 000 000   1 cm on the map = 100 km on the earth's surface   1 inch on the map = 160 miles on the earth's surface

0   100   200   300   400 km   0   100   200 miles

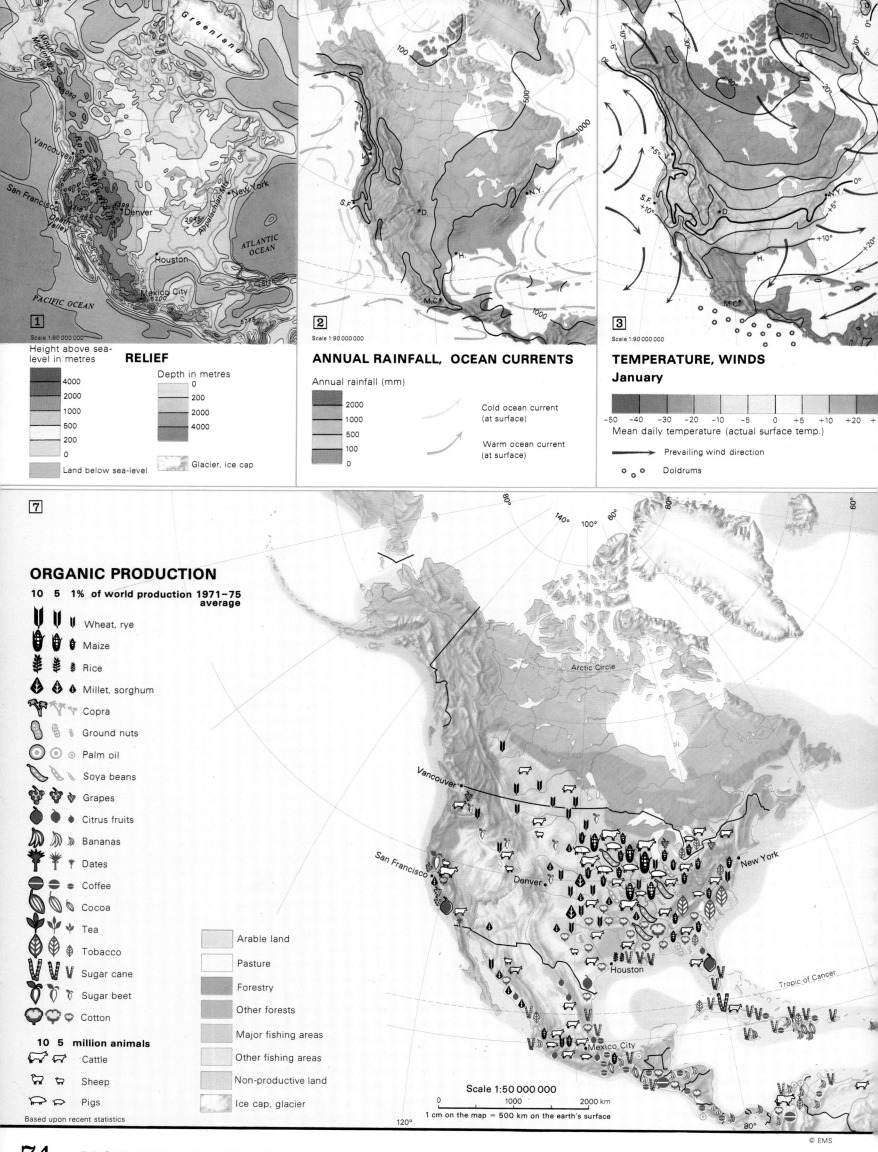

RELIEF

Height above sea-level in metres

- 4000
- 2000
- 1000
- 500
- 200
- 0

Depth in metres

- 0
- 200
- 2000
- 4000

Land below sea-level

Glacier, ice cap

Scale 1:90 000 000

ANNUAL RAINFALL, OCEAN CURRENTS

Annual rainfall (mm)

- 2000
- 1000
- 500
- 100
- 0

Cold ocean current (at surface)

Warm ocean current (at surface)

Scale 1:90 000 000

TEMPERATURE, WINDS

January

-50 -40 -30 -20 -10 -5 0 +5 +10 +20 +

Mean daily temperature (actual surface temp.)

Prevailing wind direction

Doldrums

Scale 1:90 000 000

ORGANIC PRODUCTION

10 5 1% of world production 1971–75 average

- Wheat, rye
- Maize
- Rice
- Millet, sorghum
- Copra
- Ground nuts
- Palm oil
- Soya beans
- Grapes
- Citrus fruits
- Bananas
- Dates
- Coffee
- Cocoa
- Tea
- Tobacco
- Sugar cane
- Sugar beet
- Cotton

10 5 million animals

- Cattle
- Sheep
- Pigs

Based upon recent statistics

- Arable land
- Pasture
- Forestry
- Other forests
- Major fishing areas
- Other fishing areas
- Non-productive land
- Ice cap, glacier

Scale 1:50 000 000

0   1000   2000 km

1 cm on the map = 500 km on the earth's surface

© EMS

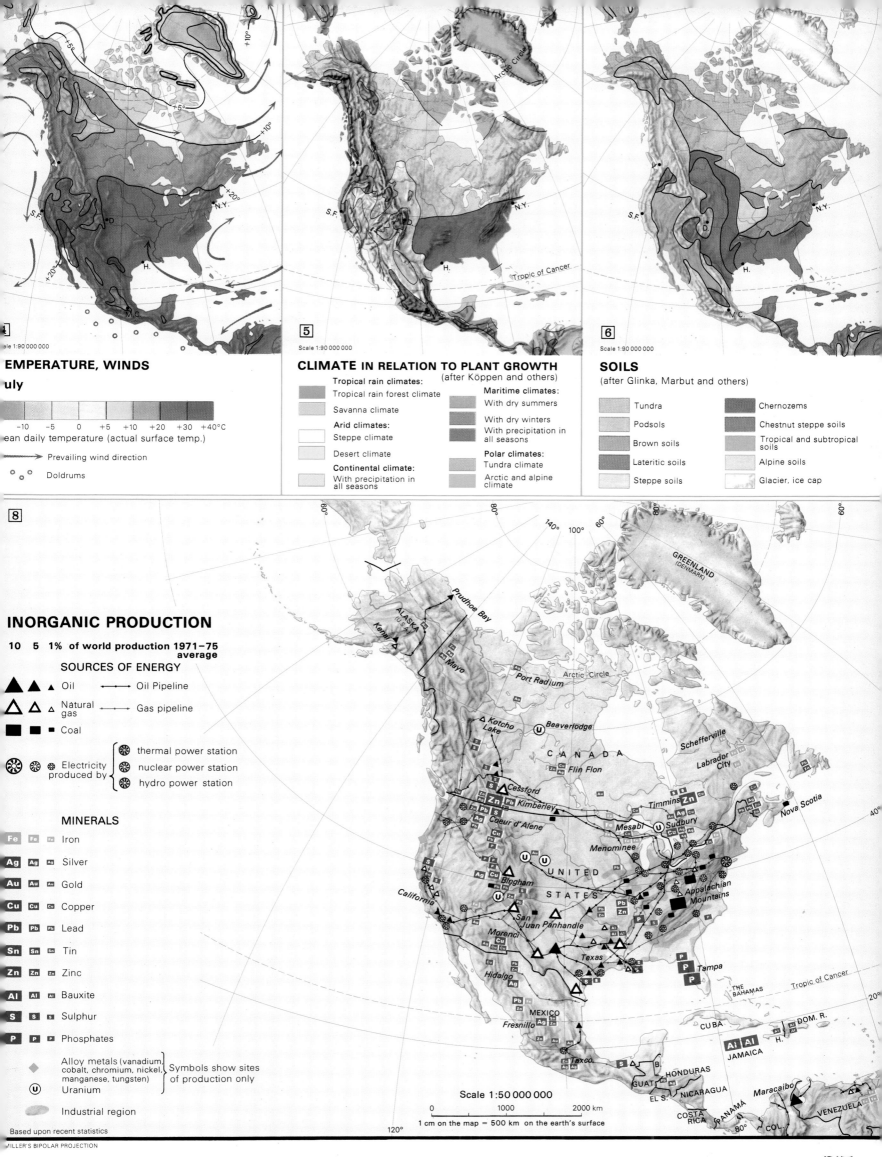

TEMPERATURE, WINDS

July

-10 -5 0 +5 +10 +20 +30 +40°C

Mean daily temperature (actual surface temp.)

→ Prevailing wind direction

∘ ⚬ ₒ Doldrums

Scale 1:90 000 000

CLIMATE IN RELATION TO PLANT GROWTH
(after Köppen and others)

Tropical rain climates:
Tropical rain forest climate
Savanna climate

Arid climates:
Steppe climate
Desert climate

Continental climate:
With precipitation in all seasons

Maritime climates:
With dry summers
With dry winters
With precipitation in all seasons

Polar climates:
Tundra climate
Arctic and alpine climate

Scale 1:90 000 000

SOILS
(after Glinka, Marbut and others)

Tundra
Podsols
Brown soils
Lateritic soils
Steppe soils

Chernozems
Chestnut steppe soils
Tropical and subtropical soils
Alpine soils
Glacier, ice cap

Scale 1:90 000 000

INORGANIC PRODUCTION

10 5 1% of world production 1971–75 average

SOURCES OF ENERGY

▲ ▲ ▴ Oil   ←—→ Oil Pipeline
△ △ △ Natural gas   ←—→ Gas pipeline
■ ■ ▪ Coal

⚙ ⚙ ⚙ Electricity produced by
  ⚙ thermal power station
  ⚙ nuclear power station
  ⚙ hydro power station

MINERALS

Fe	Fe	Fe	Iron
Ag	Ag	Ag	Silver
Au	Au	Au	Gold
Cu	Cu	Cu	Copper
Pb	Pb	Pb	Lead
Sn	Sn	Sn	Tin
Zn	Zn	Zn	Zinc
Al	Al	Al	Bauxite
S	S	S	Sulphur
P	P	P	Phosphates

◆ Alloy metals (vanadium, cobalt, chromium, nickel, manganese, tungsten) Symbols show sites of production only

Ⓤ Uranium

Industrial region

Based upon recent statistics

Scale 1:50 000 000

0   1000   2000 km

1 cm on the map = 500 km on the earth's surface

MILLER'S BIPOLAR PROJECTION

POLITICAL DIVISIONS

Scale 1:60 000 000

0   1000   2000 km

1 cm on the map = 600 km on the earth's surface

[1]

POPULATION

Population distribution 1975

• 1 million inhabitants

•⁵ Figures show populations (cities with suburbs) in millions

uninhabited (less than 1 person per sq.km)

Population increase per country 1965-1975

50 %
40
30 — Average for Latin America 29%
20
10
0

Based upon recent statistics

[2]

São Paulo   More than 5 000 000 inhabitants
Salvador   1 000 000 – 5 000 000 inhabitants
Valparaíso   250 000 – 1 000 000 inhabitants
Bahía Blanca 50 000 –   250 000 inhabitants
Ciudad Bolívar   Less than 50 000 inhabitants

Brasília Capital cities underlined   ∴ Historical site

———— International boundary   ········· Canal
- - - - Disputed intl. bdy.   Dam
———— Other Boundary   Waterfall
- - - - Disputed other bdy.   5215 • Height in metres
+—+—+ Main railway   ▾ 5630 Depth in metres
Main road   Salt pan

Arable land   Rain forest

Llanos, pampas   Chaco forest

Desert   Other forest

Semi-desert, steppe   Savanna

Marsh, swamp   Glacier

© EMS

76   SOUTH AMERICA, environment, political divisions, population

Scale 1:25 000 000

80° JAMAICA Ⓒ **70°** Puerto Rico Ⓓ Lesser Antilles **60°** Ⓔ **50°** Ⓕ **40°** Ⓖ **30°**

Caribbean Sea

Antigua (U.K.)
Guadeloupe (FR.)
Pointe-à-Pitre
Dominica (U.K.)
Martinique (FR.)
Fort-de-France
St. Lucia (U.K.)
St. Vincent (U.K.)
BARBADOS
Bridgetown
GRENADA

P. Gallinas
Aruba I.
Curaçao I. (NETH.)
Santa Marta
Barranquilla
Cartagena
Mt. Cristóbal
Colón
Lagunillas
Maracaibo
Barquisimeto
Maracay
Valencia
Caracas
Cumaná
Barcelona
Santo Tomé de Guayana
TRINIDAD AND TOBAGO
Port of Spain

ATLANTIC

Panamá
NAMA
Colón
Panamá
Medellín
Bucaramanga
Cúcuta
San Cristóbal
Ciudad Bolívar
Cerro Bolívar
Georgetown
Paramaribo
Cayenne

OCEAN

Manizales
Mt. Tolima
Bogotá
Ibagué
VENEZUELA
Angel Falls
Mt. Roraima
Kaieteur Falls
GUYANA
SURINAM
FRENCH GUIANA

Buenaventura
Cali
COLOMBIA
R. Meta
R. Orinoco
Boa Vista
RORAIMA
AMAPÁ
Macapá

St. Peter and St. Paul Rocks (BRAZ.)

Pasto
R. Guaviare
R. Putumayo
R. Casiquiare
R. Negro
R. Branco
R. Amazon
Marajó I.
Belém
Equator

Quito
Mt. Cotopaxi
ECUADOR
Guayaquil
Cuenca
Tumbes
Fonte Boa
Manaus
Santarém
R. Xingu
R. Tocantins
São Luís
Parnaíba
Fortaleza

Fernando de Noronha I. (BRAZ.)

Iquitos
R. Amazon
Leticia
AMAZONAS
Selvas
PARÁ
MARANHÃO
Teresina
Sobral
Mossoro
C. São Roque
Natal

Piura
Marañón
R. Juruá
R. Madeira
Catingas
CEARÁ
RIO GRANDE DO NORTE
Campina Grande
João Pessoa

Cajamarca
Trujillo
Chimbote
Mt. Huascarán
PERU
ACRE
Pôrto Velho
R. Tapajós
BRAZIL
PIAUÍ
PERNAMBUCO
Juàzeiro do Norte
Caruaru
Recife

Cerro de Pasco
Huánuco
Rio Branco
Cobija
RONDÔNIA
R. Xingu
Juàzeiro
ALAGOAS
SERGIPE
Garanhuns
Maceió

Lima
Callao
La Oroya
Huancayo
Guajará Mirim
R. Guaporé
R. Beni
MATO GROSSO
R. Araguaia
GOIÁS
Campos
BAHIA
Feira
Aracaju
Alagoinhas
Salvador

Huancavelica
Pisco
Ica
Ayacucho
Machu Picchu
Cuzco
Trinidad
Mato Grosso
Cuiaba
R. S. Francisco
Jequié
Itabuna
Ilhéus

Mt. Coropuna
Puno
Lake Titicaca
Mt. Ancohuma
DISTRITO FEDERAL
Anápolis
Brasília
Montes Claros
Vitória

Arequipa
La Paz
Mt. Illimani
BOLIVIA
Cochabamba
Goiânia
Brazilian
Teófilo Otôni

Mollendo
Oruro
Llallagua
Sucre
Santa Cruz
MINAS GERAIS
Governador Valadares

Tacna
Lake Poopó
Potosí
Uberlândia
Belo Horizonte
Uberaba
Itabira
ESPÍRITO SANTO
Vitória

Arica
Iquique
Tarija
Highlands
Ribeirão Prêto
Juiz de Fora
Mt. Bandeira
Campos

Tocopilla
Gran Chaco
R. Paraguay
Campo Grande
São José
PARANÁ
Presidente Prudente
Bauru
Campinas
Volta Redonda
RIO DE JANEIRO
C. Frio

Antofagasta
Mt. Llullaillaco
PARAGUAY
Ponta Porã
Londrina
Sorocaba
São Paulo
Niterói
Rio de Janeiro
Santos

Mt. Galán
Jujuy
Salta
R. Bermejo
R. Pilcomayo
Asunción
Formosa
PARANÁ
Ponta Grossa
Iguaçu Falls
SANTA CATARINA
Curitiba
Joinville
Blumenau

Copiapó
Mt. Ojos del Salado
Tucumán
Resistencia
Corrientes
Posadas
R. Uruguay
Florianópolis

La Serena
Catamarca
Santiago del Estero
R. Salado
Uruguaiana
RIO GRANDE DO SUL
Passo Fundo
Caxias do Sul

CHILE
La Rioja
R. Paraná
Santa Fé
Salto
Santa Maria
Pôrto Alegre
L. dos Patos

Mt. Aconcagua
San Juan
Córdoba
Paraná
Paysandú
Pelotas
Rio Grande

Viña del Mar
Valparaíso
Santiago
Mendoza
San Luis
Rosario
Río Cuarto
Zárate
URUGUAY
L. Mirim

Rancagua
Junín
La Plata
Montevideo
River Plate

Talca
ARGENTINA
Santa Rosa
Azul
Tandil

Chillán
Concepción
Talcahuano
R. Colorado
Pampas
Mar del Plata

Temuco
Neuquén
Bahía Blanca

Valdivia
Osorno
Plaza Huincul
Viedma
Gulf of San Matías

Puerto Montt
Chiloé I.
Rawson

Puerto Aisén
San Carlos de Bariloche
Patagonia
Gulf of San Jorge

Cerro San Valentín
Comodoro Rivadavia
Deseado

Falkland Islands (U.K.)
Stanley

Río Gallegos
Strait of Magellan

MILLER'S BIPOLAR PROJECTION

Juan Fernández Islands (CHILE)
S. Félix I. S. Ambrosio I. (CHILE)
Tierra del Fuego
Punta Arenas
Ushuaia
Cape Horn
South Georgia (U.K.)

Tropic of Capricorn
Trindade I. Martín Vaz Is. (BRAZ.)

ATLANTIC

OCEAN

250 500 750 1000 km
on the map = 250 km on the earth's surface

0 200 400 600 miles
1 inch on the map = 400 miles on the earth's surface

77

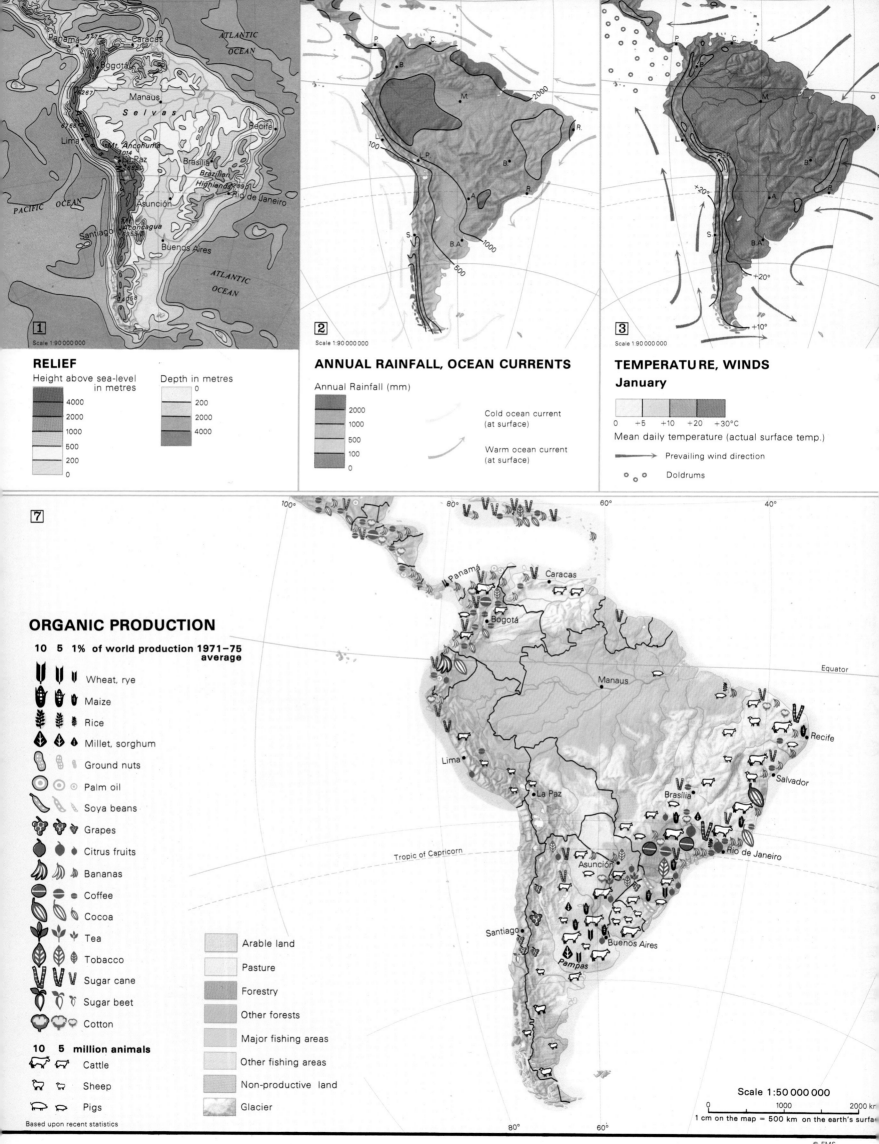

1 Scale 1:90 000 000

RELIEF

Height above sea-level in metres

- 4000
- 2000
- 1000
- 500
- 200
- 0

Depth in metres

- 0
- 200
- 2000
- 4000

2 Scale 1:90 000 000

ANNUAL RAINFALL, OCEAN CURRENTS

Annual Rainfall (mm)

- 2000
- 1000
- 500
- 100
- 0

→ Cold ocean current (at surface)

→ Warm ocean current (at surface)

3 Scale 1:90 000 000

TEMPERATURE, WINDS
January

Mean daily temperature (actual surface temp.)

0 +5 +10 +20 +30°C

→ Prevailing wind direction

∘ ∘ ∘ Doldrums

7

ORGANIC PRODUCTION

10 5 1% of world production 1971–75 average

- Wheat, rye
- Maize
- Rice
- Millet, sorghum
- Ground nuts
- Palm oil
- Soya beans
- Grapes
- Citrus fruits
- Bananas
- Coffee
- Cocoa
- Tea
- Tobacco
- Sugar cane
- Sugar beet
- Cotton

10 5 million animals

- Cattle
- Sheep
- Pigs

Based upon recent statistics

- Arable land
- Pasture
- Forestry
- Other forests
- Major fishing areas
- Other fishing areas
- Non-productive land
- Glacier

Scale 1:50 000 000

0   1000   2000 km

1 cm on the map = 500 km on the earth's surface

© EMS

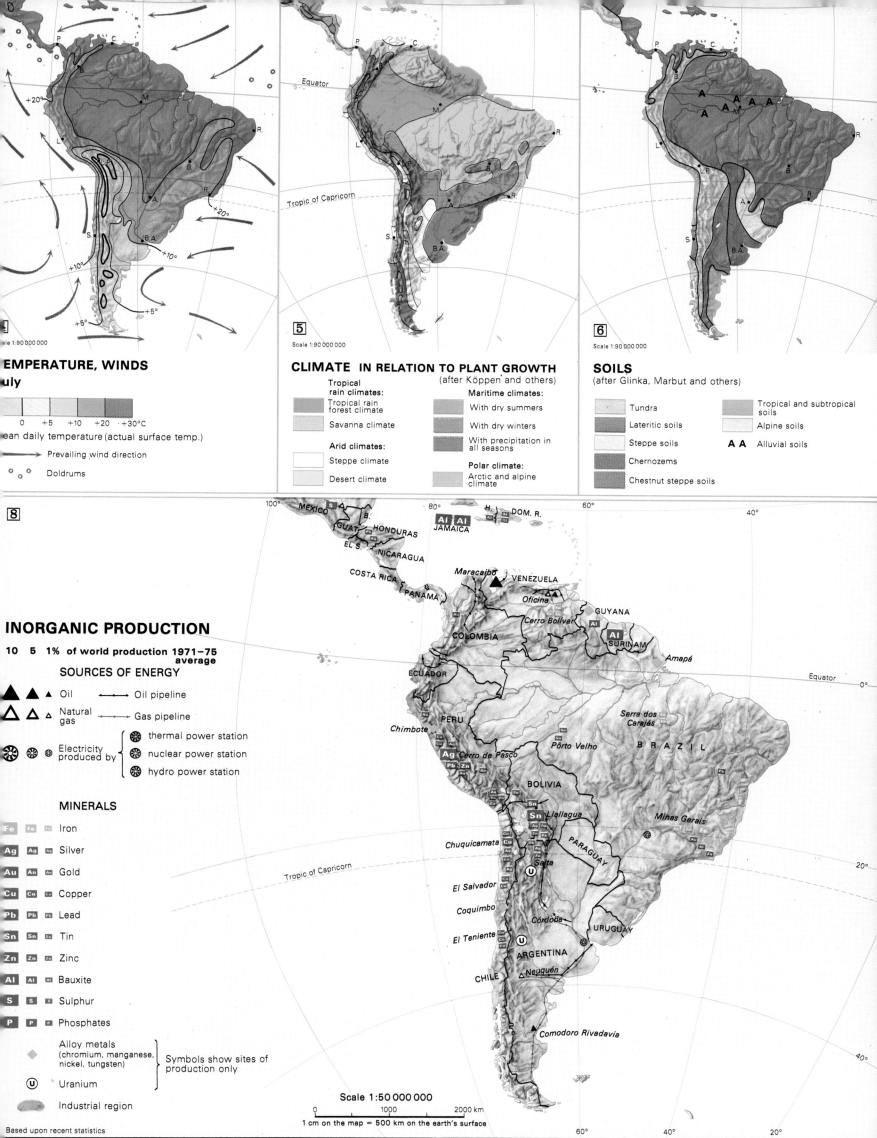

TEMPERATURE, WINDS

uly

Scale 1:90 000 000

0   +5 +10 +20 +30°C

ean daily temperature (actual surface temp.)

→ Prevailing wind direction

o o o Doldrums

4

+20°
+20°
+10°
+5°
+5°

Equator
Tropic of Capricorn

P   C.
B.
M.
R.
L.
B.
R.
A.
S.
B.A.

CLIMATE IN RELATION TO PLANT GROWTH
(after Köppen and others)

5   Scale 1:90 000 000

Equator
Tropic of Capricorn

Tropical rain climates:
- Tropical rain forest climate
- Savanna climate

Arid climates:
- Steppe climate
- Desert climate

Maritime climates:
- With dry summers
- With dry winters
- With precipitation in all seasons

Polar climate:
- Arctic and alpine climate

P   C.
M.
L.
P.
B.
A.
S.
B.A.

SOILS
(after Glinka, Marbut and others)

6   Scale 1:90 000 000

P   C.
B.
A A A A A
M.
R.
L.
L.P.
A.
S.
B.A.

- Tundra
- Lateritic soils
- Steppe soils
- Chernozems
- Chestnut steppe soils
- Tropical and subtropical soils
- Alpine soils

A A Alluvial soils

8

INORGANIC PRODUCTION

10 5 1% of world production 1971–75 average

SOURCES OF ENERGY

▲ ▲ ▲ Oil   ←→ Oil pipeline
△ △ △ Natural gas   ←→ Gas pipeline

⊛ ⊛ ⊛ Electricity produced by
- ⊛ thermal power station
- ⊛ nuclear power station
- ⊛ hydro power station

MINERALS

Fe Fe Fe Iron
Ag Ag Ag Silver
Au Au Au Gold
Cu Cu Cu Copper
Pb Pb Pb Lead
Sn Sn Sn Tin
Zn Zn Zn Zinc
Al Al Al Bauxite
S   S   S   Sulphur
P   P   P   Phosphates

◆ Alloy metals (chromium, manganese, nickel, tungsten) } Symbols show sites of production only

Ⓤ Uranium

   Industrial region

Based upon recent statistics

LLER'S BIPOLAR PROJECTION

Scale 1:50 000 000

0   1000   2000 km

1 cm on the map = 500 km on the earth's surface

100°   80°   60°   40°

MEXICO S   A.
B.
GUAT. HONDURAS
EL S. NICARAGUA
COSTA RICA PANAMA
Al Al JAMAICA
H. DOM. R.

Maracaibo ▲ VENEZUELA
Oficina △ △
Cerro Bolívar GUYANA
COLOMBIA Al SURINAM
Amapá

ECUADOR
PERU
Chimbote
Cerro de Pasco Ag
Pb Zn

Pôrto Velho
Serra dos Carajás
B R A Z I L

BOLIVIA
Llallagua Sn
Sn
Minas Gerais

Chuquicamata Cu
Salta
Ⓤ
PARAGUAY

El Salvador
Coquimbo
Córdoba
El Teniente
Ⓤ
Neuquén △
ARGENTINA
URUGUAY
CHILE

Comodoro Rivadavia ▲

Equator 0°
Tropic of Capricorn
20°
40°

60°   40°   20°

Map 1 (Arctic region) labels:

PACIFIC OCEAN

120° · San Francisco · Oakland · Los Angeles · 4418 · Portland · Seattle · Vancouver · Juneau · Whitehorse · Yukon R. · 150° · Anchorage · Mount McKinley 6194 · ALASKA · Fairbanks · Prudhoe Bay · Barrow · Wrangel I. · Bering Sea · 180° · Bering Strait · Anadyr · Arctic Circle · Sea of Magadan · Okhotsk · Nikolayevsk · Komsomolsk · Khabarovsk · Harbi · CHIN

Salt Lake City · Rocky Mountains · Calgary · Edmonton · Mackenzie River · Inuvik · Great Bear Lake · Great Slave Lake · Yellowknife · Banks Island · Beaufort Sea · Amundsen 1903–06 · Nordenskiöld 1878–79 · East Siberian Sea · R. Kolyma · Okhotsk · 3147 · S · Verkhoyansk · Yakutsk · Chita · L. Baykal · Bratsk · Irk

4399 · Denver · Omaha · Regina · Saskatchewan R. · Missouri R. · Winnipeg · Lake Winnipeg · Victoria Island · Melville Island · Queen Elizabeth Islands · 80° · Area of Magnetic North Pole · New Siberian Islands · ARCTIC OCEAN · Laptev Sea · 3809 · C. Chelyuskin · Severnaya Zemlya · Tiksi · R. Lena · Khatanga · R. Lena · R. Angara

CANADA · Minneapolis · St. Paul · Chicago · Lake Michigan · Lake Superior · Winnipeg · Churchill · Hudson Bay · Boothia Pen. · 70° · Resolute · Melville Pen. · Ellesmere I. · Lomonosov Ridge · North Pole · Peary 1909 · Byrd (air) 1926 · 5220 · Franz Josef Land (U.S.S.R.) · 80° · 70° · Dikson · R. Yenisei · Norilsk · 60° · Novosibirsk · Krasnoyars

Detroit · Lake Huron · Pittsburgh · Toronto · Washington · Ottawa · Philadelphia · Montreal · Schefferville · New York · Québec · Boston · 1917 · St. Lawrence River · Baffin Island · Baffin Bay · Nares Strait · Thule · Camp Century (U.S.A.) · Peary Land · C. Morris Jesup · West Spitsbergen · N.E. Land · Svalbard (NORWAY) · Novaya Zemlya · 1590 · Kara Sea · Taymyr Pen. · Vorkuta · R. Ob · 1894 · Naryan Mar · Ural Mountains · Tyumen · Sverdlovsk · Chelyabi · Perm

Halifax · Nova Scotia · Goose Bay · Labrador · Upernavik · Davis Strait · Egedesminde · Jakobshavn · Söndre Strömfjord · Godthåb · Greenland (DENMARK) · 3360 · 3700 · Greenland Sea · Bear I. (NORWAY) · North Cape · Hammerfest · Barents Sea · Murmansk · 1208 · Arkhangel · Kirov · Ufa · Magnitogo · Kazan · Gorki

St. Pierre and Miquelon (FR.) · 60° · Newfoundland · St. John's · Julianehåb · 3809 · Labrador Sea · C. Farewell · Ångmagssalik · Denmark Strait · Arctic Circle · Norwegian Sea · Jan Mayen I. (NORWAY) · Narvik · 2111 · FINLAND · SWEDEN · NORWAY · Umeå · Helsinki · Yaroslavl · R. Volga · R. Ural · Kuybyshev · Saratov

ATLANTIC OCEAN · 30° · Reykjavik · ICELAND · 2119 · Trondheim · 0° · 30° · Leningrad · Moscow

[1]

Map 2 (Antarctic region) labels:

Buenos Aires · Mar del Plata · ARGENTINA · Bahía Blanca · 6212 · South Georgia (U.K.) · 2915 · 30° · South Sandwich Islands (U.K.) · 0° · Antarctic Circle · 6972 · Crozet Islands (FR.) · ATLANTIC OCEAN

Stanley · Falkland Islands (U.K.) · Signy Island (U.K.) · South Orkney Islands (U.K.) · C. Norvegia · Sanae (S.AFR.) · Novolazarevskaya (U.S.S.R.) · Showa (JAPAN) · Molodeshnaya (U.S.S.R.) · INDIAN OCEAN · Kerguelen (FR.)

Comodoro Rivadavia · Patagonia · Tierra del Fuego · South Shetland Islands · Weddell Sea · Crown Princess Martha Coast · Princess Astrid Coast · Princess Ragnhild Coast · 3180 · Enderby Land · McDonald Islands (AUSTR.) · Heard

Puerto Montt · 4058 · CHILE · Strait of Magellan · Cape Horn · Drake Passage · 5486 · O'Higgins (CHILE) · Graham Land · Palmer Station (U.S.A.) · Larsen Ice Shelf · Palmer Land · Halley Bay (U.K.) · Queen Maud Land · Coats Land · MacRobertson Coast · Mawson Station (AUSTR.) · Amery Ice Shelf · Davis (AUSTR.)

Punta Arenas · Antarctic Peninsula · Stonington I. (U.K.) · Alexander I Island · General Belgrano (ARG.) · Berkner I. · Filchner Ice Shelf · Lassiter Ice Shelf · Fuchs 1957–58 · East Antarctica · Lambert Glacier · West Ice Shelf · 6089

Bellingshausen Sea · Peter I Island · 5280 · 70° · Siple Station (U.S.A.) · Ellsworth Land · Vinson Massif · 5140 · West Antarctica · Byrd Land · Amundsen-Scott Station (U.S.A.) · Amundsen 1911 · Scott 1912 · Byrd (air) 1929 · South Pole · Shackleton 1909 · 80° · Sovietskaya (U.S.S.R.) · 70° · Davis Sea · 60° · Mirnyy (U.S.S.R.) · Shackleton Ice Shelf

Amundsen Sea · Byrd Station (U.S.A.) · Queen Maud Mts. · Fuchs–Hillary 1958 · 4350 · Vostok (U.S.S.R.) · Wilkes Land · Knox Coast · Wilkes Station (AUSTR./U.S.A.) · Cape Poinsett

Mt. Sidley 4181 · 8100 · Ross Ice Shelf · Scott 1911–12 · Scott Station (N.Z.) · McMurdo Sound (U.S.A.) · 3794 · Victoria Land · Adélie Land · Dumont d'Urville (FR.) · Area of Magnetic South Pole · 5201

Ross Sea · Hallett · Cape Adare · PACIFIC OCEAN · 120° · 150° · 180° · Scott Island · Balleny Islands · d'Urville Sea · Antarctic Circle

[2]

Legend:

- ■ Philadelphia — 'Million' city
- ■ Philadelphia — capital cities underlined
- ● Arkhangel — Other town
- ▲ Molodeshnaya — Research station
- —— International boundary
- ----- Journey of exploration
- 4058 • Height in metres
- 3809 ▼ Depth in metres

Arable land	Tundra
Coniferous forest	Ice cap
Desert	Shelf ice
Steppe	Pack and drift ice

The major powers and countries with territorial claims in Antarctica (Argentin, Australia, Chile, France, New Zealand, N way and United Kingdom) agreed in 19 not to press their claims during the thir years up to 1989.

© EMS

EQUID STANT AZIMUTHAL PROJE

80 POLAR REGIONS, environment

Scale 1:40 000 000

0 · 500 · 1000 · 1500 km · 1 cm = 400 km

0 · 250 · 500 · 75 · 1 inch = 640 miles

GAZETTEER

Introduction

An index is a method for quickly finding particular items mentioned in a book. It lists important names, places, and items alphabetically, and gives the number of the page on which each item occurs.

Indexes in atlases differ from those in other books by including additional information, such as a brief description (often with abbreviations) of each item listed and its geographical location. An atlas index is therefore a gazetteer.

The geographical location of a place or feature is related to latitude and longitude, the lines of which appear on maps as superimposed grids. Latitude and longitude are called geographical co-ordinates. They are international, and the same for all maps in all languages.

Latitude and longitude are always written according to internationally agreed methods. The lines of latitude, reading North or South of latitude zero (the Equator), always precede those for longitude, which read East or West of longitude zero (Greenwich).

In this atlas, the lines of latitude and longitude are used also for letter-number co-ordinates. The longitude lines divide the maps into vertical strips, and these are lettered. The latitude lines divide the maps into horizontal strips, and these are numbered. Letter-number co-ordinates can be used very quickly, but they are not standardised and so their application and precision is limited.

Below are examples of both methods of gazetteering geographical information.

Place	Description of entry	Geographical co-ordinates	Page	
Aachen.	town, W. Germany.	50 47N 6 04E	39	using geographical
Altai.	mt.range, Mongolia.	46 40N 92 45E	53	co-ordinates
Amazon.	river, Brazil.	2 00S 53 30W	77	

Place	Description of entry	Letter-number co-ordinates	Page	
Aachen.	town, W.Germany	E 3	39	using letter-number
Altai.	mt.range, Mongolia.	M 5	53	co-ordinates
Amazon.	river, Brazil.	E 3	77	

Where practicable names in this atlas have been anglicised in the usual way; but some natural features, such as rivers and mountain ranges, straddle more than one country, in each of which they are known by different names. For example, the river Douro in Portugal is called the river Duero in Spain. As both these names are shown in the atlas, both are listed in the gazetteer, where they are cross-referenced as follows.

Douro, river, Portugal. 41 01N 8 16W 44 (as Duero in Sp.)
Duero, river, Spain. 41 37N 4 25W 44 (as Douro in Port.)

From time to time several cities and towns have been officially renamed. Constantinople, for example, has become Istanbul; St. Petersburg has been renamed Leningrad; and Saigon is now Ho Chi Minh. The maps show former or historical names in brackets under the present names, the gazetteer cross-referencing all the different versions. Only the present names, however, are provided with geographical co-ordinates.

Below is an alphabetical list of abbreviations used in the gazetteer.

ABBREVIATIONS

admin. reg.	administrative region (includes county, department, province, state, territory union etc.)
Afghan.	Afghanistan
Afr.	Africa, African
Ala.	Alabama
Alb.	Albania
Alg.	Algeria
Alta.	Alberta
Amer.	America
anch.	anchorage
Ang.	Angola
Ant.	Antarctica
Arch.	Archipelago
Arg.	Argentina
Ariz.	Arizona
Ark.	Arkansas
assoc.	associated
Atlan.	Atlantic
Aust.	Austria
Austr.	Australia
Austral.	Australasia
b.	bay, bight
Bangl.	Bangladesh
B.C.	British Columbia
Belg.	Belgium
Bol.	Bolivia
Bots.	Botswana
Braz.	Brazil
Bulg.	Bulgaria
C.	Cape
Calif.	California
Cam.	Cameroon
Cambod.	Cambodia
Cambs.	Cambridgeshire
Can.	Canada
Can. Is.	Canary Islands
cap.	capital
Carib.	Caribbean
Cent.	Central
Chan., chan.	Channel
Col.	Colombia

Colo.	Colorado
comm. nat.	commonwealth nation
Confed.	Confederation
Conn.	Connecticut
const. reg.	constituent region
cr. dep.	crown dependency
Cz.	Czechoslovakia
D.C.	District of Columbia
Del.	Delaware
Den.	Denmark
dep.	dependency, dependent
Derbys.	Derbyshire
des.	desert
dist.	district
dom.	dominion
Dom. Rep.	Dominican Republic
E.	East
Ec.	Ecuador
Eg.	Egypt
Eng.	England
Equ. Guin.	Equatorial Guinea
est.	estuary
Eur.	Europe
Falk. Is.	Falkland Islands
fd.	fiord
Fed.	Federal, Federation
Fin.	Finland
Fla.	Florida
for.	forest
Fr.	France, French
Fr. Guiana	French Guiana
G., g.	gulf
Ga.	Georgia
Gam.	The Gambia
geog. reg.	geographical region
Ger.	Germany
gl.	glacier
gov.	governing

Gr.	Greece	N. Dak.	North Dakota
Green.	Greenland	Nebr.	Nebraska
Gt.	Great	Neth.	Netherlands
Guat.	Guatemala	Nev.	Nevada
Guin.	Guinea	Newf.	Newfoundland
Guy.	Guyana	N.H.	New Hampshire
		Nic.	Nicaragua
		Nig.	Nigeria
Hants.	Hampshire	N. Ire.	Northern Ireland
hdl.	headland (includes cape, foreland, head, point, etc.)	N.J.	New Jersey
		N. Mex.	New Mexico
hist. site	historical site	Nor.	Norway
Hond.	Honduras	N.S.	Nova Scotia
hs.	hills	N.S.W.	New South Wales
Hung.	Hungary	N. Terr.	Northern Territory
		N.W. Terrs.	North West Territories
		N.Y.	New York
I., Is.	Island, Islands	N.Z.	New Zealand
Ice.	Iceland		
Ill.	Illinois		
Ind.	Indiana	Oc.	Ocean
Indon.	Indonesia	Okla.	Oklahoma
inl.	inlet	Ont.	Ontario
I.o.M.	Isle of Man	Oreg.	Oregon
I.o.W.	Isle of Wight		
Ire.	Ireland		
It.	Italy	p.	pass
		Pa.	Pennsylvania
		Pac.	Pacific
Jam.	Jamaica	Pak.	Pakistan
Jap.	Japan	Pan.	Panama
		Pap. New Guin.	Papua New Guinea
		Par.	Paraguay
Kans.	Kansas	pen.	peninsula
Kingd.	Kingdom	Phil.	Philippines
Kor.	Korea	pl.	plain
Ky.	Kentucky	plat.	plateau
		Pol.	Poland
		Port.	Portugal, Portuguese
L.	Lake, Loch, Lough	P. Rico	Puerto Rico
La.	Louisiana	prot.	protectorate
Lab.	Labrador		
Les.	Lesotho		
Lib.	Liberia	Que.	Quebec
Lr.	Lower	Queensl.	Queensland
Lux.	Luxembourg		
		R.	River
Madag.	Madagascar	reg.	region
Mal.	Malawi	Rep.	Republic
Malay.	Malaysia	resr.	reservoir
Man.	Manitoba	Rhod.	Rhodesia
Mass.	Massachusetts	R.I.	Rhode Island
Maur.	Mauritania	Rom.	Romania
Md.	Maryland		
Me.	Maine		
Medit.	Mediterranean	s.	sea
Mex.	Mexico	S.	South, Southern
Mich.	Michigan	Sar.	Sarawak
Minn.	Minnesota	Sard.	Sardinia
Miss.	Mississippi	Sask.	Saskatchewan
Mo.	Missouri	S.C.	South Carolina
Mong.	Mongolia	Scot.	Scotland
Mont.	Montana	sd.	sound
Mor.	Morocco	S. Dak.	South Dakota
Mozam.	Mozambique	Sen.	Senegal
Mt., Mts.,		Si. Arab.	Saudi Arabia
mt., mts.	mount, mountain, mountains	S. Leone	Sierra Leone
		Sp.	Spain, Spanish
		S.S.R.	Soviet Socialist Republic
Nam.	Namibia	st.	state
Nat.	National	St.	Saint
N.	North, Northern	Ste.	Sainte
N.B.	New Brunswick	str.	strait
N.C.	North Carolina	Sud.	Sudan

Sur.	Surinam		Ven.	Venezuela
Swazi.	Swaziland		Vic.	Victoria
Swed.	Sweden		Viet.	Vietnam
Switz.	Switzerland		vol.	volcano
			Vt.	Vermont
Tanz.	Tanzania			
Tas.	Tasmania			
Tenn.	Tennessee		W.	West, Western
terr., terrs.	territory, territories		Wash.	Washington
Tex.	Texas		wf.	waterfalls
Thai.	Thailand		W.I.	West Indies
tn.	town		Wilts.	Wiltshire
Tun.	Tunisia		Wis.	Wisconsin
Tur.	Turkey		W. Va.	West Virginia
			Worcs.	Worcestershire
			Wyo.	Wyoming
U.A.E.	United Arab Emirates			
Ugan.	Uganda			
UK	United Kingdom of Great Britain and Northern Ireland			
Urug.	Uruguay		Yorks.	Yorkshire
USA	United States of America		Yug.	Yugoslavia
USSR	Union of Soviet Socialist Republics			
Va.	Virginia			
val.	valley		Zam.	Zambia

A

Aachen, tn., W. Ger., 50 47N 6 04E 39
Aba, tn., Nig., 5 06N 7 21E 67
Abādān, tn., Iran, 30 20N 48 15E 52
Abakan, tn., USSR, 53 43N 91 25E 53
Abbeville, tn., Fr., 50 06N 1 51E 39
Abéché, tn., Chad, 13 49N 20 49E 67
Abeokuta, tn., Nig., 7 10N 3 26E 67
Aberdare, tn., Wales, 51 43N 3 27W 26
Aberdeen, tn., Scot., 57 10N 2 04W 22
Aberdeen, tn., S. Dak., USA, 45 28N 98 30W 72
Aberfeldy, tn., Scot., 56 37N 3 54W 23
Abergavenny, tn., Wales, 51 50N 3 00W 26
Abergele, tn., Wales, 53 17N 3 34W 26
Abertillery, tn., Wales, 51 45N 3 09W 26
Aberystwyth, tn., Wales, 52 25N 4 05W 26
Abidjan, tn., Ivory Coast, 5 19N 4 01W 66
Abilene, tn., Tex., USA, 32 27N 99 45W 72
Abingdon, tn., Eng., 51 41N 1 17W 27
Abisko, tn., Swed., 68 21N 18 50E 43
Abor Low, hist. site, Eng., 53 08N 1 57W 25
Aboyne, tn., Scot., 57 04N 2 48W 23
Abruzzi, geog. reg., It., 42 15N 14 00E 45
Abu Dhabi, tn., U.A.E., 24 28N 54 25E 52
Abu Simbel, hist. site, Eg., 22 19N 31 38E 49
Abyssinia see Ethiopia
Acapulco, tn., Mex., 16 51N 99 56W 71
Accra, tn., Ghana, 5 33N 0 15W 66
Accrington, tn., Eng., 53 46N 2 21W 25
Acireale, tn., Sicily, 37 36N 15 10E 45
Aconcagua, Mt., Arg., 32 40S 70 02W 77
Ådalen, R., Swed., 63 20N 17 50E 43
Adamaoua Mts., Cam., 7 10N 12 20E 67
Adana, tn., Tur., 37 00N 35 19E 47
Adapazari, tn., Tur., 40 45N 30 23E 47
Adare, C., hdl., Ant., 71 00S 171 00E 80
Addis Ababa, tn., Ethiopia, 9 03N 38 42E 67
Adelaide, tn., S. Austr., 34 56S 138 36E 63
Adélie Land, geog. reg., Ant., 67 00S 140 00E . . . 80
Aden, tn., S. Yemen, 12 50N 45 03E 52
Aden, Gulf of, S. Yemen, 13 00N 50 00E 52
Adige, R., It., 45 09N 11 25E 45
Adirondack Mts., N.Y., USA, 44 00N 74 15W 73
Adrar, tn., Alg., 27 51N 0 19W 48
Adriatic Sea, It./Yug., 43 00N 16 00E 45
Aegean Sea, Gr./Tur., 37 00N 25 00E 46
Afghanistan, Rep., Asia, 33 00N 65 00E 52
Afyonkarahisar, tn., Tur., 38 46N 30 32E 47
Agadèz, tn., Niger, 17 00N 7 56E 67
Agadir, tn., Mor., 30 30N 9 40W 66
Agartala, tn., India, 23 49N 91 15E 55
Agen, tn., Fr., 44 12N 0 38E 44
Agra, tn., India, 27 09N 78 00E 54
Agrigento, tn., Sicily, 37 19N 13 35E 45
Aguascalientes, tn., Mex., 22 00N 102 12W 71
Agulhas, C., hdl., Rep. S. Afr., 34 50S 20 00E . . . 67
Ahaggar, geog. reg., Alg., 23 00N 6 30E 67
Ahlen, tn., W. Ger., 51 46N 7 53E 39
Ahmadabad, tn., India, 23 03N 72 40E 54
Ahmadnagar, tn., India, 19 08N 74 48E 54
Aľpa, tn., China, 33 00N 102 00E 56
Ahwaz, tn., Iran, 31 17N 48 43E 52
Ailsa Craig, I., Scot., 55 15N 5 07W 23
Aïn Salah, tn., Alg., 27 12N 2 29E 48
Aïr, geog. reg., Niger, 18 30N 8 00E 67
Airdrie, tn., Scot., 55 52N 3 59W 23
Aire, R., Eng., 53 42N 1 30W 25
Aireborough, tn., Eng., 53 51N 1 42W 25
Aisne, R., Fr., 49 12N 4 47E 39
Aix-en-Provence, tn., Fr., 43 31N 5 27E 45
Aizuwakamatsu, tn., Jap., 37 30N 139 58E 57
Ajaccio, tn., Corsica, 41 55N 8 43E 45
Ajedabia, tn., Libya, 30 48N 20 15E 49
Ajmer, tn., India, 26 29N 74 40E 54
Akashi, tn., Jap., 34 39N 135 00E 57
Aketi, tn., Zaire, 2 42N 23 51E 67
Akhisar, tn., Tur., 38 54N 27 50E 47
Akhtubinsk, tn., USSR, 48 20N 46 10E 51
Akita, tn., Jap., 39 44N 140 05E 57
Aklavik, tn., N.W. Terrs., Can., 68 15N 135 02W . . 71
Akranes, tn., Ice., 64 19N 22 05W 43
Akron, tn., Ohio, USA, 41 04N 81 31W 73
Akşehir, tn., Tur., 38 22N 31 24E 47
Aktyubinsk, tn., USSR, 50 20N 57 00E 51
Akureyri, tn., Ice., 65 41N 18 04W 43
Akyab, tn., Burma, 20 09N 92 55E 55
Aalst, tn., Belg., 50 47N 5 12E 39
Al Mawṣil see Mosul
Ala Shan, mts., China, 40 00N 105 00E 56
Ala Tau Range, mts., China/USSR, 42 43N 71 26E . . 51
Alabama, admin. reg., USA, 32 40N 87 00W 73
Alabama, R., Ala., USA, 31 00N 87 00W 73
Alagôas, admin. reg., Braz., 9 40S 35 50W 77
Alagoinhas, tn., Braz., 12 09S 38 21W 77
Åland Is., Fin., 60 15N 20 00E 42
Alapayevsk, tn., USSR, 57 55N 61 42E 51
Alaska, admin. reg., USA, 66 30N 150 00W 71
Alaska, G. of, Alaska, USA, 58 00N 145 00W 70
Alaska Peninsula, Alaska, USA, 56 00N 160 00W . . 70

Alatyr, tn., USSR, 54 51N 46 35E 50
Albacete, tn., Sp., 39 00N 1 52W 44
Albania, Rep., Eur., 41 00N 20 00E 46
Albany, R., Ont., Can., 51 30N 87 00W 71
Albany, tn., Ga., USA, 31 37N 84 10W 73
Albany, tn., N.Y., USA, 42 40N 73 49W 73
Albany, tn., Oreg., USA, 44 38N 123 07W 72
Albany, tn., W. Austr., 34 57S 117 54E 62
Albert Canal, Belg., 50 54N 5 30E 39
Albert, L., Zaire, 1 30N 31 00E 67
Albert Lea, tn., Minn., USA, 43 38N 93 16W 73
Alberta, admin. reg., Can., 54 40N 115 00W 71
Albertville see Kalemie
Albi, tn., Fr., 43 56N 2 08E 44
Alborán I., Sp., 35 57N 3 05W 44
Ålborg, tn., Den., 57 03N 9 56E 42
Albuquerque, tn., N. Mex., USA, 35 05N 106 38W . . 72
Albury, tn.N.S.W., Austr., 36 03S 146 53E 63
Alcalá de Henares, tn., Sp., 40 28N 3 22W 44
Alcira, tn., Sp., 39 10N 0 27W 44
Alcoy, tn., Sp., 38 42N 0 29W 44
Aldabra Is., Seychelles, 9 22S 46 28E 67
Aldan, R., USSR, 62 30N 135 30E 53
Aldan, tn., USSR, 58 44N 125 22E 53
Aldeburgh, tn., Eng., 52 09N 1 35E 27
Alderney, I., Chan. Is., UK, 49 43N 2 12W 27
Aldershot, tn., Eng., 51 15N 0 47W 27
Aldridge, tn., Eng., 52 37N 1 55W 27
Aleksandrov, tn., USSR, 56 23N 38 45E 50
Aleksandrovsk, tn., USSR, 50 50N 142 20E 53
Alençon, tn., Fr., 48 25N 0 05E 44
Aleppo, tn., Syria, 36 14N 37 10E 49
Alès, tn., Fr., 44 08N 4 05E 44
Alessándria, tn., It., 44 55N 8 37E 45
Ålesund, tn., Nor., 62 28N 6 11E 42
Aleutian Is., Bering Sea, 52 00N 176 00W 70
Aleutian Trench, Bering Sea, 50 00N 174 00W . . . 70
Alexander 1 Island, Ant., 69 00S 70 00W 80
Alexandria, tn., Eg., 31 13N 29 55E 49
Alexandria, tn., Va., USA, 38 49N 77 06W 73
Alexandroúpolis, tn., Gr., 40 51N 25 53E 46
Alford, tn., Scot., 57 14N 2 42W 22
Alfreton, tn., Eng., 53 06N 1 23W 25
Algeciras, tn., Sp., 36 08N 5 27W 44
Algeria, Rep., Afr., 28 00N 1 45E 48
Algiers, tn., Alg., 36 50N 3 00E 48
Alicante, tn., Sp., 38 21N 0 29W 44
Alice Springs, tn., N. Terr., Austr., 23 42S 133 52E . . 63
Alitus, tn., USSR, 54 24N 24 03E 42
Alkmaar, tn., Neth., 52 38N 4 44E 39
Allahabad, tn., India, 25 27N 81 50E 54
Allegheny Mts., USA, 37 20N 80 00W 73
Allen, L., Rep. Ire., 54 08N 8 03W 24
Allentown, tn., Pa., USA, 40 37N 75 30W 73
Aller, R., W. Ger., 52 50N 9 29E 39
Allier, R., Fr., 46 40N 3 10E 44
Alloa, tn., Scot., 56 07N 3 49W 23
Alma Ata, tn., USSR, 43 19N 76 55E 52
Almada, tn., Port., 38 40N 9 09W 44
Almalyk, tn., USSR, 40 50N 69 40E 51
Almelo, tn., Neth., 52 21N 6 40E 39
Almeria, tn., Sp., 36 50N 2 26W 44
Almetyevsk, tn., USSR, 54 50N 52 22E 51
Alnwick, tn., Eng., 55 25N 1 42W 25
Alor Setar, tn., Malay., 6 06N 100 23E 55
Alot'ai see Sharasume
Alphen, tn., Neth., 52 08N 4 40E 39
Alps, The, mts., Eur., 46 00N 13 00E 45
Alsace, admin. reg., Fr., 48 15N 7 25E 41
Alsace, geog. reg., Fr., 48 15N 7 25E 45
Alsh, L., Scot., 57 15N 5 36W 22
Alston, tn., Eng., 54 49N 2 26W 25
Altafjord, fd., Nor., 70 10N 23 00E 43
Altai, mts., Mong., 46 40N 92 45E 53
Alton, tn., Eng., 51 09N 0 59W 27
Altoona, tn., Pa., USA, 40 32N 78 23W 73
Altrincham, tn., Eng., 53 24N 2 21W 25
Alushta, tn., USSR, 44 41N 34 24E 47
Alva, tn., Scot., 56 09N 3 49W 23
Amagasaki, tn., Jap., 34 42N 135 23E 57
Amami Group, Is., Jap., 28 00N 129 00E 57
Amami I., Jap., 28 50N 129 03E 57
Amapá, admin. reg., Braz., 1 40N 52 00W 77
Amarillo, tn., Tex., USA, 35 14N 101 50W 72
Amasya, tn., Tur., 40 37N 35 50E 47
Amazon, R., S. Amer., 2 00S 53 00W 77
Amazonas, admin. reg., Braz., 4 20S 64 00W 77
Ambarchik, tn., USSR, 69 39N 162 27E 53
Ambato, tn., Ec., 1 18S 78 39W 77
Ambleside, tn., Eng., 54 26N 2 58W 25
Ambon, tn., Indon., 3 41S 128 10E 55
Ambre, C. d', hdl., Madag., 11 58S 49 14E 67
Ameland, I., Neth., 53 27N 5 45E 39
Amersfoort, tn., Neth., 52 09N 5 23E 39
Amersham, tn., China, 31 50N 117 30E 56
Amery Ice Shelf, Ant., 68 00S 75 00E 80
Amesbury, tn., Eng., 51 10N 1 47W 27
Amiens, tn., Fr., 49 54N 2 18E 39
Amirante Is., Seychelles, 6 00S 53 00E 67
Amlwch, tn., Wales, 53 25N 4 20W 26
Ammān, tn., Jordan, 31 57N 35 56E 49
Ammanford, tn., Wales, 51 48N 3 59W 26
Amne Machin, Mt., China, 34 25N 99 40E 56

Amoy, tn., China, 24 26N 118 07E 56
Amritsar, tn., India, 31 35N 74 56E 54
Amstelveen, tn., Neth., 52 18N 4 50E 39
Amsterdam, tn., Neth., 52 21N 4 54E 39
Amu Darya, R., USSR, 37 50N 65 00E 52
Amundsen-Scott Station, USA base, Ant.,
90 00S 0 00 80
Amundsen Sea, Ant., 70 00S 110 00W 80
Amur, R., China/USSR, 53 30N 122 30E 53
(see also Heilung Kiang)
An Uaimh, tn., Rep. Ire., 53 39N 6 41W 24
Anadyr, tn., USSR, 64 35N 177 20E 53
Anaheim, tn., Calif., USA, 33 50N 117 56W 72
Anaiza, tn., Si. Arab., 26 06N 43 58E 52
Anambas Is., Indon., 3 20N 106 30E 55
Anápolis, tn., Braz., 16 19S 48 58W 77
Anatolia, geog. reg., Tur., 38 00N 29 00E 47
Anchorage, tn., Alaska, USA, 61 10N 150 00W . . . 70
Ancohuma, Mt., Bol., 15 54S 68 30W 77
Ancona, tn., It., 43 37N 13 31E 45
Andalusia, geog. reg., Sp., 37 35N 5 00W 44
Andaman Is., India, 12 30N 92 30E 55
Andaman Sea, Thai., 10 00N 96 00E 55
Andes, Mts., S. Amer., 20 00S 69 00W 77
Andizhan, tn., USSR, 40 48N 72 23E 52
Andorra, Rep., Eur., 42 30N 1 30E 44
Andorra (tn.) see Andorra La Vella
Andorra la Vella, tn., Andorra, 42 30N 1 30E 44
Andover, tn., Eng., 51 13N 1 28W 27
Andøya, I., Nor., 69 05N 15 40E 43
Andria, tn., It., 41 14N 16 18E 45
Ándros, I., Gr., 37 49N 24 54E 46
Andros I., The Bahamas, 24 30N 78 00W 73
Angara, R., USSR, 58 30N 97 00E 53
Angarsk, tn., USSR, 52 31N 103 55E 53
Angda, Rep., Afr., 12 00S 18 00E 67
Angel Falls, wf., Ven., 5 56N 62 30W 77
Angeles, tn., Phil., 15 09N 120 33E 55
Ångermanälven, R., Swed., 64 30N 17 00E 43
Angers, tn., Fr., 47 29N 0 32W 44
Angkor, hist. site, Cambod., 13 26N 103 50E 55
Anglesey, geog. reg., Wales, 53 17N 4 20W 26
Angmagssalik, tn., Green., 65 35N 38 00W 71
Angora see Ankara
Angoulême, tn., Fr., 45 40N 0 10E 44
Anhwei, admin. reg., China, 31 50N 117 30E 56
Anjou, geog. reg., Fr., 47 20N 0 30W 44
Anju, tn., N. Kor., 39 36N 125 42E 57
Ankang, tn., China, 32 40N 109 12E 56
Ankara, tn., Tur., 39 55N 32 50E 47
Ankiang, tn., China, 27 00N 110 05E 56
Anking, tn., China, 30 46N 119 40E 56
Ann Arbor, tn., Mich., USA, 42 18N 83 43W 73
Annaba, tn., Alg., 36 55N 7 47E 48
Annam, admin. reg., Viet., 16 30N 107 30E 56
Annam, geog. reg., Viet., 16 30N 107 30E 55
Annan, tn., Scot., 54 59N 3 16W 23
Annecy, tn., Fr., 45 54N 6 07E 45
Annobón see Pagalu
Ansham, tn., China, 41 05N 122 58E 57
Anshun, tn., China, 26 15N 105 51E 56
Ansi, tn., China, 40 21N 96 10E 56
Anstruther, tn., Scot., 56 14N 2 42W 23
Anta, tn., China, 46 25N 125 20E 57
Antakya, tn., Tur., 36 12N 36 10E 47
Antalya, tn., Tur., 36 53N 30 42E 47
Antarctic Peninsula, Ant., 65 00S 70 00W 80
Antequera, tn., Sp., 37 01N 4 34W 44
Antibes, tn., Fr., 43 35N 7 07E 45
Anticosti I., Que., Can., 49 20N 62 40W 71
Antigua, assoc. st. of UK, W.I., 17 09N 61 49W . . 77
Antofagasta, tn., Chile, 23 40S 70 23W 77
Antrim, tn., N. Ire., 54 43N 6 13W 24
Antrim Mts., N. Ire., 54 57N 6 08W 24
Antsirabe, tn., Madag., 19 51S 47 01E 67
Antung, tn., China, 40 06N 124 25E 57
Antwerp, tn., Belg., 51 13N 4 25E 39
Anyang, tn., China, 36 04N 114 20E 56
Aomori, tn., Jap., 40 50N 140 43E 57
Aosta, tn., It., 45 43N 7 19E 45
Apatity, tn., USSR, 67 32N 33 21E 43
Apeldoorn, tn., Neth., 52 13N 5 57E 39
Apennines, mts., It., 44 20N 10 20E 45
Apia, tn., W. Samoa, Pac. Oc., 13 48S 171 45W . . 63
Appalachian Mts., USA, 38 00N 80 00W 73
Appin, geog. reg., Scot., 56 50N 5 27W 23
Appleby, tn., Eng., 54 36N 2 29W 25
Appleton, tn., Wis., USA, 44 17N 88 24W 73
Apsheronsk, tn., USSR, 44 26N 39 45E 47
Apulia, geog. reg., It., 41 30N 15 20E 45
Aqaba, tn., Jordan, 29 32N 35 00E 49
Aqaba, Gulf of, Red Sea, 28 15N 33 20E 49
Arabian Desert, Eg., 27 40N 32 00E 49
Arabian Sea, 21 00N 61 00E 54
Aracaju, tn., Braz., 10 54S 37 07W 77
Arad., tn., Rom., 46 10N 21 19E 46
Arafura Sea, Austr./Indon., 10 00S 135 00E 55
Aragon, geog. reg., Sp., 41 25N 1 00W 44
Araguaia, R., Braz., 12 44S 50 34W 77
Aral Sea, L., USSR, 44 30N 60 00E 51
Aralsk, tn., USSR, 46 56N 61 43E 51

Aranjuez, *tn., Sp.*, 40 02N 3 37W 44
Ararat, Mt., *Tur.*, 39 44N 44 15E 49
Aras, *R., Tur.*, 40 00N 43 00E 49
Arbor Low, *hist. site, Eng.*, 53 10N 1 44W 27
Arbroath, *tn., Scot.*, 56 34N 2 35W 23
Arctic Ocean 3
Ardebil, *tn., Iran*, 38 15N 48 18E 51
Ardee, *tn., Rep. Ire.*, 53 52N 6 33W 24
Ardennes, *plat., Belg./Fr.*, 50 00N 5 15E 39
Ardnamurchan, *geog. reg., Scot.*, 56 44N 6 14W . . 23
Ardrishaig, *tn., Scot.*, 56 00N 5 27W 23
Ardrossan, *tn., Scot.*, 55 39N 4 49W 23
Ards Peninsula, *N. Ire.*, 54 30N 5 30W 24
Åre, *tn., Swed.*, 63 25N 13 05E 43
Arendal, *tn., Nor.*, 58 27N 8 56E 42
Arequipa, *tn., Peru*, 16 25S 71 32W 77
Arezzo, *tn., It.*, 43 28N 11 53E 45
Argentina, *Rep., S. Amer.*, 35 00S 66 00W 77
Arghai Bulak Pass, *Sinkiang*, 42 23N 88 32E 56
Argyll, *geog. reg., Scot.*, 56 14N 5 10W 23
Århus, *tn., Den.*, 56 10N 10 13E 42
Arica, *tn., Chile*, 18 30S 70 20W 77
Arisaig, Sound of, *Scot.*, 56 50N 5 50W 23
Arizona, *admin. reg., USA*, 34 20N 111 30W 72
Arkaig, *L., Scot.*, 56 58N 5 10W 23
Arkansas, *admin. reg., USA*, 35 00N 92 30W 73
Arkansas, *R., USA*, 35 20N 94 00W 73
Arkhangel, *tn., USSR*, 45 41N 40 16E 50
Arlberg Pass, *Aust.*, 47 09N 10 12E 45
Arles, *tn., Fr.*, 43 41N 4 38E 45
Arlington, *tn., Tex., USA*, 32 44N 97 05W 72
Arlon, *tn., Belg.*, 49 41N 5 49E 39
Arklow, *tn., Rep. Ire.*, 52 48N 6 09W 24
Armagh, *tn., N. Ire.*, 54 21N 6 39W 24
Armavir, *tn., USSR*, 44 59N 41 10E 51
Armenian S.S.R., *admin. reg., USSR*,
40 38N 44 17E 51
Armidale, *tn., N.S.W., Austr.*, 30 32S 151 40E . . . 63
Arnhem, *tn., Neth.*, 52 00N 5 53E 39
Arnhem, Cape, *hdl., N. Terr., Austr.*, 12 18S 137 00E . 63
Arnhem Land, *geog. reg., N. Terr., Austr.*,
13 15S 133 30E 62
Arno, *R., It.*, 43 44N 10 20E 45
Arran, *I., Scot.*, 55 35N 5 15W 23
Arras, *tn., Fr.*, 50 17N 2 46E 39
Árta, *tn., Gr.*, 39 10N 20 59E 46
Artem, *tn., USSR*, 43 23N 132 08E 57
Artois, *geog. reg., Fr.*, 50 20N 2 30E 39
Aru Is., *Indon.*, 6 00S 134 30E 55
Aruba I., *self-gov. Neth. terr., Lesser Antilles*,
12 30N 70 00W 77
Arusha, *tn., Tanz.*, 3 21S 36 40E 67
Arvayheer, *tn., Mong.*, 46 15N 102 46E 56
Arvidsjaur, *tn., Swed.*, 65 37N 19 10E 43
Arzamas, *tn., USSR*, 55 24N 43 48E 50
Arzew, *tn., Alg.*, 35 50N 0 19W 48
Asahi, Mt., *Jap.*, 43 42N 142 54E 57
Asahigawa, *tn., Jap.*, 43 46N 142 23E 57
Asbest, *tn., USSR*, 57 05N 61 30E 51
Ascension I., *UK cr. colony, S. Atlan. Oc.*,
8 00S 14 15W 66
Aschaffenburg, *tn., W. Ger.*, 49 58N 9 10E 39
Ascoli Piceno, *tn., It.*, 42 52N 13 35E 45
Ascot, *tn., Eng.*, 51 25N 0 41W 27
Ashbourne, *tn., Eng.*, 53 01N 1 43W 25
Ashby de la Zouch, *tn., Eng.*, 52 46N 1 28W 27
Asheville, *tn., N.C., USA*, 35 35N 82 35W 73
Ashford, *tn., Eng.*, 51 09N 0 53E 27
Ashikaga, *tn., Jap.*, 36 21N 139 26E 57
Ashington, *tn., Eng.*, 55 11N 1 34W 25
Ashkhabad, *tn., USSR*, 37 58N 58 24E 52
Ashton-in-Makerfield, *tn., Eng.*, 53 29N 2 39W . . . 25
Ashton-under-Lyne, *tn., Eng.*, 53 29N 2 06W 25
Asmara, *tn., Ethiopia*, 15 20N 38 58E 67
Assen, *tn., Neth.*, 53 00N 6 34E 39
Asti, *tn., It.*, 44 54N 8 13E 45
Astoria, *tn., Oreg., USA*, 46 12N 123 50W 72
Astrakhan, *tn., USSR*, 46 22N 48 04E 51
Asturias, *geog. reg., Sp.*, 43 15N 6 00W 44
Asuncion, *tn., Par.*, 25 15S 57 40W 77
Aswân, *tn., Eg.*, 24 05N 32 56E 49
Asyût, *tn., Eg.*, 27 14N 31 07E 49
Atacama Desert, *Chile*, 24 00S 69 20W 77
Atar, *tn., Maur.*, 20 32N 13 08W 66
Atbara, *R., Sud.*, 17 50N 34 03E 67
Atbara, *tn., Sud.*, 17 42N 34 00E 67
Athabasca, *L., Alta./Sask., Can.*, 58 50N 109 55W . 71
Athens, *tn., Gr.*, 38 00N 23 44E 46
Athínai see Athens
Athlone, *tn., Rep. Ire.*, 53 25N 7 56W 24
Áthos, *mt., Gr.*, 40 10N 24 19E 46
Athy, *tn., Rep. Ire.*, 52 59N 6 59W 24
Atlanta, *tn., Ga., USA*, 33 45N 84 23W 73
Atlantic Ocean 2
Atlas Mts., *Mor.*, 33 00N 3 00W 48
Atrek, *R., Iran/USSR*, 35 13N 52 17E 51
Auchterarder, *tn., Scot.*, 56 18N 3 43W 23
Auckland, *tn., N.Z.*, 36 55S 174 47E 63
Augsburg, *tn., W. Ger.*, 48 21N 10 54E 45
Augusta, *tn., Ga., USA*, 33 29N 82 00W 73
Augusta, *tn., Me., USA*, 44 17N 69 48W 73
Augusta, *tn., Sicily*, 37 14N 15 14E 45
Aurillac, *tn., Fr.*, 44 56N 2 26E 44
Austin, *tn., Tex., USA*, 30 18N 97 47W 72
Australia, *comm. nat., Austral.*, 25 00S 130 00E . . . 62
Australian Alps, *mts., N.S.W./Vic., Austr.*,
36 30S 148 08E 63
Austria, *Rep., Eur.*, 47 30N 14 00E 45
Auvergne, *geog. reg., Fr.*, 45 20N 3 00E 44
Auxerre, *tn., Fr.*, 47 48N 3 35E 44
Avebury, *hist. site, Eng.*, 51 27N 1 50W 27

Avellino, *tn., It.*, 40 49N 14 47E 45
Aviemore, *tn., Scot.*, 57 12N 3 50W 22
Avignon, *tn., Fr.*, 43 56N 4 48E 45
Avila, *tn., Sp.*, 40 39N 4 42W 44
Avilés, *tn., Sp.*, 43 33N 5 55W 44
Avon, *admin. reg., Eng.*, 51 25N 2 30W 26
Avon, *R., Hants., Eng.*, 50 57N 1 45W 27
Avon, *R., Scot.*, 57 09N 3 25W 22
Avon, *R., Wilts., Eng.*, 51 22N 2 20W 26
Avon, *R., Worcs., Eng.*, 52 08N 1 53W 27
Awe, *L., Scot.*, 56 15N 5 15W 23
Axel Heiberg I., *N.W. Terrs., Can.*, 80 00N 90 00W . 71
Axios, *R., Gr.*, 40 57N 22 35E 46
Axminster, *tn., Eng.*, 50 47N 3 00W 26
Ayacucho, *tn., Peru*, 13 10S 74 15W 77
Ayaguz, *tn., USSR*, 47 59N 80 27E 51
Aydın, *tn., Tur.*, 37 52N 27 50E 47
Aylesbury, *tn., Eng.*, 51 50N 0 50W 27
Aylsham, *tn., Eng.*, 52 49N 1 15E 27
Ayr, *tn., Queensl., Austr.*, 19 32S 147 25E 63
Ayr, *tn., Scot.*, 55 28N 4 38W 23
Ayre, Point of, *hdl., I.o.M.*, 54 25N 4 22W 24
Azbine see Aïr
Azerbaydzhan S.S.R., *admin. reg., USSR*,
40 43N 46 06E 51
Azores, *Is., Port. terr., Atlan. Oc.*, 38 44N 29 00W . 66
Azov, *tn., USSR*, 47 06N 39 26E 47
Azov, Sea of, *USSR*, 46 00N 36 30E 47
Azul, *tn., Arg.*, 36 46S 59 50W 77

B

Babul, *tn., Iran*, 36 32N 52 42E 51
Babylon, *hist. site, Iraq*, 32 33N 44 25E 49
Bac Ninh, *tn., Viet.*, 21 16N 106 14E 56
Bacău, *tn., Rom.*, 46 33N 26 58E 46
Back, *R., N.W. Terrs., Can.*, 65 20N 98 30W 71
Bacton, *tn., Eng.*, 52 52N 1 28E 27
Bacup, *tn., Eng.*, 53 43N 2 12W 25
Bad Salzuflen, *tn., W. Ger.*, 52 06N 8 45E 39
Badajoz, *tn., Sp.*, 38 53N 6 58W 44
Badalona, *tn., Sp.*, 41 27N 2 15E 44
Baden-Baden, *tn., W. Ger.*, 48 45N 8 15E 39
Baden-Württemberg, *admin. reg., W. Ger.*,
48 40N 9 00E 41
Badenoch, *geog. reg., Scot.*, 57 00N 4 00W 23
Baffin Bay, *Green./Can.*, 74 00N 73 00W 71
Baffin I., *N.W. Terrs., Can.*, 70 00N 80 00W 71
Bafra, *tn., Tur.*, 41 34N 35 56E 47
Bagdad see Baghdad
Baghdad, *tn., Iraq*, 33 20N 44 26E 49
Bagheria, *tn., Sicily*, 38 05N 13 31E 45
Bahamas, The, *Is., comm. nat., W.I.*, 25 30N 77 00W . 73
Baharia Oasis, *Eg.*, 28 00N 28 50E 49
Bahia, *admin. reg., Braz.*, 11 26S 42 47W 77
Bahia Blanca, *tn., Arg.*, 38 45S 62 15W 77
Bahrain, *Emirate, Persian Gulf*, 26 00N 50 35E . . . 52
Baia-Mare, *tn., Rom.*, 47 39N 23 36E 46
Baidoa, *tn., Somalia*, 3 08N 43 30E 67
Baile Atha Cliath see Dublin
Baker, *tn., Oreg., USA*, 44 46N 117 50W 72
Baker I., *Pac. Oc.*, 0 12N 176 28W 63
Bakersfield, *tn., Calif., USA*, 35 25N 119 00W . . . 72
Bakony Forest, *mts., Hung.*, 47 10N 17 30E 46
Baku, *tn., USSR*, 40 22N 49 53E 51
Balakovo, *tn., USSR*, 52 04N 47 46E 50
Balasov, *tn., USSR*, 51 30N 43 10E 50
Balaton, *L., Hung.*, 46 50N 17 40E 46
Balbriggan, *tn., Rep. Ire.*, 53 37N 6 11W 24
Baldock, *tn., Eng.*, 51 59N 0 11W 27
Balearic Is., *Sp.*, 39 21N 3 03E 44
Bali, *I., Indon.*, 8 20S 115 00E 55
Balikesir, *tn., Tur.*, 39 37N 27 51E 47
Balikpapan, *tn., Indon.*, 1 15S 116 50E 55
Balkan Mts., *Bulg.*, 43 15N 23 00E 46
Balkhash, *tn., USSR*, 46 50N 74 57E 52
Balkhash, L., *USSR*, 46 00N 74 50E 52
Ballachulish, *tn., Scot.*, 56 40N 5 09W 23
Ballantrae, *tn., Scot.*, 55 06N 5 00W 23
Ballarat, *tn., Vic., Austr.*, 37 36S 143 58E 63
Ballater, *tn., Scot.*, 57 03N 3 03W 23
Balleny Is., *Ant.*, 66 30S 163 00E 80
Ballybofey, *tn., Rep. Ire.*, 54 57N 7 47W 24
Ballycastle, *tn., N. Ire.*, 55 12N 6 15W 24
Ballyclare, *tn., N. Ire.*, 54 45N 6 00W 24
Ballymena, *tn., N. Ire.*, 54 52N 6 17W 24
Ballymoney, *tn., N. Ire.*, 55 10N 6 30W 24
Ballynahinch, *tn., Rep. Ire.*, 55 20N 9 53W 24
Ballyshannon, *tn., Rep. Ire.*, 54 30N 8 11W 24
Baltic Sea, *Eur.*, 56 00N 20 00E 42
Baltimore, *tn., Md., USA*, 39 18N 76 38W 73
Bamako, *tn., Mali*, 12 40N 7 59W 66
Bamberg, *tn., W. Ger.*, 49 54N 10 54E 41
Banbridge, *tn., N. Ire.*, 54 21N 6 16W 24
Banbury, *tn., Eng.*, 52 04N 1 20W 27
Banchory, *tn., Scot.*, 57 03N 2 30W 23
Banda Atjeh, *tn., Indon.*, 5 30N 95 20E 55
Banda Sea, *Indon.*, 6 00S 126 00E 55
Bandar Abbas, *tn., Iran*, 27 12N 56 15E 52
Bandar Seri Begawan, *tn., Brunei*, 4 56N 114 58E . 55

Bandeira, Mt., *Braz.*, 20 25S 41 45W 77
Bandırma, *tn., Tur.*, 40 21N 27 58E 47
Bandjarmasin, *tn., Indon.*, 3 20S 114 35E 55
Bandundu, *tn., Zaire*, 3 20S 17 24E 67
Bandung, *tn., Indon.*, 6 57S 107 34E 55
Banff, *tn., Scot.*, 57 40N 2 31W 22
Bangalore, *tn., India*, 12 58N 77 35E 54
Bangasson, *tn., Cent. Afr.*, 4 41N 22 48E 67
Bangka, *I., Indon.*, 2 00S 105 50E 55
Bangkok, *tn., Thai.*, 13 44N 100 30E 55
Bangladesh, *Rep., comm. nat., Asia*, 24 00N 88 00E . 55
Bangor, *tn., N. Ire.*, 54 40N 5 40W 24
Bangor, *tn., Wales*, 53 13N 4 08W 26
Bangui, *tn., Cent. Afr.*, 4 23N 18 37E 67
Bangweulu, *L., Zam.*, 11 15S 29 45E 67
Baniyás, *tn., Syria*, 35 12N 35 57E 49
Banja Luka, *tn., Yug.*, 44 47N 17 11E 46
Banjarmasin see Bandjarmasin
Banjul, *tn., Gam.*, 13 28N 16 39W 66
Banks I., *N.W. Terrs., Can.*, 73 30N 124 00W . . . 71
Bann, *R., N. Ire.*, 55 00N 6 40W 24
Banská Bystrica, *tn., Cz.*, 48 44N 19 10E 41
Baracaldo, *tn., Sp.*, 43 17N 2 59W 44
Baranovichi, *tn., USSR*, 53 09N 26 00E 50
Barbados, *comm. nat., Lesser Antillies*,
13 00N 59 30W 77
Barcelona, *tn., Sp.*, 41 25N 2 10E 44
Barcelona, *tn., Ven.*, 10 08N 64 43W 77
Bardsey I., *Wales*, 52 46N 4 48W 26
Bareilly, *tn., India*, 28 20N 79 24E 54
Barents Sea, *Arctic Oc.*, 73 00N 39 00E 52
Bari, *tn., It.*, 41 07N 16 52E 45
Barkly Tableland, *plat., N. Terr./Queensl., Austr.*,
19 00S 138 40E 63
Barletta, *tn., It.*, 41 20N 16 17E 45
Barmouth, *tn., Wales*, 52 43N 4 03W 26
Barnard Castle, *tn., Eng.*, 54 33N 1 55W 25
Barnaul, *tn., USSR*, 53 21N 83 15E 52
Barnsley, *tn., Eng.*, 53 34N 1 28W 25
Barnstaple, *tn., Eng.*, 51 05N 4 04W 26
Barnstaple Bay, *Eng.*, 51 05N 4 20W 26
Baroda, *tn., India*, 22 19N 73 14E 54
Barquisimeto, *tn., Ven.*, 10 03N 69 18W 77
Barra, *I., Scot.*, 57 00N 7 30W 23
Barra Head, *hdl., Scot.*, 56 47N 7 36W 23
Barranquilla, *tn., Col.*, 11 00N 74 50W 77
Barri, *tn., Wales*, 51 24N 3 18W 26
Barrie, *tn., Ont., Can.*, 44 22N 79 42W 73
Barrow, *R., Rep. Ire.*, 52 46N 7 00W 24
Barrow, *R., Alaska, USA*, 71 16N 156 50W 71
Barrow-in-Furness, *tn., Eng.*, 54 07N 3 14W 25
Baruun Urt, *tn., Mong.*, 46 42N 113 20E 56
Basel, *tn., Switz.*, 47 33N 7 36E 45
Basilan, *tn., Phil.*, 6 40N 121 59E 55
Basildon, *tn., Eng.*, 51 34N 0 25E 27
Basilicata, *geog. reg., It.*, 40 30N 16 00E 45
Basingstoke, *tn., Eng.*, 51 16N 1 05W 27
Basle see Basel
Basque Provinces, *geog. reg., Sp.*, 43 15N 2 50W . . 44
Basra, *tn., Iraq*, 30 30N 47 50E 52
Bass Strait, *Austr.*, 40 00S 146 00E 63
Bassein, *tn., Burma*, 16 46N 94 45E 55
Bastia, *tn., Corsica*, 42 41N 9 26E 45
Batavia see Djakarta
Bataysk, *tn., USSR*, 47 09N 39 46E 50
Bath, *tn., Eng.*, 51 23N 2 22W 26
Bathgate, *tn., Scot.*, 55 55N 3 39W 23
Bathurst see Banjul
Bathurst, *tn., N.S.W., Austr.*, 35 04S 149 12E . . . 63
Batley, *tn., Eng.*, 53 44N 1 37W 25
Batna, *tn., Alg.*, 35 34N 6 10E 48
Baton Rouge, *tn., La., USA*, 30 30N 91 10W 73
Battle, *tn., Eng.*, 50 55N 0 29E 27
Batumi, *tn., USSR*, 47 37N 41 36E 51
Bauchi, *tn., Nig.*, 10 16N 9 50E 67
Bauru, *tn., Braz.*, 22 19S 49 07W 77
Bavaria, *admin. reg., W. Ger.*, 49 07N 11 30E . . . 41
Bayamo, *tn., Cuba*, 20 23N 76 39W 73
Bayan Kara Shan, *mts., China*, 34 00N 98 00E . . . 56
Bayanhongor, *tn., Mong.*, 45 07N 100 44E 56
Bayeux, *tn., Fr.*, 49 16N 0 42W 39
Baykal, *L., USSR*, 53 00N 108 00E 53
Baykonur, *tn., USSR*, 47 50N 66 03E 51
Bayonne, *tn., Fr.*, 43 30N 1 28W 44
Bayreuth, *tn., W. Ger.*, 49 57N 11 35E 41
Bayrūt see Beirut
Beachy Head, *hdl., Eng.*, 50 44N 0 16E 27
Beaconsfield, *tn., Eng.*, 51 37N 0 39W 27
Bear I., *Nor.*, 74 30N 19 00E 52
Beaufort Sea, *Arctic Oc.*, 73 30N 155 00W 71
Beauly, *tn., Scot.*, 57 29N 4 29W 22
Beauly Firth, *Scot.*, 57 30N 4 20W 22
Beaumaris, *tn., Wales*, 53 16N 4 05W 26
Beaumont, *tn., Tex., USA*, 30 04N 94 06W 73
Beauvais, *tn., Fr.*, 49 26N 2 05E 39
Bebington, *tn., Eng.*, 52 23N 3 01W 26
Beccles, *tn., Eng.*, 52 28N 1 34E 27
Béchar, *tn., Alg.*, 31 35N 2 17W 48
Bedford, *tn., Eng.*, 52 08N 0 29W 27
Bedfordshire, *admin. reg., Eng.*, 52 03N 0 40W . . . 27
Bedlington, *tn., Eng.*, 55 08N 1 35W 25
Bedworth, *tn., Eng.*, 52 28N 1 29W 27
Beersheba, *tn., Israel*, 31 15N 34 47E 49
Beeston, *tn., Eng.*, 52 56N 1 12W 25
Beida, *tn., Libya*, 32 49N 21 45E 49
Beinn Dearg, *mt., Scot.*, 57 47N 4 55W 22
Beira, *tn., Mozam.*, 19 49S 34 52E 67
Beirut, *tn., Lebanon*, 33 52N 35 30E 49
Beith, *tn., Scot.*, 55 45N 4 38W 23
Bejá, *tn., Port.*, 38 01N 7 52W 44
Bejaïa, *tn., Alg.*, 36 49N 5 03E 48

Békéscsaba, tn., Hung., 46 40N 21 05E 46
Belaya, R., USSR, 54 45N 56 00E 51
Belaya Tserkov, tn., USSR, 49 49N 30 10E 50
Belcher Is., Hudson Bay, Can., 56 20N 79 20W . . . 71
Belém, tn., Braz., 1 27S 48 29W 77
Belfast, tn., N. Ire., 54 35N 5 55W 24
Belfast L., N. Ire., 54 40N 5 50W 24
Belford, tn., Eng., 55 36N 1 49W 25
Belfort, tn., Fr., 47 38N 6 52E 45
Belgium, Kingd., Eur., 51 30N 5 00E 39
Belgorod, tn., USSR, 50 38N 36 36E 50
Belgorod Dnestrovskiy, tn., USSR, 46 10N 30 19E . 47
Belgrade, tn., Yug., 44 50N 20 30E 46
Belize, comm. nat., Cent. Amer., 17 25N 88 00W . . 71
Bellingham, tn., Wash., USA, 48 45N 122 29W . . . 72
Bellingshausen Sea, Ant., 66 00S 80 00W 80
Belluno, tn., It., 46 08N 12 13E 45
Belmopan, tn., Belize, 17 13N 88 48W 71
Belo Horizonte, tn., Braz., 19 54S 43 54W 77
Belogorsk, tn., USSR, 51 00N 128 20E 53
Belomorsk, tn., USSR, 64 34N 34 45E 43
Beloretsk, tn., USSR, 53 59N 58 20E 51
Belper, tn., Eng., 53 01N 1 29W 25
Beltsy, tn., USSR, 47 44N 27 51E 50
Belukha, Mt., USSR, 49 50N 86 50E 52
Ben Hope, mt., Scot., 58 24N 4 36W 22
Ben Lawers, mt., Scot., 56 33N 4 15W 23
Ben Lomond, mt., Scot., 56 12N 4 38W 23
Ben Macdhui, mt., Scot., 57 04N 3 40W 23
Ben More, mt., Scot., 56 25N 6 02W 23
Ben More Assynt, mt., Scot., 58 07N 4 52W 22
Ben Nevis, mt., Scot., 56 48N 5 00W 23
Ben Wyvis, mt., Scot., 57 40N 4 35W 22
Benares see Varanasi
Benbecula, I., Scot., 57 26N 7 20W 22
Bendery, tn., USSR, 46 50N 29 29E 50
Bendigo, tn., Vic., Austr., 36 48S 144 21E 63
Benevento, tn., It., 41 08N 14 46E 45
Bengal, Bay of, Indian Oc., 15 00N 83 00E 54
Benghazi, tn., Libya, 32 07N 20 05E 49
Benguela, tn., Angu., 12 34S 13 24E 67
Beni, R., Bol., 10 30S 69 00W 77
Beni-Mellal, tn., Mor., 32 22N 6 29W 48
Beni Suef, tn., Eg., 29 05N 31 05E 49
Benidorm, tn., Sp., 38 33N 0 09W 44
Benin, Rep., Afr., 8 00N 2 00E 66
Benoni, tn., Rep. S. Afr., 26 12S 28 18E 67
Benue, R., Nig., 7 50N 6 30E 67
Beograd see Belgrade
Berbera, tn., Somalia, 10 28N 45 02E 67
Berbérati, tn., Cent. Afr., 4 19N 15 51E 67
Berdichev, tn., USSR, 49 54N 28 39E 50
Berdyansk, tn., USSR, 46 45N 36 47E 50
Berezniki, tn., USSR, 59 26N 56 49E 51
Berezovo, tn., USSR, 63 58N 65 00E 51
Bergama, tn., Tur., 39 08N 27 10E 47
Bergamo, tn., It., 45 42N 9 40E 45
Bergen, tn., Nor., 60 23N 5 20E 42
Bergen-op-Zoom, tn., Neth., 51 30N 4 17E 39
Bergisch Gladbach, tn., W. Ger., 50 59N 7 10E . . . 39
Bering Sea, Pac. Oc., 58 00N 167 00E 53
Bering Strait, USA/USSR, 66 00N 170 00W 53
Berkeley, tn., Calif., USA, 37 53N 122 17W 72
Berkner I., Ant., 79 30S 50 00W 80
Berkshire, admin. reg., Eng., 51 26N 1 20W 27
Berlin, tn., Ger., 52 32N 13 25E 41
Bermejo, R., Arg., 23 49S 62 27W 77
Bermuda see Bermuda Is.
Bermuda Is., self-gov. UK dep. terr., Atlan. Oc.,
32 45N 65 00W 71
Bern see Berne
Berne, tn., Switz., 46 57N 7 26E 45
Berneray, I., Scot., 56 47N 7 38W 22
Berry, geog. reg., Fr., 47 00N 2 00E 44
Berwick-upon-Tweed, tn., Eng., 55 46N 2 00W . . . 25
Besançon, tn., Fr., 47 14N 6 02E 45
Bessarabia, geog., USSR, 46 20N 29 00E 47
Béthune, tn., Fr., 50 32N 2 38E 39
Beverley, tn., Eng., 53 51N 0 26W 25
Bexhill, tn., Eng., 50 50N 0 29E 27
Beysehir, L., Tur., 37 40N 31 45E 47
Béziers, tn., Fr., 43 21N 3 13E 44
Bhopal, tn., India, 23 17N 77 28E 54
Bhubaneswar, tn., India, 20 13N 85 50E 54
Bhutan, Kingd., Asia, 27 00N 88 00E 55
Białystok, tn., Pol., 53 09N 23 10E 41
Biarritz, tn., Fr., 43 29N 1 33W 44
Bicester, tn., Eng., 51 54N 1 09W 27
Bideford, tn., Eng., 51 01N 4 13W 26
Bideford Bay, Eng., 51 05N 4 20W 26
Biel, tn., Switz., 47 09N 7 16E 45
Bielefeld, tn., W. Ger., 52 02N 8 32E 39
Bielsko-Biała, tn., Pol., 49 50N 19 00E 41
Big Horn Mts., Mont./Wyo., USA, 44 30N 107 30W . 72
Biggleswade, tn., Eng., 52 05N 0 17W 27
Bihać, tn., Yug., 44 49N 15 53E 46
Bikin, tn., USSR, 46 52N 134 15E 57
Bikini, I., Pac. Oc., 11 35N 165 20E 63
Bilbao, tn., Sp., 43 15N 2 56W 44
Billericay, tn., Eng., 51 38N 0 25E 27
Billings, tn., Mont., USA, 45 47N 108 30W 72
Bilma, tn., Niger, 18 46N 13 04E 67
Bingen, tn., W. Ger., 49 58N 7 55E 39
Bingham Canyon, tn., Utah, USA, 40 33N 112 09W . 72
Binghamton, tn., N.Y., USA, 42 06N 75 55W 73
Bingley, tn., Eng., 53 51N 1 50W 25
Birkenhead, tn., Eng., 53 24N 3 02W 25
Birlad, tn., Rom., 46 14N 27 40E 47
Birmingham, tn., Ala., USA, 33 30N 86 55W 73
Birmingham, tn., Eng., 52 30N 1 50W 27
Birobidzhan, tn., USSR, 48 49N 132 54E 53

Birr, tn., Rep. Ire., 53 05N 7 54W 24
Birsk, tn., USSR, 55 28N 55 31E 51
Bisbee, tn., Ariz., USA, 31 27N 109 55W 72
Biscay, Bay of, Fr./Sp., 45 00N 2 00W 44
Bishop Auckland, tn., Eng., 54 40N 1 40W 25
Bishop's Stortford, tn., Eng., 51 53N 0 09E 27
Biskra, tn., Alg., 34 50N 5 41E 48
Bismarck Archipelago, Pap., New Guin.,
3 30S 148 30E 63
Bismark, tn., N. Dak., USA, 46 50N 100 48W 72
Bissau, tn., Guinea-Bissau, 11 52N 15 39W 66
Bitola, tn., Yug., 41 01N 21 21E 46
Bitterfontein, tn., Rep. S. Afr., 31 03S 18 16E 67
Bitterroot Range, mts., Idaho, USA, 46 00N 115 00W . 72
Biwa, L., Jap., 53 15N 135 45E 57
Biysk, tn., USSR, 52 35N 85 16E 52
Bizerta, tn., Tun., 37 18N 9 52E 48
Black Forest, geog. reg., W. Ger., 48 00N 8 00E . . . 45
Black Hills, S. Dak., USA, 44 00N 103 50W 72
Black Isle, geog. reg., Scot., 57 35N 4 10W 22
Black Mts., Wales, 51 52N 3 50W 26
Black R. see Song Bo
Black Sea, Eur., 43 30N 35 00E 47
Blackburn, tn., Eng., 53 45N 2 29W 25
Blackpool, tn., Eng., 53 50N 3 03W 25
Blackwater, R., Eng., 51 53N 0 37E 27
Blaenavon, tn., Wales, 51 48N 3 05W 26
Blagoevgrad, tn., Bulg., 42 01N 23 05E 46
Blagoveshchensk, tn., USSR, 50 19N 127 30E 53
Blair Atholl, tn., Scot., 56 46N 3 51W 23
Blairgowrie, tn., Scot., 56 36N 3 21W 23
Blanc, C., hdl., Maur., 20 44N 17 05W 66
Blandford Forum, tn., Eng., 50 52N 2 11W 27
Blantyre, tn., Mal., 15 46S 35 00E 67
Blida, tn., Alg., 36 30N 2 50E 48
Bloemfontein, tn., Rep. S. Afr., 29 07S 26 14E 67
Blois, tn., Fr., 47 36N 1 20E 44
Blue Nile, R., Sud., 10 30N 35 00E 67
Blue Ridge, mts., USA, 36 30N 80 15W 73
Blue Stack Mts., Rep. Ire., 54 46N 8 05W 24
Blumenau, tn., Braz., 26 55N 49 07W 77
Blyth, tn., Eng., 55 07N 1 30W 25
Boa Vista, tn., Braz., 2 51N 60 43W 77
Bobo Dioulasso, tn., Upper Volta, 11 11N 4 18W . . 66
Bobruysk, tn., USSR, 53 08N 29 10E 50
Bocholt, tn., W. Ger., 51 49N 6 37E 39
Bochum, tn., W. Ger., 51 28N 7 11E 39
Boden, tn., Swed., 65 50N 21 44E 43
Bodmin, tn., Eng., 50 29N 4 43W 26
Bodmin Moor, geog. reg., Eng., 50 33N 4 36W . . . 26
Bodø, tn., Nor., 67 18N 14 26E 43
Bognor Regis, tn., Eng., 50 47N 0 41W 27
Bogor, tn., Indon., 6 34S 106 45E 55
Bogotá, tn., Col., 4 34N 74 00W 77
Bohemian Forest, mts., Cz., 49 20N 13 00E 41
Boise, tn., Idaho, USA, 43 38N 116 12W 72
Boknafjord, fd., Nor., 59 12N 5 15E 42
Bolgatanga, tn., Ghana, 10 44N 0 53W 66
Bolgrad, tn., USSR, 45 42N 28 35E 47
Bolivia, Rep., S. Amer., 17 06S 64 00W 77
Bologna, tn., It., 44 30N 11 20E 45
Bolson de Mapimí, des., Mex., 27 30N 103 00W . . . 72
Bolton, tn., Eng., 53 35N 2 26W 25
Bolu, tn., Tur., 40 45N 31 38E 47
Bolzano, tn., It., 46 30N 11 22E 45
Boma, tn., Congo, 5 50S 13 03E 67
Bombay, tn., India, 18 56N 72 51E 54
Bon, C., hdl., Tun., 37 01N 11 02E 45
Bonar Bridge, tn., Scot., 57 53N 4 21W 22
Bo'ness, tn., Scot., 56 01N 3 37W 23
Bonifacio, Strait of, Sard./Corsica, 41 20N 9 15E . . 45
Bonn, tn., W. Ger., 50 44N 7 06E 39
Boothia Peninsula, hdl., N.W. Terrs., Can.,
69 00N 95 00W 71
Borås, tn., Swed., 57 44N 12 55E 42
Bordeaux, tn., Fr., 44 50N 0 34W 44
Borders, admin. reg., Scot., 55 27N 3 07W 23
Borgå, tn., Fin., 60 24N 25 40E 42
Borisoglebsk, tn., USSR, 51 23N 42 02E 50
Borkum I., Neth., 53 35N 6 47E 39
Borlänge, tn., Swed., 60 29N 15 25E 42
Bornholm, I., Den., 55 02N 15 00E 42
Borovichi, tn., USSR, 58 22N 34 00E 50
Borzya, tn., USSR, 50 24N 116 35E 53
Bosnia, admin. reg., Yug., 44 00N 18 00E 46
Bosporus, str., Tur., 41 10N 29 10E 47
Boston, tn., Eng., 52 59N 0 01W 27
Boston, tn., Mass., USA, 42 20N 71 05W 73
Bothnia, Gulf of, Fin./Swed., 63 41N 21 00E 43
Botoşani, tn., Rom., 47 44N 26 41E 46
Botswana, Rep., Afr., 23 00S 24 00E 67
Bottrop, tn., W. Ger., 51 31N 6 55E 39
Bou Saâda, tn., Alg., 35 10N 4 09E 48
Bouaké, tn., Ivory Coast, 7 42N 5 00W 66
Bouar, tn., Cent. Afr., 5 58N 15 35E 67
Bougainville I., Solomon Is., Pac. Oc., 6 00S 155 0E . 63
Boulder, tn., Colo., USA, 40 02N 105 16W 72
Boulder, tn., W. Austr., 30 55S 121 32E 62
Boulogne-sur-Mer, tn., Fr., 50 43N 1 37E 39
Bourges, tn., Fr., 47 05N 2 23E 44
Bourke, tn., N.S.W. Austr., 30 09S 145 59E 63
Bourne, tn., Eng., 52 46N 0 23W 27
Bournemouth, tn., Eng., 50 43N 1 54W 27
Bowen, tn., Queensl., Austr., 20 00S 148 10E 63
Bowland Forest, Eng., 54 00N 2 30W 25
Boyne, R., Rep. Ire., 53 43N 6 15W 24
Boyoma Falls, wf., Zaire, 0 18N 25 30E 67
Bozeman, tn., Mont., USA, 45 40N 111 00W 72
Brač, I., Yug., 43 20N 16 40E 46
Bracknell, tn., Eng., 51 26N 0 46W 27

Bradford, tn., Eng., 53 48N 1 45W 25
Braemar, geog. reg., Scot., 57 02N 3 20W 23
Braemar, tn., Scot., 57 01N 3 24W 23
Braga, tn., Port., 41 32N 8 26W 44
Bragança, tn., Sp., 41 47N 6 46W 44
Brahmaputra, R., Asia, 26 00N 90 00E 55
(see also Tsangpo, R.)
Brăila, tn., Rom., 45 17N 27 58E 47
Braintree, tn., Eng., 51 53N 0 32E 27
Brandenburg, admin. reg., E. Ger., 52 42N 12 34E . 41
Brandenburg, tn., E. Ger., 52 25N 12 34E 41
Brander, Pass of, Scot., 56 24N 5 08W 23
Brandon, tn., Man., Can., 49 50N 99 57W 72
Brantford, tn., Ont., Can., 43 09N 80 17W 73
Brasília, tn., Braz., 16 13S 44 29W 77
Braşov, tn., Rom., 45 39N 25 35E 46
Bratislava, tn., Cz., 48 10N 17 10E 41
Bratsk, tn., USSR, 56 20N 101 50E 53
Braunton, tn., Eng., 51 07N 4 10W 26
Bray, tn., Rep. Ire., 53 12N 6 06W 24
Brazil, Rep., S. Amer., 9 00S 57 00W 77
Brazilian Highlands, mts., Braz., 18 00S 46 30W . . . 77
Brazos, R., Tex., USA, 32 00N 97 00W 72
Brazzaville, tn., Congo, 4 14S 15 14E 67
Breadalbane, geog. reg., Scot., 56 30N 4 15W 23
Brechin, tn., Scot., 56 44N 2 40W 23
Brecon, tn., Wales, 51 57N 3 24W 26
Breda, tn., Neth., 51 35N 4 46E 39
Breidafjördur, fd., Ice., 65 15N 24 00W 43
Bremen, admin. reg., W. Ger., 53 15N 8 40E 39
Bremen, tn., W. Ger., 53 05N 8 48E 39
Bremerhaven, tn., W. Ger., 53 33N 8 35E 39
Brenner Pass, Aust./It., 47 02N 11 32E 45
Brentwood, tn., Eng., 51 38N 0 18E 27
Brescia, tn., It., 45 33N 10 13E 45
Breslau see Wrocław
Bressay, I., Scot., 60 08N 1 05W 22
Brest, tn., Fr., 48 23N 4 30W 44
Brest, tn., USSR, 52 08N 23 40E 50
Bridgend, tn., Wales, 51 31N 3 35W 26
Bridgeport, tn., Conn., USA, 41 12N 73 12W 73
Bridgetown, tn., Barbados, 13 06N 59 37W 77
Bridgnorth, tn., Eng., 52 33N 2 25W 26
Bridgwater, tn., Eng., 51 08N 3 00W 26
Bridgwater Bay, Eng., 51 15N 3 15W 26
Bridlington, tn., Eng., 54 05N 0 12W 25
Bridport, tn., Eng., 50 44N 2 46W 26
Brighouse, tn., Eng., 53 42N 1 47W 25
Brightlingsea, tn., Eng., 51 49N 1 02E 27
Brighton, tn., Eng., 50 50N 0 10W 27
Brindisi, tn., It., 40 37N 17 57E 45
Brisbane, tn., Queensl., Austr., 27 30S 153 00E . . . 63
Bristol, tn., Eng., 51 27N 2 35W 26
Bristol Bay, Bering Sea, 58 30N 162 00W 70
Bristol Channel, Eng./Wales, 51 18N 3 30W 26
British Columbia, admin. reg., Can., 55 00N 125 15W . 71
Brittany, geog. reg., Fr., 48 00N 3 00W 44
Brive, tn., Fr., 45 09N 1 32E 44
Brixham, tn., Eng., 50 02N 3 30W 26
Brno, tn., Cz., 49 12N 16 40E 41
Broad Bay, Scot., 58 15N 6 16W 22
Broadford, tn., Scot., 57 14N 5 54W 22
Broadstairs, tn., Eng., 51 22N 1 27E 27
Brodick, tn., Scot., 55 34N 5 09W 23
Broken Hill, tn., N.S.W., Austr., 31 57S 141 30E . . . 63
Broken Hill, Zam., see Kabwe
Bromsgrove, tn., Eng., 52 20N 2 03W 27
Brønnøysund, tn., Nor., 65 38N 12 15E 43
Brooks Range, mts., Alaska, USA, 68 40N 161 00W . 71
Broom, L., Scot., 57 55N 5 15W 22
Broome, tn., W. Austr., 17 58S 122 15E 62
Brora, R., Scot., 58 04N 4 15W 22
Brora, tn., Scot., 58 01N 3 51W 22
Brownhills, tn., Eng., 52 39N 1 55W 27
Brownsville, tn., Tex., USA, 25 54N 97 30W 72
Bruges, tn., Belg., 51 13N 3 14E 39
Brunei, UK prot., Borneo, 4 52N 115 00E 55
Brunswick, tn., W. Ger., 52 15N 10 30E 41
Brussels, tn., Belg., 50 50N 4 21E 39
Bruxelles see Brussels
Bryansk, tn., USSR, 53 15N 34 09E 50
Bucaramanga, tn., Col., 7 08N 73 10W 77
Buchan Ness, hdl., Scot., 57 28N 1 47W 23
Buchanan, tn., Lib., 5 57N 10 02W 66
Bucharest, tn., Rom., 44 25N 26 07E 46
Buckhaven, tn., Scot., 56 11N 3 03W 23
Buckie, tn., Scot., 57 40N 2 58W 22
Buckingham, tn., Eng., 52 00N 0 59W 27
Buckinghamshire, admin. reg., Eng., 51 50N 1 00W . 27
Bucureşti see Bucharest
Budapest, tn., Hung., 47 30N 19 03E 46
Bude, tn., Eng., 50 50N 4 33W 26
Buenaventura, tn., Col., 3 54N 77 02W 77
Buenos Aires, tn., Arg., 34 40S 58 30W 77
Buffalo, tn., N.Y., USA, 42 52N 78 55W 73
Bug, R., Pol., 51 20N 23 40E 41
Bugulma, tn., USSR, 54 32N 52 46E 51
Buguruslan, tn., USSR, 53 36N 52 30E 51
Builth Wells, tn., Wales, 52 09N 3 24W 26
Bujnurd, tn., Iran, 37 28N 57 20E 51
Bujumbura, tn., Burundi, 3 22S 29 21E 67
Bukavu, tn., Zaire, 2 30S 28 49E 67
Bukhara, tn., USSR, 39 47N 64 26E 52
Bukittinggi, tn., Indon., 0 18S 100 20E 55
Bulawayo, tn., Rhod., 20 10S 28 43E 67
Bulgaria, Rep., Eur., 42 35N 24 30E 46
Bunbury, tn., W. Austr., 33 20S 115 34E 62
Buncrana, tn., Rep. Ire., 55 08N 7 27W 24
Bundaberg, tn., Queensl., Austr., 24 50S 152 21E . . 63
Bungay, tn., Eng., 52 28N 1 26E 27
Buraida, tn., Si. Arab., 26 20N 43 59E 52

Burdur, *tn., Tur.*, 37 44N 30 17E 47
Bure, *R., Eng.*, 52 38N 1 38E 27
Burgas, *tn., Bulg.*, 42 30N 27 29E 47
Burgess Hill, *tn., Eng.*, 50 57N 0 07W 27
Burgos, *tn., Sp.*, 42 21N 3 41W 44
Burgundy, *geog. reg., Fr.*, 47 50N 3 50E 44
Burma, *Rep., Asia*, 21 00N 94 00E 55
Burma Road, *Asia*, 23 30N 98 00E 56
Burnham, *tn., Eng.*, 51 15N 3 00W 26
Burnie, *tn., Tas., Austr.*, 41 03S 145 55E 63
Burnley, *tn., Eng.*, 53 48N 2 14W 25
Burntisland, *tn., Scot.*, 56 03N 3 15W 23
Burray, *I., Scot.*, 58 51N 2 54W 22
Burry Port, *tn., Wales*, 51 42N 4 15W 26
Bursa, *tn., Tur.*, 40 12N 29 04E 47
Burton upon Trent, *tn., Eng.*, 52 49N 1 36W 27
Buru, *I., Indon.*, 3 30S 126 30E 55
Burundi, *Rep., Afr.*, 3 15S 30 00E 67
Bury, *tn., Eng.*, 53 36N 2 17W 25
Bury St. Edmunds, *tn., Eng.*, 52 15N 0 43E 27
Bussum, *tn., Neth.*, 52 17N 5 10E 39
Buta, *tn., Zaire*, 2 49N 24 50E 67
Bute, *I., Scot.*, 55 48N 5 02W 23
Butte, *tn., Mont., USA*, 46 00N 112 31W 72
Butuan, *tn., Phil.*, 8 56N 125 31E 55
Buxton, *tn., Eng.*, 53 15N 1 55W 25
Buzău, *tn., Rom.*, 45 09N 26 49E 46
Buzuluk, *tn., USSR*, 52 49N 52 19E 51
Bydgoszcz, *tn., Pol.*, 53 16N 17 33E 41
Byrd Land, *geog. reg., Ant.*, 78 00S 120 00W 80
Byrd Station, *USA base, Ant.*, 80 30S 120 00W 80
Bytom, *tn., Pol.*, 50 21N 18 51E 41

C

Cabanatuan, *tn., Phil.*, 15 30N 120 58E 55
Cabinda, *admin. reg., Ang.*, 5 00S 12 30E 67
Čačak, *tn., Yug.*, 43 54N 20 22E 46
Cáceres, *tn., Sp.*, 39 29N 6 23W 44
Cader Idris, *mt., Wales*, 52 43N 3 56W 26
Cádiz, *tn., Sp.*, 36 32N 6 18W 44
Cádiz, Gulf of, *Sp.*, 36 35N 6 20W 44
Caen, *tn., Fr.*, 49 11N 0 22W 44
Caerleon, *tn., Wales*, 51 37N 2 57W 26
Caernarfon, *tn., Wales*, 53 08N 4 16W 26
Caernarfon Bay, *Wales*, 53 04N 4 40W 26
Caerphilly, *tn., Wales*, 51 35N 3 14W 26
Cagayan de Oro, *tn., Phil.*, 8 29N 124 40E 55
Cagliari, *tn., Sard.*, 39 13N 9 08E 45
Cairngorm Mts., *Scot.*, 57 10N 4 08W 22
Cairns, *tn., Queensl., Austr.*, 16 51S 145 43E 63
Cairo, *tn., Eg.*, 30 03N 31 15E 49
Cajamarca, *tn., Peru*, 7 09S 78 32W 77
Calabar, *tn., Nig.*, 4 56N 8 22E 67
Calabria, *geog. reg., It.*, 39 04N 16 30E 45
Calais, *tn., Fr.*, 50 57N 1 52E 39
Calatayud, *tn., Sp.*, 41 21N 1 39W 44
Calcutta, *tn., India*, 22 30N 88 20E 54
Caldy I., *Wales*, 51 38N 4 42W 26
Caledonian Canal, *Scot.*, 56 46N 5 00W 23
Calf of Man, *I., I.o.M.*, 54 04N 4 48W 24
Calgary, *tn., Alta., Can.*, 51 05N 114 05W 71
Cali, *tn., Col.*, 3 24N 76 30W 77
Calicut, *tn., India*, 11 15N 75 45E 54
California, *admin. reg., USA*, 37 25N 120 00W 72
Callander, *tn., Scot.*, 56 15N 4 13W 23
Callao, *tn., Peru*, 12 05S 77 08W 77
Callernish, *hist. site, Scot.*, 58 12N 6 43W 22
Calne, *tn., Eng.*, 51 27N 2 00W 27
Caltanissetta, *tn., Sicily*, 37 29N 14 04E 45
Calvinia, *tn., Rep. S. Afr.*, 31 25S 19 47E 67
Camagüey, *tn., Cuba*, 21 25N 77 55W 73
Camberley, *tn., Eng.*, 51 21N 0 45W 27
Cambodia, *Rep., Asia*, 13 00N 103 00E 55
Camborne, *tn., Eng.*, 50 12N 5 19W 26
Cambrai, *tn., Fr.*, 50 10N 3 14E 39
Cambrian Mts., *Wales*, 52 10N 3 52W 26
Cambridge, *tn., Eng.*, 52 12N 0 07E 27
Cambridge, *tn., Mass., USA*, 42 22N 71 06W 73
Cambridgeshire, *admin. reg., Eng.*, 52 21N 0 20W . . . 27
Camden, *tn., N.J., USA*, 39 52N 75 07W 73
Camelford, *tn., Eng.*, 50 37N 4 41W 26
Cameroon, *Rep., Afr.*, 5 50N 12 30E 67
Cameroon, Mt., *Cam.*, 4 13N 9 10E 67
Camp Century, *USA base, Green.*, 77 20N 60 30W . . 80
Campania, *geog. reg., It.*, 40 50N 14 45E 45
Campbeltown, *tn., Scot.*, 55 26N 5 36W 23
Campeche, Bay of, *Mex.*, 20 00N 95 00W 71
Campina Grande, *tn., Braz.*, 7 15S 35 53W 77
Campinas, *tn., Braz.*, 22 54S 47 06W 77
Campo Grande, *tn., Braz.*, 8 44S 59 14W 77
Campobasso, *tn., It.*, 41 33N 14 39E 45
Campos, *tn., Braz.*, 21 46S 41 21W 77
Campsie Fells, *hs., Scot.*, 56 02N 4 20W 23
Canada, *dom. N. Amer.*, 47 30N 116 00W 71
Canadian, *R., USA*, 36 00N 101 00W 72
Canary Is., *admin. reg., Sp.*, 28 30N 15 10W 66
Canaveral, Cape, *hdl., Fla., USA*, 28 22N 80 36W . . . 73
Canberra, *tn., Austr. cap. terr.*, 35 18S 149 08E . . . 63
Candia see Iráklion
Canea, *tn., Crete*, 35 31N 24 01E 46

Çankırı, *tn., Tur.*, 40 35N 33 37E 47
Canna, *I., Scot.*, 57 03N 6 33W 23
Cannes, *tn., Fr.*, 43 33N 7 00E 45
Cannock, *tn., Eng.*, 52 42N 2 01W 27
Cantabrian Mts., *Sp.*, 43 00N 5 10W 44
Canterbury, *tn., Eng.*, 51 17N 1 05E 27
Canton, *tn., China*, 23 08N 113 20E 56
Canton, *tn., Ohio, USA*, 40 48N 81 23W 73
Canvey, *tn., Eng.*, 51 32N 0 35E 27
Cape Breton I., *N.S., Can.*, 46 00N 61 00W 71
Cape Province, *admin. reg., Rep. S. Afr.*,
32 00S 23 00E 67
Cape Town, *tn., Rep. S. Afr.*, 33 56S 18 28E 67
Cape Verde Is., *Rep., Atlan. Oc.*, 17 10N 25 20W . . . 12
Cape York Peninsula, *Queensl., Austr.*,
13 30S 142 30E 63
Capri, *I., It.*, 40 34N 14 15E 45
Caprivi Strip, *S.W. Afr. (Nam.)*, 17 50S 23 00E 67
Caracas, *tn., Ven.*, 10 35N 66 56W 77
Carbonia, *tn., Sard.*, 39 11N 8 31E 45
Carcassonne, *tn., Fr.*, 43 13N 2 21E 44
Cárdenas, *tn., Cuba*, 23 02N 81 12W 73
Cardiff, *tn., Wales*, 51 30N 3 13W 26
Cardigan, *tn., Wales*, 52 06N 4 40W 26
Cardigan Bay, *Wales*, 52 30N 4 30W 26
Caribbean Sea, 15 00N 82 00W 71
Carlingford L., *N. Ire./Rep. Ire.*, 54 05N 6 14W 24
Carlisle, *tn., Eng.*, 54 54N 2 55W 25
Carlow, *admin. reg., Rep. Ire.*, 52 43N 6 55W 24
Carlow, *tn., Rep. Ire.*, 52 50N 6 55W 24
Carluke, *tn., Scot.*, 55 45N 3 51W 23
Carmarthen, *tn., Wales*, 51 52N 4 19W 26
Carmarthen Bay, *Wales*, 51 40N 4 30W 26
Carnarvon, *tn., W. Austr.*, 24 51S 113 45E 62
Carnforth, *tn., Eng.*, 54 08N 2 46W 25
Carnoustie, *tn., Scot.*, 56 30N 2 44W 23
Carnsore Point, *hdl., Rep. Ire.*, 52 10N 6 22W 26
Caroline Is., *Pac. Oc.*, 6 00N 145 00E 63
Carpathians, *mts., Eur.*, 46 20N 26 00E 46
Carpentaria, Gulf of, *N. Terr./Queensl., Austr.*,
14 00S 139 00E 63
Carrantuohill, *mt., Rep. Ire.*, 52 00N 9 45W 40
Carrara, *tn., It.*, 44 04N 10 06E 45
Carrick, *geog. reg., Scot.*, 55 12N 4 38W 23
Carrick-on-Shannon, *tn., Rep. Ire.*, 53 57N 7 25W . . . 24
Carrickfergus, *tn., N. Ire.*, 54 43N 5 49W 24
Carrickmacross, *tn., Rep. Ire.*, 53 58N 6 43W 24
Carron, *L., Scot.*, 57 22N 5 35W 22
Carson City, *tn., Nev., USA*, 39 10N 119 46W 72
Cartagena, *tn., Col.*, 10 24N 75 33W 77
Cartagena, *tn., Sp.*, 37 36N 0 59W 44
Carthage, *hist. site, Tun.*, 36 54N 10 16E 48
Caruarú, *tn., Braz.*, 8 15S 35 55W 77
Casablanca, *tn., Mor.*, 33 39N 7 35W 48
Cascade Range, *mts., USA*, 44 00N 122 10W 72
Caserta, *tn., It.*, 41 04N 14 20E 45
Casiquiare, *R., Ven.*, 3 00N 67 00W 77
Casper, *tn., Wyo., USA*, 42 50N 106 20W 72
Caspian Sea, *L., USSR*, 43 00N 50 00E 51
Castellón de la Plana, *tn., Sp.*, 39 59N 0 03W 44
Castelo Branco, *tn., Port.*, 39 50N 7 30W 44
Castle Douglas, *tn., Scot.*, 54 57N 3 56W 23
Castlebay, *tn., Scot.*, 56 58N 7 30W 23
Castleblayney, *tn., Rep. Ire.*, 54 07N 6 44W 24
Castleford, *tn., Eng.*, 53 44N 1 21W 25
Castlerigg, *hist. site, Eng.*, 54 32N 3 07W 25
Cat I., *The Bahamas*, 24 30N 75 30W 73
Catalonia, *geog. reg., Sp.*, 41 40N 1 15E 44
Catamarca, *tn., Arg.*, 28 28S 65 46W 77
Catania, *tn., Sicily*, 37 31N 15 06E 45
Catanzaro, *tn., It.*, 38 54N 16 36E 45
Caterham, *tn., Eng.*, 51 17N 0 04W 27
Catingas, *geog. reg., Braz.*, 8 18S 57 36W 77
Caucasus Mts., *USSR*, 43 00N 44 00E 51
Cavan, *admin reg., Rep. Ire.*, 53 52N 7 25W 24
Cavan, *tn., Rep. Ire.*, 54 00N 7 21W 24
Caxias do Sul, *tn., Braz.*, 29 14S 51 10W 77
Cayenne, *tn., Fr. Guiana*, 4 55N 52 18W 77
Ceanannus Mór, *tn., Rep. Ire.*, 53 44N 6 53W 24
Ceara, *admin. reg., Braz.*, 5 00S 40 00W 77
Cebu, *tn., Phil.*, 10 17N 123 56E 55
Cedar Rapids, *tn., Iowa, USA*, 41 59N 91 39W 73
Cekhira, *tn., Tun.*, 34 16N 10 03E 48
Celebes, *Is., Indon.*, 2 00S 120 00E 55
Celebes Sea, *Indon.*, 3 00N 123 00E 55
Celle, *tn., W. Ger.*, 52 37N 10 05E 41
Central, *admin. reg., Scot.*, 56 06N 4 23W 23
Central Africa, *Rep., Afr.*, 6 00N 20 00E 67
Central Massif, *plat., Fr.*, 45 30N 2 21E 44
Central Siberian Plateau, *USSR*, 65 00N 105 00E . . . 53
Cephalonia, *I., Gr.*, 38 28N 20 30E 46
Ceram, *I., Indon.*, 3 10S 129 00E 55
Cerignola, *tn., It.*, 41 16N 15 54E 45
Cerigo, *I., Gr.*, 36 09N 23 00E 46
Cerro Bolivar, *mt., Ven.*, 7 35N 62 45W 77
Cerro de Pasco, *tn., Peru*, 10 43S 76 15W 77
Cerro San Valentin, *mt., Chile*, 46 18S 72 06W 77
Cesena, *tn., It.*, 44 09N 12 15E 45
České Budějovice, *tn., Cz.*, 49 00N 14 30E 41
Ceuta, *tn., (Sp. terr.), Mor.*, 35 53N 5 19W 44
Cévennes, *mts., Fr.*, 44 10N 3 50E 44
Ceyhan, *R., Tur.*, 37 20N 36 30E 47
Ceyhan, *tn., Tur.*, 37 02N 35 48E 47
Ceylon see Sri Lanka
Chad, *L., Chad*, 13 20N 14 20E 67
Chad, *Rep., Afr.*, 12 30N 17 15E 67
Chagos Archipelago, *UK terr., Indian Oc.*,
6 00S 72 00E 54
Chalcis, *tn., Gr.*, 38 28N 23 36E 46
Challenger Deep, *trench, Pac. Oc.*,
11 19N 142 15E 63

Chalon-sur-Saône, *tn., Fr.*, 46 47N 4 51E 45
Châlons-sur-Marne, *tn., Fr.*, 48 58N 4 22E 39
Chambéry, *tn., Fr.*, 45 34N 5 55E 45
Chamdo, *tn., China*, 31 21N 97 02E 56
Champagne, *geog. reg., Fr.*, 49 00N 4 50E 45
Champlain, *L., N.Y./Vt., USA*, 44 30N 73 20W 73
Chandigarh, *tn., India*, 30 43N 76 47E 54
Chang Tang, *plat., Tibet*, 34 00N 85 00E 52
Changchih, *tn., China*, 36 05N 113 12E 56
Changchow, *tn., Fukien, China*, 24 31N 117 40E . . . 56
Changchow, *tn., Kiangsu, China*, 31 45N 119 57E . . . 57
Changchun, *tn., China*, 43 50N 125 20E 57
Changhua, *tn., Taiwan*, 24 06N 120 31E 57
Changjin, *tn., N. Kor.*, 41 50N 129 55E 57
Changkiakow, *tn., China*, 41 00N 115 00E 56
Changli, *tn., China*, 39 44N 119 13E 57
Changpai Shan, *mts., China*, 42 00N 128 00E 57
Changping, *tn., China*, 25 18N 117 23E 56
Changsha, *tn., China*, 28 10N 113 00E 56
Changteh, *tn., China*, 29 03N 111 35E 56
Changting, *tn., China*, 25 47N 116 17E 56
Changyeh, *tn., China*, 38 58N 100 30E 56
Channel Is., *Calif., USA*, 33 30N 120 00W 72
Channel Is., *cr. dep., UK*, 49 30N 2 40W 27
Chaotung, *tn., China*, 27 20N 103 39E 56
Chaoyang, *tn., Kwangtung, China*, 23 17N 116 33E . . 56
Chaoyang, *tn., Liaoning, China*, 41 36N 120 25E . . . 57
Chapayevsk, *tn., USSR*, 52 58N 49 44E 51
Charchan, *tn., China*, 38 04N 85 16E 52
Chard, *tn., Eng.*, 50 53N 2 58W 26
Chardzhou, *tn., USSR*, 39 09N 63 34E 51
Charente, *R., Fr.*, 45 41N 0 30W 44
Chari, *R., Cam./Chad*, 10 55N 16 15E 67
Charkhlik, *tn., Sinkiang, China*, 39 02N 88 02E 56
Charleroi, *tn., Belg.*, 50 25N 4 27E 39
Charles, Cape, *hdl., Va., USA*, 37 17N 76 01W 73
Charleston, *tn., S.C., USA*, 32 48N 79 58W 73
Charleston, *tn., W. Va., USA*, 38 23N 81 40W 73
Charleville, *tn., Queensl., Austr.*, 26 25S 146 13E . . . 63
Charleville-Mézières, *tn., Fr.*, 49 46N 4 43E 39
Charlotte, *tn., N.C., USA*, 35 03N 80 50W 73
Charters Towers, *tn., Queensl., Austr.*,
20 02S 146 20E 63
Chartres, *tn., Fr.*, 48 27N 1 30E 44
Château Thierry, *tn., Fr.*, 49 03N 3 24E 39
Châteauroux, *tn., Fr.*, 46 49N 1 41E 44
Châtellerault, *tn., Fr.*, 46 49N 0 33E 44
Chatham, *tn., Eng.*, 51 23N 0 32E 27
Chatham Is., *Pac. Oc.*, 44 00S 176 40W 63
Chattanooga, *tn., Tenn., USA*, 35 02N 85 18W 73
Chaumont, *tn., Fr.*, 48 07N 5 08E 45
Chaykovskiy, *tn., USSR*, 56 54N 54 10E 51
Cheboksary, *tn., USSR*, 56 08N 47 12E 50
Chechon, *tn., S. Kor.*, 37 05N 128 09E 57
Chekiang, *admin. reg., China*, 29 15N 120 00E 57
Cheli, *tn., China*, 22 01N 100 50E 56
Chéliff, *R., Alg.*, 36 00N 0 40E 48
Chelmsford, *tn., Eng.*, 51 44N 0 28E 27
Cheltenham, *tn., Eng.*, 51 54N 2 04W 27
Chelyabinsk, *tn., USSR*, 55 12N 61 25E 51
Chelyuskin, C., *hdl., USSR*, 77 44N 103 55E 53
Chengchow, *tn., China*, 34 45N 113 38E 56
Chengteh, *tn., China*, 40 59N 117 52E 57
Chengting, *tn., China*, 38 10N 114 30E 56
Chengtu, *tn., China*, 30 37N 104 06E 56
Chenhsien, *tn., China*, 25 34N 112 57E 56
Chepstow, *tn., Wales*, 51 39N 2 41W 26
Cher, *R., Fr.*, 47 10N 2 10E 44
Cherbourg, *tn., Fr.*, 49 38N 1 37W 44
Cheremkhovo, *tn., USSR*, 53 08N 103 01E 53
Cherepovets, *tn., USSR*, 59 09N 37 50E 50
Cherkassy, *tn., USSR*, 49 27N 32 04E 50
Cherkessk, *tn., USSR*, 44 14N 42 05E 51
Chernigov, *tn., USSR*, 51 30N 31 18E 50
Chernovtsy, *tn., USSR*, 48 19N 25 52E 50
Chernyakhovsk, *tn., USSR*, 54 36N 21 48E 42
Cherskiy Range, *mts., USSR*, 65 00N 143 00E 53
Cherwell, *R., Eng.*, 51 56N 1 18W 27
Chesapeake Bay, *USA*, 38 00N 76 12W 73
Chesham, *tn., Eng.*, 51 43N 0 38W 27
Cheshire, *admin. reg., Eng.*, 53 13N 2 47W 25
Cheshunt, *tn., Eng.*, 51 43N 0 02W 27
Chester, *tn., Eng.*, 53 12N 2 54W 25
Chester-le-Street, *tn., Eng.*, 54 52N 1 34W 25
Chesterfield, *tn., Eng.*, 53 15N 1 25W 25
Chesterfield Is., *Coral Sea*, 19 52S 158 15E 63
Cheviot Hills, *Eng.*, 55 28N 2 08W 25
Cheyenne, *tn., Wyo., USA*, 41 08N 104 50W 72
Chiai, *tn., Taiwan*, 23 38N 120 27E 57
Chiang Mai, *tn., Thai.*, 18 48N 98 59E 55
Chiang Rai, *tn., Thai.*, 19 56N 99 51E 57
Chiba, *tn., Jap.*, 35 38N 140 07E 57
Chicago, *tn., Ill., USA*, 41 50N 87 45W 73
Chichén Itzá, *hist. site, Mex.*, 20 40N 88 32W 71
Chichester, *tn., Eng.*, 50 50N 0 48W 27
Chiclayo, *tn., Peru*, 6 47S 79 47W 77
Chidley, Cape, *hdl., Newf. and Lab., Can.*,
60 30N 64 30W 71
Chifeng, *tn., China*, 42 17N 118 56E 57
Chihli, Gulf of, *China*, 38 30N 119 00E 57
Chihuahua, *tn., Mex.*, 28 40N 106 06W 72
Chile, *Rep., S. Amer.*, 31 00S 70 00W 77
Chillán, *tn., Chile*, 36 37S 72 10W 77
Chiloé I., *Chile*, 42 50S 73 45W 77
Chiltern Hills, *Eng.*, 51 44N 0 42W 27
Chilung, *tn., Taiwan*, 25 10N 121 43E 57
Chimborazo, Mt., *Ec.*, 1 29S 78 52W 77
Chimbote, *tn., Peru*, 9 04S 78 34W 77
Chimkent, *tn., USSR*, 42 16N 69 05E 51
China, *Rep. Asia*, 35 00N 100 00E 56
Chinchow, *tn., China*, 41 07N 121 06E 57

Chindwin, R., *Burma*, 25 00N 95 00E 56
Chinkiang, *tn.*, *China*, 32 02N 119 29E 57
Chinling Shan, *mts.*, *China*, 34 00N 106 00E 56
Chinsha, *tn.*, *China*, 27 29N 106 12E 56
Chinsi, *tn.*, *China*, 40 48N 120 51E 57
Chinwangtao, *tn.*, *China*, 39 55N 119 37E 57
Chioggia, *tn.*, *It.*, 45 13N 12 17E 45
Chios, *I.*, *Gr.*, 38 27N 26 09E 46
Chios, *tn.*, *Gr.*, 38 23N 26 07E 46
Chippenham, *tn.*, *Eng.*, 51 28N 2 07W 27
Chipping Norton, *tn.*, *Eng.*, 51 56N 1 32W 27
Chirchik, *tn.*, *USSR*, 41 28N 69 31E 51
Chistopol, *tn.*, *USSR*, 55 21N 50 32E 51
Chita, *tn.*, *USSR*, 52 00N 113 25E 53
Chittagong, *tn.*, *Bangl.*, 22 20N 91 48E 55
Choiseul I., *Solomon Is.*, *Pac. Oc.*, 6 48S 157 00E . 63
Cholet, *tn.*, *Fr.*, 47 04N 0 53W 44
Chomo Dzong, *tn.*, *China*, 29 40N 94 16E 56
Chongju, *tn.*, *S. Kor.*, 36 39N 127 27E 57
Chonju, *tn.*, *S. Kor.*, 35 50N 127 05E 57
Chorley, *tn.*, *Eng.*, 53 40N 2 38W 25
Chorzów, *tn.*, *Pol.*, 50 19N 18 56E 41
Chott Djerid, *L.*, *Tun.*, 33 40N 8 00E 48
Chott ech Chergui, *L.*, *Alg.*, 34 00N 0 10E 48
Chott el Hodna, *L.*, *Alg.*, 36 00N 4 00E 48
Chott Melrhir, *L.*, *Alg.*, 34 00N 6 30E 48
Chowkow, *tn.*, *China*, 33 42N 114 90E. 56
Choybalsan, *tn.*, *Mong.*, 48 02N 114 32E 57
Christchurch, *tn.*, *Eng.*, 50 44N 1 45W 27
Christchurch, *tn.*, *N.Z.*, 43 33S 172 40E 63
Christmas I., *Austr. terr.*, *Austral.*, 10 00S 105 40E . 55
Chuanchow, *tn.*, *China*, 24 53N 118 36E 56
Chuchow, *tn.*, *China*, 27 53N 113 07E 56
Chukotsk Peninsula, *USSR*, 60 00N 175 00W 53
Chuksien, *tn.*, *China*, 28 55N 118 54E. 57
Chumatien, *tn.*, *China*, 33 00N 114 04E 56
Chunchon, *tn.*, *S. Kor.*, 37 56N 127 40E 57
Ch'ungch'ing see Chungking
Chungking, *tn.*, *China*, 29 30N 106 35E 56
Chungli, *tn.*, *Taiwan*, 24 55N 121 08E 57
Chur, *tn.*, *Switz.*, 46 52N 9 32E 45
Churchill, *tn.*, *Man.*, *Can.*, 58 45N 94 00W 71
Chushan, *tn.*, *China*, 30 00N 122 00E 57
Chusovoy, *tn.*, *USSR*, 58 18N 57 50E 51
Ciego de Avila, *tn.*, *Cuba*, 21 51N 78 47W 73
Cienfuegos, *tn.*, *Cuba*, 22 10N 80 27W 73
Cilician Gates, *pass*, *Tur.*, 37 17N 34 46E 47
Cimarron, *R.*, *USA*, 36 30N 98 45W 72
Cincinnati, *tn.*, *Ohio*, *USA*, 39 10N 84 30W 73
Cinto, Mt., *Corsica*, 42 24N 8 54E 45
Cirencester, *tn.*, *Eng.*, 51 44N 1 59W 27
Citlaltepetl, Mt., *vol.*, *Mex.*, 18 00N 97 18W 71
Ciudad Bolivar, *tn.*, *Ven.*, 8 06S 63 36W 77
Ciudad Juárez, *tn.*, *Mex.*, 31 42N 106 29W 72
Ciudad Obregón, *tn.*, *Mex.*, 27 28N 109 59W 72
Ciudad Real, *tn.*, *Sp.*, 38 59N 3 55W 44
Ciudad Victoria, *tn.*, *Mex.*, 23 43N 99 10W 72
Civitavecchia, *tn.*, *It.*, 42 05N 11 47E 45
Clacton-on-Sea, *tn.*, *Eng.*, 51 48N 1 09E 27
Clay Cross, *tn.*, *Eng.*, 53 10N 1 24W 25
Cleethorpes, *tn.*, *Eng.*, 53 34N 0 02W 25
Clermont-Ferrand, *tn.*, *Fr.*, 45 47N 3 05E 44
Clevedon, *tn.*, *Eng.*, 51 27N 2 51W 26
Cleveland, *admin. reg.*, *Eng.*, 54 38N 1 32W 25
Cleveland, *tn.*, *Ohio*, *USA*, 41 30N 81 41W 73
Cleveland Hills, *Eng.*, 54 25N 1 11W 25
Clitheroe, *tn.*, *Eng.*, 53 53N 2 23W 25
Clones, *tn.*, *Rep. Ire.*, 54 11N 7 14W 24
Clonmel, *tn.*, *Rep. Ire.*, 52 21N 7 42W 40
Cluj, *tn.*, *Rom.*, 46 47N 23 37E 46
Clwyd, *admin. reg.*, *Wales*, 53 05N 3 28W 26
Clyde, Firth of, *Scot.*, 55 20N 5 00W 23
Clyde, *R.*, *Scot.*, 55 46N 3 58W 23
Clydebank, *tn.*, *Scot.*, 55 54N 4 24W 23
Coalville, *tn.*, *Eng.*, 52 44N 1 20W 27
Coast Mts., *B.C./Alaska, Can./USA*,
55 00N 128 00W 71
Coast Ranges, *mts.*, *USA*, 40 00N 124 00W 72
Coatbridge, *tn.*, *Scot.*, 55 52N 4 01W 23
Coats Land, *geog. reg.*, *Ant.*, 77 00S 25 00W 80
Cobar, *tn.*, *N.S.W. Austr.*, 31 32S 145 51E 63
Cobija, *tn.*, *Bol.*, 11 01S 68 45W 77
Cochabamba, *tn.*, *Bol.*, 17 26S 66 10W 77
Cochin, *tn.*, *India*, 9 56N 76 15E 54
Cochin China, *geog. reg.*, *Viet.*, 10 00N 105 00E . . 55
Cockermouth, *tn.*, *Eng.*, 54 40N 3 21W 25
Coco I., *Pac. Oc.*, 5 33N 87 00W 76
Cod, Cape, *hdl.*, *Mass.*, *USA*, 42 08N 70 10W . . . 73
Coeur d'Alene, *tn.*, *Idaho*, *USA*, 47 40N 116 46W . 72
Coimbatore, *tn.*, *India*, 11 00N 76 57E 54
Coimbra, *tn.*, *Port.*, 40 12N 8 25W 44
Colchester, *tn.*, *Eng.*, 51 54N 0 54E 27
Coleraine, *tn.*, *N. Ire.*, 55 08N 6 40W 24
Coleshill, *tn.*, *Eng.*, 52 30N 1 42W 27
Coll, *I.*, *Scot.*, 56 40N 6 35W 23
Colne, *tn.*, *Eng.*, 53 52N 2 09W 25
Cologne, *tn.*, *W. Ger.*, 50 56N 6 57E 39
Colombia, *Rep.*, *S. Amer.*, 3 45N 73 00W 77
Colombo, *tn.*, *Sri Lanka*, 6 55N 79 52E 54
Colón, *tn.*, *Pan.*, 9 21N 80 00W 71
Colon, *tn.*, *Ven.*, 8 02N 72 17W 77
Colonsay, *I.*, *Scot.*, 56 05N 6 10W 23
Colorado, *admin. reg.*, *USA*, 39 00N 106 30W 72
Colorado, *R.*, *Arg.*, 37 30S 69 00W 77
Colorado, *R.*, *Ariz./Calif.*, *USA*, 33 30N 114 30W . 72
Colorado, *R.*, *Tex.*, *USA*, 31 20N 99 00W 72
Colorado Plateau, *Colo.*, *USA*, 38 00N 106 00W . . 72
Colorado Springs, *tn.*, *Colo.*, *USA*,
38 50N 104 50W 72
Columbia, *R.*, *Oreg./Wash.*, *USA*, 45 50N 122 00W . 72
Columbia, *tn.*, *S.C.*, *USA*, 34 00N 81 00W 73

Columbia, District of, *Fed. dist.*, *USA*,
38 55N 77 00W 73
Columbia Plateau, *Idaho/Oreg.*, *USA*,
45 00N 118 30W 72
Columbus, *tn.*, *Ga.*, *USA*, 32 28N 84 59W 73
Columbus, *tn.*, *Ohio*, *USA*, 39 59N 83 03W 73
Colwyn Bay, *tn.*, *Wales*, 53 18N 3 43W 26
Communism, Mt., *USSR*, 39 00N 72 00E 52
Como, *tn.*, *It.*, 45 48N 9 05E 45
Comodoro Rivadavia, *tn.*, *Arg.*, 45 50S 67 30W . . 77
Comorin, Cape, *India*, 8 03N 77 40E 54
Comoro Is., *Rep.*, *Afr.*, 10 00S 50 00E 67
Compiègne, *tn.*, *Fr.*, 49 25N 2 50E 39
Conakry, *tn.*, *Guin.*, 9 30N 13 43W 66
Conceptión, *tn.*, *Chile*, 36 50S 73 03W 77
Conchos, *R.*, *Mex.*, 29 20N 106 00W 72
Concord, *tn.*, *N.H.*, *USA*, 43 13N 71 34W 73
Congleton, *tn.*, *Eng.*, 53 10N 2 13W 25
Congo, *Rep.*, *Afr.*, 6 05S 15 45E 67
Congo, *R.*, *Congo*, 4 50S 15 00E 67
Connacht, *geog. reg.*, *Rep. Ire.*, 53 23N 8 40W . . . 40
Connah's Quay, *tn.*, *Wales*, 53 13N 3 03W 26
Connecticut, *admin. reg.*, *USA*, 41 40N 72 40W . . . 73
Consett, *tn.*, *Eng.*, 54 51N 1 49W 25
Constance, L., *Switz.*, 47 44N 9 19E 41
Constanţa, *tn.*, *Rom.*, 44 12N 28 40E 47
Constantine, *tn.*, *Alg.*, 36 22N 6 40E. 48
Constantinople see Istanbul
Conwy, *tn.*, *Wales*, 53 17N 3 50W 26
Cook, Mt., *N.Z.*, 43 37S 170 08E 63
Cook Strait, *N.Z.*, 41 15S 174 29E 63
Cookstown, *tn.*, *N. Ire.*, 54 39N 6 45W 24
Copenhagen, *tn.*, *Den.*, 55 43N 12 34E 42
Copiapó, *tn.*, *Chile*, 27 20S 70 23W 77
Coquet, *R.*, *Eng.*, 55 10N 2 00W 25
Coral Sea, *Pac. Oc.*, 15 00S 155 00E 63
Corbridge, *tn.*, *Eng.*, 54 58N 2 01W 25
Corby, *tn.*, *Eng.*, 52 29N 0 40W 27
Cordoba, *tn.*, *Arg.*, 31 25S 64 11W 77
Córdoba, *tn.*, *Sp.*, 37 53N 4 46W 44
Corfu, *I.*, *Gr.*, 39 30N 19 40E 46
Corfu, *tn.*, *Gr.*, 39 38N 19 50E 46
Corinth, Gulf of, *Gr.*, 38 16N 22 30E. 46
Corinth, *tn.*, *Gr.*, 37 56N 22 55E 46
Cork, *tn.*, *Rep. Ire.*, 51 54N 8 28W 40
Corner Brook, *tn.*, *Newf. and Lab.*, *Can.*,
48 58N 57 58W 71
Cornwall, *admin. reg.*, *Eng.*, 50 26N 4 40W 26
Cornwall, *tn.*, *Ont.*, *Can.*, 45 02N 74 45W 73
Coromandel Coast, *India*, 12 30N 81 00E 54
Coropuna, Mt., *Peru*, 15 58S 71 49W 77
Corpus Christi, *tn.*, *Tex.*, *USA*, 27 47N 97 26W . . 72
Corrientes, *tn.*, *Arg.*, 27 30S 58 48W 77
Corsica, *I.*, *Fr.*, 42 00N 9 00E 45
Corte, *tn.*, *Corsica*, 42 18N 9 08E 45
Çoruh, *R.*, *Tur.*, 40 40N 40 05E 47
Çorum, *tn.*, *Tur.*, 40 31N 34 57E 47
Corunna, *tn.*, *Sp.*, 43 22N 8 24W 44
Cosenza, *tn.*, *It.*, 39 17N 16 16E 45
Costa Brava, *geog. reg.*, *Sp.*, 41 30N 3 00E 44
Costa del Sol, *geog. reg.*, *Sp.*, 36 30N 4 30W 44
Costa Rica, *Rep.*, *Cent. Amer.*, 10 00N 85 00W . . . 71
Côte d'Azur, *geog. reg.*, *Fr.*, 43 25N 6 30E 45
Cotentin, *pen.*, *Fr.*, 49 20N 2 00W 44
Cotonou, *tn.*, *Benin*, 6 24N 2 31E 66
Cotopaxi, Mt., *vol.*, *Ec.*, 0 45S 78 28W 77
Cotswold Hills, *Eng.*, 51 42N 2 10W 27
Cottbus, *tn.*, *E. Ger.*, 51 43N 14 21E. 41
Council Bluffs, *tn.*, *Iowa*, *USA*, 41 14N 95 54W . . 73
Coventry, *tn.*, *Eng.*, 52 25N 1 30W 27
Cowal, *geog. reg.*, *Scot.*, 56 05N 5 08W 23
Cowdenbeath, *tn.*, *Scot.*, 56 07N 3 21W 23
Cowes, *tn.*, *I.o.W.*, *Eng.*, 50 45N 1 18W 27
Cracow, *tn.*, *Pol.*, 50 03N 19 55E. 41
Craigavon, *tn.*, *N. Ire.*, 54 28N 6 25W 24
Craignure, *tn.*, *Scot.*, 56 28N 5 42W 23
Craiova, *tn.*, *Rom.*, 44 18N 23 47E 46
Cramlington, *tn.*, *Eng.*, 55 05N 1 35W 25
Crawley, *tn.*, *Eng.*, 51 07N 0 12W 27
Cremona, *tn.*, *It.*, 45 08N 10 01E 45
Cres, *tn.*, *Yug.*, 44 58N 14 25E 46
Crete, *I.*, *Gr.*, 35 15N 25 00E 46
Crete, Sea of, *Eur.*, 36 00N 25 00E 46
Creus, C., *hdl.*, *Sp.*, 42 19N 3 19E 44
Creuse, *R.*, *Fr.*, 46 55N 1 40E 44
Crewe, *tn.*, *Eng.*, 53 05N 2 27W 25
Criccieth, *tn.*, *Wales*, 52 55N 4 14W 26
Crieff, *tn.*, *Scot.*, 56 23N 3 52W 23
Criel, *tn.*, *Fr.*, 49 16N 2 29E. 39
Crimea, *pen.*, *USSR*, 45 00N 34 00E 47
Crinan Canal, *Scot.*, 56 04N 5 30W 23
Cristóbal, Mt., *Col.*, 10 53N 73 48W 77
Croatia, *admin. reg.*, *Yug.*, 45 20N 16 00E 46
Cromarty, *tn.*, *Scot.*, 57 40N 4 02W 22
Cromarty Firth, *Scot.*, 57 36N 4 24W 22
Cromer, *tn.*, *Eng.*, 52 56N 1 18E 27
Crook, *tn.*, *Eng.*, 54 43N 1 44W 25
Crotone, *tn.*, *It.*, 39 05N 17 08E 45
Crown Princess Märtha Coast, *Ant.*,
73 00S 10 00W 80
Crozet Is., *Fr. terr.*, *Indian Oc.*, 46 27S 52 00E . . . 80
Cruden Bay, *tn.*, *Scot.*, 57 24N 1 51W 22
Crumlin, *tn.*, *N. Ire.*, 54 37N 6 14W 24
Cuanza, *R.*, *Ang.*, 9 02S 13 30E 67
Cuba, *Rep.*, *W.I.*, 22 00N 80 00W 73
Cubango, *R.*, *Ang.*, 17 00S 18 00E 67
Cúcuta, *tn.*, *Col.*, 7 55N 72 31W 77
Cuenca, *tn.*, *Ec.*, 2 45S 79 00W 77
Cuenca, *tn.*, *Sp.*, 40 04N 2 07W 44
Cuiaba, *tn.*, *Braz.*, 15 32S 56 05W 77
Cuillin Hills, *Scot.*, 57 18N 6 20W 22

Cuillin Sound, *Scot.*, 57 04N 6 20W 23
Culiacán, *tn.*, *Mex.*, 24 50N 107 23W 72
Cumaná, *tn.*, *Ven.*, 10 29N 64 12W 77
Cumberland, *R.*, *Ky./Tenn.*, *USA*, 36 15N 87 00W . 73
Cumberland Plateau, *USA*, 36 00N 84 30W 73
Cumbernauld, *tn.*, *Scot.*, 55 57N 4 00W 23
Cumbria, *admin. reg.*, *Eng.*, 54 46N 3 16W 25
Cumbrian Mts., *Eng.*, 54 30N 3 05W 25
Cumnock, *tn.*, *Scot.*, 55 27N 4 16W 23
Cunene, *R.*, *Ang.*, 17 00S 15 00E 67
Cunnamulla, *tn.*, *Queensl.*, *Austr.*, 28 04S 145 40E . 63
Cunningham, *geog. reg.*, *Scot.*, 55 40N 4 50W . . . 23
Cupar, *tn.*, *Scot.*, 56 19N 3 01W 23
Curaçao I., *self-gov. Neth. terr.*, *W.I.*,
12 10N 69 00W 77
Curitiba, *tn.*, *Braz.*, 25 24S 49 16W 77
Cuttack, *tn.*, *India*, 20 26N 85 56E 54
Cuxhaven, *tn.*, *W. Ger.*, 53 52N 8 42E 39
Cuzco, *tn.*, *Peru*, 13 32S 71 57W 77
Cwmbran, *tn.*, *Wales*, 51 39N 3 00W 26
Cyclades, *Is.*, *Gr.*, 37 20N 24 30E 46
Cyprus, *Rep.*, *Eur.*, 35 00N 33 00E 47
Cyrenaica, *geog. reg.*, *Libya*, 31 00N 21 00E 49
Cyrene, *hist. site*, *Libya*, 32 29N 21 18E 49
Czech Republic, *admin. reg.*, *Cz.*, 49 48N 15 00E . 41
Czechoslovakia, *Rep.*, *Eur.*, 49 00N 17 00E 41
Częstochowa, *tn.*, *Pol.*, 50 49N 19 07E 41

D

Da Lat, *tn.*, *Viet.*, 11 56N 108 25E 55
Da Nang, *tn.*, *Viet.*, 16 04N 108 14E 55
Dacca, *tn.*, *Bangl.*, 23 42N 90 22E. 55
Dagö see Hiiumaa
Dahomey see Benin
Dairen see Lüta
Dakar, *tn.*, *Sen.*, 14 38N 17 27W 66
Dakhla Oasis, *Eg.*, 25 30N 27 50E 49
Dakhlah, *tn.*, *Maur.*, 24 00N 15 58W 66
Dalälven, *R.*, *Swed.*, 60 05N 16 30E 42
Dalandzadgad, *tn.*, *Mong.*, 43 34N 104 20E 56
Dalbeattie, *tn.*, *Scot.*, 54 56N 3 49W 23
Dalby, *tn.*, *Queensl.*, *Austr.*, 27 11S 151 12E 63
Dalkeith, *tn.*, *Scot.*, 55 51N 3 04W 23
Dallas, *tn.*, *Tex.*, *USA*, 32 47N 96 48W 73
Dalmally, *tn.*, *Scot.*, 56 24N 4 58W 23
Dalmatia, *geog. reg.*, *Yug.*, 43 20N 17 00E 46
Dalmellington, *tn.*, *Scot.*, 55 19N 4 24W 23
Dalnergorsk, *tn.*, *USSR*, 44 31N 135 31E 57
Daloa, *tn.*, *Ivory Coast*, 6 56N 6 28W 66
Dalton-in-Furness, *tn.*, *Eng.*, 54 10N 3 11W 25
Daly Waters, *tn.*, *N. Terr.*, *Austr.*, 16 13S 133 20E . 62
Damanhûr, *tn.*, *Eg.*, 31 03N 30 28E 49
Damascus, *tn.*, *Syria*, 33 30N 36 19E 49
Damietta, *tn.*, *Eg.*, 31 26N 31 48E. 49
Dampier, *tn.*, *W. Austr.*, 20 45S 116 48E. 62
Danube, *R.*, *Eur.*, 48 00N 15 00E 48
Danube Delta, *Rom.*, 46 00N 29 00E. 47
Dar es Salaam, *tn.*, *Tanz.*, 6 51S 39 18E 67
Dardanelles, *str.*, *Tur.*, 40 00N 26 20E 46
Darling, *R.*, *N.S.W.*, *Austr.*, 34 00S 144 30E 63
Darlington, *tn.*, *Eng.*, 54 31N 1 34W 25
Darmstadt, *tn.*, *W. Ger.*, 49 52N 8 39E 39
Dartford, *tn.*, *Eng.*, 51 27N 0 14E 27
Dartmoor, *geog. reg.*, *Eng.*, 50 36N 4 00W 26
Dartmouth, *tn.*, *Eng.*, 50 21N 3 35W 26
Darwen, *tn.*, *Eng.*, 53 42N 2 28W 25
Darwin, *tn.*, *N. Terr.*, *Austr.*, 12 23S 130 44E 62
Dasht-i-Kavir, *des.*, *Iran*, 34 30N 55 00E 52
Daugava, *R.*, *USSR*, 56 30N 25 00E 42
(See also W. Dvina, R.)
Daugavpils, *tn.*, *USSR*, 55 52N 26 31E 50
Dauphiné, *geog. reg.*, *Fr.*, 45 15N 5 25E 45
Davao, *tn.*, *Phil.*, 7 05N 125 38E 55
Davenport, *tn.*, *Iowa*, *USA*, 41 32N 90 36W 73
Daventry, *tn.*, *Eng.*, 52 16N 1 09W 27
Davis, *Austr. base*, *Ant.*, 69 20S 79 00E 80
Davis Sea, *Ant.*, 65 00S 90 00E 80
Davis Strait, *Green./Can.*, 67 30N 81 00W 71
Dawlish, *tn.*, *Eng.*, 50 35N 3 28W 26
Dawson, *tn.*, *Yukon*, *Can.*, 64 04N 139 24W 71
Dawson Creek, *tn.*, *B.C.*, *Can.*, 55 45N 120 15W . 71
Dayton, *tn.*, *Ohio*, *USA*, 39 45N 84 10W 73
Dead Sea, *Israel/Jordan*, 31 30N 35 30E 49
Deal, *tn.*, *Eng.*, 51 14N 1 24E 27
Dean, Forest of, *geog. reg.*, *Eng.*, 51 50N 2 35W . . 26
Death Valley, *Calif.*, *USA*, 36 00N 116 40W 72
Debrecen, *Hung.*, 47 30N 21 37E 46
Decatur, *tn.*, *Ill.*, *USA*, 39 51N 88 57W 73
Deccan, *plat.*, *India*, 16 00N 75 00E 54
Dee, *R.*, *Scot.*, 57 08N 2 15W 23
Dee, *R.*, *Wales*, 53 15N 3 07W 26
Deir Ez Zor, *tn.*, *Syria*, 35 20N 40 08E 49
Delaware, *admin. reg.*, *USA*, 39 00N 75 40W 73
Delft, *tn.*, *Neth.*, 52 01N 4 21E 39
Delhi, *tn.*, *India*, 28 40N 77 14E 54
Delicias, *tn.*, *Mex.*, 28 10N 105 30W 72
Delmenhorst, *tn.*, *W. Ger.*, 53 03N 8 37E 39
Delos, *hist. site*, *Gr.*, 37 30N 25 05E 46
Delphi, *hist. site*, *Gr.*, 38 29N 22 30E 46

Demavend, Mt., *Iran*, 36 00N 53 00E 52
Den Helder, *tn., Neth.*, 52 58N 4 46E 39
Denain, *tn., Fr.*, 50 19N 3 24E 39
Denbigh, *tn., Wales*, 53 11N 3 25W 26
Denizli, *tn., Tur.*, 37 46N 29 05E 47
Denmark, *Kingd., Eur.*, 55 30N 9 00E 42
Denmark Strait, *Green./Ice.*, 66 00N 30 00W 80
Denver, *tn., Colo., USA*, 39 45N 105 00W 72
Derbent, *tn., USSR*, 42 03N 48 18E 51
Derby, *tn., Eng.*, 52 55N 1 30W 25
Derby, *tn., W. Austr.*, 17 19S 123 38E 62
Derbyshire, *admin. reg., Eng.*, 53 08N 1 45W 25
Derna, *tn., Libya*, 32 40N 22 35E 49
Derryveagh Mts., *Rep. Ire.*, 55 00N 8 40W 24
Derwent, *R., Derbys., Eng.*, 53 26N 1 44W 27
Derwent, *R., Yorks., Eng.*, 54 13N 0 35W 25
Des Moines, *tn., Iowa, USA*, 41 35N 93 35W 73
Deseado *tn., Arg*, 47 44S 65 56W 77
Dessau, *tn., E. Ger.*, 51 51N 12 15E 41
Dessye, *tn., Ethiopia*, 11 05N 39 40E 67
Detmold, *tn., W. Ger.*, 51 55N 8 50E 39
Detroit, *tn., Mich., USA*, 42 23N 83 05W 73
Deventer, *tn., Neth.*, 52 15N 6 10E 39
Deveron, *R., Scot.*, 57 22N 3 00W 22
Devil's Elbow, *pass, Scot.*, 56 52N 3 25W 23
Devizes, *tn., Eng.*, 51 22N 1 59W 27
Devon, *admin. reg., Eng.*, 50 50N 3 40W 26
Devon I., *N.W. Terrs., Can.*, 75 00N 87 00W 71
Devonport, *tn., Tas., Austr.*, 41 09S 146 16E 63
Dewsbury, *tn., Eng.*, 53 42N 1 37W 25
Dhahran, *tn., Si. Arab.*, 26 18N 50 05E 52
Dhaulagiri, Mt., *Nepal*, 28 45N 83 45E 54
Dibrugarh, *tn., India*, 27 29N 94 56E 56
Didcot, *tn., Eng.*, 51 37N 1 15W 27
Diégo Suarez, *tn., Madag.*, 12 19S 49 17E 67
Dien Bien Phu, *tn., Viet.*, 21 23N 103 02E 56
Dieppe, *tn., Fr.*, 49 55N 1 5E 39
Digboi, *tn., India*, 27 22N 95 34E 56
Digne, *tn., Fr.*, 44 05N 6 14E 45
Dijon, *tn., Fr.*, 47 20N 5 02E 45
Dikson, *tn., USSR*, 73 32N 80 09E 52
Dili, *tn., Indon.*, 8 35S 125 35E 55
Dimitrovgrad, *tn., Bulg.*, 42 03N 25 34E 46
Dinaric Alps, *mts., Yug.*, 44 00N 17 30E 46
Dingwall, *tn., Scot.*, 57 35N 4 26W 22
Dinslaken, *tn, W. Ger.*, 51 34N 6 43E 39
Diredawa, *tn., Ethiopia*, 9 35N 41 50E 67
Disko, I., *Green.*, 69 00N 54 00W 71
Diss, *tn., Eng.*, 52 23N 1 06E 27
Distrito Federal, *admin. reg., Braz.*, 15 58S 49 37W . . 77
Diyarbakir, *tn., Tur.*, 37 55N 40 14E 49
Djaja Peak, *mt., W. Irian, Indon.*, 4 05S 137 09E 55
Djajapura, *tn., W. Irian, Indon.*, 2 37S 140 39E 55
Djakarta, *tn., Indon.*, 6 08S 106 45E 55
Djambi *see Telanaipura*
Djanet, *tn. Alg.*, 24 34N 9 30E 48
Djelfa, *tn., Alg.*, 34 43N 3 14E 48
Djibouti, *Rep., Afr.*, 11 35N 43 11E 67
Djibouti, *tn., Rep. Djibouti*, 11 35N 43 11E 67
Dneprodzerzhinsk, *tn., USSR*, 48 30N 34 37W 50
Dnepropetrovsk, *tn., USSR*, 48 29N 35 00E 50
Dnestr *see Dniester*
Dnieper, *R., USSR*, 50 00N 31 00E 50
Dniester, *R., USSR*, 48 30N 26 30E 50
Dobrogea, *geog. reg., Rom.*, 44 30N 28 15E 47
Dodecanese, *Is., Gr.*, 36 35N 27 00E 46
Dodge City, *tn., Kans., USA*, 37 45N 100 02W 72
Dodman Point, *hdl., Eng.*, 50 13N 4 48W 26
Dodoma, *tn., Tanz.*, 6 10S 35 40E 67
Dogger Bank, *North Sea*, 54 30N 1 10E 40
Doha, *tn., Qatar*, 25 15N 51 36E 52
Dolak I., *see Kolepom I.*
Dolgellau, *tn., Wales*, 52 44N 3 53W 26
Dolisle, *tn., Congo*, 4 09S 12 47E 67
Dollard, *R., Neth.*, 53 27N 6 57E 39
Dolomites, *mts., It.*, 46 30N 11 40E 45
Dominica, I., *assoc. st. of UK, W.I.*,
15 20N 61 20W 77
Dominican Republic, *W.I.*, 19 00N 70 30W 71
Don, *R., Scot.*, 57 12N 2 15W 22
Don, *R., USSR*, 49 35N 41 40E 50
Don Benito, *tn., Sp.*, 38 57N 5 52W 44
Donaghadee, *tn., N. Ire.*, 54 39N 5 33W 24
Donau *see Danube*
Doncaster, *tn., Eng.*, 53 32N 1 07W 25
Donegal, *admin. reg., Rep. Ire.*, 54 48N 8 10W 24
Donegal, *tn., Rep. Ire.*, 54 39N 8 06W 24
Donegal Bay, *Rep. Ire.*, 54 31N 8 30W 40
Denets Basin, *USSR*, 46 59N 38 06E 50
Donetsk, *tn., USSR*, 48 00N 37 50E 50
Doon, L., *Scot.*, 55 15N 4 21W 23
Dorchester, *tn., Eng.*, 50 43N 2 26W 26
Dordrecht, *tn., Neth.*, 51 48N 4 40E 39
Dordogne, *R., Fr.*, 44 50N 0 05E 44
Dorking, *tn., Eng.*, 51 14N 0 20W 27
Dornoch, *tn., Scot.*, 57 52N 4 02W 22
Dornoch Firth, *Scot.*, 57 51N 4 13W 22
Dorset, *admin. reg., Eng.*, 50 48N 2 25W 26
Dortmund, *tn., W. Ger.*, 51 32N 7 27E 39
Douai, *tn., Fr.*, 50 22N 3 05E 39
Douala, *tn., Cam.*, 4 04N 9 43E 67
Doubs, *R., Fr.*, 47 08N 6 40E 45
Douglas, *tn., I.o.M.*, 54 09N 4 29W 24
Douro, *R., Port.*, 41 01N 8 16W 44
(as Duero in Sp.)
Dove, *R., Eng.*, 53 00N 1 80W 25
Dover, *tn., Eng.*, 51 08N 1 19E 27
Dover, Strait of, *Eng.*, 51 00N 1 30E 27
Dovrefjell, *plat., Nor.*, 62 25N 9 30E 42
Downham Market, *tn., Eng.*, 52 36N 0 23E 27
Downpatrick, *tn., N. Ire.*, 54 20N 9 20W 24

Drake Passage, *str., S. Amer./Ant.*,
58 00S 68 00W 80
Drakensberg, *mts., Rep. S. Afr.*, 31 00S 25 00E 67
Dráma. *tn., Gr.*, 41 10N 24 11E 46
Drammen, *tn., Nor.*, 59 45N 10 15E 42
Drau, *R., Aust.*, 47 46N 13 33E 45
Drava, *R., Yug.*, 45 50N 18 00E 46
Dresden, *tn., E. Ger.*, 51 03N 13 45E 41
Dreux, *tn., Fr.*, 48 44N 1 23E 39
Drina, *R., Yug.*, 44 00N 19 10E 46
Drogheda, *tn., Rep. Ire.*, 53 43N 6 21W 24
Drogobych, *tn., USSR*, 49 22N 23 32E 41
Droichead Nua, *tn., Rep. Ire.*, 53 11N 6 48W 24
Droitwich, *tn., Eng.*, 52 16N 2 09W 27
Dronfield, *tn., Eng.*, 53 19N 1 27W 25
Drumochter, Pass of, *Scot.*, 56 50N 4 15W 23
Dubai, *tn., U.A.E.*, 25 14N 55 17E 52
Dubbo, *tn., N.S.W., Austr.*, 32 16S 148 41E 63
Dublin, *admin. reg., Rep. Ire.*, 53 22N 6 21W 24
Dublin, *tn., Rep. Ire.*, 53 20N 6 15W 24
Dubno, *tn., USSR*, 50 28N 25 40E 42
Dubrovnik, *tn., Yug.*, 42 40N 18 07E 46
Dubuque, *tn., Iowa, USA*, 42 31N 90 41W 73
Dudinka, *tn., USSR*, 69 27N 86 13E 52
Dudley, *tn., Eng.*, 52 30N 2 05W 27
Duero, *R., Sp.*, 41 37N 4 25W 44
(as Douro in Port.)
Dufftown, *tn., Scot.*, 57 27N 3 09W 22
Duirinish, *geog. reg., Scot.*, 57 30N 6 45W 22
Duisburg, *tn., W. Ger.*, 51 26N 6 45E 39
Duluth, *tn., Minn., USA*, 46 45N 92 10W 73
Dumbarton, *tn., Scot.*, 55 57N 4 35W 23
Dumfries, *tn., Scot.*, 55 04N 3 37W 23
Dumfries & Galloway, *admin. reg., Scot.*,
55 05N 4 00W 23
Dumont d'Urville, *Fr. base, Ant.*, 66 40S 140 01E . . . 80
Dún Laoghaire, *tn., Rep. Ire.*, 53 17N 6 08W 24
Dunbar, *tn., Scot.*, 56 00N 2 31W 23
Dunblane, *tn., Scot.*, 56 12N 3 59W 23
Duncansby Head, *hdl., Scot.*, 58 39N 3 01W 22
Dundalk, *tn., Rep. Ire.*, 54 01N 6 25W 24
Dundalk Bay, *Rep. Ire.*, 53 55N 6 45W 24
Dundee, *tn., Scot.*, 56 28N 3 00W 23
Dunedin, *tn., N.Z.*, 45 52S 170 30E 63
Dunfermline, *tn., Scot.*, 56 04N 3 29W 23
Dungannon, *tn., N. Ire.*, 54 31N 6 46W 24
Dungeness, *hdl., Eng.*, 50 55N 0 58E 27
Dunkeld, *tn., Scot.*, 56 34N 3 36W 23
Dunkirk, *tn., Fr.*, 51 02N 2 23E 39
Dunnet Head, *hdl., Scot.*, 58 39N 3 23W 22
Dunoon, *tn., Scot.*, 55 57N 4 56W 23
Duns, *tn., Scot.*, 55 47N 2 20W 23
Dunstable, *tn., Eng.*, 51 53N 0 32W 27
Durance, *R., Fr.*, 44 30N 6 00E 45
Durango, *tn., Mex.*, 24 10N 104 40W 72
Durban, *tn., Rep. S. Afr.*, 29 53S 31 00E 67
Düren, *tn., W. Ger.*, 50 48N 6 30E 39
Durham, *admin. reg., Eng.*, 54 38N 2 10W 25
Durham, *tn., Eng.*, 54 47N 1 34W 25
Durham, *tn., N.C., USA*, 36 00N 78 54W 73
Durmitor, Mt., *Yug.*, 43 18N 19 00E 46
Durrës, *tn., Alb.*, 41 18N 19 28E 46
d'Urville Sea, *Ant.*, 63 00S 145 00E 80
Dushanbe, *tn., USSR*, 38 38N 68 51E 52
Düsseldorf, *tn., W. Ger.*, 51 13N 6 47E 39
Dutch Harbour, *tn., Aleutian Is.*, 53 55N 166 36W . . . 70
Dyfed, *admin. reg., Wales*, 52 00N 4 30W 26
Dzambul, *tn., USSR*, 42 50N 71 25E 51
Dzerzhinsk, *tn., USSR*, 48 21N 37 50E 50
Dzezkazgan, *tn., USSR*, 47 48N 67 24E 51
Dzhankoy, *tn., USSR*, 45 40N 34 20E 47
Dzhugdzhur Range, *mts., USSR*, 57 30N 138 00E . . . 53
Dzungaria, *geog. reg., China*, 46 00N 88 00E 52

E

Earn, L., *Scot.*, 56 30N 4 20W 23
Easington, *tn., Eng.*, 53 40N 0 07E 25
East Antarctica, *geog. reg., Ant.*, 80 00S 75 00E 80
East China Sea, *Asia*, 30 05N 126 00E 57
East Dereham, *tn., Eng.*, 52 41N 0 56E 27
East Frisian Is., *W. Ger.*, 53 45N 7 15E 39
East Germany, *Rep., Eur.*, 52 00N 12 00E 41
East Grinstead, *tn., Eng.*, 51 08N 0 01W 27
East Kilbride, *tn., Scot.*, 55 46N 4 10W 23
East London, *tn., Rep. S. Africa*, 33 00S 27 54E 67
East Retford, *tn., Eng.*, 53 19N 0 56W 25
East St. Louis, *tn., Ill., USA*, 38 34N 90 04W 73
East Siberian Sea, *Arctic Oc.*, 73 00N 160 00E 53
East Sussex, *admin. reg., Eng.*, 51 00N 0 04E 27
East Turkistan, *geog. reg., China*, 39 00N 83 00E . . . 52
Eastbourne, *tn., Eng.*, 50 46N 0 17E 27
Eastern Ghats, *mts., India*, 14 00N 79 00E 54
Eastern Sierra Madre, *mts., Mex.*, 25 00N 100 30W . . 72
Eastleigh, *tn., Eng.*, 50 58N 1 22W 27
Ebbw Vale, *tn., Wales*, 51 47N 3 12W 26
Ebro, *R., Sp.*, 41 49N 0 50W 44
Ebro Delta, *Sp.*, 41 00N 1 00E 44
Eccles, *tn., Eng.*, 53 29N 2 21W 26
Ecuador, *Rep., S. Amer.*, 2 00S 80 00W 77

Eday, I., *Scot.*, 59 11N 2 47W 22
Ede, *tn., Neth.*, 52 03N 5 40E 39
Eden, *R., Eng.*, 54 32N 2 25W 25
Edenferry, *tn., Rep. Ire.*, 53 21N 7 03W 24
Edinburgh, *tn., Scot.*, 55 57N 3 13W 23
Edirne, *tn., Tur.*, 41 40N 26 34E 46
Edmonton, *tn., Alta., Can.*, 53 34N 113 25W 71
Edsin Gol, *R., China*, 42 00N 101 00E 56
Edward, L., *Zaire*, 0 20S 29 40E 67
Edwards Plateau, *Tex., USA*, 30 30N 101 00W 72
Efate I., *New Hebrides, Pac. Oc.*, 17 00S 168 00E . . . 63
Egadi Is., *Sicily*, 37 55N 12 10E 45
Egedesminde, *tn., Green.*, 68 50N 53 00W 71
Egremont, *tn., Eng.*, 54 29N 3 33W 25
Eğridir, L., *Tur.*, 37 53N 30 50E 47
Egypt, *Rep., Afr.*, 26 40N 27 30E 49
Eigg, I., *Scot.*, 56 54N 6 10W 23
Eilat, *tn., Israel*, 29 30N 34 56E 49
Eindhoven, *tn., Neth.*, 51 26N 5 30E 39
El Aaiún, *tn., Mor.*, 27 10N 13 11W 66
El Asnam, *tn., Alg.*, 36 00N 0 02E 48
El Faiyûm, *tn., Eg.*, 29 08N 30 40E 49
El Fasher, *tn., Sud.*, 13 37N 25 22E 67
El Ferrol del Caudillo, *tn., Sp.*, 43 29N 8 14W 44
El Goléa, *tn., Alg.*, 30 30N 2 50E 48
El Jof, *tn., Libya*, 24 09N 23 19E 49
El Khârga, *tn., Eg.*, 25 27N 30 32E 49
El Mansûra, *tn., Eg.*, 31 00N 31 19E 49
El Mars, *tn., Libya*, 33 00N 21 00E 49
El Minya, *tn., Eg.*, 28 06N 30 45E 49
El Obeid, *tn., Sud.*, 13 11N 30 10E 67
El Paso, *tn., Tex., USA*, 31 50N 106 30W 72
El Salvador, *Rep., Cent. Amer.*, 13 50N 89 00W 71
Elâzig, *tn., Tur.*, 38 41N 39 14E 49
Elba, I., *It.*, 42 48N 10 15E 45
Elbasan, *tn., Alb.*, 41 07N 20 05E 46
Elbe, *R., W. Ger.*, 53 25N 10 07E 41
(as Labe in Cz.)
Elbert Mt., *Colo., USA*, 39 05N 106 27W 72
Elbląg, *tn., Pol.*, 54 10N 19 25E 41
Elbrus, Mt., *USSR*, 43 21N 42 29E 51
Elburz Mts., *Iran*, 36 00N 52 00E 52
Elche, *tn., Sp.*, 38 16N 0 41W 44
Elda, *tn., Sp.*, 38 29N 0 47W 44
Elekrostal, *tn., USSR*, 55 46N 38 30E 50
Eleuthera I., *The Bahamas*, 25 00N 76 20W 73
Elgin, *tn., Scot.*, 57 39N 3 20W 22
Elgon, Mt., *Kenya/Ugan.*, 1 07N 34 35E 67
Elisabethville *see Lubumbashi*
Elista, *tn., USSR*, 46 18N 44 14E 51
Ełk, *tn., Pol.*, 53 51N 22 20E 41
Elko, *tn., Nev., USA*, 40 50N 115 46W 72
Ellesmere I., *N.W. Terrs., Can.*, 82 00N 81 00W 71
Ellesmere Port, *tn., Eng.*, 53 17N 2 54W 25
Ellice Is. *see Tuvalu*
Ellon, *tn., Scot.*, 57 22N 2 05W 22
Ellsworth Land, *geog. reg., Ant.*, 74 00S 80 00W 80
Ely, *tn., Eng.*, 52 24N 0 16E 27
Ely, *tn., Nev., USA*, 39 15N 114 53W 72
Emba, *R., USSR*, 47 38N 56 12E 51
Emden, *tn., W. Ger.*, 53 23N 7 13E 39
Emi Koussi, Mt., *Chad*, 19 52N 18 31E 49
Emilia Romagna, *geog. reg., It.*, 44 33N 10 40E 45
Emmen, *tn., Neth.*, 52 47N 6 55E 39
Ems, *R., W. Ger.*, 52 37N 7 16E 39
Enard Bay, *Scot.*, 58 05N 5 20W 22
Ende, *tn., Indon.*, 8 51S 121 40E 55
Enderby Land, *geog. reg., Ant.*, 69 00S 53 00E 80
Engels, *tn., USSR*, 51 30N 46 07E 51
England, *Kingd., UK*, 52 00N 2 00W 40
English Channel, *Eur.*, 50 00N 2 00W 40
Enid, *tn., Okla., USA*, 36 26N 97 54W 72
Eniwetok, I., *Pac. Oc.*, 11 30N 162 15E 63
Enniscorthy, *tn., Rep. Ire.*, 52 30N 6 34W 26
Enniskillen, *tn., N. Ire.*, 54 21N 7 38W 24
Enschede, *tn., Neth.*, 52 13N 6 55E 39
Ensenada, *tn., Mex.*, 31 53N 116 38W 72
Entebbe, *tn., Ugan.*, 0 05N 32 29E 67
Enugu, *tn., Nig.*, 6 20N 7 29E 67
Épernay, *tn., Fr.*, 49 02N 3 58E 39
Ephesus, *hist. site, Tur.*, 37 55N 27 19E 47
Épinal, *tn., Fr.*, 48 10N 6 28E 45
Epping, *tn., Eng.*, 51 42N 0 08E 27
Epsom, *tn., Eng.*, 51 20N 0 16W 27
Equatorial Guinea, *Rep., Afr.*, 2 00N 8 00E 67
Erbil, *tn., Iraq*, 36 12N 44 00E 49
Ereğli, *tn., Tur.*, 37 30N 34 02E 47
Erfurt, *tn., E. Ger.*, 50 58N 11 02E 41
Eriboll, L., *Scot.*, 58 28N 4 41W 22
Ericht, L., *Scot.*, 56 50N 4 25W 23
Erie, *tn., Pa., USA*, 42 07N 80 05W 73
Erie, L., *Can./USA*, 42 30N 81 00W 73
Erimo, C., *hdl., Jap.*, 41 55N 143 13E 57
Eriskay, I., *Scot.*, 57 04N 7 18W 23
Eritrea, *geog. reg., Ethiopia*, 14 00N 41 00E 67
Erlangen, *tn., W. Ger.*, 49 36N 11 02E 41
Ermoúpolis, *tn., Gr.*, 37 26N 24 56E 46
Erne, *R., N. Ire./Rep. Ire.*, 54 24N 8 10W 24
Erne, L., Lower, *Rep. Ire.*, 54 30N 7 50W 24
Erne, L., Upper, *N. Ire.*, 54 15N 7 35W 24
Erzincan, *tn., Tur.*, 39 44N 39 30E 49
Erzurum, *tn., Tur.*, 39 57N 41 17E 49
Esbjerg, *tn., Den.*, 55 28N 8 28E 42
Esch, *tn., Lux.*, 49 30N 5 59E 39
Esfahán *see Isfahan*
Esh Sham *see Damascus*
Eskdale, *val., Scot.*, 55 04N 3 10W 23
Eskilstuna, *tn., Swed.*, 59 22N 16 31E 42
Eskişehir, *tn., Tur.*, 39 46N 30 30E 47
Esla, *R., Sp.*, 42 00N 5 50W 44
Esperance, *tn., W. Austr.*, 33 49S 121 52E 62

Espirito Santo., *admin. reg., Braz.,* 20 23S 40 18W ... 77
Espíritu Santo I., *New Hebrides, Pac. Oc.,*
15 30S 167 00E 63
Espoo, *tn., Fin.,* 60 10N 24 42E 42
Essen, *tn., W. Ger.,* 51 27N 6 57E 39
Essex, *admin. reg., Eng.,* 51 48N 0 30E 27
Esslingen, *tn., W. Ger.,* 48 45N 9 19E 41
Estevan, *tn., Sask., USA,* 49 09N 102 59W ... 72
Estonia, *geog. reg., USSR,* 58 45N 24 00E 42
Estonian S.S.R., *admin. reg., USSR,* 58 30N 25 30E ... 50
Estrela, Mt., *Port.,* 40 19N 7 36W 44
Estremadura, *geog. reg., Sp.,* 39 30N 6 05W 44
Esztergom, *tn., Hung.,* 47 46N 18 42E 46
Ethiopia, *Rep., Afr.,* 8 00N 40 00E 67
Etive, L., *Scot.,* 56 30N 5 12W 23
Etna, Mt., *vol., Sicily,* 37 45N 15 00E 45
Euboea, I., *Gr.,* 38 30N 24 00E 46
Eugene, *tn., Oreg., USA,* 44 03N 123 04W 72
Euphrates, R., *Iraq/Syria/Tur.,* 33 30N 43 00E .. 67
Eure, R., *Fr.,* 49 10N 1 10W 39
Eureka, *tn., Calif., USA,* 40 49N 124 10W 72
Europort, *tn., Neth.,* 51 59N 4 06E 39
Evanston, *tn., Ill., USA,* 42 02N 87 41W 73
Evansville, *tn., Ind., USA,* 38 00N 87 33W 73
Everest, Mt., *Nepal/Tibet,* 28 05N 86 58E 54
Everett, *tn., Wash., USA,* 47 59N 122 14W 72
Everglades National Park, *Fla., USA,*
25 30N 80 30W 73
Everglades, The, *swamp reg., Fla., USA,*
26 00N 80 30W 73
Evesham, *tn., Eng.,* 52 06N 1 56W 27
Evesham, Vale of, *geog. reg., Eng.,*
52 07N 2 04W 27
Évora, *tn., Port.,* 38 34N 7 54W 44
Evreux, *tn., Fr.,* 49 03N 1 11E 44
Ewe, L., *Scot.,* 57 49N 5 38W 22
Exe, R., *Scot.,* 50 38N 3 27W 26
Exeter, *tn., Eng.,* 50 43N 3 31W 26
Exmoor, *geog. reg., Eng.,* 51 10N 3 55W 26
Exmouth, *tn., Eng.,* 50 37N 3 25W 26
Eye Peninsula, *Scot.,* 58 13N 6 12W 22
Eyemouth, *tn., Scot.,* 55 52N 2 06W 23
Eyre, L., *S. Austr.,* 28 30S 138 00E 63
Eysturoy, *mt., Faeroe Is.,* 62 14N 6 59W 43

F

Faenza, *tn., It.,* 44 17N 11 53E 45
Faeroe Is., *I. terr. of Den., N. Atlan. Oc.,*
62 00N 7 00W 43
Fair Isle, *Scot.,* 59 32N 1 38W 22
Fairbanks, *tn., Alaska, USA,* 64 50N 147 50W 71
Fais, I., *Pac. Oc.,* 9 45N 140 31E 63
Faisalabad, *tn., Pak.,* 31 25N 73 09E 54
Fakenham, *tn., Eng.,* 52 50N 0 51E 27
Faku, *tn., China,* 42 30N 123 24E 57
Falkirk, *tn., Scot.,* 56 00N 3 48W 23
Falkland Is., *UK dep. terr., Atlan. Oc.,*
51 30S 59 00W 77
Falmouth, *tn., Eng.,* 50 08N 5 04W 26
Falmouth Bay, *Eng.,* 50 07N 5 03W 26
Falster, I., *Den.,* 54 49N 12 00E 42
Falun, *tn., Swed.,* 60 37N 15 40E 42
Famagusta, *tn., Cyprus,* 35 07N 33 57E 47
Farafra Oasis, *Eg.,* 27 15N 28 20E 49
Faraulep, I., *Pac. Oc.,* 8 36N 144 33E 63
Fareham, *tn., Eng.,* 50 51N 1 10W 27
Farewell, C., *hdl., Green.,* 59 45N 43 30W 71
Fargo, *tn., N. Dak., USA,* 47 00N 97 00W 72
Farnborough, *tn., Eng.,* 51 17N 0 46W 27
Farnham, *tn., Eng.,* 51 13N 0 49W 27
Farnworth, *tn., Eng.,* 53 33N 2 24W 25
Faro, *tn., Port.,* 37 01N 7 56W 44
Fårö, I., *Swed.,* 57 55N 19 10E 42
Fårö, *tn., Swed.,* 57 55N 19 10E 41
Fatshan, *tn., China,* 23 03N 113 08E 56
Fauské, *tn., Nor.,* 67 17N 15 25E 43
Faxaflói, *b., Ice.,* 64 28N 23 20W 43
F Dérik, *tn., Maur.,* 22 40N 12 41W 66
Fear, Cape, *hdl., N.C., USA,* 33 45N 78 00W 73
Fécamp, *tn., Fr.,* 49 45N 0 23E 39
Fehmarn, I., *W. Ger.,* 54 26N 11 10E 42
Fehmarn, *str., Den./Ger.,* 54 35N 11 20E 41
Felixstowe, *tn., Eng.,* 51 58N 1 20E 27
Femunden, L., *Nor.,* 62 05N 11 55E 42
Fen Ho, R., *China,* 37 00N 111 50E 56
Fengchen, *tn., China,* 40 28N 113 06E 56
Fengcheng, *tn., China,* 28 11N 115 47E 56
Fengfeng, *tn., China,* 36 50N 114 00E 56
Fengkieh, *tn., China,* 31 00N 109 33E 56
Fens, The, *geog. reg., Eng.,* 52 45N 0 02E 27
Fensi, *tn., China,* 36 50N 111 00E 56
Fenyang, *tn., China,* 37 14N 111 43E 56
Feodosiya, *tn., USSR,* 45 03N 35 23E 47
Fernando de Noronha I., *Atlan. Oc.,* 3 50S 32 25W ... 77
Fernando Poo see Macias Nguema I.
Ferrara, *tn., It.,* 44 50N 11 38E 45
Fès, *tn., Mor.,* 34 05N 5 00W 48
Fetlar, I., *Scot.,* 60 37N 0 52W 22
Fezzan, *geog. reg., Libya,* 26 30N 15 00E 48
Ffestiniog, *tn., Wales,* 52 58N 3 55W 26

Fianarantsoa, *tn., Madag.,* 21 27S 47 05E 67
Fife, *admin. reg., Scot.,* 56 14N 3 07W 23
Fife Ness, *hdl., Scot.,* 56 17N 2 36W 23
Figuig, *tn., Mor.,* 32 10N 1 15W 48
Fiji, Is., *comm. nat., Pac. Oc.,* 17 20S 179 00E .. 63
Filchner Ice Shelf, *Ant.,* 78 00S 45 00W 80
Filey, *tn., Eng.,* 54 12N 0 17W 25
Findhorn, R., *Scot.,* 57 15N 4 10W 22
Finisterre, C., *hdl., Sp.,* 42 52N 9 16W 44
Finland, *Rep., Eur.,* 63 00N 25 00E 43
Finland, Gulf of, *Fin./USSR,* 60 00N 26 00E 42
Finnmark, *geog. reg., Nor.,* 69 30N 25 00E 50
Finnmarksvidda, *geog. reg., Nor.,* 69 15N 23 00E .. 43
Firat, R., *Tur.,* 39 30N 38 00E 49
Firenze see Florence
Fishguard, *tn., Wales,* 51 59N 4 49W 26
Flagstaff, *tn., Ariz., USA,* 35 12N 111 38W 72
Flamborough Head, *hdl., Eng.,* 54 06N 0 04W .. 25
Flanders, *geog. reg., Belg.,* 51 00N 4 00E 39
Flannan Isles, *Scot.,* 58 16N 7 35W 22
Fleet, *tn., Eng.,* 51 16N 0 50W 27
Fleetwood, *tn., Eng.,* 53 56N 3 01W 25
Flensburg, *tn., W. Ger.,* 54 47N 9 27E 41
Flinders Range, *mts., S. Austr.,* 31 30S 138 30E .. 63
Flint, *tn., Mich., USA,* 43 03N 83 04W 73
Flint, *tn., Wales,* 53 15N 3 07W 26
Flora, *tn., Nor.,* 61 36N 5 04E 42
Florence, *tn., It.,* 43 47N 11 15E 45
Flores, I., *Indon.,* 8 35S 121 00E 55
Flores Sea, *Indon.,* 7 00S 119 30E 55
Florianópolis, *tn., Braz.,* 27 35S 48 31W 77
Florida, *admin. reg., USA,* 29 00N 82 30W 73
Florida Keys, *Is., Fla., USA,* 25 00N 80 40W 73
Florida, Straits of, *USA,* 24 45N 79 30W 73
Flotta, I., *Scot.,* 58 49N 3 07W 22
Flushing, *tn., Neth.,* 51 27N 3 35E 39
Foggia, *tn., It.,* 41 28N 15 33E 45
Folkestone, *tn., Eng.,* 51 05N 1 11E 27
Fontainebleau, *tn., Fr.,* 48 24N 2 42E 44
Fonte Boa, *tn., Braz.,* 2 33S 65 59W 77
Forbach, *tn., W. Ger.,* 48 40N 8 21E 39
Forest Fawr, *geog. reg., Wales,* 51 50N 3 45W ... 26
Forfar, *tn., Scot.,* 56 38N 2 54W 23
Forli, *tn., It.,* 44 13N 12 02E 45
Formby, *tn., Eng.,* 53 34N 3 05W 25
Formentera, I., *Balearic Is., Sp.,* 38 40N 1 30E ... 44
Formosa, *tn., Arg.,* 26 07S 58 14W 77
Formosa see Taiwan
Formosa Strait, *Asia,* 23 30N 118 20E 56
Forres, *tn., Scot.,* 57 37N 3 38W 22
Forsayth, *tn., Queensl., Austr.,* 18 31S 143 32E .. 63
Fort Archambault see Sarh
Fort Augustus, *tn., Scot.,* 57 09N 4 41W 22
Fort Dauphin, *tn., Madag.,* 25 01S 47 00E 67
Fort-de-France, *tn., Martinique,* 14 36N 61 05W .. 77
Fort Lamy see N'Djamena
Fort Lauderdale, *tn., Fla., USA,* 26 08N 80 08W .. 73
Fort Peck Dam, *Mont., USA,* 48 00N 106 20W .. 72
Fort Smith, *tn., Ark., USA,* 35 22N 94 27W 73
Fort Wayne, *tn., Ind., USA,* 41 05N 85 08W 73
Fort William, *tn., Scot.,* 56 49N 5 07W 23
Fort Worth, *tn., Tex., USA,* 32 45N 97 20W 72
Fortaleza, *tn., Braz.,* 3 45S 38 35W 77
Forth, R., *Scot.,* 56 08N 4 20W 23
Forth, Firth of, *Scot.,* 56 05N 2 55W 23
Foula, I., *Scot.,* 60 08N 2 05W 22
Foulness I., *Eng.,* 51 36N 0 55E 27
Fowey, *tn., Eng.,* 50 20N 4 38W 26
Fowling, *tn., China,* 29 39N 107 29E 56
Fowyang, *tn., China,* 33 00N 116 00E 56
Foxe Basin, *N.W. Terrs., Can.,* 66 00N 83 00W .. 71
Foyle, L., *N. Ire./Rep. Ire.,* 55 05N 7 10W 24
Foyle, R., *N. Ire./Rep. Ire.,* 54 58N 7 22W 24
France, *Rep., Eur.,* 46 00N 3 00E 44
Frankfort, *tn., Ky., USA,* 38 11N 84 53W 73
Frankfurt am Main, *tn., W. Ger.,* 50 06N 8 41E ... 39
Frankfurt an der Oder, *tn., E. Ger.,* 52 20N 14 32E .. 41
Franz Josef Land, *USSR I. terr., Arctic Oc.,*
76 00N 62 00E 52
Fraserburgh, *tn., Scot.,* 57 42N 2 00W 22
Frazer, R., *B.C., Can.,* 53 40N 123 00W 71
Fredericton, *tn., N.B., Can.,* 45 57N 66 40W 73
Frederikshåb, *tn., Green.,* 62 00N 49 47W 71
Frederikshavn, *tn., Den.,* 57 28N 10 33E 42
Fredrikstad, *tn., Nor.,* 59 15N 10 55E 42
Freeport, *tn., Grand Bahama I., The Bahamas,*
26 30N 78 47W 73
Freetown, *tn., S. Leone,* 8 30N 13 17W 66
Freiburg, *tn., W. Ger.,* 48 00N 7 52E 41
Freemantle, *tn., W. Austr.,* 32 07S 115 44E 62
French Guiana, *Fr. terr., S. Amer.,* 4 00N 53 00W ... 77
Fresnillo, *tn., Mex.,* 23 10N 102 54W 72
Fresno, *tn., Calif., USA,* 36 41N 119 47W 72
Frinton, *tn., Eng.,* 51 50N 1 14E 27
Frio, C., *hdl., Braz.,* 22 59S 42 00W 77
Frisian Is., *Neth./W. Ger.,* 53 30N 6 00E 41
Friuli-Venezia Guilia, *geog. reg., It.,* 46 00N 13 00E .. 45
Frolovo, *tn., USSR,* 49 45N 43 40E 51
Frome, *tn., Eng.,* 51 14N 2 20W 27
Front Range, *mts., Colo., USA,* 40 00N 105 10W .. 72
Froya, I., *Nor.,* 63 45N 8 45E 43
Frunze, *tn., USSR,* 42 53N 74 46E 52
Fuan, *tn., China,* 27 06N 119 36E 57
Fuchin, *tn., China,* 47 15N 131 59E 57
Fuchow, *tn., Fukien, China,* 26 09N 119 17E 57
Fuchow, *tn., Kiangsi, China,* 28 03N 116 15E 56
Fuhsien, *tn., China,* 39 36N 122 00E 57
Fujiyama, *vol., Jap.,* 35 23N 138 42E 57
Fukien, *admin. reg., China,* 25 55N 117 40E 56
Fukui, *tn., Jap.,* 36 04N 136 12E 57
Fukuoka, *tn., Jap.,* 33 39N 130 21E 57

Fukushima, *tn., Jap.,* 37 44N 140 28E 57
Fukuyama, *tn., Jap.,* 34 29N 133 21E 57
Fulda, R., *W. Ger.,* 51 05N 9 30E 39
Fulda, *tn., W. Ger.,* 50 33N 9 41E 39
Funabashi, *tn., Jap.,* 35 42N 139 59E 57
Funafuti, Is., *Tuvalu,* 8 30S 179 12E 63
Funen, I., *Den.,* 55 18N 10 20E 42
Fürth, *tn., W. Ger.,* 49 28N 11 00E 41
Fushun, *tn., Szechwan, China,* 29 12N 104 52E .. 56
Fushun, *tn., Liaoning, China,* 41 51N 123 53E ... 57
Fusin, *tn., China,* 42 08N 121 39E 57
Futuna I., *Pac. Oc.,* 14 25S 178 20W 63
Fuyu, *tn., China,* 45 10N 124 40E 57
Fyne, L., *Scot.,* 56 00N 5 20W 23

G

Gabès, *tn., Tun.,* 33 52N 10 06E 48
Gabon, *Rep., Afr.,* 0 10S 10 00E 67
Gaborone, *tn., Bots.,* 24 00S 26 00E 67
Gabrovo, *tn., Bulg.,* 42 52N 25 19E 46
Gafsa, *tn., Tun.,* 34 28N 8 43E 48
Gagnon, *tn., Que., Can.,* 51 56N 68 16W 71
Gainesville, *tn., Fla., USA,* 29 40N 82 20W 73
Gainsborough, *tn., Eng.,* 53 24N 0 48W 25
Gairloch, *tn., Scot.,* 57 43N 5 40W 22
Galán, Mt., *Arg.,* 26 22S 67 55W 77
Galápagos Is., *Pac. Oc.,* 0 00 89 00W 76
Galashiels, *tn., Scot.,* 55 37N 2 49W 23
Galathea Depth, *Kermadec Trench, Pac. Oc.,*
32 10S 177 00W 63
Galați, *geog. reg., Rom.,* 45 12N 28 00E 47
Galați, *tn., Rom.,* 45 27N 28 02E 50
Galdhøpiggen, Mt., *Nor.,* 61 38N 8 19E 42
Galicia, *geog. reg., Sp.,* 42 43N 8 00W 44
Gallan Head, *hdl., Scot.,* 58 14N 7 01W 22
Gallinas, P., *hdl., Col.,* 12 27N 71 44W 77
Gallipoli Peninsula, *Tur.,* 40 30N 26 40E 46
Gällivare, *tn., Swed.,* 67 10N 20 40E 43
Galloway, *geog. reg., Scot.,* 55 00N 4 25 W 23
Galloway, Mull of, *hdl., Scot.,* 54 38N 4 50W ... 23
Gallup, *tn., N. Mex., USA,* 35 30N 108 45W 72
Galveston, *tn., Tex., USA,* 29 17N 94 48W 73
Galway, *tn., Rep. Ire.,* 53 16N 9 03W 40
Gambia, The, *Rep., Afr.,* 13 25N 16 00W 66
Ganges, R., *India,* 25 00N 87 00E 54
Gao, *tn., Mali,* 16 19N 0 09W 66
Gao Bang, *tn., Viet.,* 22 37N 106 18E 56
Gap, *tn., Fr.,* 44 33N 6 05E 45
Garanhuns, *tn., Braz.,* 8 53S 36 28W 77
Garda, L., *It.,* 45 40N 10 40E 45
Garonne, R., *Fr.,* 44 45N 0 32W 44
Garrison Dam, *tn., N. Dak., USA,* 47 30N 101 26W .. 72
Gary, *tn., Ind., USA,* 41 34N 87 20W 73
Gascony, *geog. reg., Fr.,* 43 45N 0 20E 44
Gata, C. de, *hdl., Sp.,* 36 44N 2 10W 44
Gatchina, *tn., USSR,* 59 32N 30 05E 42
Gatehouse of Fleet, *tn., Scot.,* 54 53N 4 11W .. 23
Gatooma, *tn., Rhod.,* 18 16S 29 55E 67
Gaula, R., *Nor.,* 62 57N 11 00E 43
Gausta, Mt., *Nor.,* 59 51N 8 42E 42
Gävle, *tn., Swed.,* 60 41N 17 10E 42
Gaziantep, *tn., Tur.,* 37 04N 37 21E 47
Gdańsk, *tn., Pol.,* 54 22N 18 41E 41
Gdynia, *tn., Pol.,* 54 31N 18 30E 41
Geelong, *tn., Vic., Austr.,* 38 10S 144 26E 63
Gela, *tn., Sicily,* 37 04N 14 15E 45
Gelsenkirchen, *tn., W. Ger.,* 51 30N 7 05E 39
General Belgrano, *Arg. base, Ant.,* 78 00S 42 00W .. 80
Geneva, *tn., Switz.,* 46 13N 6 09E 45
Geneva, L., *Switz.,* 46 26N 6 30E 45
Genève see Geneva
Genichesk, *tn., USSR,* 46 10N 34 49E 47
Genk, *tn., Neth.,* 50 58N 5 30E 39
Genoa, *tn., It.,* 44 24N 8 56E 45
Genoa, Gulf of, *It.,* 44 00N 9 00E 45
Genova see Genoa
Gent, *tn., Belg.,* 51 02N 3 42E 39
Georgetown, *tn., Guy.,* 6 50N 58 12W 77
Georgia, *admin. reg., USA,* 32 00N 83 00W 73
Georgian Bay, *Ont., Can.,* 45 15N 81 00W 73
Georgian S.S.R., *admin. reg., USSR,* 41 00N 45 00E . 51
Georgiu-Dezh, *tn., USSR,* 51 00N 39 30E 50
Georgiyevsk, *tn., USSR,* 44 10N 43 30E 51
Gera, *tn., E. Ger.,* 50 51N 12 11E 41
Geraldton, *tn., W. Austr.,* 28 49S 114 36E 62
Germiston, *tn., Rep. S. Afr.,* 26 15S 28 10E 67
Gerona, *tn., Sp.,* 41 59N 2 49E 44
Getafe, *tn., Sp.,* 40 18N 3 44W 44
Ghadames, *tn., Libya,* 30 10N 9 30E 48
Ghana, *Rep. Afr.,* 6 00N 1 00W 66
Ghardaïa, *tn., Alg.,* 32 20N 3 40E 48
Ghent see Gent
Gibraltar, *UK dep. terr., Eur.,* 36 09N 5 21W 48
Gibraltar, Strait of, *Afr./Eur.,* 35 55N 5 40W 48
Gibson Desert, *W. Austr.,* 24 00S 125 00E 62
Giessen, *tn., W. Ger.,* 50 35N 8 42E 39
Gifu, *tn., Jap.,* 35 27N 136 46E 57
Gigha, I., *Scot.,* 55 41N 5 45W 23
Gigüela, R., *Sp.,* 39 00N 4 00W 44

Gijón, tn., Sp., 43 32N 5 40W 44
Gila, R., Ariz., USA, 33 20N 112 00W 72
Gilbert Is., Pac. Oc., 2 00N 175 00E 63
Gillingham, tn., Eng., 51 24N 0 33E 27
Girdle Ness, hdl., Scot., 57 08N 2 02W 22
Girga, tn., Eg., 26 17N 31 58E 49
Girvan, tn., Scot., 55 15N 4 51W 23
Gisborne, tn., N.Z., 38 41S 178 02E 63
Giurgiu, tn., Rom., 43 53N 25 58E 46
Giza, tn., Eg., 30 01N 31 12E 49
Gjirokastër, tn., Alb., 40 05N 20 10E 46
Gjøvik, tn., Nor., 60 47N 10 41E 42
Glacier National Park, Mont., USA,
48 30N 113 08W 72
Gladbeck, tn., W. Ger., 51 34N 6 59E 39
Gladstone, tn., Queensl., Austr., 23 52S 151 16E .. 63
Glåma, R., Nor., 59 30N 11 15E 42
Glasgow, tn., Scot., 55 53N 4 15W 23
Glastonbury, tn., Eng., 51 09N 2 43W 26
Glazov, tn., USSR, 58 09N 52 42E 51
Glen Coe, Pass of, Scot., 56 40N 5 00W 23
Glen Garry, val., Scot., 56 47N 4 05W 23
Glen Lyon, val., Scot., 56 35N 4 20W 23
Glen More, val., Scot., 57 05N 4 48W 23
Glendale, tn., Calif., USA, 34 09N 118 20W 72
Glenrothes, tn., Scot., 56 12N 3 10W 23
Glittertind, Mt., Nor., 61 40N 8 32E 42
Gliwice, tn., Pol., 50 20N 18 40E 41
Globe, tn., Ariz., USA, 33 23N 110 48W 72
Glossop, tn., Eng., 53 27N 1 57W 25
Gloucester, tn., Eng., 51 53N 2 14W 27
Gloucestershire, admin. reg., Eng.,
51 45N 2 10W 26
Gniezno, tn., Pol., 52 32N 17 32E 41
Gobabis, tn., S.W. Afr. (Nam.), 22 30S 18 58E .. 67
Gobi, des., Asia, 44 00N 111 00E 56
Godalming, tn., Eng., 51 11N 0 37W 27
Godavari, R., India, 19 00N 77 00E 54
Godthåb, tn., Green., 64 15N 51 35W 71
Gogebic Range, mts., Mich., USA, 46 40N 90 00W . 73
Goiânia, tn., Braz., 16 43S 49 18W 77
Goiás, admin. reg., Braz., 15 55S 50 10W 77
Golmo, tn., China, 36 30N 95 10E 56
Golspie, tn., Scot., 57 58N 3 58W 22
Gomel, tn., USSR, 52 25N 31 00E 50
Gómez Palacio, tn., Mex., 25 39N 103 30W 72
Gondar, tn., Ethiopia, 12 39N 37 29E 67
Good Hope, C. of, hdl., Rep. S. Afr., 34 20S 18 25E . 67
Goole, tn., Eng., 53 42N 0 52W 25
Goose Bay, tn., Newf. and Lab., Can.,
53 15N 60 20W 71
Gorakhpur, tn., India, 26 45N 83 23E 54
Gordium, hist. site, Tur., 39 36N 32 00E 47
Gorebridge, tn., Scot., 55 51N 3 02W 23
Gorey, tn., Rep. Ire., 52 40N 6 18W 24
Gorinchem, tn., Neth., 51 50N 4 59E 39
Gorki, tn., USSR, 57 36N 45 04E 50
Görlitz, tn., E. Ger., 51 09N 15 00E 41
Gorlovka, tn., USSR, 48 17N 38 05E 50
Gorseinon, tn., Wales, 51 39N 4 03W 26
Gorzów Wielkopolski, tn., Pol., 52 42N 15 12E .. 41
Gosport, tn., Eng., 50 48N 1 08W 27
Göta, R., Sweden, 57 50N 12 01E 42
Göta Canal, Swed., 58 30N 14 00E 42
Götaland, geog. reg., Swed., 57 10N 12 55E ... 42
Gotha, tn., E. Ger., 50 57N 10 43E 41
Gothenburg, tn., Swed., 57 45N 12 00E 42
Gotland, I., Swed., 57 15N 18 30E 42
Goto Is., Jap., 32 55N 129 05E 57
Göttingen, tn., W. Ger., 51 32N 9 57E 41
Gottwaldov, tn., Cz., 49 14N 17 40E 41
Gouda, tn., Neth., 52 01N 4 43E 39
Goulburn, tn., N.S.W., Austr., 34 47S 149 43E .. 63
Gourock, tn., Scot., 55 58N 4 49W 23
Governador Valadares, tn., Braz., 18 51S 41 57W . 77
Gower, pen., Wales, 51 35N 4 10W 26
Gozo, I., Malta, 36 00N 14 13E 46
Graaff-Reinet, tn., Rep. S. Afr., 32 15S 24 32E . 67
Grafton, tn., N.S.W., Austr., 29 40S 152 56E ... 63
Graham Land, geog reg., Ant., 63 30S 65 00W ... 80
Grahamstown, tn., Rep. S. Afr., 33 19S 26 43E . 67
Grampian, admin. reg., Scot., 57 16N 2 53W ... 22
Grampian Mts., Scot., 56 32N 4 55W 23
Gran Chaco, geog. reg., Arg./Par., 25 00S 61 00W . 77
Gran Sasso d'Italia, mts., It., 42 25N 13 30E ... 45
Granada, tn., Sp., 37 10N 3 35W 44
Granby, tn., Que., Can., 45 23N 72 44W 73
Grand Bahama I., The Bahamas, 26 40N 78 30W . 73
Grand Canal, Rep. Ire., 53 15N 8 10W 24
Grand Canyon, gorge, Ariz., USA, 36 15N 112 30W . 72
Grand Canyon National Park, Ariz., USA,
36 10N 112 10W 72
Grand Coulee Dam, Wash., USA, 47 59N 118 58W . 72
Grand Forks, tn., N. Dak., USA, 47 57N 97 05W . 72
Grand Island, tn., Nebr., USA, 40 56N 98 21W .. 72
Grand Junction, tn., Colo., USA, 39 04N 108 33W . 72
Grand Rapids, tn., Mich., USA, 42 57N 86 40W .. 73
Grand Teton, mt., Wyo., USA, 43 45N 110 50W ... 72
Grangemouth, tn., Scot., 56 01N 3 44W 23
Grantham, tn., Eng., 52 55N 0 39W 27
Grantown-on-Spey, tn., Scot., 57 20N 3 38W ... 22
Gravesend, tn., Eng., 51 27N 0 24E 27
Grays, tn., Eng., 51 29N 0 20E 27
Graz, tn., Aust., 47 05N 15 22E 45
Great Abaco I., The Bahamas, 26 15N 77 10W ... 73
Great Australian Bight, b., Austr., 34 00S 130 00E . 62
Great Barrier Reef, Austr., 19 00S 149 00E ... 63
Great Basin, geog. reg., Nev., USA,
40 00N 116 30W 72
Great Bear, L., N.W. Terrs., Can.,
66 00N 120 00W 71

Great Belt, str., Den., 55 20N 11 00E 42
Great Dividing Range, mts., Queensl./N.S.W., Austr.
26 00S 150 00E 63
Great Driffield, tn., Eng., 54 01N 0 26W 25
Great Eastern Erg, des., Alg., 30 00N 6 30E ... 48
Great Falls, tn., Mont., USA, 47 30N 111 16W ... 72
Great Fisher Bank, North Sea, 55 30N 3 00E ... 40
Great Khingan Mts., China, 48 00N 121 00E ... 57
Great Malvern, tn., Eng., 52 07N 2 19W 27
Great Plains, geog. reg., USA, 41 00N 102 00W .. 72
Great Salt L., Utah, USA, 41 10N 112 40W 72
Great Salt L. Des., Utah, USA, 40 20N 113 50W . 72
Great Sandy Desert, W. Austr., 20 30S 124 00E . 62
Great Slave L., N.W. Terrs., Can.,
61 30N 114 20W 71
Great Victoria Desert, S. Austr./W. Austr.,
28 30S 127 30E 62
Great Wall, hist. site, China, 38 30N 109 30E .. 56
Great Western Erg., des., Alg., 31 30N 2 00E .. 48
Greater Antilles, Is., W.I., 21 00N 80 00W ... 71
Greater Manchester, admin. reg., Eng.,
53 30N 2 39W 25
Greater Sunda Is., Indon., 4 00S 115 00E 55
Greece, Rep., Eur., 40 00N 23 00E 46
Greeley, tn., Colo., USA, 40 26N 104 43W 72
Green, R., USA, 39 30N 109 55W 72
Green Bay, tn., Wis., USA, 44 32N 88 00W 73
Greenland, admin. reg., Den., Arctic Oc.,
76 00N 45 00W 71
Greenland Sea, Arctic Oc., 76 00N 7 00W 52
Greenlaw, tn., Scot., 55 43N 2 28W 23
Greenock, tn., Scot., 55 57N 4 45W 23
Greensboro, tn., N.C., USA, 36 03N 79 50W 73
Greenville, tn., Miss., USA, 33 23N 91 03W 73
Greenville, tn., S.C., USA, 34 52N 82 25W 73
Greifswald, tn., E. Ger., 54 06N 13 24E 41
Grenada, comm. nat., W.I., 12 10N 61 40W 77
Grenoble, tn., Fr., 45 11N 5 43E 45
Grimsby, tn., Eng., 53 35N 0 05W 25
Grimsey, I., Ice., 66 33N 18 00W 43
Grodno, tn., USSR, 53 40N 23 50E 50
Groningen, tn., Neth., 53 13N 6 35E 39
Grootfontein, tn., S.W. Afr., 19 32S 18 05E ... 67
Grosseto, tn., It., 42 46N 11 07E 45
Grossglockner, Mt., Aust., 47 05N 12 44E 45
Groznyy, tn., USSR, 43 21N 45 42E 51
Grudziądz, tn., Pol., 53 29N 18 45E 41
Guadalajara, tn., Mex., 20 40N 103 20W 71
Guadalajara, tn., Sp., 40 37N 3 10W 44
Guadalcanal I., Solomon Is., Pac. Oc.,
10 00S 160 00E 63
Guadalquivir, R., Sp., 37 20N 6 00W 44
Guadeloupe, Fr. terr., Lesser Antilles,
16 20N 61 40W 77
Guadiana, R., Port./Sp., 39 00N 5 30W 44
Guajará Mirim, tn., Braz., 10 50S 65 21W 77
Guam I., USA terr., Pac. Oc., 13 30N 144 45E .. 63
Guantánamo, tn., Cuba, 20 09N 75 14W 73
Guaporé, R., Braz., 13 00S 63 00W 77
Guardafui, C., hdl., Somalia, 11 50N 51 16E ... 67
Guasave, tn., Mex., 25 33N 108 30W 72
Guatemala, Rep., Cent. Amer., 15 40N 90 30W .. 71
Guatemala, tn., Guat., 14 38N 90 22W 71
Guaviare, R., Col., 3 30N 71 00W 77
Guaymas, tn., Mex., 27 59N 110 54W 72
Guayquil, tn., Ec., 2 13S 79 54W 77
Gubkin, tn., USSR, 51 17N 37 32E 50
Gudbrandsdalen, val., Nor., 61 30N 10 20E 42
Guelma, tn., Alg., 36 29N 7 25E 48
Guienne, geog. reg., Fr., 44 30N 0 40E 44
Guildford, tn., Eng., 51 14N 0 35W 27
Guinea, Rep., Afr., 10 20N 10 00W 66
Guinea-Bissau, Rep., Afr., 12 00N 15 00W 66
Guinea, Gulf of, Afr., 3 00N 2 30E 67
Guisborough, tn., Eng., 54 32N 1 04W 25
Gulistan, tn., USSR, 40 31N 68 47E 51
Guntur, tn., India, 16 20N 80 27E 54
Gurgan, tn., Iran, 36 51N 54 25E 52
Gurgan, tn., USSR, 36 51N 54 25E 51
Guryev, tn., USSR, 47 08N 51 59E 51
Gus Khrustalnyy, tn., USSR, 55 38N 40 44E 50
Gütersloh, tn., W. Ger., 51 54N 8 22E 39
Guyana, Rep., S. Amer., 4 36N 58 54W 77
Gwalior, tn., India, 26 12N 78 09E 54
Gwelo, tn., Rhod., 19 25S 29 50E 67
Gwent, admin. reg., Wales, 51 40N 3 00W 26
Gwynedd, admin. reg., Wales, 52 50N 4 00W ... 26
Gympie, tn., Queensl., Austr., 26 10S 152 35E .. 63
Győr, tn., Hung., 47 41N 17 40E 46

H

Haapsalu, tn., USSR, 58 58N 23 33E 42
Haarlem, tn., Neth., 52 23N 4 38E 39
Haarlemmermeer, tn., Neth., 52 20N 4 00E ... 39
Hachijo I., Jap., 33 00N 139 45E 57
Hachinohe, tn., Jap., 40 30N 141 30E 57
Hachioji, tn., Jap., 35 40N 139 20E 57
Haddington, tn., Scot., 55 58N 2 47W 23
Hadramaut, geog. reg., S. Yemen,
15 30N 49 30E 52

Hadrian's Wall, hist. site, Eng., 55 00N 2 40W . 23
Hafnarfjördur, tn., Ice., 64 04N 21 58W 43
Hagen, tn., W. Ger., 51 22N 7 27E 39
Hague, C. de la, hdl., Fr., 49 44N 1 56W 27
Hague, The, tn., Neth., 52 05N 4 16E 39
Haguenau, tn., Fr., 48 49N 7 47E 39
Haifa, tn., Israel, 32 49N 34 59E 49
Hailsham, tn., Eng., 50 52N 0 16E 27
Hailung, tn., China, 42 39N 125 48E 57
Hailuoto, I., Fin., 65 01N 24 45E 43
Haimen, tn., China, 31 48N 121 08E 57
Hainan, I., China, 19 00N 110 00E 56
Haiphong, tn., Viet., 20 50N 106 41E 55
Haiti, Rep., W.I., 19 00N 72 30W 71
Haiyen, tn., China, 36 45N 101 50E 56
Hakodate, tn., Jap., 41 46N 140 44E 57
Halab see Aleppo
Halden, tn., Nor., 59 08N 11 13E 42
Haleb see Aleppo
Halesowen, tn., Eng., 52 26N 2 05W 27
Halicarnassus, hist. site, Tur., 37 03N 27 28E .. 47
Halifax, tn., Eng., 53 44N 1 52W 25
Halifax, tn., N.S., Can., 44 38N 63 35W 71
Halle, tn., E. Ger., 51 28N 11 58E 41
Hallett, USA base, Ant., 72 30S 170 00E 80
Halley Bay, UK base, Ant., 76 00S 26 00W 80
Hallingdal, R., Nor., 60 34N 9 12E 42
Halmahera, I., Indon., 0 40N 128 00E 55
Halmstad, tn., Swed., 56 41N 12 55E 42
Halstead, tn., Eng., 51 57N 0 38E 27
Halti, Mt., Fin., 69 17N 21 21E 43
Hama, tn., Syria, 35 09N 36 44E 49
Hamamatsu, tn., Jap., 34 42N 137 42E 57
Hamar, tn., Nor., 60 57N 10 55E 42
Hamburg, admin. reg., W. Ger., 53 38N 10 00E .. 41
Hamburg, tn., W. Ger., 53 33N 10 00E 41
Hämeenlinna, tn., Fin., 61 00N 24 25E 42
Hameln, tn., W. Ger., 52 07N 9 24E 39
Hamersley Range, hs., W. Austr., 22 00S 117 45E . 62
Hamhung, tn., N. Kor., 39 54N 127 35E 57
Hami, tn., Sinkiang, China, 42 37N 93 32E 56
Hamilton, tn., N.Z., 37 46S 175 18E 63
Hamilton, tn., Ont., Can., 43 15N 79 50W 73
Hamilton, tn., Scot., 55 47N 4 03W 23
Hamm, tn., W. Ger., 51 40N 7 49E 39
Hammerfest, tn., Nor., 70 40N 23 44E 43
Hammond, tn., Ind., USA, 41 37N 87 30W 73
Hampshire, admin. reg., Eng., 52 21N 1 34W ... 27
Hampton, tn., Va., USA, 37 02N 76 23W 73
Han Kiang, R., China, 31 40N 12 20E 56
Hanau, tn., W. Ger., 50 08N 8 56E 39
Hanchung, tn., China, 33 09N 107 03E 56
Hangchow, tn., China, 30 18N 120 07E 57
Hangchow Bay, China, 30 30N 121 30E 57
Hangö, tn., Fin., 59 50N 23 00E 42
Hankow see Wuhan
Hanoi, tn., Viet., 21 01N 105 52E 55
Hanover, tn., W. Ger., 52 23N 9 44E 41
Hantan, tn., China, 36 37N 114 25E 56
Haparanda, tn., Swed., 65 50N 24 10E 43
Harar, tn., Ethiopia, 9 20N 42 10E 67
Harbin, tn., China, 45 50N 126 40E 57
Hardangerfjord, fd., Nor., 60 15N 6 00E 42
Hardangervidda, plat., Nor., 60 20N 7 20E 42
Hargeisa, tn., Somalia, 9 31N 44 02E 67
Harlow, tn., Eng., 51 47N 0 08E 27
Harney Basin, geog. reg., Oreg., USA,
43 30N 119 00W 72
Härnösand, tn., Swed., 62 37N 17 55E 43
Harpenden, tn., Eng., 51 49N 0 22W 27
Harris, I., Scot., 57 54N 7 00W 22
Harris, Sound of, Scot., 57 44N 7 06W 22
Harrisburg, tn., Pa., USA, 40 18N 76 49W 73
Harrogate, tn., Eng., 54 00N 1 33W 25
Harstad, tn., Nor., 68 48N 16 30E 43
Hartford, tn., Conn., USA, 41 45N 72 42W 73
Hartland Point, hdl., Eng., 51 02N 4 31W 26
Hartlepool, tn., Eng., 54 41N 1 13W 25
Harwich, tn., Eng., 51 57N 1 17E 27
Harz Mts., Ger., 51 40N 10 40E 41
Haslemere, tn., Eng., 51 06N 0 43W 27
Hassi Messaoud, tn., Alg., 31 52N 5 43E 67
Hastings, tn., Eng., 50 51N 0 36E 27
Hastings, tn., Nebr., USA, 40 37N 98 22W 72
Hatfield, tn., Eng., 51 46N 0 13W 27
Hatteras, Cape, hdl., N.C., USA, 35 14N 75 31W . 73
Haugesund, tn., Nor., 59 25N 5 15E 42
Haukivesi, L., Fin., 62 10N 28 30E 43
Havana, tn., Cuba, 23 07N 82 25W 73
Havant, tn., Eng., 50 51N 0 59W 27
Havel, R., E. Ger., 52 32N 12 25E 41
Haverfordwest, tn., Wales, 51 49N 4 58W 26
Haverhill, tn., Eng., 52 05N 0 26E 27
Havre, le, tn., Fr., 49 30N 0 06E 39
Hawick, tn., Scot., 55 25N 2 47W 23
Hay-on-Wye, tn., Eng., 52 04N 3 07W 26
Hay River, tn., N.W. Terrs., Can., 60 51N 115 42W . 71
Hayward's Heath, tn., Eng., 51 00N 0 06W 27
Hazel Grove, tn., Eng., 53 23N 2 05W 25
Heanor, tn., Eng., 53 01N 1 22W 25
Heard I., Indian Oc., 53 00S 74 00E 80
Hebburn, tn., Eng., 54 59N 1 30W 25
Hebrides, Inner, Is., Scot., 58 00N 7 00W 23
Hebrides, Outer, Is., Scot., 57 30N 7 40W 22
Hebrides, Sea of the, Scot., 57 12N 6 50W ... 23
Heerenveen, tn., Neth., 52 57N 5 55E 39
Heerlen, tn., Neth., 50 53N 5 59E 39
Heidelberg, tn., W. Ger., 49 25N 8 42E 41
Heilbronn, tn., W. Ger., 49 08N 9 14E 41
Heilung Kiang, R., China/USSR, 53 30N 122 30E . 53
(see also Amur, R.)

Heilungkiang, *admin. reg., China,* 47 30N 129 00E . . . 57
Hejaz, *geog. reg., Si. Arab.,* 26 00N 37 30E 52
Hekla, Mt., *vol., Ice.,* 64 01N 19 39W 43
Helagsfjället, *mt., Swed.,* 62 58N 12 25E 43
Helena, *tn., Mont., USA,* 46 35N 112 00W . . . 72
Helensburgh, *tn., Scot.,* 56 01N 4 44W 23
Heligoland, *I., W. Ger.,* 54 09N 7 52E 41
Helmond, *tn., Neth.,* 51 28N 5 40E 39
Helmsdale, *tn., Scot.,* 58 07N 3 40W 22
Helsingborg, *tn., Swed.,* 56 05N 12 45E 42
Helsingør, *tn., Den.,* 56 03N 12 38E 42
Helsinki, *tn., Fin.,* 60 08N 25 00E 42
Helston, *tn., Eng.,* 50 05N 5 16W 26
Helwan, *tn., Eg.,* 29 51N 31 20E 49
Hemel Hempstead, *tn., Eng.,* 51 46N 0 28W 27
Hengelo, *tn., Neth.,* 52 16N 6 46E 39
Hengshui, *tn., China,* 37 45N 115 44E 56
Hengyang, *tn., China,* 26 58N 112 31E 56
Herat, *tn., Afghan.,* 34 20N 62 10E 52
Hercegovina, *admin. reg., Yug.,* 43 20N 18 00E . . . 46
Hereford, *tn., Eng.,* 52 04N 2 43W 26
Hereford & Worcester, *admin. reg., Eng.,*
52 13N 2 90W 26
Herford, *tn., W. Ger.,* 52 07N 8 40E 39
Herlen Gol *see* Kerulen, R.
Herm, *I., Chan. Is., UK,* 49 28N 2 27W 27
Herma Ness, *hdl., Scot.,* 60 50N 0 54W 22
Hermosillo, *tn., Mex.,* 29 15N 110 59W . . . 72
Herne, *tn., W. Ger.,* 51 32N 7 12E 39
Herne Bay, *tn., Eng.,* 51 23N 1 08E 27
Hertford, *tn., Eng.,* 51 48N 0 05W 27
Hertfordshire, *admin. reg., Eng.,* 51 51N 0 19W 27
Hesse, *admin. reg., W. Ger.,* 50 28N 8 15E 39
Hexham, *tn., Eng.,* 54 58N 2 06W 25
Heysham, *tn., Eng.,* 54 02N 2 54W 25
Heywood, *tn., Eng.,* 53 36N 2 13W 25
Hidalgo del Parral, *tn., Mex.,* 26 58N 105 40W . . . 72
High Wycombe, *tn., Eng.,* 51 38N 0 46W 27
Highland, *admin. reg., Scot.,* 57 21N 5 13W 22
Hiiumaa I., *USSR,* 58 50N 22 45E 42
Hildesheim, *tn., W. Ger.,* 52 09N 9 58E 39
Hilversum, *tn., Neth.,* 52 14N 5 10E 39
Himalayas, *mts., Asia,* 30 00N 82 00E 54
Himeji, *tn., Jap.,* 34 50N 134 40E 57
Hinckley, *tn., Eng.,* 52 33N 1 21W 27
Hindu Kush, *mts., Afghan.,* 36 00N 70 00E 52
Hindustan, *geog. reg., India,* 27 00N 81 00E 54
Hinghwa, *tn., China,* 32 56N 119 55E 57
Hinnøya, *I., Nor.,* 68 35N 15 50E 43
Hirosaki, *tn., Jap.,* 40 34N 140 28E 57
Hiroshima, *tn., Jap.,* 34 23N 132 27E 57
Hirtshals, *tn., Den.,* 57 36N 9 58E 42
Hispaniola, *I., W.I.,* 19 00N 71 00W 71
Hitachi, *tn., Jap.,* 36 35N 140 40E 57
Hitchin, *tn., Eng.,* 51 57N 0 17W 27
Hitra, *I., Nor.,* 63 30N 8 45E 43
Hkakabo Razi, Mt., *Burma,* 28 17N 97 46E 56
Ho Chi Minh, *tn., Viet.,* 10 46N 106 43E 55
Hobart, *tn., Tas., Austr.,* 42 54S 147 18E 63
Hochwan, *tn., China,* 30 02N 106 15E 56
Hoddesdon, *tn., Eng.,* 51 46N 0 01W 27
Hodeida, *tn., Yemen,* 14 50N 42 58E 52
Hódmezővásárhely, *tn., Hung.,* 46 26N 20 21E . . . 46
Hofei, *tn., China,* 31 45N 116 36E 56
Hofsjökull, *ice-cap, Ice.,* 64 50N 18 50W 43
Hofuf, *tn., Si. Arab.,* 25 20N 49 34E 52
Hogland I., *USSR,* 60 05N 27 00E 43
Hoihow, *tn., China,* 20 05N 110 25E 56
Hokang, *tn., China,* 47 36N 130 30E 57
Hokiang, *tn., China,* 28 50N 105 50E 56
Hokkaido, *I., Jap.,* 43 30N 143 00E 57
Hokow, *tn., China,* 22 30N 103 54E 56
Holguín, *tn., Cuba,* 20 54N 76 15W 73
Holstebro, *tn., Den.,* 56 22N 8 38E 42
Holsworthy, *tn., Eng.,* 50 49N 4 21W 26
Holy I., *Eng.,* 55 41N 1 48W 25
Holy I., *Wales,* 53 16N 4 39W 26
Holyhead, *tn., Wales,* 53 19N 4 38W 26
Holywood, *tn., N. Ire.,* 54 38N 5 50W 24
Homs, *tn., Libya,* 32 29N 14 15E 48
Homs, *tn., Syria,* 34 44N 36 43E 49
Hon Gay, *tn., Viet.,* 20 57N 107 06E 56
Honan, *admin. reg., China,* 33 50N 113 15E 56
Honduras, *Rep., Cent. Amer.,* 14 40N 86 30W 71
Hønefoss, *tn., Nor.,* 60 05N 10 10E 42
Hong Kong, *UK colony, China,* 22 11N 114 14E 56
Honiara, *tn., Solomon Is., Pac. Oc.,* 9 28S 159 57E . . . 63
Honiton, *tn., Eng.,* 50 48N 3 13W 26
Honshu, *I., Jap.,* 36 00N 138 00E 57
Hoogeveen, *tn., Neth.,* 52 43N 6 29E 39
Hook of Holland, *tn., Neth.,* 51 59N 4 07E 39
Hoover Dam, *Ariz./Nev., USA,* 36 01N 114 45W . . . 72
Hopeh, *admin. reg., China,* 39 25N 116 45E 56
Hopi, *tn., China,* 35 57N 114 08E 56
Horizon Depth, *Pac. Oc.,* 23 15S 174 46W 63
Horley, *tn., Eng.,* 51 11N 0 11W 27
Horn, Cape, *hdl., S. Amer.,* 56 00S 67 15W 77
Hornavan, *L., Swed.,* 66 15N 17 40E 43
Horncastle, *tn., Eng.,* 53 13N 0 07W 25
Horsens, *tn., Den.,* 55 53N 9 53E 42
Horsham, *tn., Eng.,* 51 04N 0 21W 27
Horsham, *tn., Vic., Austr.,* 36 45S 142 15E 63
Hospitalet, *tn., Sp.,* 41 21N 2 06E 44
Hot Springs, *tn., Ark., USA,* 34 30N 93 02W 73
Hotazel, *tn., Rep. S. Afr.,* 27 17S 23 00E 67
Hotseh, *tn., China,* 35 40N 115 50E 56
Houghton-le-Spring, *tn., Eng.,* 54 51N 1 28W 25
Hourn, *L., Scot.,* 57 07N 5 35W 23
Houston, *tn., Tex., USA,* 29 45N 95 25W 73
Hove, *tn., Eng.,* 50 49N 0 10W 27
Hovd, *tn., Mong.,* 48 00N 91 43E 53
Howe, Cape, *hdl., N.S.W., Austr.,* 37 20S 149 59E . . . 63

Howland I., *Pac. Oc.,* 0 48N 176 38W 63
Howth Head, *hdl., Rep. Ire.,* 53 21N 6 00W 24
Höxter, *tn., W. Ger.,* 51 47N 9 22E 39
Hoy, *I., Scot.,* 58 50N 3 43W 22
Hoylake, *tn., Eng.,* 53 23N 3 11W 25
Hradec Králové, *tn., Cz.,* 50 13N 15 50E 41
Hsiamen *see* Amoy
Hsian *see* Sian
Hsiapachen, *tn., China,* 41 00N 106 00E 56
Hsinchu, *tn., Taiwan,* 24 48N 120 59E 57
Hsuchang, *tn., China,* 34 03N 113 48E 56
Hualien, *tn., Taiwan,* 23 58N 121 35E 57
Huambo, *tn., Ang.,* 12 47S 15 44E 67
Huancavelica, *tn., Peru,* 12 45S 75 03W 77
Huancayo, *tn., Peru,* 12 05S 72 12W 77
Huánuco, *tn., Peru,* 9 55S 76 11W 77
Huascaran, Mt., *Peru,* 9 08S 77 36W 77
Hubli, *tn., India,* 15 20N 75 14E 54
Huchow, *tn., China,* 30 56N 120 04E 57
Hucknall Torkard, *tn., Eng.,* 53 02N 1 11W 27
Huddersfield, *tn., Eng.,* 53 39N 1 47W 25
Hudiksvall, *tn., Swed.,* 61 45N 17 10E 42
Hudson, *R., N.Y., USA,* 43 00N 73 50W 73
Hudson Bay, *Can.,* 60 00N 86 00W 71
Hudson Strait, *Can.,* 65 00N 75 00W 71
Hue, *tn., Viet.,* 16 28N 107 35E 55
Huelva, *tn., Sp.,* 37 15N 6 56W 44
Huesca, *tn., Sp.,* 42 08N 0 25W 44
Hugh Town, *tn., Eng.,* 49 55N 6 19W 26
Hughenden, *tn., Queensl., Austr.,* 20 50S 144 10E . . . 63
Huhehot, *tn., China,* 40 49N 111 37E 56
Huiyang, *tn., China,* 23 00N 114 50E 56
Hull, *tn., Que., Can.,* 45 26N 75 45W 73
Hulin, *tn., China,* 45 44N 132 59E 57
Humber, *R., Eng.,* 53 42N 0 20W 25
Humberside, *admin. reg., Eng.,* 53 46N 0 50W 25
Humboldt, *R., Nev., USA,* 40 55N 118 00W 72
Hunan, *admin. reg., China,* 27 30N 111 30E 56
Hunan *see* Loyang
Hunedoara, *tn., Rom.,* 45 45N 22 54E 46
Hungarian Plain, *geog. reg., Hung.,* 47 00N 20 00E . . . 46
Hungary, *Rep., Eur.,* 47 20N 19 20E 46
Hungerford, *tn., Eng.,* 51 26N 1 30W 27
Hungkiang, *tn., China,* 27 08N 109 51E 56
Hungnam, *tn., N. Kor.,* 39 49N 127 40E 57
Hungshui Ho, *R., China,* 24 20N 107 10E 56
Hungtze, *L., China,* 33 20N 118 35E 57
Hunsrück, *mts., W. Ger.,* 50 00N 7 30E 39
Huntingdon, *tn., Eng.,* 52 20N 0 12W 27
Huntingdon, *tn., W. Va., USA,* 38 24N 82 26W 73
Huntly, *tn., Scot.,* 57 27N 2 47W 22
Huntsville, *tn., Ala., USA,* 34 44N 86 35W 73
Hupeh, *admin. reg., China,* 31 05N 113 05E 56
Huron, L., *Can./USA,* 44 34N 82 30W 73
Húsavik, *tn., Ice.,* 66 03N 17 17W 43
Hutchinson, *tn., Kans., USA,* 38 03N 97 56W 72
Hvar, *I., Yug.,* 43 11N 16 28E 46
Hwai Ho, *R., China,* 34 00N 119 50E 57
Hwaian, *tn., China,* 33 50N 119 40E 57
Hwainan, *tn., China,* 32 44N 117 01E 56
Hwang Ho, *R., China,* 37 15N 117 40E 56
Hwangchwan, *tn., China,* 32 00N 115 04E 56
Hwangshih, *tn., China,* 30 13N 115 05E 56
Hwangyen, *tn., China,* 28 34N 121 12E 57
Hweitseh, *tn., China,* 26 24N 103 08E 56
Hyderabad, *tn., India,* 17 22N 78 26E 54
Hyesan, *tn., N. Kor.,* 41 48N 129 50E 57
Hythe, *tn., Eng.,* 51 05N 1 05E 27
Hyvinkää, *tn., Fin.,* 60 37N 24 50E 42

I

Iaşi, *tn., Rom.,* 47 09N 27 38E 47
Ibadan, *tn., Nig.,* 7 23N 3 56E 67
Ibagué, *tn., Col.,* 4 35N 75 30W 77
Iberian Mts., *Sp.,* 47 20N 3 00W 44
Ibiza, *I., Balearic Is., Sp.,* 38 54N 1 26E 44
Ibiza, *tn., Ibiza, Sp.,* 38 52N 1 25E 44
Ica, *tn., Peru,* 14 05S 75 43W 77
Iceland, *Rep., Eur.,* 65 00N 19 00W 43
Ichang, *tn., China,* 30 43N 111 22E 56
Ichun, *tn., Heilungkiang, China,* 47 41N 129 10E . . . 57
Ichun, *tn., Kiangsi, China,* 27 45N 114 22E 56
Idaho, *admin. reg., USA,* 44 00N 114 30W 72
Idar-Oberstein, *tn., W. Ger.,* 49 43N 7 19E 39
Idfu, *tn., Eg.,* 24 58N 32 50E 49
Idlib, *tn., Syria,* 36 00N 36 30E 47
Igarka, *tn., USSR,* 67 31N 86 33E 52
Iguaçu Falls, *wf., Braz.,* 25 35S 54 22W 77
Ihsien, *tn., China,* 41 21N 121 03E 57
Iialmi, *tn., Fin.,* 63 33N 27 14E 43
IJmuiden, *tn., Neth.,* 52 28N 4 39E 39
IJssel, *R., Neth.,* 52 35N 6 05E 39
IJsselmeer, *L., Neth.,* 52 45N 5 20E 39
Ikaria, *I., Gr.,* 37 35N 26 10E 46
Ilagan, *tn., Phil.,* 17 07N 121 53E 55
Île de France, *geog. reg., Fr.,* 49 00N 2 20E 44
Ilebo, *tn., Zaire,* 4 23S 20 23E 67

Ilfracombe, *tn., Eng.,* 51 13N 4 08W 26
Ilhéus, *tn., Braz.,* 14 50S 39 06W 77
Ili, *R., USSR,* 43 51N 77 14E 51
Ilkeston, *tn., Eng.,* 52 59N 1 18W 25
Ilkley, *tn., Eng.,* 53 55N 1 50W 25
Illimani, Mt., *Bol.,* 16 37S 67 48W 77
Illinois, *admin. reg., USA,* 40 15N 89 30W 73
Illinois, *R., Ill., USA,* 40 30N 90 00W 73
Ilmen, *L., USSR,* 58 15N 31 10E 50
Iloilo, *tn., Phil.,* 10 41N 122 33E 55
Ilorin, *tn., Nig.,* 8 32N 4 34E 67
Imandra, *L., USSR,* 67 45N 33 00E 43
Imatra, *tn., Fin.,* 61 14N 28 50E 43
Imbaba, *tn., Eg.,* 30 00N 30 00E 49
Imola, *tn., It.,* 44 22N 11 43E 45
Imperial Valley, *Calif., USA,* 32 50N 115 30W . . . 72
Inari, *L., Fin.,* 69 00N 28 00E 43
Inari, *tn., Fin.,* 68 54N 27 05E 43
Inchon, *tn., S. Kor.,* 37 30N 126 38E 57
Indalsälven, *R., Swed.,* 63 10N 16 05E 43
Independence, *tn., Mo., USA,* 39 04N 94 27W . . . 73
India, *Rep.—comm. nat., Asia,* 24 00N 75 00E 54
Indian Ocean 3
Indiana, *admin. reg., USA,* 40 30N 86 00W 73
Indianapolis, *tn., Ind., USA,* 39 45N 86 10W 73
Indigirka, *R., USSR,* 69 00N 147 00E 53
Indonesia, *Rep., Austral.,* 3 00S 115 00E 55
Indore, *tn., India,* 22 42N 75 54E 54
Indus, *R., Pak.,* 27 00N 67 00E 54
İnegöl, *tn., Tur.,* 40 06N 29 31E 47
Ingolstadt, *tn., W. Ger.,* 48 46N 11 27E 41
Inhambane, *tn., Mozam.,* 23 51S 35 29E 67
Ining, *tn., China,* 42 52N 81 20E 52
Inishowen, *pen., Rep. Ire.,* 55 13N 7 30W 24
Inishowen Head, *hdl., Rep. Ire.,* 55 09N 6 56W . . . 24
Inishtrahull, *I., Rep. Ire.,* 55 27N 7 14W 24
Inland Sea, *Jap.,* 34 10N 133 10E 57
Inn, *R., Aust.,* 48 00N 13 00E 45
Inner Mongolia, *admin. reg., China,* 44 50N 117 40E . . 56
Inner Sound, *Scot.,* 57 30N 5 55W 22
Innerleithen, *tn., Scot.,* 55 38N 3 05W 23
Innsbruck, *tn., Aust.,* 47 17N 11 25E 45
Inowrocław, *tn., Pol.,* 52 49N 18 12E 41
Inuvik, *tn., N.W. Terrs., Can.,* 68 16N 133 40W . . . 71
Inveraray, *tn., Scot.,* 56 13N 5 05W 23
Invercargill, *tn., N.Z.,* 46 26S 168 21E 63
Invergordon, *tn., Scot.,* 57 42N 4 10W 22
Inverness, *tn., Scot.,* 57 27N 4 15W 22
Inverness, Firth of, *Scot.,* 57 34N 4 10W 22
Inverurie, *tn., Scot.,* 57 17N 2 23W 22
Iona, *I., Scot.,* 56 19N 6 25W 23
Ionian Is., *Gr.,* 38 40N 20 00E 46
Ionian Sea, *Eur.,* 37 30N 17 30E 46
Iowa, *admin. reg., USA,* 42 00N 93 30W 73
Ipin, *tn., China,* 28 50N 104 35E 56
Ipoh, *tn., Malay.,* 4 36N 101 02E 55
Ipswich, *tn., Eng.,* 52 04N 1 10E 27
Ipswich, *tn., Queensl., Austr.,* 27 38S 152 40E . . . 63
Iquique, *tn., Chile,* 20 15S 70 08W 77
Iquitos, *tn., Peru,* 3 51S 73 13W 77
Iráklion, *tn., Crete,* 35 20N 25 08E 46
Iran, *Kingd., Asia,* 33 00N 53 00E 52
Iraq, *Rep., Asia,* 33 00N 44 00E 49
Irbid, *tn., Jordan,* 32 33N 35 51E 49
Irbit, *tn., USSR,* 57 44N 63 02E 51
Ireland, Republic of, *Eur.,* 53 00N 8 00W 40
Iringa, *tn., Tanz.,* 7 49S 35 39E 67
Irish Sea, 54 00N 5 00W 24
Irkutsk, *tn., USSR,* 52 18N 104 15E 53
Irlam, *tn., Eng.,* 53 28N 2 25W 25
Iron Gate, *gorge, Rom.,* 44 42N 22 30E 46
Iron Knob, *tn., S. Austr.,* 32 44S 137 08E 63
Irrawaddy, *R., Burma,* 23 00N 96 00E 55
Irshih, *tn., China,* 47 08N 119 57E 57
Irtysh, *R., USSR,* 60 00N 70 00E 52
Irun, *tn., Sp.,* 43 20N 1 48W 44
Irvine, *tn., Scot.,* 55 37N 4 40W 23
Isabela I., *Galápagos Is.,* 0 00 91 21W 77
Isafjördur, *tn., Ice.,* 66 05N 23 06W 43
Ise, *tn., Jap.,* 34 29N 136 41E 57
Isère, *R., Fr.,* 45 15N 5 30E 45
Iserlohn, *tn., W. Ger.,* 51 23N 7 42E 39
Isfahan, *tn., Iran,* 32 41N 51 41E 52
Ishim, *R., USSR,* 56 45N 70 40E 51
Ishim, *tn., USSR,* 56 10N 69 30E 51
Ishimbay, *tn., USSR,* 53 30N 55 59E 51
Ishinomaki, *tn., Jap.,* 38 25N 141 18E 57
Isiro, *tn., Zaire,* 2 50N 27 40E 67
İskenderun, *tn., Tur.,* 36 37N 36 08E 47
Islamabad, *tn., Pak.,* 33 40N 73 08E 54
Island Magee, *pen., N. Ire.,* 54 48N 5 44W 24
Islay, *I., Scot.,* 55 46N 6 10W 23
Isle of Man, *cr. dep., UK,* 54 15N 4 30W 24
Isle Royale, *Mich., USA,* 48 00N 88 50W 73
Ismailia, *tn., Eg.,* 30 36N 32 15E 49
Isna, *tn., Eg.,* 25 16N 32 30E 49
isparta, *tn., Tur.,* 37 46N 30 32E 47
Israel, *Rep., Asia,* 33 00N 33 40E 49
İstanbul, *tn., Tur.,* 41 02N 28 57E 47
Istria, *geog. reg., Yug.,* 45 10N 14 00E 46
Itabira, *tn., Braz.,* 19 39S 43 14W 77
Itabuna, *tn., Braz.,* 14 48S 39 18W 77
Italy, *Rep., Eur.,* 42 00N 13 00E 45
Itu, *tn., China,* 30 24N 111 32E 56
Ivalo, *tn., Fin.,* 68 40N 27 40E 43
Ivano Frankovsk, *tn., USSR,* 48 55N 24 42E 50
Ivanovo, *tn., USSR,* 57 00N 41 00E 50
Ivdel, *tn., USSR,* 60 45N 60 30E 51
Ivory Coast, *Rep., Afr.,* 7 30N 5 00W 66
Iwaki, *tn., Jap.,* 37 00N 141 00E 57
Izhevsk, *tn., USSR,* 56 49N 53 11E 51
Izmail, *tn., USSR,* 45 20N 28 48E 47

İzmir, *tn., Tur.*, 38 25N 27 10E 47
İzmit, *tn., Tur.*, 40 47N 29 55E 47
Izu Is., *Jap.*, 34 00N 139 50E 57

J

Jabalpur, *tn., India*, 23 10N 79 59E 54
Jackson, *tn., Miss., USA*, 32 20N 90 11W 73
Jacksonville, *tn., Fla., USA*, 30 20N 81 40W 73
Jadebusen, *b., W. Ger.*, 53 30N 8 15E 39
Jaén, *tn., Sp.*, 37 46N 3 48W 44
Jaffna, *tn., Sri Lanka*, 9 40N 80 01E 54
Jaipur, *tn., India*, 26 53N 75 50E 54
Jakarta see Djakarta
Jakobshavn, *tn., Green.*, 69 16N 51 05W 71
Jaluit, *I., Pac. Oc.*, 6 00N 169 35E 63
Jamaica, *I., comm. nat., Carib. Sea*,
18 10N 77 30W 71
James, *R., Va., USA*, 37 20N 78 00W 73
James, *R., USA*, 46 20N 98 00W 72
James Bay, *Hudson Bay, Can.*, 53 30N 80 30W . . . 71
Jamshedpur, *tn., India*, 22 47N 86 12E 54
Jan Mayen I., *Arctic Oc.*, 71 00N 8 00W 52
Jaoping, *tn., China*, 23 55N 116 45E 56
Japan, *empire, Asia*, 36 04N 136 00E 57
Japan, Sea of, *E. Asia*, 40 00N 135 00E 57
Jarlshof, *hist. site, Scot.*, 59 51N 1 25W 22
Jarrow, *tn., Eng.*, 54 59N 1 29W 25
Java, *I., Indon.*, 7 00S 113 00E 55
Jedburgh, *tn., Scot.*, 55 29N 2 34W 23
Jefferson City, *tn., Mo., USA*, 38 33N 92 10W . . . 73
Jelenia Góra, *tn., Pol.*, 50 55N 15 45E 41
Jelgava, *tn., USSR*, 56 39N 23 40 42
Jena, *tn., E. Ger.*, 50 56N 11 35E 41
Jequié, *tn., Braz.*, 13 52S 40 06W 77
Jerez de la Frontera, *tn., Sp.*, 36 41N 6 08W 44
Jersey, *I., Chan. Is., UK*, 49 13N 2 07W 27
Jerusalem, *tn., Israel*, 31 47N 35 13E 49
Jidda, *tn., Si. Arab.*, 21 30N 39 10E 52
Jihlava, *tn., Cz.*, 49 24N 15 35E 41
Jimma, *tn., Ethiopia*, 7 39N 36 47E 67
Jinja, *tn., Ugan.*, 0 27N 33 14E 67
João Pessoa, *tn., Braz.*, 7 06S 34 53W 77
Jodhpur, *tn., India*, 26 18N 73 08E 54
Joensuu, *tn., Fin.*, 62 36N 29 45E 43
Jogjakarta, *tn., Indon.*, 7 48S 110 24E 55
Johannesburg, *tn., Rep. S. Afr.*, 26 10S 28 02E . . . 67
Johnstone, *tn., Scot.*, 55 50N 4 31W 23
Johore Bahru, *tn., Malay.*, 1 29N 103 44E 55
Joinville, *tn., Braz.*, 26 20S 48 49W 77
Jokkmokk, *tn., Swed.*, 66 37N 19 50E 43
Jönköping, *tn., Swed.*, 57 45N 14 10E 42
Jordan, *Kingd., Asia*, 31 00N 36 00E 49
Jorhat, *tn., India*, 26 45N 94 12E 56
Jos., *tn., Nig.*, 9 54N 8 53E 67
Jostedalsbreen, *gl., Nor.*, 61 45N 7 00E 42
Jotunheimen Mts., *Nor.*, 61 30N 9 00E 42
Juan de Fuca, Strait of, *Can./USA*,
48 15N 124 00W 72
Juan Fernandez Is., *Pac. Oc.*, 33 50S 80 00W 77
Juàzeiro, *tn., Braz.*, 9 25S 40 30W 77
Juàzeiro do Norte, *tn., Braz.*, 7 10S 39 18W 77
Juba, *R., Som.*, 1 30N 42 35E 67
Juba, *tn., Sud.*, 4 50N 31 35E 67
Jucar, *R., Sp.*, 39 00N 2 13W 44
Juikin, *tn., China*, 26 00N 116 00E 56
Juiz de Fora, *tn., Braz.*, 21 47S 43 23W 77
Jujuy, *admin. reg., Arg.*, 23 20S 65 40W 77
Jukao, *tn., China*, 31 10N 120 32E 57
Julianehåb, *tn., Green.*, 60 40N 46 00W 71
Jumet, *tn., Belg.*, 50 27N 4 26E 39
Junan, *tn., China*, 33 00N 114 20E 56
Juneau, *tn., Alaska, USA*, 58 20N 134 20W 71
Junin, *tn., Arg.*, 34 34S 60 55W 77
Junk'atse see Shigatse
Jura, *I., Scot.*, 56 00N 5 50W 23
Jura Mts., *Fr./Switz.*, 46 35N 6 05E 45
Jura, Sound of, *Scot.*, 55 57N 5 45W 23
Jūrmala, *tn., USSR*, 56 59N 23 35E 42
Juruá, *R., Braz.*, 5 20S 67 40W 77
Jutland, *pen., Den.*, 56 00N 8 00E 42
Jyekundo see Yüshu
Jyväskylä, *tn., Fin.*, 62 16N 25 50E 43

K

K2, Mt., *China/India*, 36 00N 77 00E 54
Kabalo, *tn., Zaire*, 6 02S 26 55E 67
Kabarega Falls, *wf., Ugan.*, 2 17N 31 41E 67
Kabul, *tn., Afghan.*, 34 30N 69 10E 52

Kabwe, *tn., Zam.*, 14 29S 28 25E 67
Kadiyevka, *tn., USSR*, 48 34N 38 40E 50
Kaduna, *tn., Nig.*, 10 28N 7 25E 67
Kaesong, *tn., N. Kor.*, 37 59N 126 30E 57
Kafue, *R., Zam.*, 15 45S 28 12E 67
Kagoshima, *tn., Jap.*, 31 37N 130 32E 57
Kaieteur Falls, *wf., Guy.*, 5 09N 59 29W 77
Kaifeng, *tn., China*, 34 47N 114 20E 56
Kaiping, *tn., China*, 40 24N 122 17E 57
Kairouan, *tn., Tun.*, 35 42N 10 01E 48
Kaiserslautern, *tn., W. Ger.*, 49 27N 7 47E 39
Kaiyuan, *tn., China*, 42 39N 124 04E 57
Kajaani, *tn., Fin.*, 64 12N 27 45E 43
Kakhovka Reservoir, *USSR*, 46 50N 33 30E 47
Kalahari Desert, *Bots.*, 24 00S 22 00E 67
Kalamata, *tn., Gr.*, 37 02N 22 07E 46
Kalamazoo, *tn., Mich., USA*, 42 17N 85 36W 73
Kalemie, *tn., Zaire*, 5 57S 29 10E 67
Kalevala, *tn., USSR*, 65 13N 31 12E 43
Kalgoorlie, *tn., W. Austr.*, 30 49S 121 29E 62
Kalinin, *tn., USSR*, 56 49N 35 57E 50
Kaliningrad, *tn., USSR*, 54 40N 20 30E 42
Kalispell, *tn., Mont.*, 48 12N 114 19W 72
Kalisz, *tn., Pol.*, 51 46N 18 02E 41
Kalix, *tn., Swed.*, 65 51N 23 14E 43
Kalixälven, *R., Swed.*, 66 00N 23 00E 43
Kalmar, *tn., Swed.*, 56 39N 16 20E 42
Kaluga, *tn., USSR*, 54 31N 36 16E 50
Kama, *R., USSR*, 60 00N 53 00E 51
Kamchatka, *pen., USSR*, 57 00N 160 00E 53
Kamenets Podolskiy, *tn., USSR*, 48 40N 26 36E . . 46
Kamensk Uralskiy, *tn., USSR*, 59 29N 61 49E 51
Kamina, *tn., Zaire*, 8 46S 25 00E 67
Kampala, *tn., Ugan.*, 0 19N 32 35E 67
Kamyshin, *tn., USSR*, 50 05N 45 24E 51
Kan Kiang, *R., China*, 27 50N 116 00E 56
Kananga, *tn., Zaire*, 5 53S 22 26E 67
Kanazawa, *tn., Jap.*, 36 35N 136 38E 57
Kanchow, *tn., China*, 25 52N 114 51E 56
Kandahar, *tn., Afghan.*, 31 36N 65 47E 52
Kandalaksha, *tn., USSR*, 67 09N 32 31E 43
Kandalaksha, Gulf of, *USSR*, 66 30N 33 50E 43
Kandavu, *I., Fiji*, 19 01S 178 24E 63
Kandy, *tn., Sri Lanka*, 7 17N 80 40E 54
Kanggye, *tn., N. Kor.*, 40 58N 126 38E 57
Kangnung, *tn., S. Kor.*, 37 48N 127 52E 57
Kangting, *tn., China*, 30 05N 102 04E 56
Kanin Peninsula, *USSR*, 68 00N 45 00E 50
Kankan, *tn., Guin.*, 10 22N 9 11W 66
Kano, *tn., Nig.*, 12 00N 8 31E 67
Kanpur, *tn., India*, 26 27N 80 14E 54
Kansas, *admin. reg., USA*, 38 40N 98 00W 72
Kansas City, *tn., Miss., USA*, 39 02N 94 33W 73
Kansas City, *tn., Kans., USA*, 39 05N 94 37W 73
Kansk, *tn., USSR*, 56 20N 95 37E 53
Kansu, *admin. reg., China*, 35 30N 104 30E 56
Kantse, *tn., China*, 31 30N 100 29E 56
Kaolack, *tn., Sen.*, 14 09N 16 08W 66
Kaosiung, *tn., Taiwan*, 22 36N 120 17E 57
Kapingamaringi, *I., Pac. Oc.*, 1 00N 125 00E 63
Kaposvár, *tn., Hung.*, 46 21N 17 49E 46
Kapuskasing, *tn., Ont., Can.*, 49 25N 82 26W 73
Kara-Bogaz-Gol, *b., USSR*, 41 44N 53 05E 51
Kara-Kum, *des., USSR*, 38 57N 57 18E 51
Kara Sea, *USSR*, 74 00N 67 00E 52
Karabük, *tn., Tur.*, 41 12N 32 36E 47
Karachi, *tn., Pak.*, 24 51N 67 02E 54
Karaganda, *tn., USSR*, 49 53N 73 07E 51
Karakoram, *mts., Kashmir*, 37 00N 75 00E 54
Karamai, *tn., China*, 45 48N 84 30E 52
Karaman, *tn., Tur.*, 37 11N 33 13E 47
Karashahr, *tn., Sinkiang*, 42 04N 86 34E 56
Karbala, *tn., Iraq*, 32 37N 44 03E 49
Karelia, *admin. reg., USSR*, 63 40N 29 50E 43
Karelian Isthmus, *USSR*, 60 30N 29 35E 42
Kariba, L., *Rhod./Zam.*, 16 31S 28 50E 67
Karl-Marx-Stadt, *tn., E. Ger.*, 50 50N 12 55E 41
Karlovac, *tn., Yug.*, 45 30N 15 34E 46
Karlovy Vary, *tn., Cz.*, 50 14N 12 53E 41
Karlskoga, *tn., Swed.*, 59 19N 14 33E 42
Karlskrona, *tn., Swed.*, 56 10N 15 35E 42
Karlsruhe, *tn., W. Ger.*, 49 00N 8 24E 41
Karlstad, *tn., Swed.*, 59 24N 13 32E 42
Kárpathos, *I., Gr.*, 35 37N 27 10E 47
Karroo, *geog. reg., Rep. S. Afr.*,
33 45S 21 30E 67
Kars, *tn., Tur.*, 40 35N 43 05E 49
Karsakpay, *tn., USSR*, 47 47N 66 43E 51
Karshi, *tn., USSR*, 38 53N 64 45E 51
Kartaly, *tn., USSR*, 53 06N 60 37E 51
Karviná, *tn., Cz.*, 49 50N 18 30E 41
Kasai, *R., Zaire*, 4 00S 19 10E 67
Kasama, *tn., Zam.*, 10 10S 31 11E 67
Kashgar, *tn., China*, 39 29N 76 02E 52
K'ashih see Kashgar
Kashing, *tn., China*, 30 45N 120 41E 57
Kashmir, *geog. reg., Asia*, 34 00N 75 00E 54
Kasimov, *tn., USSR*, 54 55N 41 25E 50
Kasr es Souk, *tn., Mor.*, 32 30N 5 00W 48
Kassala, *tn., Sud.*, 15 24N 36 30E 67
Kassel, *tn., W. Ger.*, 51 18N 9 30E 41
Kastamonu, *tn., Tur.*, 41 22N 33 47E 47
Katanga see Shaba
Katerina, *tn., Gr.*, 40 15N 22 30E 46
Kathmandu see Katmandu
Katmandu, *tn., Nepal*, 27 42N 85 19E 54
Katowice, *tn., Pol.*, 50 15N 18 59E 41
Katrine, L., *Scot.*, 56 15N 4 30W 23
Kattegat, *chan., Den./Swed.*, 56 50N 11 20E 42
Kaunas, *tn., USSR*, 54 52N 25 55E 50

Kautokeino, *tn., Nor.*, 69 00N 23 06E 43
Kaválla, *tn., Gr.*, 40 57N 24 28E 46
Kavieng, *tn., Pap. New Guin.*, 2 34S 150 48E 63
Kayes, *tn., Mali*, 14 26N 11 28W 66
Kayseri, *tn., Tur.*, 38 42N 35 28E 47
Kazakh S.S.R., *admin. reg., USSR*, 47 12N 59 03E . . 51
Kazan, *R., N.W. Terrs., Can.*, 62 00N 100 00W . . . 71
Kazan, *tn., USSR*, 55 45N 49 10E 51
Kazanlŭk, *tn., Bulg.*, 42 37N 25 23E 46
Kebnekaise, Mt., *Swed.*, 67 55N 18 35E 43
Kecskemét, *tn., Hung.*, 46 56N 19 43E 46
Keetmanshoop, *tn., S.W. Afr. (Nam.)*, 26 36S 18 08E . 67
Keflavik, *tn., Ice.*, 64 01N 22 35W 43
Keighley, *tn., Eng.*, 53 52N 1 54W 25
Keitele, L., *Fin.*, 63 10N 26 24E 43
Keith, *tn., Scot.*, 57 32N 2 57W 22
Kelkit, *R., Tur.*, 40 40N 37 30E 47
Kells see Ceanannus Mór
Kelso, *tn., Scot.*, 55 36N 2 25W 23
Kem, *R., USSR*, 64 58N 33 10E 43
Kem, *tn., USSR*, 64 58N 34 39E 43
Kemerovo, *tn., USSR*, 55 25N 86 05E 52
Kemi, *tn., Fin.*, 65 46N 24 34E 43
Kemijärvi, L., *Fin.*, 66 35N 27 28E 43
Kemijärvi, *tn., Fin.*, 66 42N 27 30E 43
Kemijoki, *R., Fin.*, 66 00N 25 00E 43
Kempten, *tn., W. Ger.*, 47 44N 10 19E 41
Kendal, *tn., Eng.*, 54 20N 2 45W 25
Kendari, *tn., Indon.*, 3 57S 122 36E 55
Kenilworth, *tn., Eng.*, 52 21N 1 34W 27
Kenitra, *tn., Mor.*, 34 20N 6 34W 48
Kennet, *R., Eng.*, 51 28N 1 30W 27
Kenora, *tn., Ont., Can.*, 49 47N 94 26W 73
Kenosha, *tn., Wis., USA*, 42 34N 87 50W 73
Kent, *admin. reg., Eng.*, 51 12N 0 40E 27
Kentucky, *admin. reg., USA*, 37 20N 86 00W 73
Kenya, *Rep., Afr.*, 0 05N 37 00E 67
Kenya, Mt., *Kenya*, 0 10S 37 19E 67
Kerch, *tn., USSR*, 45 22N 36 27E· 50
Kerguelen I., *Fr. terr., Indian Oc.*, 49 30S 69 30E . . 80
Kerintji see Kerintji
Kermadec Is., *Pac. Oc.*, 30 00S 178 30W 63
Kermadec Trench, *Pac. Oc.*, 31 00S 177 00W 63
Kerman, *tn., Iran*, 30 18N 57 05E 52
Kermanshah, *tn., Iran*, 34 19N 47 04E 52
Kerulen, *R., Mong.*, 48 00N 114 00E 56
Keswick, *tn., Eng.*, 54 37N 3 08W 25
Kettering, *tn., Eng.*, 52 24N 0 44W 27
Key West, *tn., Fla., USA*, 24 34N 81 48W 73
Keynsham, *tn., Eng.*, 51 26N 2 30W 26
Khabarovsk, *tn., USSR*, 48 32N 135 08E 53
Khalkís see Chalcis
Khaniá see Canea
Khanka, L., *USSR*, 45 00N 132 30E 57
Khanty Mansiysk, *tn., USSR*, 61 01N 69 00E 52
Kharga Oasis, *Eg.*, 25 00N 30 00E 49
Kharkov, *tn., USSR*, 50 00N 36 15E 50
Khartoum, *tn., Sud.*, 15 33N 32 35E 67
Khaskovo, *tn., Bulg.*, 41 57N 25 32E 46
Khatanga, *tn., USSR*, 71 59N 102 31E 53
Khenifra, *tn., Mor.*, 33 00N 5 40W 48
Kherson, *tn., USSR*, 46 39N 32 38E 50
Khibiny, Mt., *USSR*, 67 48N 33 48E 43
Khimki, *tn., USSR*, 55 53N 37 26E 50
Khmelnitskiy, *tn., USSR*, 49 25N 26 59E 50
Khoi, *tn., Iran*, 38 40N 45 00E 49
Kholmsk, *tn., USSR*, 47 02N 142 03E 57
Khon Kaen, *tn., Thai.*, 16 30N 102 47E 56
Khoper, *R., USSR*, 52 00N 43 20E 50
Khouribga, *tn., Mor.*, 32 54N 32 35E 48
Khurasan, *geog. reg., Iran*, 34 00N 57 00E 51
Khurramshahr, *tn., Iran*, 30 25N 48 09E 52
Khust, *tn., USSR*, 48 11N 23 19E 46
Kialing Kiang, *R., China*, 32 00N 106 00E 56
Kiamusze, *tn., China*, 46 59N 130 29E 57
Kian, *tn., China*, 27 01N 114 58E 56
Kiangling, *tn., China*, 30 28N 113 16E 56
Kiangsi, *admin. reg., China*, 27 20N 115 40E 56
Kiangsu, *admin. reg., China*, 33 00N 119 50E 57
Kiangtsing, *tn., China*, 29 00N 106 00E 56
Kiaoho, *tn., China*, 43 36N 127 23E 57
Kiawang, *tn., China*, 34 30N 117 26E 57
Kiayukwan, *tn., China*, 39 47N 98 14E 56
Kidderminster, *tn., Eng.*, 52 23N 2 14W 27
Kidwelly, *tn., Wales*, 51 45N 4 18W 26
Kiel, *tn., W. Ger.*, 54 20N 10 08E 41
Kiel Canal, *W. Ger.*, 54 15N 9 40E 41
Kielce, *tn., Pol.*, 50 51N 20 39E 41
Kienow, *tn., China*, 27 04N 118 20E 56
Kienshui, *tn., China*, 23 40N 102 50E 56
Kiev, *tn., USSR*, 50 28N 30 29E 50
Kigali, *tn., Rwanda*, 1 59S 30 05E 67
Kigoma, *tn., Tanz.*, 4 52S 29 36E 67
Kilbrannan Sound, *Scot.*, 55 40N 5 23W 23
Kildare, *admin. reg., Rep. Ire.*, 53 13N 7 00W 24
Kildare, *tn., Rep. Ire.*, 53 10N 6 55W 24
Kilien Shan, *mts., China*, 38 50N 100 00E 56
Kilimanjaro, Mt., *Tanz.*, 3 02S 37 20E 67
Kilis, *tn., Tur.*, 36 43N 37 07E 47
Kilkeel, *tn., N. Ire.*, 54 04N 6 00W 24
Kilkenny, *admin. reg., Rep. Ire.*, 52 38N 7 28W . . . 24
Kilkenny, *tn., Rep. Ire.*, 52 39N 7 15W 24
Killarney, *tn., Rep. Ire.*, 52 03N 9 30W 40
Killiecrankie, Pass of, *Scot.*, 56 43N 3 40W 23
Killin, *tn., Scot.*, 56 28N 4 20W 23
Kilmarnock, *tn., Scot.*, 55 37N 4 30W 23
Kilosa, *tn., Tanz.*, 6 49S 37 00E 67
Kimberley, *tn., B.C., Can.*, 49 40N 115 58W 72
Kimberley, *tn., Rep. S. Afr.*, 28 45S 24 46E 67
Kimberley Plateau, *W. Austr.*, 17 30S 126 00E 62
Kimchaek, *tn., N. Kor.*, 40 40N 129 10E 57

Kimovsk, *tn., USSR,* 53 58N 38 35E 50
Kimry, *tn., USSR,* 56 51N 37 20E 50
Kinabalu Mt., *Malay.,* 6 03N 116 32E 55
Kindu, *tn., Zaire,* 3 00S 25 55E 67
Kineshma, *tn., USSR,* 57 28N 42 08E 50
King Ho, *R., China,* 36 00N 108 00E 56
Kingisepp, *tn., USSR,* 58 12N 22 30E 42
King's Lynn, *tn., Eng.,* 52 45N 0 24E 27
Kingsbridge, *tn., Eng.,* 50 17N 3 46W 26
Kingsmill Group, *Is., Pac. Oc.,* 1 00S 176 30E . . 63
Kingsteignton, *tn., Eng.,* 50 33N 3 35W 26
Kingston, *tn., Jam.,* 17 58N 76 48W 71
Kingston, *tn., Ont., Can.,* 44 14N 76 30W 73
Kingston upon Hull, *tn., Eng.,* 53 45N 0 20W . . . 25
Kingtehchen, *tn., China,* 29 17N 117 12E 56
Kingussie, *tn., Scot.,* 57 05N 4 04W 23
Kinhwa, *tn., China,* 29 06N 119 40E 56
Kinnaird's Head, *hdl., Scot.,* 57 42N 2 00W 22
Kinross, *tn., Scot.,* 56 13N 3 27W 23
Kinsha Kiang, *R., China,* 28 30N 99 00E 56
Kinshasa, *tn., Zaire,* 4 18S 15 18E 67
Kintyre, *geog. reg., Scot.,* 55 32N 5 35W 23
Kintyre, Mull of, *hdl., Scot.,* 55 17N 5 04W 23
Kirensk, *tn., USSR,* 57 45N 108 02E 53
Kirghiz S.S.R., *admin. reg., USSR,* 42 00N 75 00E . . 52
Kirghiz Steppe, *pl., USSR,* 48 41N 54 27E 51
Kirikkale, *tn., Tur.,* 39 51N 33 32E 47
Kirin, *admin. reg., China,* 43 45N 125 20E 57
Kirin, *tn., China,* 43 53N 126 35E 57
Kirkcaldy, *tn., Scot.,* 56 07N 3 10W 23
Kirkcudbright, *tn., Scot.,* 54 50N 4 03W 23
Kirkenes, *tn., Nor.,* 69 41N 30 00E 43
Kirkintilloch, *tn., Scot.,* 55 57N 4 10W 23
Kirklareli, *tn., Tur.,* 41 45N 27 12E 47
Kirkuk, *tn., Iraq,* 35 28N 44 26E 49
Kirkwall, *tn., Scot.,* 58 59N 2 58W 22
Kirov, *tn., USSR,* 54 05N 34 20E 50
Kirov, *tn., USSR,* 58 38N 49 38E 50
Kirovabad, *tn., USSR,* 37 19N 69 05E 49
Kirovabad, *tn., USSR,* 40 39N 46 20E 51
Kirovakan, *tn., USSR,* 40 49N 44 30E 51
Kirovo Chepetsk, *tn., USSR,* 58 38N 49 38E . . . 50
Kirovograd, *tn., USSR,* 48 31N 32 15E 50
Kirovsk, *tn., USSR,* 67 37N 33 39E 43
Kirşehir, *tn., Tur.,* 39 09N 34 08E 47
Kiruna, *tn., Swed.,* 67 53N 20 15E 43
Kisangani, *tn., Zaire,* 0 33N 25 14E 67
Kishinev, *tn., USSR,* 47 00N 28 50E 50
Kisi, *tn., China,* 45 21N 121 00E 57
Kislovodsk, *tn., USSR,* 43 56N 42 44E 51
Kismayu, *tn., Somalia,* 0 25S 42 31E 67
Kisumu, *tn., Kenya,* 0 03S 34 47E 67
Kitakyushu, *tn., Jap.,* 33 52N 130 49E 57
Kitami, *tn., Jap.,* 43 51N 143 54E 57
Kitchener, *tn., Ont., Can.,* 43 27N 80 30W 73
Kit's Coty House, *hist. site, Eng.,* 51 20N 0 30E . . 27
Kitwe, *tn., Zam.,* 12 48S 28 14E 67
Kityang, *tn., China,* 23 32N 116 20E 56
Kiuchuan, *tn., China,* 39 47N 98 30E 56
Kiukiang, *tn., China,* 29 37N 116 02E 56
Kiunglai, *tn., China,* 30 35N 103 30E 56
Kiungtung, *tn., China,* 19 00N 110 50E 56
Kivu, L., *Zaire,* 1 50S 29 10E 67
Kizel, *tn., USSR,* 59 01N 57 42E 51
Kızıl Irmak, *R., Tur.,* 39 15N 36 00E 47
Kladno, *tn., Cz.,* 50 10N 14 05E 41
Klagenfurt, *tn., Aust.,* 46 38N 14 20E 45
Klaipéda, *tn., USSR,* 55 43N 21 07E 42
Klarälven, *R., Swed.,* 60 32N 13 15E 42
Klerksdorp, *tn., Rep. S. Afr.,* 26 52S 26 39E 67
Kleve, *tn., W. Ger.,* 51 47N 6 11E 39
Klin, *tn., USSR,* 56 20N 36 45E 50
Klintsy, *tn., USSR,* 52 45N 32 15E 50
Klyuchevskaya Sopka, Mt., *USSR,*
55 50N 160 30E 53
Knaresborough, *tn., Eng.,* 54 00N 1 27W 25
Knossos, *hist. site, Crete,* 35 18N 25 10E 46
Knox Coast, *Ant.,* 66 30S 108 00E 80
Knoxville, *tn., Tenn., USA,* 36 00N 83 57W 73
Knoydart, *geog. reg., Scot.,* 57 03N 5 33W 23
Kobe, *tn., Jap.,* 34 40N 135 12E 57
Koblenz, *tn., W. Ger.,* 50 21N 7 36E 39
Kobrin, *tn., USSR,* 52 16N 24 22E 42
Kochi, *tn., Jap.,* 33 33N 133 32E 57
Kodiak I., *Alaska, USA,* 57 20N 153 40W 70
Koforidua, *tn., Ghana,* 6 01N 0 12W 66
Kofu, *tn., Jap.,* 35 42N 138 34E 57
Kohtla-Järve, *tn., USSR,* 59 28N 27 20E 50
Kokand, *tn., USSR,* 40 33N 70 55E 51
Kokchetav, *tn., USSR,* 53 18N 69 25E 51
Kokiu, *tn., China,* 23 25N 103 05E 56
Kokkola, *tn., Fin.,* 63 50N 23 10E 43
Koko Nor, L., *China,* 37 00N 100 00E 56
Kokonselkä, L., *Fin.,* 61 50N 28 25E 43
Kola Peninsula, *USSR,* 67 30N 34 30E 43
Köln see Cologne
Kolomna, *tn., USSR,* 55 05N 38 45E 50
Kolomyya, *tn., USSR,* 48 31N 25 00E 46
Kolwezi, *tn., Zaire,* 10 44S 25 28E 67
Kolyma, *R., USSR,* 64 40N 153 00E 53
Kolyma Range, *mts., USSR,* 63 00N 157 00E . . . 53
Komsomolsk na Amure, *tn., USSR,*
50 32N 136 59E 53
Kondopoga, *tn., USSR,* 62 12N 34 17E 43
Kongmoon, *tn., China,* 22 35N 113 01E 56
Kongolo, *tn., Zaire,* 5 20S 27 00E 67
Konotop, *tn., USSR,* 51 15N 33 14E 50
Konstantinovka, *tn., USSR,* 48 33N 37 45E 50

Konya, *tn., Tur.,* 37 51N 32 30E 47
Konzhakovskiy Kamen, *mt., USSR,* 59 40N 59 05E . . 51
Kopet Dagh, *geog. reg., Iran,* 38 04N 56 23E . . . 51
Kopeysk, *tn., USSR,* 55 08N 61 39E 51
Korçë, *tn., Alb.,* 40 38N 20 44E 46
Korčula, I., *Yug.,* 42 56N 17 00E 46
Korea Strait, *Jap./Kor.,* 34 00N 129 30E 57
Koriyama, *tn., Jap.,* 37 23N 140 22E 57
Korkino, *tn., USSR,* 54 55N 61 25E 51
Korsakov, *tn., USSR,* 46 36N 142 50E 57
Kortrijk, *tn., Belg.,* 50 50N 3 17E 39
Koryak Range, *mts., USSR,* 61 00N 171 00E 53
Kosciusko, Mt., *N.S.W., Austr.,* 36 28S 148 17E . . . 63
Koshan, *tn., China,* 48 03N 125 55E 57
Košice, *tn., Cz.,* 48 44N 21 15E 41
Kosovo-Metohija, *geog. reg., Yug.,*
42 30N 21 00E 46
Kosovska Mitrovica, *tn., Yug.,* 42 54N 20 52E . . 46
Kostroma, *tn., USSR,* 57 46N 40 59E 50
Koszalin, *tn., Pol.,* 54 10N 16 10E 41
Kota Baharu, *tn., Malay.,* 6 07N 102 15E 55
Kota Kinabalu, *tn., Malay.,* 5 59N 116 04E 55
Kotka, *tn., Fin.,* 60 26N 26 55E 42
Kotlas, *tn., USSR,* 61 15N 46 35E 50
Kotovsk, *tn., USSR,* 47 42N 29 30E 47
Koudougou, *tn., Upper Volta,* 12 15N 2 23W . . . 66
Kouvola, *tn., Fin.,* 60 54N 26 45E 42
Kovd, L., *USSR,* 66 40N 32 00E 43
Kovel, *tn., USSR,* 51 12N 24 48E 42
Kovrov, *tn., USSR,* 56 23N 41 21E 50
Kowloon, *tn., China,* 22 20N 114 15E 56
Koyiu, *tn., China,* 23 02N 112 28E 56
Kozhikode see Calicut
Kra, Isthmus of, *Thai.,* 11 00N 98 00E 55
Kragujevac, *tn., Yug.,* 44 01N 20 55E 46
Krakatau, I., *Indon.,* 6 10S 105 20E 55
Kramatorsk, *tn., USSR,* 48 43N 37 33E 50
Kramfors, *tn., Swed.,* 62 55N 17 50E 43
Krasnodar, *tn., USSR,* 45 02N 39 00E 50
Krasnokamsk, *tn., USSR,* 58 05N 55 49E 51
Krasnoturinsk, *tn., USSR,* 59 46N 60 10E 51
Krasnovodsk, *tn., USSR,* 40 01N 53 00E 51
Krasnoyarsk, *tn., USSR,* 56 05N 92 46E 53
Krasnyy Luch, *tn., USSR,* 48 10N 39 00E 50
Krasnyy Lugh, *tn., USSR,* 48 14N 38 46E 47
Krefeld, *tn., W. Ger.,* 51 20N 6 32E 39
Kremenchug, *tn., USSR,* 49 03N 33 25E 50
Krishna, *R., India,* 17 00N 77 00E 54
Kristiansand, *tn., Nor.,* 58 08N 8 01E 42
Kristianstad, *tn., Swed.,* 56 02N 14 10E 42
Kristiansund, *tn., Nor.,* 63 06N 7 58E 43
Krivoy Rog, *tn., USSR,* 47 55N 33 24E 50
Kronshtadt, *tn., USSR,* 60 00N 29 40E 42
Kropotkin, *tn., USSR,* 45 25N 40 35E 51
Kruger Nat. Park, *Rep. S. Afr.,* 24 00S 31 40E . . . 67
Krugersdorp, *tn., Rep. S. Afr.,* 26 06S 27 46E . . . 67
Krung Thep see Bangkok
Kruševac, *tn., Yug.,* 43 34N 21 20E 46
Krymsk, *tn., USSR,* 44 56N 38 00E 47
Ksar-el-Kebir, *tn., Mor.,* 35 04N 5 56W 48
Kuala Lumpur, *tn., Malay.,* 3 08N 101 42E 55
Kualøy, I., *Nor.,* 69 40N 18 30E 43
Kuban, *R., USSR,* 45 16N 41 19E 51
Kucenangen, *fd., Nor.,* 70 15N 20 58E 43
Kuching, *tn., Sar., Malay.,* 1 32N 110 20E 55
Kudymkar, *tn., USSR,* 59 01N 54 40E 51
Kufra Oasis, *Libya,* 24 00N 23 00E 49
Kuldja see Ining
Kuma, *R., USSR,* 45 04N 45 39E 51
Kumamoto, *tn., Jap.,* 32 50N 130 42E 57
Kumanovo, *tn., Yug.,* 42 07N 21 40E 46
Kumasi, *tn., Ghana,* 6 45N 1 35W 66
Kumertau, *tn., USSR,* 52 48N 55 46E 51
Kunashir I., *USSR,* 44 00N 146 00E 57
Kungchuling, *tn., China,* 43 30N 124 48E 57
Kungka Shan, *mts., China,* 29 00N 101 00E 56
Kungrad, *tn., USSR,* 43 05N 58 23E 51
Kungur, *tn., USSR,* 57 27N 56 10E 51
Kunlun Shan, *mts., China,* 36 00N 86 30E 52
Kunming, *tn., China,* 25 04N 102 41E 56
Kunsan, *tn., S. Kor.,* 35 57N 126 42E 57
Kuopio, *tn., Fin.,* 62 54N 27 40E 43
Kupang, *tn., Indon.,* 10 13S 123 38E 55
Kurashiki, *tn., Jap.,* 34 36N 133 43E 57
Kurdistan, *geog. reg., Tur.,* 37 00N 43 00E 49
Kure, *tn., Jap.,* 34 14N 132 32E 57
Kurgan, *tn., USSR,* 55 30N 65 20E 51
Kuril Is., *USSR,* 45 00N 150 00E 53
Kuril Trench, *Pac. Oc.,* 44 00N 153 00E 53
Kurland, *geog. reg., USSR,* 56 50N 21 30E 42
Kursk, *tn., USSR,* 51 45N 36 14E 50
Kurume, *tn., Jap.,* 33 20N 130 29E 57
Kushiro, *tn., Jap.,* 42 58N 144 24E 57
Kushka, *tn., USSR,* 35 18N 62 22E 51
Kustanay, *tn., USSR,* 53 15N 63 40E 51
Kütahya, *tn., Tur.,* 39 25N 29 56E 47
Kutaisi, *tn., USSR,* 42 15N 42 44E 51
Kutch, *geog. reg., India,* 22 30N 69 00E 54
Kutsing, *tn., China,* 25 29N 103 47E 56
Kuwait, *Sheikhdom, Persian Gulf,* 29 00N 47 30E . . 52
Kuwait, *tn., Kuwait,* 29 20N 48 00E 52
Kuybyshev, *tn., USSR,* 53 10N 50 10E 51
Kuybyshev Reservoir, *USSR,* 54 44N 49 02E . . . 51
Kuyto, L., *USSR,* 64 40N 31 00E 43
Kuyuan, *tn., China,* 35 56N 106 50E 56
Kvarken, *chan., Fin./Swed.,* 63 30N 20 00E 43
Kwajalein, I., *Pac. Oc.,* 9 15N 167 30E 63
Kwangchow see Canton
Kwanghan, *tn., China,* 31 00N 104 30E 56
Kwanghua, *tn., China,* 32 10N 111 50E 56
Kwangju, *tn., S. Kor.,* 35 07N 126 52E 57

Kwango, *R., Zaire,* 3 58S 16 40E 67
Kwangsi Chuang, *admin. reg., China,*
23 30N 108 55E 56
Kwangtung, *admin. reg., China,* 23 35N 114 00E . . 56
Kwangtung Peninsula, *China,* 39 00N 122 00E . . 57
Kwangyuan, *tn., China,* 32 30N 105 49E 56
Kwanhsien, *tn., China,* 30 59N 103 40E 56
Kweichow, *admin. reg., China,* 26 40N 107 00E . . 56
Kweihsien, *tn., China,* 22 59N 109 44E 56
Kweilin, *tn., China,* 25 21N 110 11E 56
Kweiting, *tn., China,* 26 30N 107 00E 56
Kweiyang, *tn., China,* 26 35N 106 40E 56
Kyakhta, *tn., USSR,* 50 30N 106 25E 53
Kyle of Lochalsh, *tn., Scot.,* 57 17N 5 43W 22
Kyoto, *tn., Jap.,* 35 02N 135 45E 57
Kyrenia, *tn., Cyprus,* 35 20N 33 20E 47
Kyrinia see Kyrenia
Kyushu, I., *Jap.,* 32 30N 131 00E 57
Kyzyl, *tn., USSR,* 51 54N 94 28E 53
Kyzyl-Kum, *des., USSR,* 43 50N 65 00E 51
Kzyl Orda, *tn., USSR,* 44 50N 65 10E 51

L

La Coruna see Corunna
La Linea, *tn., Sp.,* 36 10N 5 21W 44
La Mancha, *geog. reg., Sp.,* 39 10N 2 54W 48
La Oroya, *tn., Peru,* 11 36S 75 54W 77
La Paz, *tn., Bol.,* 16 30S 68 10W 77
La Paz, *tn., Mex.,* 24 10N 110 17W 72
La Plata, *tn., Arg.,* 34 52S 57 55W 77
La Rioja, *tn., Arg.,* 29 26S 66 50W 77
La Serena, *tn., Chile,* 29 54S 71 18W 77
La Spezia, *tn., It.,* 44 08N 9 50E 48
La Tuque, *tn., Que., Can.,* 47 26N 72 47W 73
Labe, *R., Cz.,* 50 03N 15 20E 41
(as Elbe in W. Ger.)
Labinsk, *tn., USSR,* 44 39N 40 44E 51
Labrador, *geog. reg., Newf. and Lab., Can.,*
54 00N 70 00W 71
Labrador Sea, *Green.,* 56 00N 56 00W 71
Laccadive Is., *India,* 10 00N 72 30E 54
Lachlan, *R., N.S.W., Austr.,* 34 00S 144 45E . . . 63
Ladoga, L., *USSR,* 61 15N 30 30E 50
Lae, *tn., Pap., New Guin.,* 6 45S 147 00E 63
Laesø, I., *Den.,* 57 15N 10 53E 42
Lafayette, *tn., La., USA,* 30 12N 92 01W 73
Laggan, L., *Scot.,* 56 57N 4 30W 23
Laghouat, *tn., Alg.,* 33 49N 2 55E 48
Lagos, *tn., Nig.,* 6 27N 3 28E 67
Lagunillas, *tn., Ven.,* 10 07N 71 16W 77
Lahn, *R., W. Ger.,* 50 52N 8 35E 39
Lahore, *tn., Pak.,* 31 34N 74 22E 54
Lahti, *tn., Fin.,* 61 00N 25 40E 42
Lairg, *tn., Scot.,* 58 01N 4 25W 22
Laiyang, *tn., China,* 36 58N 120 40E 57
Lake Charles, *tn., La., USA,* 30 13N 93 13W . . . 73
Lake District, *geog. reg., Eng.,* 54 45N 3 15W . . 25
Laksefjord, *fd., Nor.,* 70 58N 26 58E 43
Lambay, I., *Rep. Ire.,* 53 29N 6 01W 24
Lambert Glacier, *Ant.,* 74 00S 70 00E 80
Lamezia Terme, *tn., It.,* 37 10N 16 08E 45
Lamia, *tn., Gr.,* 38 55N 22 26E 46
Lammermuir Hills, *Scot.,* 55 50N 2 40W 23
Lamotrek, I., *Pac. Oc.,* 7 28N 146 23E 63
Lampang, *tn., Thai.,* 18 40N 98 53E 56
Lampeter, *tn., Wales,* 52 07N 4 05W 26
Lanark, *tn., Scot.,* 55 41N 3 48W 23
Lancashire, *admin. reg., Eng.,* 53 52N 2 56W . . 25
Lancaster, *tn., Eng.,* 54 03N 2 48W 25
Lanchi, *tn., China,* 29 12N 119 27E 57
Lanchow, *tn., China,* 36 01N 103 45E 56
Land's End, *hdl., Eng.,* 50 03N 5 44W 26
Langanes, *pen., Ice.,* 66 16N 15 00W 43
Langholm, *tn., Scot.,* 55 09N 3 00W 23
Langjökull, *ice-cap, Ice.,* 64 43N 20 30W 43
Langøya, I., *Nor.,* 68 45N 15 00E 43
Langreo, *tn., Sp.,* 43 20N 5 48W 44
Languedoc, *geog. reg., Fr.,* 43 58N 3 22E 44
Lansing, *tn., Mich., USA,* 42 44N 85 34W 73
Lantsang Kiang, *R., China,* 31 00N 97 00E 55
Laoag, *tn., Phil.,* 18 14N 120 36E 55
Laoha Ho, *R., China,* 43 00N 120 00E 57
Laois, *admin. reg., Rep. Ire.,* 52 54N 7 32W . . . 24
Laon, *tn., Fr.,* 49 34N 3 37E 39
Laos, *Rep., Asia,* 19 00N 103 30E 55
Lapland, *geog. reg., N. Scandinavia,*
66 30N 20 05E 43
Lappajärvi, L., *Fin.,* 63 13N 23 40E 43
Lappeenranta, *tn., Fin.,* 61 04N 28 15E 42
Laptev Sea, *Arctic Oc.,* 76 00N 125 00E 53
L'Aquila, *tn., It.,* 42 22N 13 22E 45
Larache, *tn., Mor.,* 35 12N 6 10W 48
Laramie, *tn., Wyo., USA,* 41 20N 105 38W 72
Laramie Mts., *Wyo., USA,* 42 00N 105 30W . . . 72
Laredo, *tn., Tex., USA,* 27 32N 99 22W 72
Largeau, *tn., Chad,* 17 58N 19 06E 67
Largs, *tn., Scot.,* 55 48N 4 52W 23
Lárisa, *tn., Gr.,* 39 38N 22 25E 46
Larissa see Lárisa

Larnaca, tn., Cyprus, 34 54N 33 39E 47
Larne, tn., N. Ire., 54 50N 5 48W 24
Larsen Ice Shelf, Ant., 68 00S 63 00W 80
Larvik, tn., Nor., 59 04N 10 02E 42
Las Cruces, tn., N. Mex., USA; 32 18N 106 47W . . . 72
Las Palmas, tn., Can. Is., 28 08N 15 27W 66
Las Vegas, tn., Nev., USA, 36 10N 115 10W 72
Lashio, tn., Burma, 22 58N 97 48E 56
Lassen Peak, Calif., 40 30N 121 30W 72
Lassiter Ice Shelf, Ant., 78 00S 63 00W 80
Latakia, tn., Syria, 35 31N 35 47E 49
Latina, tn., It., 41 28N 12 53E 45
Latium, geog. reg., It., 42 00N 12 30E 45
Latvia, geog. reg., USSR, 56 38N 23 42E 42
Latvian S.S.R., admin. reg., USSR, 56 45N 24 30E . . 42
Lauder, tn., Scot., 55 43N 2 45W 23
Launceston, tn., Eng., 50 38N 4 21W 26
Launceston, tn., Tas., Austr., 41 25S 147 07E 63
Lausanne, tn., Switz., 46 32N 6 39E 45
Laval, tn., Fr., 48 04N 0 45W 44
Laval, tn., Que., Can., 45 34N 73 40W 73
Lawton, tn., Okla., USA, 34 36N 98 25W 72
le Mans, tn., Fr., 48 00N 0 12E 44
Leatherhead, tn., Eng., 51 18N 0 20W 27
Lebanon, Rep., Asia, 36 00N 33 50E 49
Lecce, tn., It., 40 21N 18 11E 45
Leeds, tn., Eng., 53 50N 1 35W 25
Leek, tn., Eng., 53 06N 2 01W 25
Leer, tn., W. Ger., 53 14N 7 27E 39
Leeuwarden, tn., Neth., 53 12N 5 48E 39
Leeuwin, Cape, hdl., W. Austr., 34 24S 115 09E . . . 62
Legaspi, tn., Phil., 13 10N 123 45E 55
Leghorn see Livorno
Legnica, tn., Pol., 51 12N 16 10E 41
Leicester, tn., Eng., 52 38N 1 05W 27
Leicestershire, admin. reg., Eng., 52 40N 1 15W . . . 27
Leiden, tn., Neth., 52 10N 4 30E 39
Leigh, tn., Eng., 53 30N 2 33W 26
Leigh Eccles, tn., Eng., 53 30N 2 33W 25
Leighton Buzzard, tn., Eng., 51 55N 0 40W 27
Leinster, geog. reg., Rep. Ire., 53 00N 7 10W 40
Leipzig, tn., E. Ger., 51 20N 12 20E 41
Leith, tn., Scot., 55 59N 3 10W 23
Leitrim, admin. reg., Rep. Ire., 54 08N 8 00W 24
Leixlip, tn., Rep. Ire., 53 22N 6 30W 24
Lek, R., Neth., 51 56N 4 50E 39
Lemnos, I., Gr., 39 57N 24 50E 46
Lena, R., USSR, 64 30N 127 00E 53
Lenghu, tn., China, 38 50N 93 30E 56
Lenin Canal, USSR, 60 35N 36 55E 50
Leninabad, tn., USSR, 40 14N 69 40E 51
Leninakan, R., USSR, 40 47N 43 49E 51
Leningrad, tn., USSR, 59 55N 30 25E 42
Lens, tn., Fr., 50 26N 2 50E 39
Lensk, tn., USSR, 60 48N 114 55E 53
Leoben, tn., Aust., 47 23N 15 06E 45
Leominster, tn., Eng., 52 14N 2 45W 26
León, geog. reg., Sp., 41 40N 5 55W 44
León, tn., Mex., 21 10N 101 42W 71
León, tn., Nic., 12 24N 86 52W 71
León, tn., Sp., 42 35N 5 34W 44
Leonora, tn., W. Austr., 28 54S 121 20E 62
Léopold II, L. see Mai Ndombe, L.
Léopoldville see Kinshasa
Leptis Magna, hist. site, Libya, 32 59N 14 15E . . . 48
Lérida, tn., Sp., 41 37N 0 38E 44
Lerwick, tn., Scot., 60 09N 1 09W 22
Les Landes, geog. reg., Fr., 44 20N 1 00W 44
Lesbos, I., Gr., 39 00N 26 20E 46
Leskovac, tn., Yug., 43 00N 21 57E 46
Lesnoy, tn., Murmansk, USSR, 66 40N 34 20E . . . 43
Lesotho, Kingd./comm. nat., Afr., 30 00S 26 00E . . . 67
Lesozavodsk, tn., USSR, 45 30N 133 29E 57
Lesser Antilles, Is., W.I., 12 30N 61 00W 77
Lesser Sunda Is., Indon., 9 30S 120 00E 55
Letchworth, tn., Eng., 51 58N 0 14W 27
Lethbridge, tn., Alta., Can., 49 43N 112 48W 72
Leticia, tn., Col., 4 00S 70 00W 77
Letterkenny, tn., Rep. Ire., 54 57N 7 44W 24
Leuven, tn., Belg., 50 53N 4 42E 39
Leven, L., Scot., 56 12N 3 22W 23
Leverkusen, tn., W. Ger., 51 02N 6 59E 39
Lévis, tn., Que., Can., 46 47N 71 12W 73
Lewes, tn., Eng., 50 52N 0 01E 27
Lewis, I., Scot., 58 10N 6 40W 22
Lewis, Butt of, hdl., Scot., 58 30N 6 12W 22
Lewiston, tn., Idaho, USA, 46 25N 117 00W 72
Lexington, tn., Ky., USA, 38 02N 84 30W 73
Leyland, tn., Eng., 53 42N 2 42W 25
Leyte, I., Phil., 11 00N 125 00E 55
Lgov, tn., USSR, 51 41N 35 16E 50
Lhasa, tn., Tibet, 29 41N 91 10E 55
Liao Ho, R., China, 42 20N 123 20E 57
Liaocheng, tn., China, 36 29N 115 55E 56
Liaoning, admin. reg., China, 41 40N 122 30E 57
Liaotung Bay, China, 40 00N 120 45E 57
Liaoyuan, tn., China, 42 53N 125 10E 57
Liard, R., N.W. Terrs./Yukon/B.C., Can., 59 00N 125 00W 71
Liberec, tn., Cz., 50 48N 15 05E 41
Liberia, Rep., Afr., 6 30N 9 30W 66
Libreville, tn., Gabon, 0 30N 9 25E 67
Libya, Rep., Afr., 27 35N 25 00E 48
Libyan Desert, Eg./Libya, 27 35N 25 00E 49
Lichfield, tn., Eng., 52 42N 1 48W 27
Lichinga, tn., Mozam., 13 12S 35 22E 67
Lida, tn., USSR, 53 50N 25 19E 42
Liechtenstein, Principality, Eur., 47 08N 9 35E 45
Liège, tn., Belg., 50 38N 5 35E 39
Lienyunkang, tn., China, 34 42N 119 28E 57
Liepāja, tn., USSR, 56 30N 21 00E 42

Liévin, tn., Fr., 50 25N 2 48E 39
Liffey, R., Rep. Ire., 53 21N 6 20W 24
Lifford, tn., Rep. Ire., 54 50N 7 29W 24
Liguria, geog. reg., It., 44 30N 9 00E 45
Ligurian Sea, It/Corsica, 43 20N 9 00E 45
Likasi, tn., Zaire, 10 58S 26 47E 67
Likiang, tn., China, 26 50N 100 15E 56
Lille, tn., Fr., 50 39N 3 05E 39
Lillehammer, tn., Nor., 61 06N 10 27E 42
Lilongwe, tn., Mal., 13 58S 33 49E 67
Lima, tn., Peru, 12 06S 77 03W 77
Limassol, tn., Cyprus, 34 40N 33 03E 47
Limavady, tn., N. Ire., 55 03N 6 57W 24
Limbe, tn., Mal., 15 50S 35 03E 67
Limerick, tn., Rep. Ire., 52 40N 8 38W 40
Limfjord, fd., Den., 56 52N 9 00E 42
Limoges, tn., Fr., 45 50N 1 15E 44
Limousin, geog. reg., Fr., 46 00N 1 00E 44
Limpopo, R., Moz., 24 15S 32 45E 67
Linares, tn., Mex., 24 54N 99 38W 72
Linares, tn., Sp., 38 05N 3 38W 44
Lincoln, tn., Eng., 53 14N 0 33W 25
Lincoln, tn., Nebr., USA, 40 49N 96 41W 72
Lincoln Wolds, hs., Eng., 53 20N 0 05W 25
Lincolnshire, admin. reg., Eng., 53 06N 0 38W 25
Lindesnes, hdl., Nor., 58 00N 7 05E 42
Lindisfarne see Holy I.
Linfen, tn., China, 36 08N 111 34E 56
Lingling, tn., China, 26 15N 111 33E 56
Linhai, tn., China, 28 50N 121 08E 57
Lini, tn., China, 35 10N 118 18E 56
Linköping, tn., Swed., 58 25N 15 35E 42
Linlithgow, tn., Scot., 55 59N 3 37W 23
Linnhe, L., Scot., 56 36N 5 25W 23
Linsia, tn., China, 35 31N 103 08E 56
Lintsing, tn., China, 36 51N 115 42E 56
Linz, tn., Aust., 48 19N 14 18E 45
Linz, tn., W. Ger., 50 34N 7 18E 48
Lions, Gulf of, Fr., 43 00N 4 00E 44
Lipari Is., It., 38 40N 15 00E 45
Lipetsk, tn., USSR, 52 37N 39 36E 50
Lippe, R., W. Ger., 51 40N 8 15E 39
Lisboa see Lisbon
Lisbon, tn., Port., 38 44N 9 08W 44
Lisburn, tn., N. Ire., 54 31N 6 03W 24
Lishui, tn., China, 28 30N 119 59E 57
Lisichansk, tn., USSR, 48 53N 38 25E 50
Lisieux, tn., Fr., 49 09N 0 14E 39
Liskeard, tn., Eng., 50 28N 4 28W 26
Lismore, I., Scot., 56 30N 5 30W 23
Litang, tn., China, 23 06N 109 02E 56
Lithuania, geog. reg., USSR, 55 40N 22 10E 42
Lithuanian S.S.R., admin. reg., USSR, 55 30N 24 00E 42
Little Belt, str., Den., 55 08N 9 55E 42
Little Minch, sd., Scot., 57 35N 6 45W 22
Little Rock, tn., Ark., USA, 34 42N 92 17W 73
Littlehampton, tn., Eng., 50 48N 0 33W 27
Liuan, tn., China, 31 48N 116 30E 56
Liuchow, tn., China, 24 17N 109 15E 56
Liverpool, tn., Eng., 53 25N 2 55W 25
Livingston, tn., Scot., 55 51N 3 31W 23
Livingstone, Zam., see Maramba
Livonia, geog. reg., USSR, 57 30N 25 00E 42
Livorno, tn., It., 43 33N 10 18E 45
Lizard Point, hdl., Eng., 49 56N 5 13W 26
Lizard, The, pen., Eng., 50 00N 5 20W 26
Ljubljana, tn., Yug., 46 04N 14 30E 46
Ljusnan, R., Swed., 62 10N 15 05E 42
Llallagua, tn., Bol., 17 41S 66 32W 77
Llandovery, tn., Wales, 51 59N 3 48W 26
Llandrindod Wells, tn., Wales, 52 15N 3 23W 26
Llandudno, tn., Wales, 53 19N 3 49W 26
Llanelli, tn., Wales, 51 42N 4 10W 26
Llanfairfechan, tn., Wales, 53 15N 3 58W 26
Llangefni, tn., Wales, 53 16N 4 18W 26
Llangollen, tn., Wales, 52 58N 3 10W 26
Llanidloes, tn., Wales, 52 27N 3 32W 26
Llano Estacado, plat., N. Mex./Tex., USA, 34 00N 103 00W 72
Llanos, geog. reg., Col./Ven., 3 25N 71 35W 77
Llanrwst, tn., Wales, 53 08N 3 48W 26
Lleyn, pen., Wales, 52 55N 4 35W 26
Lliang, tn., China, 24 53N 103 07E 56
Llullaillaco, Mt., vol., Arg., 24 43S 68 30W 77
Lobito, tn., Ang., 12 20S 13 34E 67
Lochaber, geog. reg., Scot., 56 55N 5 00W 23
Lochboisdale, tn., Scot., 57 09N 7 19W 22
Lochinver, tn., Scot., 58 09N 5 15W 22
Lochmaddy, tn., Scot., 57 36N 7 10W 22
Lochnagar, mt., Scot., 56 57N 3 14W 23
Lochy, L., Scot., 56 58N 4 55W 23
Lockerbie, tn., Scot., 55 07N 3 22W 23
Łódź, tn., Pol., 51 49N 19 28E 41
Lofoten Is., Nor., 68 20N 14 00E 43
Logan, tn., Utah, USA, 41 45N 111 50W 72
Logan, Mount, Yukon, Can., 60 31N 140 22W 71
Logroño, tn., Sp., 42 28N 2 25W 44
Loho, tn., China, 33 42N 114 09E 56
Loibl Pass, Aust./Yug., 46 25N 14 17E 46
Loikaw, tn., Burma, 19 40N 97 17E 56
Loire, R., Fr., 47 25N 0 20W 44
Lolland, I., Den., 54 45N 11 30E 42
Lombardy, geog. reg., It., 45 35N 9 45E 45
Lombok, I., Indon., 8 35S 116 20E 55
Lomé, tn., Togo, 6 10N 1 21E 66
Lomond, L., Scot., 56 08N 4 38W 23
Lomonosov, tn., USSR, 59 50N 29 48E 42
Lomonosov Ridge, Arctic Oc., 89 30N 115 00W . . . 80
London, tn., Eng., 51 30N 0 10W 27
London, tn., Ont., Can., 42 58N 91 15W 73

Londonderry, tn., N. Ire., 55 00N 7 19W 24
Londonderry, Cape, hdl., W. Austr., 13 45S 126 56E 62
Londrina, tn., Braz., 23 18S 51 13W 77
Long Beach, tn., Calif., USA, 33 47N 118 15W . . . 72
Long Eaton, tn., Eng., 52 54N 1 15W 25
Long I., The Bahamas, 23 20N 75 10W 73
Long I., N.Y., USA, 40 50N 73 20W 73
Long, L., Scot., 56 04N 4 50W 23
Longford, admin. reg., Rep. Ire., 53 43N 7 43W . . . 24
Longford, tn., Rep. Ire., 53 04N 7 44E 24
Longreach, tn., Queensl., Austr., 23 30S 144 15E . . 63
Longs Peak, mt., Colo., USA, 40 16N 105 37W . . . 72
Longwy, tn., Fr., 49 32N 5 46E 39
Looe, tn., Eng., 50 21N 4 26W 26
Lop Nor, L., China, 40 20N 90 10E 56
Lopez, C., hdl., Gabon, 0 36S 8 45E 67
Lorca, tn., Sp., 37 40N 1 41W 44
Lord Howe I., Pac. Oc., 31 28S 159 09E 63
Lorian, tn., Ohio, USA, 41 28N 82 11W 73
Lorient, tn., Fr., 47 45N 3 21W 44
Lorn, geog. reg., Scot., 56 20N 5 30W 23
Lorn, Firth of, Scot., 56 20N 5 40W 23
Lorraine, geog. reg., Fr., 49 00N 6 00E 45
Los Angeles, tn., Calif., USA, 34 00N 119 15W . . . 72
Los Mochis, tn., Mex., 25 48N 109 00W 72
Loshan, tn., China, 29 34N 103 42E 56
Lossiemouth, tn., Scot., 57 43N 3 18W 22
Lot, R., Fr., 44 27N 0 38E 44
Lothian, admin. reg., Scot., 55 48N 3 19W 23
Lotung, tn., Taiwan, 24 40N 121 45E 57
Loughborough, tn., Eng., 52 47N 1 11W 27
Louisiana, admin. reg., USA, 30 50N 92 00W 73
Louisville, tn., Ky., USA, 38 13N 85 45W 73
Loukhi, tn., USSR, 66 05N 33 04E 43
Lourenço Marques see Maputo
Louth, admin. reg., Rep. Ire., 53 50N 6 35W 24
Louth, tn., Eng., 53 22N 0 01W 25
Lower Saxony, admin. reg., W. Ger., 52 45N 9 00E 41
Lower Tunguska, R., USSR, 64 20N 93 00E 53
Lowestoft, tn., Eng., 52 29N 1 45E 27
Loyalty Is., Pac. Oc., 21 00S 167 30E 63
Loyang, tn., China, 34 47N 112 26E 56
Lualaba, R., Zaire, 1 00S 25 56E 67
Luanda, tn., Ang., 8 50S 13 15E 67
Luang Prabang, tn., Laos, 19 53N 102 10E 55
Luanshya, tn., Zam., 13 09S 28 24E 67
Lubango, tn., Ang., 14 55S 13 30E 67
Lubbock, tn., Tex., USA, 33 35N 101 53W 72
Lübeck, tn., W. Ger., 53 52N 10 40E 41
Lublin, tn., Pol., 51 18N 22 31E 41
Lubumbashi, tn., Zaire, 11 32S 27 28E 67
Lucan, tn., Rep. Ire., 53 22N 6 27W 24
Lucca, tn., It., 43 50N 10 30E 45
Luce Bay, Scot., 54 45N 4 48W 23
Lucerne, tn., Switz., 47 03N 8 17E 45
Luchou see Luchow
Luchow, tn., China, 28 55N 105 25E 56
Lucknow, tn., India, 26 50N 80 54E 54
Lüdenscheid, tn., W. Ger., 51 13N 7 38E 39
Lüderitz, tn., S.W. Afr. (Nam.), 26 38S 15 10E . . . 67
Ludhiana, tn., India, 30 56N 75 52E 54
Ludlow, tn., Eng., 52 22N 2 43W 26
Ludwigsburg, tn., W. Ger., 48 54N 9 12E 39
Ludwigshafen, tn., W. Ger., 49 29N 8 27E 39
Luga, R., USSR, 59 12N 29 05E 42
Luga, tn., USSR, 58 42N 29 49E 42
Lugano, tn., Switz., 46 01N 8 57E 45
Lugansk see Voroshilovgrad
Lugo, tn., Sp., 43 00N 7 33W 44
Luichow Peninsula, China, 20 30N 110 00E 56
Luing, I., Scot., 56 13N 5 39W 23
Luleå, tn., Swed., 65 35N 22 10E 43
Luleälven, R., Swed., 66 30N 20 50E 43
Luliang Shan, mts., China, 38 00N 111 00E 56
Luluabourg see Kananga
Lulworth Cove, b., Eng., 50 37N 2 15W 27
Lund, tn., Swed., 55 42N 13 10E 42
Lundy I., Eng., 51 11N 4 40W 26
Lune, R., Eng., 54 00N 2 51W 25
Lüneburg, tn., W. Ger., 53 15N 10 24E 41
Lüneburg Heath, geog. reg., W. Ger., 53 00N 10 00E 39
Lünen, tn., W. Ger., 51 37N 7 31E 39
Lungching, tn., China, 42 45N 129 25E 57
Lungyen, tn., China, 25 10N 117 00E 56
Lurgan, tn., N. Ire., 54 28N 6 20W 24
Lusaka, tn., Zam., 15 26S 28 20E 67
Lushuiho, tn., China, 42 30N 127 80E 57
Lüshun, tn., China, 38 46N 121 15E 57
Luso, tn., Ang., 11 48S 19 55E 67
Lüta, tn., China, 39 00N 121 31E 57
Luton, tn., Eng., 51 53N 0 25W 27
Lutsk, tn., USSR, 50 42N 25 15E 50
Luxembourg, Grand Duchy, Eur., 49 45N 5 45E . . . 39
Luxembourg, tn., Lux., 49 37N 6 08E 39
Luxor, tn., Eg., 25 41N 32 24E 49
Luzern see Lucerne
Luzon, I., Phil., 16 30N 121 30E 55
Luzon Strait, Phil., 20 30N 120 00E 55
Lvov, tn., USSR, 49 50N 24 00E 50
Lyallpur, see Faisalabad
Lycksele, tn., Swed., 64 34N 18 40E 43
Lyme Bay, Eng., 50 36N 2 55W 26
Lyme Regis, tn., Eng., 50 44N 2 57W 26
Lymington, tn., Eng., 50 46N 1 33W 27
Lyngen, fd., Nor., 70 02N 20 30E 43
Lynn Lake, tn., Man., Can., 56 51N 101 01W 71
Lynton, tn., Eng., 51 15N 3 50W 26
Lyon, tn., Fr., 45 46N 4 50E 45

Lyons see Lyon
Lys, R., Fr., 50 35N 2 30E 39
Lyso Gory, mts., Pol., 50 58N 20 39E 41
Lysva, tn., USSR, 58 07N 57 49E 51
Lytham St. Anne's, tn., Eng., 53 45N 3 01W 25

M

Maanshan, tn., China, 31 49N 118 32E 57
Maas, R., Neth., 51 48N 5 30E 39
(as Meuse in Belg./Fr.)
Maastricht, tn., Neth., 50 51N 5 42E 39
Mablethorpe, tn., Eng., 53 21N 0 15E 25
Macao, Port. dep. terr., Asia, 22 16N 113 35E . . . 56
Macao, tn., China, 22 13N 113 36E 56
Macapá, tn., Braz., 0 01N 51 01W 77
Macclesfield, tn., Eng., 53 16N 2 07W 25
McDonald Is., Austr. terr., Indian Oc., 54 00S 73 00E. . . 80
Macdonnell Ranges, hs., N. Terr., Austr.,
23 40S 133 00E 62
Macedonia, admin. reg., Yug., 43 00N 21 00E 46
Macedonia, geog. reg., Yug., 42 39N 22 00E 46
Maceió, tn., Braz., 9 40S 35 44W 77
Machu Picchu, hist. site, Peru, 13 08S 72 30W . . . 77
Machynlleth, tn., Wales, 52 35N 3 51W 26
Macias Nguema I., Equ. Guin., 3 30N 8 40E 67
Mackay, L., N. Terr./W. Austr., 22 40S 128 35E . . . 62
Mackay, tn., Queensl., Austr., 21 10S 149 10E . . . 63
Mackenzie, R., N.W. Terrs., Can., 66 30N 130 00W . . . 71
Mackenzie Mts., Yukon/N.W. Terrs., Can.,
64 00N 134 00W 71
McKinley, Mount, mt., Alaska, USA, 63 02N 151 01W . 70
McMurdo Sound, Ant., 77 00S 170 00E 80
McMurray, tn., Alta., USA, 56 41N 111 23W 71
Mâcon, tn., Fr., 46 18N 4 50E 45
Macon, tn., Ga., USA, 32 49N 83 37W 73
MacRobertson Coast, Ant., 68 30S 63 00E 80
Madagascar, I., Rep., Afr., 21 00S 46 00E. 67
Madang, tn., Pap. New Guin., 5 14S ,145 45E 63
Madeira, I., Port. terr., Atlan. Oc., 32 45N 17 00W . . 66
Madeira, R., Braz., 5 30S 61 20W 77
Madison, tn., Wis., USA, 43 04N 89 22W 73
Madiun, tn., Indon., 7 37S 111 33E 55
Madras, tn., India, 13 05N 80 18E 54
Madrid, tn., Sp., 40 25N 3 43W 44
Madurai, tn., India, 9 55N 78 07E 54
Mae Sot, tn., Thai., 16 43N 98 34E 56
Maebashi, tn., Jap., 36 24N 139 04E 57
Maes Howe, hist. site, Scot., 59 02N 3 10W 22
Maesteg, tn., Wales, 51 36N 3 40W 26
Magadan, tn., USSR, 59 38N 150 50E 53
Magdalena, R., Col., 9 00N 74 20W 77
Magdeburg, tn., E. Ger., 52 08N 11 37E 41
Magellan, Strait of, S. Amer., 53 30S 75 00W . . . 77
Magerøya, I., Nor., 71 00N 25 40E 43
Maghera, tn., N. Irel., 54 51N 6 40W 24
Magherafelt, tn., N. Ire., 54 45N 6 36W 24
Magnitogorsk, tn., USSR, 53 28N 59 06E 51
Mahon, tn., Minorca, 39 54N 4 15E 44
Mai Ndombe, L., Zaire, 2 00S 18 20E 67
Maidenhead, tn., Eng., 51 32N 0 44W 27
Maidstone, tn., Eng., 51 17N 0 32E 27
Maiduguri, tn., Nig., 11 53N 13 16E 67
Main, R., W. Ger., 50 13N 11 00E 41
Maine, admin. reg., USA, 45 20N 69 00W 73
Mainland Orkney, I., Scot., 59 00N 3 00W 22
Mainland, Shetland, I., Scot., 60 15N 1 22W 22
Mainz, tn., W. Ger., 50 00N 8 16E 39
Maitland, tn., N.S.W., Austr., 32 33S 151 33E . . . 63
Maizuru, tn., Jap., 35 30N 135 20E 57
Majorca, I., Balearic Is., Sp., 39 30N 3 00E 44
Majunga, tn., Madag., 15 40S 46 20E 67
Majuro, I., Pac. Oc., 7 05N 171 08E 63
Makarikari Pan, Salt Pan, Bots., 20 40S 25 30E . . . 67
Makassar see Udjung Pandang
Makassar, Strait of, Indon., 1 00S 118 20E 55
Makeyevka, tn., USSR, 48 01N 38 00E 50
Makhachkala, tn., USSR, 43 00N 47 30E 51
Makin, I., Pac. Oc., 3 10N 172 45E 63
Malabar Coast, India, 11 00N 75 00E 54
Malabo, tn., Macias Nguema I., 3 45N 8 48E 67
Malacca, tn., Malay., 21 14N 102 14E 55
Malacca, Strait of, Indon./Malay., 3 00N 101 00E . . 55
Málaga, tn., Sp., 36 43N 4 25W 44
Malaita I., Solomon Is., Pac. Oc., 9 00S 161 30E . . 63
Malakal, tn., Sud., 9 31N 31 40E 67
Malang, tn., Indon., 7 59S 112 45E 55
Malanje, tn., Ang., 9 36S 16 21E 67
Mälaren, L., Swed., 59 30N 17 30E 42
Malatya, tn., Tur., 38 22N 38 18E 49
Malawi, Rep., Afr., 13 00S 34 00E 67
Malawi, L., Mal., 12 00S 34 30E 67
Malaya, admin. reg., Malay., 6 00N 101 00E 55
Malaysia, East, comm. nat., Asia, 5 00N 113 00E . . 55
Malaysia, West, comm. nat., Asia, 5 00N 102 00E . . 55
Malbork, tn., Pol., 54 02N 19 01E 41
Maldives, Rep., Indian Oc., 2 00N 73 00E 54
Maldon, tn., Eng., 51 45N 0 40E 27
Male, tn., Maldives, 4 00N 73 28E 54

Malekula I., New Hebrides, Pac. Oc.,
16 30S 167 30E 63
Mali, Rep., Afr., 15 00N 5 00W 66
Malin Head, hdl., Rep. Ire., 55 23N 7 24W 24
Mallaig, tn., Scot., 57 00N 5 50W 23
Mallawi, tn., Eg., 27 44N 30 50E 49
Malmberget, tn., Swed., 67 11N 20 40E 43
Malmö, tn., Swed., 55 35N 13 00E 42
Maloelap, I., Pac. Oc., 8 45N 171 00E 63
Måløy, tn., Nor., 61 57N 5 06E 42
Malpelo I., Pac. Oc., 4 00N 81 35W 77
Malta, Rep., Eur., 35 50N 14 30E 48
Mamou, tn., Guin., 10 24N 12 05W 66
Man, tn., Ivory Coast, 7 31N 7 37W 66
Manado, tn., Indon., 1 32N 124 55E 55
Managua, tn., Nic., 12 06N 86 18W 71
Manama, tn., Bahrain, 26 12N 50 38E 52
Manass see Manassu
Manassu, tn., China, 44 20N 86 14E 52
Manaus, tn., Braz., 3 06S 60 00W 77
Mancha, La, geog. reg., Sp., 39 10N 2 54W 44
Manchester, tn., Eng., 53 30N 2 15W 25
Manchester, tn., N.H., USA, 42 59N 71 28W 73
Manchuria, admin. reg., China, 45 11N 125 00E . . . 57
Mandalay, tn., Burma, 21 57N 96 04E 55
Mandalgovi, tn., Mong., 45 40N 106 10E 56
Mangalore, tn., India, 12 54N 74 51E 54
Mangyai, tn., China, 37 52N 91 26E 56
Manila, tn., Phil., 14 37N 120 58E 55
Manipur, tn., India, 24 47N 93 55E 55
Manisa, tn., Tur., 38 36N 27 29E 47
Manitoba, admin. reg., Can., 55 30N 100 00W . . . 71
Manitoba, L., Man., Can., 50 40N 98 30W 71
Manitoulin I., Ont., Can., 45 40N 82 30W 73
Manizales, tn., Col., 5 03N 75 32W 77
Mannheim, tn., W. Ger., 49 30N 8 28E 39
Manresa, tn., Sp., 41 43N 1 50E 44
Mansfield, tn., Eng., 53 09N 1 11W 25
Mantes, tn., Fr., 48 59N 1 43E 39
Mantova see Mantua
Mantua, tn., It., 45 10N 10 47E 45
Manus I., Bismarck Arch., Pap., New Guin.,
2 00S 147 00E 63
Maoke Mts., W. Irian., Indon., 4 00S 138 00E . . . 55
Maputo, tn., Mozam., 25 58S 32 35E 67
Mar del Plata, tn., Arg., 38 04S 57 51W 77
Maracaibo, tn., Ven., 10 44N 71 37W 77
Maracay, tn., Ven., 10 20N 67 28W 77
Maradi, tn., Niger, 13 29N 7 10E 67
Marajó I., Braz., 1 00S 49 30W 77
Maramba, tn., Zam., 17 50S 25 53E 67
Maranhão, admin. reg., Braz., 5 00S 47 00W 77
Marañón, R., Peru, 4 50S 75 35W 77
Maraş, tn., Tur., 37 34N 36 54E 47
Marbella, tn., Sp., 36 31N 4 53W 44
Marburg, tn., W. Ger., 50 49N 8 36E 39
March, tn., Eng., 52 33N 0 06E 27
Marches, The, geog. reg., It., 43 22N 13 10E . . . 45
Maree, L., Scot., 57 40N 5 30W 22
Marganets, tn., USSR, 47 35N 34 37E 47
Margate, tn., Eng., 51 24N 1 24E 27
Mariana Is., Pac. Oc., 15 00N 146 00E 63
Mariana Trench, Pac. Oc., 13 00N 145 00E 63
Marianao, tn., Cuba, 23 05N 82 29W 73
Maribor, tn., Yug., 46 35N 15 40E 46
Mariehamn, tn., Fin., 60 05N 19 55E 42
Maritsa, R., Bulg., 42 15N 24 00E 46
Market Drayton, tn., Eng., 52 54N 2 29W 26
Market Harborough, tn., Eng., 52 29N 0 55W . . . 27
Market Rasen, tn., Eng., 53 24N 0 21W 25
Marl, tn., W. Ger., 51 38N 7 06E 39
Marlborough, tn., Eng., 51 26N 1 43W 27
Marmara, Sea of, Tur., 40 45N 28 15E 47
Marne, R., Fr., 48 53N 3 25E 44
Maroua, tn., Cam., 10 35N 14 20E 67
Marra Mts., Sud., 12 00N 21 00E 67
Marrakesh, tn., Mor., 31 49N 8 00W 48
Marsala, tn., Sicily, 37 48N 12 27E 45
Marseille, tn., Fr., 43 18N 5 22E 45
Marseilles see Marseille
Marshall Is., Pac. Oc., 11 00N 170 00E 63
Martin Vaz Is., Atlan. Oc., 20 42S 28 29W 77
Martinique, Fr. terr., Lesser Antilles,
14 40N 61 00W 77
Mary, tn., USSR, 37 42N 61 54E 51
Maryborough, tn., Queensl., Austr.,
25 32S 152 36E 63
Maryland, admin. reg., USA, 39 10N 76 40W . . . 73
Maryport, tn., Eng., 54 43N 3 30W 25
Masai Steppe, plat., Tanz., 4 00S 36 30E 67
Masan, tn., S. Kor., 35 10N 128 35E 57
Mascara, tn., Alg., 35 20N 0 09E 48
Maseru, tn., Lsotho, 29 19S 27 29E 67
Mashhad, tn., Iran, 36 16N 59 34E 52
Massa, tn., It., 44 02N 10 09E 45
Massachusetts, admin. reg., USA, 42 25N 72 00W . 73
Massawa, tn., Ethiopia, 15 37N 39 28E 67
Masurian Lakes, Pol., 53 51N 21 50E 41
Matadi, tn., Zaire, 5 50S 13 32E 67
Matamoros, tn., Mex., 25 50N 97 31W 71
Matanzas, tn., Cuba, 23 04N 81 35W 73
Matapan, C., hdl., Gr., 36 23N 22 29E 46
Mataram, tn., Indon., 8 36S 116 07E 55
Mataro, tn., Sp., 41 32N 2 27E 44
Matehuala, tn., Mex., 23 40N 100 40W 72
Matera, tn., It., 40 40N 16 37E 45
Matlock, tn., Eng., 53 08N 1 32W 25
Mato Grosso, admin. reg., Braz., 14 00S 55 00W . . 77
Mato Grosso, geog. reg., Braz., 15 00S 54 00W . . 77
Matozinhos, tn., Port., 41 11N 8 42W 44
Matrûh, tn., Eg., 31 21N 27 15E 49

Matsu I., China, 26 10N 119 59E 57
Matsue, tn., Jap., 35 29N 133 04E 57
Matsuyama, tn., Jap., 33 50N 132 47E 57
Maubeuge, tn., Fr., 50 17N 3 58E 39
Mauritania, Rep., Afr., 20 50N 10 00W 66
Mauritius, I., comm. nat., Indian Oc.,
20 00S 57 00E 67
Mawson Station, Austr. base, Ant., 67 30S 65 00E . 80
Maybole, tn., Scot., 55 21N 4 41W 23
Maykop, tn., USSR, 44 37N 40 48E 51
Maymyo, tn., Burma, 22 05N 96 33E 56
Mazar-i-Sharif, tn., Afghan., 36 43N 67 05E 52
Mazatlán, tn., Mex., 23 10N 106 30W 71
Mbabane, tn., Swazi., 26 20S 31 08E 67
Mbandaka, tn., Zaire, 0 03N 18 28E 67
Mbeya, tn., Tanz., 8 54S 33 29E 67
Mbuji-Mayi, tn., Zaire, 6 10S 23 39E 67
Mead, L., Ariz./Nev., USA, 36 10N 114 10W 72
Mearns, The, geog. reg., Scot., 56 52N 2 46W . . . 23
Meath, admin. reg., Rep. Ire., 53 60N 6 90W . . . 24
Meaux, tn., Fr., 48 58N 2 54E 39
Mecca, tn., Si. Arab., 21 26N 39 49E 52
Mechelen, tn., Belg., 51 02N 4 29E 39
Mecklenburg, geog. reg., E. Ger., 53 30N 11 40E . 41
Medan, tn., Indon., 3 35N 98 39E 55
Médéa, tn., Alg., 36 15N 2 48E 48
Medellin, tn., Col., 6 15N 75 36W 77
Medenine, tn., Tun., 33 24N 10 25E 48
Medford, tn., Oreg., USA, 42 20N 122 52W 72
Mediaş, tn., Rom., 46 10N 24 21E 46
Medicine Hat, tn., Alta., Can., 50 03N 110 41W . . 72
Medina, tn., Si. Arab., 24 30N 39 35E 52
Mediterranean Sea, 36 00N 14 00E 48
Mednogorsk, tn., USSR, 51 23N 57 36E 51
Medveditsa, R., USSR, 50 50N 44 00E 51
Medvezhyegorsk, tn., USSR, 62 56N 34 28N . . . 43
Medway, R., Eng., 51 12N 0 23E 27
Meekatharra, tn., W. Austr., 26 30S 118 30E . . . 62
Meerut, tn., India, 29 00N 77 42E 54
Megista I., Gr., 36 20N 29 50E 47
Meihsien, tn., China, 24 19N 116 13E 56
Meissen, tn., E. Ger., 51 10N 13 28E 41
Meknès, tn., Mor., 33 53N 5 37W 48
Mekong, R., Cambod., 12 00N 105 00E 55
Melanesia, ethnic reg. & Is., Pac. Oc.,
4 00S 155 00E 63
Melbourne, tn., Vic., Austr., 37 45S 144 58E . . . 63
Melekess, tn., USSR, 54 14N 49 37E 51
Melilla, tn., Sp., 35 20N 3 00W 48
Melitopol, tn., USSR, 46 51N 35 22E 50
Melksham, tn., Eng., 51 23N 2 09W 27
Melrose, tn., Scot., 53 36N 2 44W 23
Melton Mowbray, tn., Eng., 52 46N 0 53W 27
Melun, tn., Fr., 48 32N 2 40E 44
Melvich, tn., Scot., 58 33N 3 55W 22
Melville I., N.W. Terrs., Can., 75 30N 111 00W . . . 71
Melville Peninsula, hdl., N.W. Terrs., Can.,
68 00N 84 00W 71
Memphis, tn., Tenn., USA, 35 10N 90 00W 73
Menai Strait, Wales, 53 14N 4 10W 26
Menderes, R., Tur., 37 52N 28 45E 47
Mendip Hills, Eng., 51 17N 2 40W 26
Mendocino, Cape, hdl., Calif., USA,
40 26N 124 24W 72
Mendoza, tn., Arg., 32 48S 68 52W 77
Mengtz, tn., China, 23 20N 103 21E 56
Mentawai Is., Indon., 2 00S 99 00E 55
Menzel Bourgiba, tn., Tun., 37 10N 9 49E 48
Merano, tn., It., 46 41N 11 10E 45
Mérida, tn., Mex., 20 59N 89 39W 71
Mérida, tn., Sp., 38 55N 6 20W 44
Merrick, mt., Scot., 55 08N 4 29W 23
Merse, The, geog. reg., Scot., 55 40N 2 30W . . . 23
Merseburg, tn., E. Ger., 51 22N 12 00E 41
Mersey, R., Eng., 53 20N 2 56W 25
Merseyside, admin. reg., Eng., 53 22N 3 26W . . . 25
Mersin, tn., Tur., 36 47N 34 37E 47
Merthyr Tydfil, tn., Wales, 51 46N 3 23W 26
Mesa, tn., Ariz., USA, 33 25N 115 50W 72
Mesabi Range, mts., Minn., USA, 47 00N 92 30W . 73
Mesopotamia, geog. reg., Iraq, 34 00N 42 00E . . . 49
Messina, tn., Sicily, 38 13N 15 33E 45
Messina, Straits of, It./Sicily, 38 05N 15 35E . . . 45
Meta, R., Col., 5 30N 71 00W 77
Metz, tn., Fr., 49 07N 6 11E 45
Meuse, R., Belg., 50 32N 5 20E 39
(as Maas in Neth.)
Meuse, R., Fr., 49 15N 5 20E 45
(as Maas in Neth.)
Mexborough, tn., Eng., 53 30N 1 17W 25
Mexicali, tn., Mex., 32 36N 115 30W 72
Mexico, Rep., N. Ameri., 22 30N 105 00W 71
Mexico City, tn., Mex., 19 25N 99 10W 71
Mexico, Gulf of, Mex./USA, 27 00N 95 00W 71
Mezen, tn., USSR, 65 50N 44 20E 50
Mezhdurechenskiy, tn., USSR, 59 38N 65 48E . . 51
Miami, tn., Fla., USA, 25 45N 80 15W 73
Miass, tn., USSR, 55 00N 60 00E 51
Michigan, admin. reg., USA, 45 00N 85 00W . . . 73
Michigan, L., Can./USA, 44 00N 87 00W 73
Michurinsk, tn., USSR, 52 54N 40 30E 50
Micronesia, ethnic reg. & Is., Pac. Oc.,
7 00N 160 00E 63
Mid Glamorgan, admin. reg., Wales,
51 30N 3 40W 26
Middle America Trench, Pac. Oc., 26 00N 100 00W . 71
Middlesbrough, tn., Eng., 54 35N 1 14W 25
Middleton, tn., Eng., 53 33N 2 12W 25
Middlewich, tn., Eng., 53 11N 2 27W 25
Midland, tn., Tex., USA, 32 00N 102 09W 72
Mienyang, tn., China, 31 25N 104 45E 56

Mieres, tn., Sp., 43 15N 5 46W 44
Mikhaylovka, tn., USSR, 50 05N 43 15E 51
Mikkeli, tn., Fin., 61 44N 27 15E 43
Milan, tn., It., 45 28N 9 12E 45
Milano see Milan
Mildenhall, tn., Eng., 52 21N 0 30E 27
Mildura, tn., Vic., Austr., 34 14S 142 13E 63
Miles City, tn., Mont., USA, 46 24N 105 48W . . 72
Miletus, hist. site, Tur., 37 30N 27 18E 47
Milford Haven, est., Wales, 51 44N 5 02W 26
Milford Haven, tn., Wales, 51 44N 5 02W 26
Mili, I., Pac. Oc., 6 08N 171 59E 63
Milk, R., Can./USA, 48 30N 108 30W 72
Milos, I., Gr., 36 44N 24 25E 46
Milton Keynes, tn., Eng., 52 02N 0 42W 27
Milwaukee, tn., Wis., USA, 43 03N 87 56W . . . 73
Min Kiang, R., China, 32 00N 103 50E 56
Min Shan, mts., China, 34 00N 103 00E 56
Minas Gerais, admin. reg., Braz., 18 50S 46 00W . 77
Mindanao, I., Phil., 8 00N 125 00E 55
Minden, tn., W. Ger., 52 18N 8 54E 39
Mindoro, I., Phil., 13 00N 121 00E 55
Minehead, tn., Eng., 51 13N 3 29W 26
Mineralnyye Vody, tn., USSR, 44 14N 43 10E . . 51
Mingulay, I., Scot., 56 48N 7 37W 23
Minneapolis, tn., Minn., USA, 45 00N 93 15W . . 73
Minnesota, admin. reg., USA, 46 40N 94 00W . . 73
Miño, R., Sp., 41 58N 8 10W 44
Minorca, I., Balearic Is., Sp., 40 00N 4 00E . . . 44
Minot, tn., N. Dak., USA, 48 16N 101 19W . . . 72
Minsk, tn., USSR, 53 51N 27 30E 50
Miranda de Ebro, tn., Sp., 42 41N 2 57W 44
Mirim, L., Braz., 32 47S 52 50W 77
Mirnyy, tn., USSR, 62 30N 113 58E 53
Mirnyy, USSR base, Ant., 66 30S 98 00E 80
Mirtoan Sea, Gr., 36 40N 22 50E 46
Miskolc, tn., Hung., 48 07N 20 47E 46
Mississippi, admin. reg., USA, 33 00N 90 00W . . 73
Mississippi, R., USA, 33 23N 91 00W 73
Missouri, admin. reg., USA, 38 25N 92 30W . . . 73
Missouri, R., USA, 40 20N 95 40W 73
Missouri Coteau, hs., N. Dak., USA,
47 30N 101 15W 72
Misurata, tn., Libya, 32 24N 15 04E 48
Mitchell, Mt., N.C., USA, 35 47N 82 16W 73
Mittelland Canal, W. Ger., 52 23N 7 45E 41
Miyako Group, Is., Jap., 24 45N 125 25E 57
Miyakonojo, tn., Jap., 31 32N 131 05E 57
Miyazaki, tn., Jap., 31 56N 131 27E 57
Mizen Head, hdl., Rep. Ire., 51 27N 9 49W . . . 40
Mo i Rana, tn., Nor., 6 19N 14 10E 43
Mobile, tn., Ala., USA, 30 40N 88 05W 73
Moçâmedes, tn., Ang., 15 10S 12 10E 67
Modena, tn., It., 44 39N 10 55E 45
Modesto, tn., Calif., USA, 37 37N 121 00W . . . 72
Moers, tn., W. Ger., 51 27N 6 36E 39
Moffat, tn., Scot., 55 20N 3 27W 23
Mogadishu, tn., Somalia, 2 02N 45 21E 67
Mogilev, tn., USSR, 53 54N 30 20E 50
Mogilev Podolskiy, tn., USSR, 48 29N 27 49E . . 47
Mohammedia, tn., Mor., 33 43N 7 20W 48
Mohenjo Daro, hist. site, Pak., 27 17N 68 14E . . 54
Moidart, geog. reg., Scot., 56 47N 5 52W 23
Mojave Desert, Calif., USA, 35 00N 117 30W . . 72
Mokpo, tn., S. Kor., 34 50N 126 25E 57
Mold, tn., Wales, 53 10N 3 08W 26
Moldavia, geog. reg., Rom., 46 30N 27 00E . . . 47
Moldavian S.S.R., admin. reg., USSR,
47 00N 28 00E 47
Molde, tn., Nor., 62 44N 7 08E 43
Molfetta, tn., It., 41 12N 16 36E 45
Mollendo, tn., Peru, 17 00S 72 00W 77
Molodechno, tn., USSR, 54 16N 26 50E 42
Molodeshnaya, USSR base, Ant., 67 45S 46 00E . 80
Moluccas, Is., Indon., 0 00 127 00E 55
Mombasa, tn., Kenya, 4 04S 39 40E 67
Monach Isles, Scot., 57 32N 7 36W 22
Monaco, Principality, Eur., 43 36N 7 23E 45
Monadhliath Mts., Scot., 57 05N 4 10W 23
Monaghan, admin. reg., Rep. Ire., 54 06N 7 16W . 24
Monaghan, tn., Rep. Ire., 54 15N 6 58W 24
Monasterevin, tn., Rep. Ire., 53 08N 7 03W . . . 24
Monchegorsk, tn., USSR, 67 55N 33 01E 43
Mönchen Gladbach, tn., W. Ger., 51 12N 6 25E . 39
Monclova, tn., Mex., 26 55N 101 25W 72
Mongolia, Rep., Asia, 47 00N 103 00E 53
Mongu, tn., Zam., 15 13S 23 09E 67
Monmouth, tn., Wales, 51 50N 2 43W 26
Monravia, tn., Lib., 6 20N 10 46W 66
Mons., tn., Belg., 50 28N 3 58E 39
Mont Blanc, mt., Fr./It., 45 50N 6 52E 45
Mont-de-Marsin, tn., Fr., 43 54N 0 30W 44
Mont St Michel, I., Fr., 48 38N 1 30W 44
Montana, admin. reg., USA, 47 00N 110 00W . . 72
Montauban, tn., Fr., 44 01N 1 20E 44
Montenegro, admin. reg., Yug., 42 40N 19 20E . . 46
Monterey, tn., Calif., USA, 36 35N 121 55W . . . 72
Monterrey, tn., Mex., 25 40N 100 20W 72
Montes Claros, tn., Braz., 16 45S 43 52W 77
Montevideo, tn., Urug., 34 55S 56 10W 77
Montgomery, tn., Ala., USA, 32 22N 86 20W . . 73
Montluçon, tn., Fr., 46 20N 2 36E 44
Montpelier, tn., Vt., USA, 44 16N 72 34W 73
Montpellier, tn., Fr., 43 36N 3 53E 44
Montreal, tn., Que., Can., 45 38N 73 33W 73
Montrose, tn., Scot., 56 43N 2 29W 23
Monza, tn., It., 45 35N 9 16E 45
Moorfoot Hills, Scot., 55 44N 3 08W 23
Moose Jaw, tn., Sask., Can., 50 23N 105 35W . . 72
Moosonee, tn., Ont., Can., 51 18N 80 40W . . . 71
Mopti, tn., Mali, 14 29N 4 10W 66

Mora, tn., Swed., 61 00N 14 30E 42
Moradabad, tn., India, 28 50N 78 45E 54
Morar, L., Scot., 56 57N 5 40W 23
Morava, R., Cz., 49 50N 16 50E 41
Moray Firth, Scot., 57 50N 3 25W 22
Morecambe, tn., Eng., 54 04N 2 53W 25
Morecambe Bay, Eng., 54 07N 3 05W 25
Morelia, tn., Mex., 19 40N 101 11W 71
Morioka, tn., Jap., 39 43N 141 08E 57
Morley, tn., Eng., 53 46N 1 36W 25
Morocco, Kingd., Afr., 32 00N 5 50W 48
Moroni, tn., Madag., 11 40S 43 16E 67
Morpeth, tn., Eng., 55 10N 1 41W 25
Morris Jesup, C., hdl., Green., 83 40N 34 00W . 80
Morshansk, tn., USSR, 53 26N 41 48E 50
Morvern, geog. reg., Scot., 56 38N 5 44W 23
Moscow, tn., USSR, 55 45N 37 42E 50
Mosel R., W. Ger., 49 48N 6 45E 41
(as Moselle in Fr.)
Moselle, R., Fr., 48 10N 6 30E 45
(as Mosel in W. Ger.)
Mosjøen, tn., Nor., 65 50N 13 10E 43
Moss, tn., Nor., 59 26N 10 41E 42
Mossoro, tn., Braz., 5 10S 37 20W 77
Most, tn., Cz., 50 31N 13 39E 41
Mostaganem, tn., Alg., 35 54N 0 05E 48
Mostar, tn., Yug., 43 20N 17 50E 46
Mosul, tn., Iraq, 36 21N 43 08E 49
Motala, tn., Swed., 58 34N 15 05E 42
Motherwell, tn., Scot., 55 48N 4 00W 23
Motril, tn., Sp., 36 45N 3 31W 44
Moulmein, tn., Burma, 16 30N 97 39E 55
Moulouya, R., Mor., 34 45N 2 51W 48
Moundou, tn., Chad, 8 36N 16 02E 67
Mount Gambier, tn., S. Austr., 37 51S 140 50E . 63
Mount Isa, tn., Queensl., Austr., 20 50S 139 29E . 63
Mountain Ash, tn., Wales, 51 42N 3 24W 26
Mountmellick, tn., Rep. Ire., 53 07N 7 20W . . . 24
Mount's Bay, Eng., 50 03N 5 27W 26
Mourne Mts., N. Ire., 54 10N 6 00W 24
Moville, tn., Rep. Ire., 55 11N 7 03W 24
Mowming, tn., China, 21 50N 110 32E 56
Mozambique, Rep., Afr., 17 00S 35 00E 67
Mozambique, tn., Mozam., 15 00S 40 44E 67
Mozambique Channel, Madag./Mozam.,
17 00S 43 00E 67
Mozhga, tn., USSR, 56 25N 52 10E 51
Mtwara, tn., Tanz., 10 17S 40 11E 67
Muck, I., Scot., 56 50N 6 14W 23
Muine Bheag, tn., Rep. Ire., 52 42N 6 57W . . . 24
Mukacheve, tn., USSR, 48 26N 22 45E 50
Mukalla, tn., S. Yemen, 14 34N 49 09E 52
Mukden see Shenyang
Mulhacén, Mt., Sp., 37 04N 3 19W 44
Mulheim, tn., W. Ger., 51 25N 6 50E 39
Mulhouse, tn., Fr., 47 45N 7 21E 45
Mull, I., Scot., 56 27N 6 00W 23
Mull, Sound of, Scot., 56 30N 5 50W 23
Mullingar, tn., Rep. Ire., 53 32N 7 20W 24
Multan, tn., Pak., 30 10N 71 36E 54
München see Munich
Muncie, tn., Ind., USA, 40 11N 85 22W 73
Munich, tn., W. Ger., 48 08N 11 35E 41
Munster, geog. reg., Rep. Ire., 52 20N 8 40W . . 40
Münster, tn., W. Ger., 51 58N 7 37E 39
Muong Sing, tn., Laos, 21 12N 101 12E 56
Mur, R., Aust., 47 00N 15 23E 45
Murat, R., Tur., 39 00N 42 00E 49
Murchison Falls see Kabarega Falls
Murcia, geog. reg., Sp., 38 35N 1 50W 44
Murcia, tn., Sp., 37 59N 1 08W 44
Mures, R., Rom., 46 00N 22 00E 46
Murmansk, tn., USSR, 68 59N 33 08E 43
Murom, tn., USSR, 55 04N 22 04E 50
Muroran, tn., Jap., 42 21N 140 59E 57
Murray, R., N.S.W./S. Austr., 33 55S 140 00E . . 63
Murray Bridge, tn., S. Austr., 35 10S 139 17E . . 63
Murzuch, tn., Libya, 25 56N 13 57E 48
Musala, Mt., Bulg., 42 10N 23 35E 46
Muscat, tn., Oman, 23 37N 58 38E 52
Mutankiang, tn., China, 44 35N 129 30E 57
Mwanza, tn., Tanz., 2 30S 32 54E 67
Mweru, L., Zaire/Zam., 9 00S 28 40E 67
Mycenae, hist. site, Gr., 37 44N 22 45E 46
Myitkyina, tn., Burma, 25 24N 97 25E 55
Mýrdalsjökull, ice-cap, Ice., 63 40N 19 00W . . . 43
Mytilini, tn., Gr., 39 06N 26 34E 46
Mytishchi, tn., USSR, 55 54N 37 47E 50
Mývatn, L., Ice., 65 36N 17 00W 43
Mzuzu, tn., Mal., 11 31S 33 50E 67

N

Naas, tn., Rep. Ire., 53 13N 6 39W 24
Nabeul, tn., Tun., 36 30N 10 44E 48
Nador, tn., Mor., 35 10N 3 00W 48
Naestved, tn., Den., 55 14N 11 47E 42
Nafud, des., Si. Arab., 28 00N 41 00E 52

Nagano, tn., Jap., 36 39N 138 10E 57
Nagaoka, tn., Jap., 37 27N 138 50E 57
Nagasaki, tn., Jap., 32 45N 129 52E 57
Nagchu Dzong, tn., China, 31 22N 91 54E 56
Nagoya, tn., Jap., 35 08N 136 53E 57
Nagpur, tn., India, 21 10N 79 12E 54
Nagykanizsa, tn., Hung., 46 27N 17 00E 46
Naha, tn., Jap., 26 10N 127 40E 57
Nairn, tn., Scot., 57 35N 3 53W 22
Nairobi, tn., Kenya, 1 17S 36 50E 67
Najaf, tn., Iraq, 31 59N 44 19E 49
Najin, tn., N. Kor., 42 10N 130 20E 57
Nakhichevan, tn., USSR, 39 12N 45 24E 51
Nakhodka, tn., USSR, 42 53N 132 54E 57
Nakhon Ratchasima, tn., Thai., 15 00N 102 06E . 55
Nakhon Sawan, tn., Thai., 15 35N 100 10E . . . 55
Nakuru, tn., Kenya, 0 16S 36 04E 67
Nalayh, tn., Mong., 47 40N 107 12E 56
Nalchik, tn., USSR, 43 31N 48 38E 51
Nam Dinh, tn., Viet., 20 25N 106 12E 56
Namangan, tn., USSR, 40 59N 71 41E 51
Namcha Barwa, Mt., China, 29 38N 95 48E . . . 56
Namib Desert, S.W. Afr. (Nam.), 22 30S 15 00E . 67
Nampa, tn., Idaho, USA, 43 35N 116 34W 72
Nampo, tn., N. Kor., 38 52N 125 28E 57
Namsen, R., Nor., 64 40N 13 00E 43
Namsos, tn., Nor., 64 28N 11 30E 43
Namur, tn., Belg., 50 28N 4 52E 39
Nan Ling, mts., China, 26 00N 111 00E 56
Nan Shan, mts., China, 38 00N 98 00E 56
Nanchang, tn., China, 28 38N 115 56E 56
Nanchung, tn., China, 30 54N 106 06E 56
Nancy, tn., Fr., 48 42N 6 12E 45
Nandoma, tn., USSR, 61 35N 40 35E 50
Nanga Parbat, Mt., Kashmir, 35 10N 74 35E . . . 54
Nangchien, tn., China, 32 05N 96 25E 56
Nanking, tn., China, 32 03N 118 47E 57
Nanning, tn., China, 22 50N 108 19E 56
Nanping, tn., China, 26 40N 118 07E 56
Nantes, tn., Fr., 47 14N 1 35W 44
Nantucket I., Mass., USA, 41 16N 70 00W . . . 73
Nantung, tn., China, 32 05N 120 51E 57
Nanumea, I., Tuvalu, Pac. Oc.,
5 40S 176 10E 63
Nanyang, tn., China, 33 06N 112 31E 56
Nanyuki, tn., Kenya, 0 01N 37 05E 67
Napier, tn., N.Z., 39 29S 176 58E 63
Naples, tn., It., 40 50N 14 15E 45
Napoli see Naples
Nara, tn., Jap., 34 41N 135 49E 57
Nara, tn., Mali, 15 13N 7 20W 66
Narbonne, tn., Fr., 43 11N 3 00E 44
Nares Srait, N.W. Terrs., Can., 80 00N 70 00W . 71
Narew, R., Pol., 53 01N 21 22E 41
Narmada, R., India, 22 00N 73 00E 54
Narodnaya, Mt., USSR, 65 05N 60 00E 52
Narrogin, tn., W. Austr., 32 57S 117 07E 62
Narva, R., USSR, 59 10N 27 50E 42
Narva, tn., USSR, 59 22N 28 17E 42
Narvik, tn., Nor., 68 26N 17 25E 43
Naryan Mar, tn., USSR, 67 37N 53 02E 50
Nashville, tn., Tenn., USA, 36 10N 86 50W . . . 73
Näsijärvi, L., Fin., 61 45N 23 45E 43
Nassau, tn., The Bahamas, 25 05N 77 20W . . . 73
Nasser, L., Eg., 23 40N 32 00E 49
Nässjö, tn., Swed., 57 39N 14 40E 42
Natal, admin. reg., Rep. S. Afr., 28 30S 30 30E . 67
Natal, tn., Braz., 5 46S 35 15W 77
Natuna Is., Indon., 4 00N 108 00E 55
Nauru, I., Rep.—comm. nat., Pac. Oc.,
0 25N 166 00E 63
Navarre, geog. reg., Sp., 42 40N 1 40W 44
Navojoa, tn., Mex., 27 04N 109 28W 72
Nazas, R., Mex., 25 20N 104 04W 72
Naze, tn., Jap., 28 21N 129 30E 57
Nazilli, tn., Tur., 37 55N 28 20E 47
N'Djamena, tn., Chad, 12 10N 14 59E 67
Ndola, tn., Zamb., 13 00S 28 39E 67
Neagh, L., N. Ire., 54 40N 6 25W 24
Neath, tn., Wales, 51 40N 3 48W 26
Nebraska, admin. reg., USA, 41 30N 100 00W . . 72
Neckar, R., W. Ger., 49 30N 9 03E 39
Needles, The, hdl., Eng., 50 39N 1 34W 27
Neftekamsk, tn., USSR, 66 03N 54 12E 51
Negro, R., Braz., 0 25S 64 00W 77
Negros, I., Phil., 10 00N 123 00E 55
Neikiang, tn., China, 29 32N 105 03E 56
Neishabur, tn., Iran, 36 18N 58 51E 51
Nejd, geog. reg., Si. Arab., 23 50N 46 00E . . . 52
Nelson, R., Man., Can., 56 00N 96 30W 71
Nelson, tn., Eng., 53 51N 2 13W 25
Nelson, tn., N.Z., 41 18S 173 17E 63
Neman, R., USSR, 53 30N 25 10E 50
(see also Nemunas, R.)
Nemunas, R., USSR, 55 03N 22 00E 42
(see also Neman, R.)
Nemuro, tn., Jap., 43 32N 145 36E 57
Nene, R., Eng., 52 38N 0 07E 27
Nepal, Kingd., Asia, 28 00N 83 00E 54
Neskaupstadur, tn., Ice., 65 10N 13 43W 43
Ness, L., Scot., 57 15N 4 30W 22
Netherlands, Kingd., Eur., 52 00N 5 30E 39
Neubrandenburg, tn., E. Ger., 53 33N 13 16E . . 41
Neumünster, tn., W. Ger., 54 05N 9 59E 41
Neuquén, tn., Arg., 38 55S 68 55W 77
Neuss, tn., W. Ger., 51 12N 6 42E 39
Neustadt, tn., W. Ger., 49 21N 8 09E 39
Neuwied, tn., W. Ger., 50 26N 7 28E 39
Neva, R., USSR, 59 50N 30 30E 50
Nevada, admin. reg., USA, 39 20N 117 00W . . . 72

Nevel, *tn., USSR,* 56 00N 29 59E 42
Nevers, *tn., Fr.,* 47 00N 3 09E 44
Nevinnomyssk, *tn., USSR,* 44 38N 41 59E 51
Nevis, L., *Scot.,* 57 00N 5 43W 23
Nevşehir, *tn., Tur.,* 38 38N 34 43E 47
New Bedford, *tn., Mass., USA,* 41 38N 70 55W . . .73
New Britain, *I., Bismarck Arch., Pap. New Guin.,*
6 00S 150 00E 63
New Brunswick, *admin. reg., Can.,*
46 50N 66 30W 71
New Caledonia, *I., Pac. Oc.,* 21 00S 165 00E. 63
New Castile, *geog. reg., Sp.,* 39 45N 3 20W 44
New Cumnock, *tn., Scot.,* 55 24N 4 12W 23
New Forest, *geog. reg., Eng.,* 50 53N 1 40W 27
New Galloway, *tn., Scot.,* 55 05N 4 10W 23
New Guinea, *I., Austral./Indon.,* 5 00S 141 00E . . .63
New Hampshire, *admin. reg., USA,* 43 40N 71 40W . .73
New Haven, *tn., Conn., USA,* 41 18N 72 55W. 73
New Hebrides, *Is., Pac. Oc.,* 15 00S 168 00E 63
New Hunstanton, *tn., Eng.,* 52 56N 0 30E 27
New Ireland, *I., Bismarck Arch., Pap. New Guin.,*
3 00S 151 30E 63
New Jersey, *admin. reg., USA,* 40 00N 74 10W 73
New Mexico, *admin. reg., USA,* 34 30N 107 00W 72
New Orleans, *tn., La., USA,* 30 00N 90 03W 73
New Plymouth, *tn., N.Z.,* 39 03S 174 04E 63
New Siberian Is., *USSR,* 75 00N 140 00E 53
New South Wales, *admin. reg., Austr.,*
33 00S 146 00E 63
New York, *admin. reg., USA,* 42 40N 77 00W 73
New York, *tn., N.Y., USA,* 40 45N 74 00W 73
New Zealand, *comm. nat., Austral.,*
40 00S 175 00E 63
Newark, *tn., N.J., USA,* 40 44N 74 12W 73
Newark on Trent, *tn., Eng.,* 53 05N 0 49W 25
Newbiggin-by-the-Sea, *tn., Eng.,* 55 11N 1 30W 25
Newbury, *tn., Eng.,* 51 25N 1 20W 27
Newcastle, *tn., N.S.W., Austr.,* 32 55S 151 46E 63
Newcastle, *tn., N. Ire.,* 54 12N 5 54W 24
Newcastle-under-Lyme, *tn., Eng.,* 53 00N 2 14W 25
Newcastle upon Tyne, *tn., Eng.,* 54 59N 1 35W 25
Newchwang see Anshan
Newfoundland, *I., Newf. and Lab., Can.,*
48 30N 56 00W 71
Newfoundland and Labrador, *admin. reg., Can.,*
56 00N 62 00W 71
Newgrange, *hist. site, Rep. Ire.,* 53 42N 6 28W 24
Newhaven, *tn., Eng.,* 50 47N 0 03E 27
Newmarket, *tn., Eng.,* 52 15N 0 25E 27
Newport, *tn., Eng.,* 52 47N 2 22W 26
Newport, *tn., I.o.W., Eng.,* 50 42N 1 18W 27
Newport, *tn., Wales* 51 35N 3 00W 26
Newport News, *tn., Va., USA,* 36 59N 76 26W 73
Newquay, *tn., Eng.,* 50 25N 5 05W 26
Newry, *tn., N. Ire.,* 54 11N 6 20W 24
Newton Abbot, *tn., Eng.,* 50 32N 3 36W 26
Newton Aycliffe, *tn., Eng.,* 54 37N 1 34W 25
Newton-le-Willows, *tn., Eng.,* 53 28N 3 27W 25
Newton Stewart, *tn., Scot.,* 54 57N 4 29W 23
Newtown, *tn., Wales,* 52 32N 3 19W 26
Newtownabbey, *tn., N. Ire.,* 54 40N 5 57W 24
Newtownards, *tn., N. Ire.,* 54 36N 5 41W 24
Neyland, *tn., Wales,* 51 43N 4 57W 26
Nezhin, *tn., USSR,* 51 03N 31 54E 50
N'Gaoundéré, *tn., Cam.,* 7 20N 13 35E 67
Ngoring Nor, *L., China,* 34 50N 98 00E 56
Niagara Falls, *tn., N.Y., USA,* 43 06N 79 04W 73
Niagara Falls, *wf., Can./USA,* 43 06N 79 02W 71
Niamey, *tn., Niger,* 13 32N 2 05E 67
Nias, *I., Indon.,* 1 00N 97 40E 55
Nicaragua, *Rep., Cent. Amer.,* 13 00N 85 30W 71
Nicaragua, L., *Cent. Amer.,* 12 50N 85 30W 71
Nice, *tn., Fr.,* 43 42N 7 16E 45
Nicobar Is., *India,* 9 00N 93 00E 55
Nicosia, *tn., Cyprus,* 35 11N 33 23E 47
Nidd, R., *Eng.,* 45 01N 1 32W 25
Nienburg, *tn., W. Ger.,* 52 38N 9 13E 39
Niğde, *tn., Tur.,* 37 58N 34 42E 47
Niger, R., *Afr.,* 11 00N 4 00E 67
Niger, *Rep., Afr.,* 13 30N 10 00E 67
Nigeria, *Rep., Afr.,* 8 30N 8 00E 67
Nijmegen, *tn., Neth.,* 51 50N 5 52E 39
Nikel, *tn., USSR,* 69 20N 29 44E 43
Nikolayev, *tn., USSR,* 46 57N 32 00E 50
Nikolayevsk na Amure, *tn., USSR,* 53 40N 140 50E . . .53
Nikopol, *tn., USSR,* 47 34N 34 25E 50
Nile, R., *Eg.,* 27 30N 30 30E 49
Nile Delta, *Eg.,* 31 40N 31 00E 49
Nimba Mts., *Guin./Lib.,* 7 39N 8 30W 66
Nîmes, *tn., Fr.,* 43 50N 4 21E 45
Ningpo, *tn., China,* 29 54N 121 33E 57
Ningsia Hui, *admin. reg., China,* 37 20N 106 00E 56
Niniveh, *hist. site, Iraq,* 37 00N 43 00E 49
Niort, *tn., Fr.,* 46 19N 0 27W 44
Nipigon L., *Ont., Can.,* 49 40N 88 30W 73
Nishinomiya, *tn., Jap.,* 34 44N 135 22E 57
Niterói, *tn., Braz.,* 22 54S 43 06W 77
Nithsdale, *val., Scot.,* 55 14N 3 50W 23
Nitra, *tn., Cz.,* 48 20N 18 05E 41
Niuafou, *I., Pac. Oc.,* 15 36S 175 39W 63
Niue I., *Pac. Oc.,* 19 02S 169 55W 63
Nizhnekamsk, *tn., USSR,* 55 32N 51 56E 51
Nizhniy Tagil, *tn., USSR,* 58 00N 59 58E 51
N'Kongsamba, *tn., Cam.,* 4 59N 9 53E 67
Nobeoka, *tn., Jap.,* 32 36N 131 40E 57
Nogales, *tn., Ariz., USA,* 31 20N 110 56W 72
Noginsk, *tn., USSR,* 55 52N 38 29E 50
Nokia, *tn., Fin.,* 61 29N 23 31E 42
Nome, *tn., Alaska, USA,* 64 30N 165 30W 70
Nong Khai, *tn., Thai.,* 17 50N 102 46E 56
Nordfjord, *fd., Nor.,* 61 50N 5 25E 42

Nordhorn, *tn., W. Ger.,* 52 27N 7 05E. 39
Nordkinn, *hdl., Nor.,* 71 07N 27 40E 43
Nordoyar, *tn., Faeroe Is.,* 62 12N 6 30W 43
Nore, R., *Rep. Ire.,* 52 26N 7 20W. 24
Norfolk, *admin. reg., Eng.,* 52 39N 1 00E. 27
Norfolk, *tn., Va., USA,* 36 54N 76 18W 73
Norfolk I., *Pac. Oc.,* 29 05S 167 59E 63
Norilsk, *tn., USSR,* 69 21N 88 02E 52
Normandy, *geog. reg., Fr.,* 49 00N 0 00 44
Norra Storfjället, *mt., Swed.,* 65 54N 15 10E 43
Norrköping, *tn., Swed.,* 58 35N 16 10E 42
Norrland, *geog. reg., Swed.,* 62 27N 13 45E 43
Norrtälje, *tn., Swed.,* 59 46N 18 43E 42
Norseman, *tn., W. Austr.,* 32 15S 121 47E 62
North Bay, *tn., Ont., Can.,* 46 20N 79 28W 73
North Berwick, *tn., Scot.,* 56 04N 2 44W 23
North Cape, *hdl., N.Z.,* 34 23S 173 04E 63
North Cape, *hdl., Nor.,* 71 11N 25 40E 43
North Carolina, *admin. reg., USA,* 35 30N 80 00W . . .73
North Channel, *N. Ire./Scot.,* 55 00N 5 30W 24
North Dakota, *admin. reg., USA,* 47 30N 100 00W . . .72
North Donets R., *USSR,* 48 50N 38 45E 50
North Downs, *hs., Eng.,* 51 17N 0 05E 27
North Dvina, R., *USSR,* 61 40N 45 30E 50
North East Land, *geog. reg., Spitzbergen,*
80 00N 25 00E 80
North Foreland, *hdl., Eng.,* 51 23N 1 27E 27
North Frisian Is., *W. Ger.,* 54 50N 8 20E 41
North I., *N.Z.,* 38 00S 175 00E 63
North Korea, *Rep., Asia,* 40 00N 127 00E 57
North Minch, *sd., Scot.,* 58 07N 6 10W 22
North Pole, *Arctic Oc.,* 90 00N 0 00 80
North Rhine—Westphalia, *admin. reg., W. Ger.,*
51 00N 7 00E 39
North Rona, *I., Scot.,* 59 05N 5 51W 22
North Ronaldsay, *I., Scot.,* 59 23N 2 26W 22
North Saskatchewan, R., *Alta./Sask., Can.,*
53 40N 109 00W 71
North Sea, *Eur.,* 56 00N 1 00E 40
North Tyne, R., *Eng.,* 55 20N 2 15W. 25
North Uist, *I., Scot.,* 57 40N 7 15W 22
North Walsham, *tn., Eng.,* 52 50N 1 24E 27
North West Cape, *hdl., W. Austr.,* 21 48S 114 10E. . .62
North West Highlands, *mts., Scot.,* 56 43N 5 40W . . .22
North Yorkshire, *admin. reg., Eng.,* 54 08N 2 10W . . .25
Northallerton, *tn., Eng.,* 54 20N 1 26W 25
Northam, *tn., W. Austr.,* 31 40S 116 40E 62
Northampton, *tn., Eng.,* 52 14N 0 54W. 27
Northamptonshire, *admin. reg., Eng.,* 52 09N 1 09W . . .27
Northern Ireland, *const. reg., UK,* 54 45N 7 00W 24
Northern Sporades, *Is., Gr.,* 39 00N 23 50N 46
Northern Territory, *admin. reg., Austr.,*
8 30S 133 00E 62
Northumberland, *admin. reg., Eng.,* 55 12N 2 27W . . .25
Northwest Territories, *admin. reg., Can.,*
67 00N 115 00W 71
Northwich, *tn., Eng.,* 53 16N 2 32W 25
Norvegia, C., *hdl., Ant.,* 72 00S 22 30W 80
Norway, *Kingd., Eur.,* 67 00N 11 00E 43
Norwegian Sea, 66 00N 1 00E 50
Norwich, *tn., Eng.,* 52 38N 1 18E 27
Noteć, R., *Pol.,* 53 16N 16 00E 41
Noto Peninsula, *Jap.,* 37 00N 137 00E 57
Notodden, *tn., Nor.,* 59 35N 9 18E 42
Nottingham, *tn., Eng.,* 52 58N 1 10W. 25
Nottinghamshire, *admin. reg., Eng.,*
53 10N 1 00W 25
Nouadhibou, *tn., Maur.,* 20 54N 17 01W. 66
Nouakchott, *tn., Maur.,* 18 09N 15 58W 66
Nouméa, *tn., New Caledonia,* 22 16S 166 26E 63
Nova Lisboa see Huambo
Nova Scotia, *admin. reg., Can.,* 45 00N 63 00W 71
Novaja Kakhovka, *tn., USSR,* 46 40N 33 00E 47
Novara, *tn., It.,* 45 27N 8 37E 45
Novaya Zemlya, *USSR I. terr., Kara Sea,*
75 00N 56 00E 52
Novgorod, *tn., USSR,* 58 30N 31 20E 50
Novi Sad, *tn., Yug.,* 45 15N 19 51E 46
Novo-Kuznetsk, *tn., USSR,* 53 45N 87 12E. 52
Novocherkassk, *tn., USSR,* 47 25N 40 05E 47
Novokuybyshevsk, *tn., USSR,* 52 55N 50 00E 51
Novolazarevskaya, *USSR base, Ant.,* 71 00S 11 00E . . .80
Novomoskovsk, *tn., USSR,* 54 06N 38 15E 50
Novorossiysk, *tn., USSR,* 44 44N 37 46E 47
Novoshakhtinsk, *tn., USSR,* 47 46N 39 55E 47
Novosibirsk, *tn., USSR,* 55 04N 83 05E 52
Novotroitsk, *tn., USSR,* 51 11N 58 16E 51
Novovolynsk, *tn., USSR,* 50 40N 24 19E. 42
Nu Kiang, R., *China,* 30 00N 97 30E 56
(as Salween, R. in Burma)
Nu Shan, *mts., China,* 26 30N 99 00E. 56
Nubia, *geog. reg., Sud.,* 18 46N 29 00E 67
Nubian Desert, *Sud.,* 21 30N 33 30E 67
Nueva Rosita, *tn., Mex.,* 27 58N 101 11W. 72
Nuevo Laredo, *tn., Mex.,* 27 30N 99 30W 72
Nügata, *tn., Jap.,* 37 58N 139 02E. 57
Nühama, *tn., Jap.,* 33 57N 133 15E. 57
Nukualofa, *tn., Tonga, Pac. Oc.,*
21 09S 175 14W. 63
Nukufetau, *I., Tuvalu, Pac. Oc.,* 8 00S 178 30E 63
Nukulaelae, *I., Tuvalu, Pac. Oc.,* 9 20S 179 50E 63
Nukus, *tn., USSR,* 42 28N 59 07E 51
Nullarbor Plain, *geog. reg., S. Austr./W. Austr.,*
31 00S 128 00E 62
Nun Kiang, R., *China,* 46 00N 124 00E 57
Nuneaton, *tn., Eng.,* 52 32N 1 28W 27
Nunkiang, *tn., China,* 49 10N 125 15E 57
Nuoro, *tn., Sard.,* 40 20N 9 21E 45
Nuremberg, *tn., W. Ger.,* 49 27N 11 05E 41
Nyala, *tn., Sud.,* 12 01N 24 50E 67
Nyíregyháza, *tn., Hung.,* 47 57N 21 43E. 46

O

Oa, Mull of, *hdl., Scot.,* 55 35N 6 20W 23
Oakham, *tn., Eng.,* 52 40N 0 43W. 27
Oakland, *tn., Calif., USA,* 37 50N 122 15W 72
Ob, R., *USSR,* 67 00N 65 00E 52
Ob, Gulf of, *USSR,* 70 00N 73 00E 52
Oban, *tn., Scot.,* 56 25N 5 29W. 23
Oberhausen, *tn., W. Ger.,* 51 27N 6 50E 39
Obihiro, *tn., Jap.,* 42 56N 143 10E 57
Ocean I., *Pac. Oc.,* 0 45S 169 50E 63
Ochil Hills, *Scot.,* 56 14N 3 40W 23
Odadahraun, *geog. reg., Ice.,* 65 05N 17 00W 43
Odense, *tn., Den.,* 55 24N 10 25E 42
Odenwald, *mts., W. Ger.,* 49 18N 9 00E 39
Oder, R., *E. Ger./Pol.,* 53 00N 12 29E. 41
Odessa, *tn., Tex., USA,* 31 50N 102 23W 72
Odessa, *tn., USSR,* 46 30N 30 46E 47
Offaly, *admin. reg., Rep. Ire.,* 53 09N 7 50W 24
Offenbach am Main, *tn., W. Ger.,* 50 06N 8 46E . . .39
Ofotfjord, *fd., Nor.,* 68 27N 16 00E 43
Ogaden, *geog. reg., Ethiopia,* 5 00N 45 00E 67
Ogaki, *tn., Jap.,* 35 22N 136 36E 57
Ogbomosho, *tn., Nig.,* 8 05N 4 11E 67
Ogden, *tn., Utah, USA,* 41 14N 111 59W 72
O'Higgins, *Chile base, Ant.,* 63 40S 58 00W. 80
Ohio, *admin. reg., USA,* 40 20N 83 00W 73
Ohio, R., *USA,* 37 20N 87 40W 73
Oise, R., *Fr.,* 49 53N 3 50E. 39
Oita, *tn., Jap.,* 33 15N 131 36E 57
Ojos del Salado, Mt., *Arg./Chile,* 27 05S 68 05W . . .77
Oka, R., *USSR,* 54 50N 38 00E 50
Okavango Swamp, *Bots.,* 19 30S 23 00E 67
Okayama, *tn., Jap.,* 34 40N 133 54E 57
Okeechobee L., *Fla., USA,* 27 00N 80 50W 73
Okehampton, *tn., Eng.,* 50 44N 4 00W 26
Okha, *tn., USSR,* 53 35N 143 01E 53
Okhotsk, *tn., USSR,* 59 20N 143 15E 53
Okhotsk, Sea of, *USSR,* 55 00N 145 00E 53
Oki Is., *Jap.,* 36 05N 133 00E 57
Okinawa I., *Jap.,* 26 40N 128 00E 57
Oklahoma, *admin. reg., USA,* 35 40N 97 30W 72
Oklahoma City, *tn., Okla., USA,* 35 28N 97 33W 72
Okstindan, Mt., *Nor.,* 66 00N 14 24E. 43
Oktyabrskiy, *tn., USSR,* 54 30N 53 30E 51
Öland, *I., Swed.,* 56 45N 16 50E 42
Olbia, *tn., Sard.,* 40 56N 9 30E 45
Old Castile, *geog. reg., Sp.,* 41 55N 4 00W 44
Oldenburg, *tn., W. Ger.,* 54 17N 10 52E 39
Oldham, *tn., Eng.,* 53 33N 2 07W 25
Olenegorsk, *tn., USSR,* 68 04N 33 15E 43
Olenek, R., *USSR,* 69 00N 123 00E 53
Olomouc, *tn., Cz.,* 49 48N 17 15E 41
Olsztyn, *tn., Pol.,* 53 48N 20 29E 41
Olt, R., *Rom.,* 43 50N 24 40E. 46
Olympia, *hist. site, Gr.,* 37 38N 21 39E. 46
Olympia, *tn., Wash., USA,* 47 03N 122 53W 72
Olympia Nat. Park, *Wash., USA,* 48 00N 123 30W . . .72
Olympus, Mt., *Gr.,* 40 05N 22 21E 46
Omagh, *tn., N. Ire.,* 54 36N 7 18W 24
Omaha, *tn., Nebr., USA,* 41 15N 96 00W 73
Oman, *Sheikhdom, Asia,* 19 00N 55 00E 52
Oman, Gulf of, *Iran/Oman,* 24 30N 58 30E 52
Omdurman, *tn., Sud.,* 15 37N 32 29E 67
Omiya, *tn., Jap.,* 35 54N 139 39E 57
Omsk, *tn., USSR,* 55 00N 73 22E 51
Öndörhaan, *tn., Mong.,* 47 20N 110 35E 56
Onega, *tn., USSR,* 63 57N 38 11E 50
Onega, L., *USSR,* 62 00N 35 30E 50
Onitsha, *tn., Nig.,* 6 10N 6 47E 67
Ontario, *admin. reg., Can.,* 52 00N 89 30W 71
Ontario L., *Can./USA,* 43 40N 78 00W 73
Opava, *tn., Cz.,* 49 58N 17 55E 41
Opole, *tn., Pol.,* 50 40N 17 56E 41
Oporto see Porto
Oradea, *tn., Rom.,* 47 03N 21 55E 46
Öraefajökull, *ice-cap, Ice.,* 64 02N 16 41W. 43
Oran, *tn., Alg.,* 35 45N 0 38W 48
Orange, R., *S.W. Afr./Rep. S. Afr.,* 28 30S 18 00E . . .67
Orange, *tn., N.S.W., Austr.,* 33 19S 149 10E 63
Orange Free State, *admin. reg., Rep. S. Afr.,*
28 30S 27 00E 67
Ord, R., *W. Austr.,* 16 20S 128 37E 62
Ordos Plateau, *China,* 39 25N 108 45E 56
Ordu, *tn., Tur.,* 41 00N 37 52E 47
Ordzhonikidze, *tn., USSR,* 43 02N 44 43E 51
Ore Mts., *Cz./E. Ger.,* 50 25N 13 00E 41
Örebro, *tn., Swed.,* 59 17N 15 13E 42
Oregon, *admin. reg., USA,* 44 00N 120 00W 72
Orekhovo Zuyevo, *tn., USSR,* 55 47N 39 00E 50
Orel, *tn., USSR,* 52 58N 36 04E. 50
Orenburg, *tn., USSR,* 51 50N 55 00E 51
Orense, *tn., Sp.,* 42 20N 7 52W 44
Orinoco, R., *Ven.,* 8 00N 65 30W 77
Oristano, *tn., Sard.,* 39 54N 8 36E 45
Orkney, *admin. reg., Scot.,* 59 00N 3 00W 22
Orkney Is., *Scot.,* 59 18N 3 42W 22
Orlando, *tn., Fla., USA,* 28 33N 81 21W 73
Orléans, *tn., Fr.,* 47 54N 1 54E 44
Ormskirk, *tn., Eng.,* 53 35N 2 54W 25
Orne, R., *Fr.,* 48 57N 0 55W 39
Örnsköldsvik, *tn., Swed.,* 63 19N 18 45E. 43
Orsha, *tn., USSR,* 54 30N 30 23E 50
Orsk, *tn., USSR,* 51 13N 58 35E 51
Oruro, *tn., Bol.,* 17 59S 67 08W 77
Osaka, *tn., Jap.,* 35 08N 137 00E 57
Ösel see Saaremaa
Oshawa, *tn., Ont., Can.,* 43 53N 78 51W 73
Osijek, *tn., Yug.,* 45 33N 18 41E 46
Oskarshamm, *tn., Swed.,* 57 16N 16 25E 42
Oslo, *tn., Nor.,* 59 56N 19 45E 42

Osmaniye, tn., Tur., 38 17N 39 44E 47
Osnabrück, tn., W. Ger., 52 17N 8 03E 39
Osorno, tn., Chile, 40 35S 73 14W 77
Oss, tn., Neth., 51 46N 5 31E 39
Ostend, tn., Belg., 51 13N 2 55E 39
Österdalälven, R., Swed., 61 50N 13 05E 42
Östersund, tn., Swed., 63 10N 14 40E 43
Ostia, hist. site, It., 41 46N 12 18E 45
Ostrava, tn., Cz., 49 50N 18 15E 41
Ostrov, tn., USSR, 57 22N 28 22E 42
Ostrów Wielkopolski, tn., Pol., 51 39N 17 50E . 41
Ostrowiec Swietokrzyski, tn., Pol., 50 58N 21 22E . 41
Osumi Is., Jap., 30 30N 130 45E 57
Oswestry, tn., Eng., 52 52N 3 04W 26
Otaru, tn., Jap., 43 14N 140 59E 57
Otranto, Strait of, Alb./It., 40 15N 18 40E .. 46
Ottawa, R., Ont./Que., Can., 46 20N 79 00W ... 73
Ottawa, tn., Ont., Can., 45 25N 75 43W 73
Ouachita Mts., Ark./Okla., USA, 35 00N 94 30W . 73
Ouagadougou, tn., Upper Volta, 12 20N 1 40W .. 66
Ouargla, tn., Alg., 32 00N 5 16E 48
Ouarzazate, tn., Mor., 30 57N 6 50W 48
Oubangui, R., Congo, 0 50S 18 00E 67
Oubangui-Chari, admin. reg., Cent. Afr.,
7 40N 19 00E 67
Oued Dra, R., Mor., 29 40N 7 00E 48
Ouezzane, tn., Mor., 34 52N 5 35W 48
Oujda, tn., Mor., 34 41N 1 45W 48
Oulu, tn., Fin., 65 00N 25 26E 43
Oulujärvi, L., Fin., 64 25N 27 30E 43
Oulujoki, R., Fin., 64 50N 26 20E 43
Oum er Rbia, R., Mor., 33 00N 7 00W 48
Ounasjoki, R., Fin., 67 30N 25 00E 43
Ouse, R., Cambs., Eng., 52 21N 0 07E 27
Ouse, R., Humberside, Eng., 53 45N -1 02W 25
Ouse, Little, R., Eng., 52 25N 0 45E 27
Outokumpu, tn., Fin., 62 43N 29 05E 43
Ovambo, geog. reg., S.W. Afr. (Nam.),
17 20S 16 30E 67
Oviedo, tn., Sp., 43 21N 5 50W 44
Owen Sound, tn., Ont., Can., 44 34N 80 56W ... 73
Owen Stanley Range, hs., Pap. New Guin.,
8 30S 148 00E 63
Oxelösund, tn., Swed., 58 40N 17 10E 42
Oxford, tn., Eng., 51 46N 1 15W 27
Oxfordshire, admin. reg., Eng., 51 46N 1 15W . 27
Oxnard, tn., Calif., USA, 34 11N 119 10W 72
Oxus see Amu Darya
Ozark Plateau, Ark./Mo., USA, 36 40N 93 00W .. 73

P

Paan, tn., China, 30 02N 99 01E 56
Paarl, tn., Rep. S. Afr., 33 45S 18 58E 67
Pacific Ocean 2
Padang, tn., Indon., 1 00S 100 21E 55
Paderborn, tn., W. Ger., 51 43N 8 44E 39
Padova see Padua
Padstow, tn., Eng., 50 33N 4 56W 26
Padua, tn., It., 45 24N 11 53E 45
Paektu, Mt., N. Kor., 42 00N 128 50E 57
Paestum, hist. site, It., 40 24N 15 00E 45
Pag, I., Yug., 44 50N 15 00E 46
Pagalu, I., Equ. Guin., 1 24S 5 37E 67
Pahlevi Resht, tn., Tur., 35 51N 46 01E 51
Paicheng, tn., China, 45 37N 122 48E 57
Paignton, tn., Eng., 50 26N 3 34W 26
Päijänne, L., Fin., 61 35N 25 30E 42
Painted Desert, Ariz., USA, 36 40N 112 00W ... 72
Paisley, tn., Scot., 55 50N 4 26W 23
Paiyunopo, tn., China, 42 10N 109 28E 56
Pakanbaru, tn., Indon., 0 33N 101 30E 55
Pakhoi, tn., China, 21 29N 109 10E 56
Pakistan, Rep., S. Asia, 28 50N 64 00E 54
Palagruža Is., Yug., 42 20N 16 20E 46
Palatinate, admin. reg., W. Ger., 49 51N 7 07E . 39
Palau Is., Pac. Oc., 7 30N 134 35E 62
Palawan, I., Phil., 10 00N 119 00E 55
Palembang, tn., Indon., 2 59S 104 45E 55
Palencia, tn., Sp., 41 01N 4 32W 44
Palermo, tn., Sicily, 38 08N 13 23E 45
Pallastunturi, mt., Fin., 68 04N 24 01E 43
Palma, tn., Majorca, 39 35N 2 39E 44
Palmas, C., hdl., Lib., 4 25N 7 50W 66
Palmer Land, geog. reg., Ant., 73 00S 61 00W . 80
Palmer Station, USA base, Ant., 64 00S 65 00W . 80
Palmerston North, tn., N.Z., 40 20S 175 39E .. 63
Palmyra, hist. site, Syria, 34 36N 38 15E 49
Palomar Mt., Calif., USA, 33 22N 116 50W 72
Palos, C. de, hdl., Sp., 37 38N 0 40W 44
Pamirs, mts., Afghan./USSR, 37 40N 73 00E 52
Pamlico Sound, N.C., USA, 35 20N 76 00W 73
Pampas, geog. reg., Arg., 37 42S 64 00W 77
Pamplona, tn., Sp., 42 49N 1 39W 44
Panama, Rep., Cent. Amer., 9 00N 79 25W 77
Panamá, Rep., Cent. Amer., 9 10N 79 00W 71
Panamá, tn., Pan., 8 57N 79 30W 71
Panamá Canal, Pan., 9 10N 79 56W 71
Panay, I., Phil., 11 00N 122 30E 55
Pančevo, tn., Yug., 44 52N 20 40E 46

Panevežys, tn., USSR, 55 44N 24 24E 42
Panhandle, tn., Tex., USA, 35 21N 101 24W 72
Pantelleria I., It., 36 05N 11 57E 45
Paoki, tn., China, 34 23N 107 16E 56
Paoshan, tn., China, 25 07N 99 08E 55
Paoting, tn., China, 38 54N 115 26E 56
Paotow, tn., China, 40 45N 110 00E 56
Papa Stour, I., Scot., 60 20N 1 42W 22
Papa Westray, I., Scot., 59 22N 2 54W 22
Papua New Guinea, comm. nat., Austral.,
5 00S 150 00E 63
Pará, admin. reg., Braz., 3 20S 52 00W 77
Paraguay, Rep., S. Amer., 23 00S 61 00W 77
Paraguay, R., Braz./Par., 24 30S 58 20W 77
Paraíba, admin. reg., Braz., 7 00S 37 00W 77
Paramaribo, tn., Sur., 5 52N 55 14W 77
Parana, admin. reg., Braz., 24 30S 51 00W 77
Paraná, R., Braz./Para., 22 25S 53 01W 77
Paraná, tn., Arg., 31 45S 60 30W 77
Paranaíba, R., Braz., 18 00S 49 12W 77
Pardubice, tn., Cz., 50 03N 15 45E 41
Paris, tn., Fr., 48 52N 2 20E 44
Parkes, tn., N.S.W. Austr., 33 10S 148 13E ... 63
Parma, tn., It., 44 48N 10 19E 45
Parnaíba, tn., Braz., 19 44S 51 12W 77
Pärnu, tn., USSR, 58 28N 24 30E 42
Parry Is., N.W. Terrs., Can., 77 00N 110 30W . 71
Partizansk, tn., USSR, 43 03N 133 05E 57
Pasadena, tn., Calif., USA, 34 13N 118 09W ... 72
Passero, C., hdl., Sicily, 36 42N 15 09E 45
Passo Fundo, tn., Braz., 28 16S 52 20W 77
Pasto, tn., Col., 1 12N 77 17W 77
Patagonia, geog. reg., Arg., 45 00S 69 00W ... 77
Paterson, tn., N.J., USA, 40 56N 74 09W 73
Patna, tn., India, 25 37N 85 12E 54
Patos. L. dos, Braz., 21 30S 51 00W 77
Pátrai see Patras
Patras, tn., Gr., 38 14N 21 44E 46
Pau, tn., Fr., 43 18N 0 22W 44
Pavia, tn., It., 45 59N 13 19E 45
Pavlodar, tn., USSR, 52 21N 76 59E 51
Pavlovo, tn., USSR, 55 58N 43 05E 50
Pays de Caux, geog. reg., Fr., 49 38N 0 35E .. 39
Paysandú, tn., Urug., 32 21S 58 05W 77
Pazardzhik, tn., Bulg., 42 10N 24 20E 46
Peace, R., Alta./B.C., Can., 58 30N 116 30W .. 71
Peak District, geog. reg., Eng., 53 24N 1 53W . 25
Peary Land, geog. reg., Green., 83 00N 40 00W . 80
Pechenga, tn., USSR, 69 28N 31 04E 43
Pechora, R., USSR, 62 30N 56 30E 50
Pechora, tn., USSR, 65 14N 57 18E 50
Pecos, R., USA, 32 30N 104 20W 72
Pécs, tn., Hung., 46 04N 18 15E 46
Peebles, tn., Scot., 55 39N 3 12W 23
Peel, tn., I.o.M., 54 14N 4 40W 24
Pehpiao, tn., China, 41 52N 120 40E 57
Pelan, tn., China, 48 16N 126 36E 57
Peiping see Peking
Peipus, L., USSR, 58 13N 27 30E 42
Peking, admin. reg., China, 40 02N 116 00E ... 57
Pelagic Is., It., 36 00N 13 00E 48
Peloponnese, geog. reg., Gr., 37 10N 22 00E .. 46
Pelotas, tn., Braz., 31 45S 52 21W 77
Pematangsiantar, tn., Indon., 2 59N 99 01E ... 55
Pemba I., Tanz., 5 20S 39 40E 67
Pembroke, tn., Ont., Can., 45 49N 77 08W 73
Pembroke, tn., Wales, 51 41N 4 55W 26
Penarth, tn., Wales, 51 27N 3 11W 26
Pend Oreille, R., Can./USA, 48 30N 117 00W ... 72
Penglai, tn., China, 37 50N 120 45E 57
Pengpu, tn., China, 32 56N 117 27E 57
Pengshan, tn., China, 30 14N 103 58E 56
Penicuik, tn., Scot., 55 50N 3 14W 23
Penki, tn., China, 41 21N 123 45E 57
Penmaenmawr, tn., Wales, 53 16N 3 54W 26
Pennine Chain, mts., Eng., 54 40N 2 20W 25
Pennsylvania, admin. reg., USA, 40 50N 78 00W . 73
Penrith, tn., Eng., 54 40N 2 44W 25
Penryn, tn., Eng., 50 10N 5 07W 26
Pensacola, tn., Fla., USA, 30 26N 87 12W 73
Penticton, tn., B.C., Can., 49 29N 119 38W ... 72
Pentland Firth, Scot., 58 43N 3 10W 22
Pentland Hills, Scot., 55 48N 3 25W 23
Penza, tn., USSR, 53 11N 45 00E 50
Penzance, tn., Eng., 50 07N 5 33W 26
Peoria, tn., Ill., USA, 40 43N 89 38W 73
Pergamum, hist. site, Tur., 39 08N 27 10E 47
Périgueux, tn., Fr., 45 12N 0 44E 44
Perm, tn., USSR, 58 01N 56 10E 51
Pernambuco, admin. reg., Braz., 8 30S 38 00W . 77
Pernik, tn., Bulg., 42 36N 23 03E 46
Perpignan, tn., Fr., 42 42N 2 54E 44
Persepolis, hist. site, Iran, 29 57N 52 52E . 52
Persia see Iran
Persian Gulf, Asia, 27 00N 50 00E 52
Perth, tn., Scot., 56 24N 3 28W 23
Perth, tn., W. Austr., 31 58S 115 49E 62
Peru, Rep., S. Amer., 10 00S 77 00W 77
Peru-Chile Trench, Pac. Oc., 23 00S 72 00W ... 77
Perugia, tn., It., 43 07N 12 23E 45
Pervomaysk, tn., USSR, 48 03N 30 50E 50
Pervouralsk, tn., USSR, 56 59N 59 58E 51
Pesaro, tn., It., 43 54N 12 54E 45
Pescara, tn., It., 42 27N 14 13E 45
Peshawar, tn., Pak., 34 01N 71 40E 54
Peter 1 Island, Ant., 69 00S 91 00W 80
Peterborough, tn., Eng., 52 35N 0 15W 27
Peterborough, tn., Ont., Can., 44 19N 78 20W . 73
Peterhead, tn., Scot., 57 30N 1 46W 22
Peterlee, tn., Eng., 54 46N 1 19W 25

Petersfield, tn., Eng., 51 00N 0 56W 27
Petra, hist. site, Jordan, 30 20N 35 26E 49
Petropavlovsk, tn., USSR, 54 53N 69 13E 51
Petropavlovsk Kamchatskiy, tn., USSR,
53 03N 158 43E 53
Petroşeni, tn., Rom., 45 25N 23 22E 46
Petrozavodsk, tn., USSR, 61 46N 34 19E 50
Pevek, tn., USSR, 69 41N 170 19E 53
Pforzheim, tn., W. Ger., 48 53N 8 41E 39
Philadelphia, tn., Pa., USA, 40 00N 75 10W ... 73
Philae, hist. site, Eg., 24 02N 32 59E 49
Philippi, hist. site, Gr., 41 00N 24 00E 46
Philippine Trench, Pac. Oc., 10 00N 128 00E .. 55
Phillipines, Rep., Austral., 12 00N 123 00E .. 55
Philippopolis see Plovdiv
Phitsanulok, tn., Thai., 16 50N 100 12E 56
Phnom Penh, tn., Cambod., 11 35N 104 55E 55
Phoenix, tn., Ariz., USA, 33 30N 112 03W 72
Phoenix Is., Pac. Oc., 3 30S 174 00W 63
Phong Saly, tn., Laos, 21 40N 102 06E 56
Piacenza, tn., It., 45 03N 9 41E 45
Piatra-Neamt, tn., Rom., 46 53N 26 23E 46
Piauí, admin. reg., Braz., 7 20S 42 30W 77
Picardy, geog. reg., Fr., 50 00N 2 00E 44
Pickering, tn., Eng., 54 14N 0 46W 25
Piedmont, geog. reg., It., 45 00N 7 50E 45
Piedras Negras, tn., Mex., 28 40N 100 32W 72
Pielinen, L., Fin., 63 20N 30 15E 43
Pierre, tn., S. Dak., USA, 44 23N 100 20W 72
Pietarsaari, tn., Fin., 63 41N 22 40E 43
Pietermaritzburg, tn., Rep. S. Afr.,
29 36S 30 24E 67
Pietersburg, tn., Rep. S. Afr., 23 54S 29 23E . 67
Pihsien, tn., China, 31 00N 104 00E 56
Pila, tn., Pol., 53 09N 16 44E 41
Pilcomayo, R., Arg./Par., 23 31S 61 00W 77
Pilica, R., Pol., 50 30N 19 24E 41
Pinang, tn., Malay., 5 30N 100 28E 55
Pinar del Rio, tn., Cuba, 22 24N 83 42W 73
Pindus Mts., Gr., 40 00N 21 00E 46
Pine Bluff, tn., Ark., USA, 34 13N 92 00W 73
Pingliang, tn., China, 35 27N 106 31E 56
Pingsiang, tn., China, 22 02N 106 55E 56
Pingtingshan, tn., China, 33 50N 113 20E 56
Pingtung, tn., Taiwan, 22 40N 120 30E 57
Pinhai, tn., China, 34 00N 119 51E 57
Pinos, I. de, Cuba, 21 40N 82 40W 73
Pinsk, tn., USSR, 52 08N 26 01E 50
Piombino, tn., It., 42 56N 10 32E 45
Piotrków Trybunalski, tn., Pol., 51 27N 19 40E . 41
Piraeus, tn., Gr., 37 57N 23 42E 46
Piraiévs see Piraeus
Pirmasens, tn., W. Ger., 49 12N 7 37E 39
Pisa, tn., It., 43 43N 10 24E 45
Pisco, tn., Peru, 13 46S 76 12W 77
Pistoia, tn., It., 43 56N 10 55E 45
Piteå, tn., Swed., 65 19N 21 30E 43
Piteälven, R., Swed., 66 45N 17 20E 43
Piteşti, tn., Rom., 44 51N 24 51E 46
Pitlochry, tn., Scot., 56 43N 3 45W 23
Pittsburg, tn., Pa., USA, 40 26N 80 00W 73
Piura, tn., Peru, 5 15S 80 38W 77
Pizeň, tn., Cz., 45 20N 13 28E 50
Pjorśa, R., Ice., 64 05N 19 45W 43
Planet Deep, Solomon Sea, 7 00S 154 00E 63
Plasencia, tn., Sp., 40 02N 6 05W 44
Plate, R., Arg./Urug., 35 30S 56 00W 77
Platte, R., USA, 40 50N 100 00W 72
Platte, North, R., USA, 41 45N 103 20W 72
Platte, South, R., USA, 40 26N 103 14W 72
Plauen, tn., E. Ger., 50 29N 12 08E 41
Plaza Huincul, tn., Arg., 38 55S 69 14W 77
Pleven, tn., Bulg., 43 25N 24 40E 46
Ploče, tn., Yug., 43 02N 17 27E 46
Plock, tn., Pol., 52 32N 19 40E 41
Ploieşti, tn., Rom., 44 57N 26 01E 46
Plovdiv, tn., Bulg., 42 08N 24 45E 46
Plymouth, tn., Eng., 50 23N 4 10W 26
Plymouth Sound, est., Eng., 50 21N 4 10W 26
Plzen, tn., Cz., 49 45N 13 25E 41
Po, R., It., 45 00N 10 45E 45
Po Delta, It., 44 58N 12 28E 45
Pocatello, tn., Idaho, USA, 42 53N 112 26W ... 72
Podolsk, tn., USSR, 55 23N 37 32E 50
Pohang, tn., S. Kor., 36 00N 129 26E 57
Pohsien, tn., China, 33 55N 115 41E 56
Poinsett, C. hdl., Ant., 66 00S 123 00E 80
Pointe-a-Pitre, tn., Guadeloupe, 16 14N 61 32W . 77
Pointe Noire, hdl., Congo, 4 46S 11 53E 67
Poitiers, tn., Fr., 46 35N 0 20E 44
Poitou, geog. reg., Fr., 46 30N 0 01W 44
Poland, Rep., Eur., 52 00N 20 00E 41
Polatli, tn., Tur., 39 34N 32 08E 47
Polevskoy, tn., USSR, 56 28N 60 15E 51
Polotsk, tn., USSR, 55 30N 28 43E 50
Poltava, tn., USSR, 49 35N 34 35E 50
Polyarnyy, tn., Murmansk, USSR, 69 14N 33 30E . 43
Polynesia, ethnic reg. & Is., Pac. Oc.,
14 00S 171 45W 63
Pomerania, geog. reg., Pol., 53 45N 15 03E ... 41
Pompei, hist. site, It., 40 45N 14 27E 45
Ponape, I., Pac. Oc., 6 55N 158 10E 63
Ponferrada, tn., Sp., 42 33N 6 35W 44
Ponoy, R., USSR, 67 10N 39 00E 43
Ponta Grossa, tn., Braz., 25 07S 50 09W 77
Ponta Porã, tn., Braz., 22 27S 55 39W 77
Pontarddulais, tn., Wales, 51 43N 4 02W 26
Pontefract, tn., Eng., 53 42N 1 18W 25
Pontevedra, tn., Sp., 42 25N 8 39W 44
Pontianak, tn., Indon., 0 05S 109 16E 55
Pontine Is., It., 40 55N 13 00E 45

Pontine Mts., *Tur.*, 42 00N 35 00E 47
Pontoise, *tn.*, *Fr.*, 49 03N 2 05E 39
Pontypool, *tn.*, *Wales*, 51 43N 3 02W 26
Pontypridd, *tn.*, *Wales*, 51 37N 3 22W 26
Poole, *tn.*, *Eng.*, 50 43N 1 59W 27
Poona, *tn.*, *India*, 18 34N 73 58E 54
Poopó, L., *Bol.*, 18 23S 66 58W 77
Popocatepetl, Mt., *vol.*, *Mex.*, 19 02N 98 38W . . 71
Pordenone, *tn.*, *It.*, 45 58N 12 39E 45
Pori, *tn.*, *Fin.*, 61 28N 21 45E 42
Porsangen, *fd.*, *Nor.*, 70 30N 25 35E 43
Port Arthur, *tn.*, *Tex.*, *USA*, 29 55N 93 56W . . 73
Port-au-Prince, *tn.*, *Haiti*, 18 33N 72 20W 71
Port Augusta, *tn.*, *S. Austr.*, 32 30S 137 27E . . 63
Port Cartier, *tn.*, *Que.*, *Can.*, 50 03N 66 46W . . 71
Port Elizabeth, *tn.*, *Rep. S. Afr.*, 33 58S 25 36E . 67
Port Ellen, *tn.*, *Scot.*, 55 39N 6 12W 23
Port Erin, *tn.*, *I.o.M.*, 54 05N 4 45W 24
Port Glasgow, *tn.*, *Scot.*, 55 56N 4 41W 23
Port Harcourt, *tn.*, *Nig.*, 4 43N 7 05E 67
Port Hedland, *tn.*, *W. Austr.*, 20 24S 118 36E . . 62
Port Laoise, *tn.*, *Rep. Ire.*, 53 02N 7 17W 24
Port Lincoln, *tn.*, *S. Austr.*, 34 43S 135 49E . . . 63
Port Louis, *tn.*, *Mauritius*, 20 10S 57 30E 67
Port Moresby, *tn.*, *Pap. New Guin.*, 9 30S 147 07E . 63
Port Nelson, *tn.*, *Man.*, *Can.*, 57 05N 92 56W . . 71
Port of Spain, *tn.*, *Trinidad*, 10 38N 61 31W . . 77
Port Pirie, *tn.*, *S. Austr.*, 33 11S 138 01E 63
Port Radium, *tn.*, *N.W. Terrs.*, *Can.*, 66 04N 118 00W . 71
Port Said, *tn.*, *Eg.*, 31 17N 32 18E 49
Port Sudan, *tn.*, *Sud.*, 19 38N 37 07E 49
Port Talbot, *tn.*, *Wales*, 51 36N 3 47W 26
Portadown, *tn.*, *N. Ire.*, 54 26N 6 27W 24
Portage La Prairie, *tn.*, *Man.*, *Can.*, 49 58N 98 20W . 72
Portarlington, *tn.*, *Rep. Ire.*, 53 10N 7 11W . . . 24
Porthcawl, *tn.*, *Wales*, 51 29N 3 43W 26
Porthmadog, *tn.*, *Wales*, 52 51N 4 08W 26
Portishead, *tn.*, *Eng.*, 51 30N 2 46W 26
Portland, *tn.*, *Me.*, *USA*, 43 41N 70 18W 73
Portland, *tn.*, *Oreg.*, *USA*, 45 32N 122 40W . . . 72
Portland Bill, *hdl.*, *Eng.*, 50 31N 2 27W 26
Porto, *tn.*, *Port.*, 41 10N 6 53W 44
Pôrto Alegre, *tn.*, *Braz.*, 20 03S 51 10W 77
Porto Novo, *tn.*, *Benin*, 6 30N 2 47E 67
Pôrto Velho, *tn.*, *Braz.*, 8 45S 63 54W 77
Portpatrick, *tn.*, *Scot.*, 54 51N 5 07W 23
Portree, *tn.*, *Scot.*, 57 24N 6 12W 22
Portrush, *tn.*, *N. Ire.*, 55 12N 6 40W 24
Portsmouth, *tn.*, *Eng.*, 50 48N 1 05W 27
Portsmouth, *tn.*, *Va.*, *USA*, 36 50N 76 20W . . . 73
Portstewart, *tn.*, *N. Ire.*, 55 11N 6 43W 24
Portugal, *Rep.*, *Eur.*, 40 00N 7 00W 44
Portugalete, *tn.*, *Sp.*, 43 19N 3 01W 44
Porz am Rhein, *tn.*, *W. Ger.*, 50 50N 7 06E . . . 39
Posadas, *tn.*, *Arg.*, 27 25S 55 48W 77
Poseh, *tn.*, *China*, 23 50N 106 00E 56
Poshan, *tn.*, *China*, 36 32N 117 47E 57
Potenza, *tn.*, *It.*, 40 38N 15 48E 45
Potomac, R., *Md./Va.*, *USA*, 39 10N 77 30W . . . 73
Potosi, *tn.*, *Bol.*, 19 34S 65 45W 77
Potow, *tn.*, *China*, 38 08N 116 31E 57
Potsdam, *tn.*, *E. Ger.*, 52 24N 13 04E 41
Potters Bar, *tn.*, *Eng.*, 51 42N 0 11W 27
Powell, L., *Ariz./Utah*, *USA*, 37 20N 115 50W . . 72
Powys, *admin. reg.*, *Wales*, 52 25N 3 35W . . . 26
Poyang, *tn.*, *China*, 29 00N 116 38E 56
Poyang, L., *China*, 29 10N 116 10E 56
Poznán, *tn.*, *Pol.*, 52 25N 16 53E 41
Pozzuoli, *tn.*, *It.*, 40 99N 14 07E 45
Prague, *tn.*, *Cz.*, 50 05N 14 25E 41
Prato, *tn.*, *It.*, 43 53N 11 06E 45
Presidente Prudente, *tn.*, *Braz.*, 22 09S 51 24W . 77
Pressburg see Bratislava
Preston, *tn.*, *Eng.*, 53 46N 2 42W 25
Prestwick, *tn.*, *Scot.*, 55 30N 4 37W 23
Pretoria, *tn.*, *Rep. S. Afr.*, 25 45S 28 12E 67
Pribilof Is., *Bering Sea*, 56 00N 170 00W 70
Prilep, *tn.*, *Yug.*, 41 20N 21 32E 46
Primorsko Akhtarsk, *tn.*, *USSR*, 46 03N 38 11E . 47
Prince Edward I., *admin. reg.*, *Can.*, 45 00N 66 00W . 71
Prince George, *tn.*, *B.C.*, *Can.*, 53 55N 122 49W . 71
Prince of Wales I., *N.W. Terrs.*, *Can.*, 73 00N 99 00W . 71
Prince Patrick I., *N.W. Terrs.*, *Can.*, 77 00N 120 00W . 71
Prince Rupert, *tn.*, *B.C.*, *Can.*, 54 18N 130 17W . 71
Princes Risborough, *tn.*, *Eng.*, 51 44N 0 51W . . 27
Princess Astrid Coast, *Ant.*, 70 00S 12 00E . . . 80
Princess Ragnhild Coast, *Ant.*, 70 00S 30 00E . . 80
Principe, I., *G. of Guin.*, 1 37N 7 27E 67
Priozersk, *tn.*, *USSR*, 61 01N 50 08E 43
Pripet, R., *USSR*, 51 30N 30 00E 50
Pripet Marshes, *geog. reg.*, *USSR*, 52 00N 28 30E . 50
Pristina, *tn.*, *Yug.*, 42 39N 21 10E 46
Prokopyeusk, *tn.*, *USSR*, 53 55N 86 45E 52
Prome, *tn.*, *Burma*, 18 50N 95 14E 55
Provence, *geog. reg.*, *Fr.*, 43 40N 5 46E 45
Providence, *tn.*, *R.I.*, *USA*, 41 50N 71 28W . . . 73
Provideniya, *tn.*, *USSR*, 64 30N 173 11W 53
Provo, *tn.*, *Utah*, *USA*, 40 15N 111 40W 72
Prudhoe Bay, *tn.*, *Alaska*, *USA*, 71 20N 148 25W . 71
Prut, R., *USSR*, 46 03N 28 10E 50
Przemyśl, *tn.*, *Pol.*, 49 28N 22 48E 41
Pskov, *tn.*, *USSR*, 57 48N 28 26E 50
Pudsey, *tn.*, *Eng.*, 53 48N 1 40W 25
Puebla, *tn.*, *Mex.*, 19 03N 98 10W 71
Pueblo, *tn.*, *Colo.*, *USA*, 38 17N 104 38W 72
Puente Genil, *tn.*, *Sp.*, 37 24N 4 46W 44
Puerto Aisén, *tn.*, *Chile*, 45 27S 72 58W 77
Puerto Montt, *tn.*, *Chile*, 41 28S 73 00W 77
Puerto Rico, *self-gov. USA terr.*, *W.I.*,
18 10N 66 30W 71
Puerto Rico Trench, *W.I.*, 20 00N 67 00W 71

Puertollano, *tn.*, *Sp.*, 38 47N 4 07W 44
Pula, *tn.*, *Yug.*, 44 52N 13 52E 46
Pulap, I., *Pac. Oc.*, 7 38N 149 25E 63
Puno, *tn.*, *Bol.*, 15 53S 70 03W 77
Punta Arenas, *tn.*, *Chile*, 53 10S 70 56W 77
Purus, R., *Braz.*, 5 25S 64 00W 77
Pusan, *tn.*, *S. Kor.*, 35 05N 129 02E 57
Putao, *tn.*, *Burma*, 27 22N 97 27E 56
Putomayo, R., *Col./Peru*, 2 20S 74 10W 77
Puulavesi, L., *Fin.*, 61 50N 26 40E 43
Puy de Sancy, *mt.*, *Fr.*, 45 32N 2 48E 44
Puy, le, *tn.*, *Fr.*, 45 03N 3 53E 44
Pwllheli, *tn.*, *Wales*, 52 53N 4 25W 26
Pya, L., *USSR*, 66 08N 31 22E 43
Pyatigorsk, *tn.*, *USSR*, 44 04N 43 06E 51
Pyhäselkä, L., *Fin.*, 62 25N 29 55E 43
Pyongyang, *tn.*, *N. Kor.*, 39 00N 125 47E 57
Pyramids, *hist. site*, *Eg.*, 29 58N 31 09E 49
Pyrenees, *mts.*, *Fr./Sp.*, 42 45N 0 18E 44

Q

Qasr El Buraiqa, *tn.*, *Libya*, 31 00N 20 00E . . . 49
Qatar, *Sheikhdom*, *Persian Gulf*, 25 30N 51 15E . 52
Qattara Depression, *Eg.*, 29 00N 26 50E 49
Qena, *tn.*, *Eg.*, 26 08N 32 42E 49
Que Que, *tn.*, *Rhod.*, 18 55S 29 51E 67
Québec, *admin. reg.*, *Can.*, 52 00N 75 00W . . . 71
Québec, *tn.*, *Que.*, *Can.*, 46 50N 71 15W 71
Queen Charlotte Is., *B.C.*, *Can.*, 53 10N 132 00W . 71
Queen Elizabeth Is., *N.W. Terrs.*, *Can.*,
78 00N 114 30W 71
Queen Maud Land, *geog. reg.*, *Ant.*, 76 00S 15 00E . 80
Queen Maud Mts., *Ant.*, 86 00S 170 00W 80
Queensland, *admin. reg.*, *Austr.*, 22 30S 144 00E . 63
Queenstown, *tn.*, *Rep. S. Afr.*, 31 54S 26 53E . . 67
Quelimane, *tn.*, *Mozam.*, 17 53S 36 51E 67
Quelpart I., *S. Kor.*, 33 29N 126 34E 57
Quemoy I., *China*, 24 25N 118 24E 56
Quetta, *tn.*, *Pak.*, 30 15N 67 00E 54
Quezaltenango, *tn.*, *Guat.*, 14 50N 91 30W . . . 71
Quezon City, *tn.*, *Phil.*, 10 26N 123 19E 55
Qui Nhon, *tn.*, *Viet.*, 13 47N 109 11E 55
Quilpie, *tn.*, *Queensl.*, *Austr.*, 26 35S 144 14E . 63
Quimper, *tn.*, *Fr.*, 48 00N 4 06W 44
Quito, *tn.*, *Ec.*, 0 14S 78 30W 77
Qum, *tn.*, *Iran*, 34 39N 50 57E 52
Qunfidha, *tn.*, *Si. Arab.*, 19 09N 41 07E 52
Qus, *tn.*, *Eg.*, 25 53N 32 48E 49

R

Raasay, I., *Scot.*, 57 25N 6 04W 22
Raasay, Sound of, *Scot.*, 57 30N 6 08W 22
Rabat, *tn.*, *Mor.*, 34 02N 6 51W 48
Rabaul, *tn.*, *Pap. New Guin.*, 4 13S 152 11E . . 63
Racine, *tn.*, *Wis.*, *USA*, 42 42N 87 50W 73
Radom, *tn.*, *Pol.*, 51 26N 21 10E 41
Ragusa, *tn.*, *Sicily*, 36 56N 14 44E 45
Rainier, Mt., *Wash.*, *USA*, 46 50N 122 30W . . . 72
Raipur, *tn.*, *India*, 21 16N 81 42E 54
Rajkot, *tn.*, *India*, 22 18N 70 53E 54
Raleigh, *tn.*, *N.C.*, *USA*, 35 42N 78 40W 73
Ralik Chain, Is., *Pac. Oc.*, 9 30N 167 30E 63
Ramsey, *tn.*, *I.o.M.*, 54 19N 4 23W 24
Ramsey I., *Wales*, 51 53N 5 20W 26
Ramsgate, *tn.*, *Eng.*, 51 20N 1 25E 27
Rancagua, *tn.*, *Chile*, 34 10S 70 45W 77
Randalstown, *tn.*, *N. Ire.*, 54 45N 6 19W 24
Randers, *tn.*, *Den.*, 56 28N 10 03E 42
Rangoon, *tn.*, *Burma*, 16 47N 96 10E 55
Rannoch, L., *Scot.*, 56 41N 4 20W 23
Rannoch, Moor of, *geog. reg.*, *Scot.*, 56 38N 4 48W . 23
Rapid City, *tn.*, *S. Dak.*, *USA*, 44 06N 103 14W . 72
Raqqa, *tn.*, *Syria*, 35 57N 39 03E 49
Ras Dashan, *mt.*, *Ethiopia*, 13 15N 38 27E . . . 67
Ras el Unuf, *tn.*, *Libya*, 31 00N 18 00E 48
Ratak Chain, Is., *Pac. Oc.*, 9 00N 170 00E 63
Rathlin I., *N. Ire.*, 55 17N 6 15W 24
Rauma, *tn.*, *Fin.*, 61 09N 21 30E 42
Ravenna, *tn.*, *It.*, 44 25N 12 12E 45
Rawalpindi, *tn.*, *Pak.*, 33 40N 73 08E 54
Rawson, *tn.*, *Arg.*, 43 15S 65 53W 77
Rawtenstall, *tn.*, *Eng.*, 53 42N 2 18W 25
Rayleigh, *tn.*, *Eng.*, 51 36N 0 36E 27
Reading, *tn.*, *Eng.*, 51 28N 0 59W 27
Reading, *tn.*, *Pa.*, *USA*, 40 20N 75 55W 73

Recife, *tn.*, *Braz.*, 8 06S 34 53W 77
Recklinghausen, *tn.*, *W. Ger.*, 51 37N 7 11E . . . 39
Red, R., *Can./USA*, 47 57N 97 00W 72
Red, R., *USA*, 31 40N 93 00W 73
Red Basin, *China*, 30 00N 105 00E 56
Red R. see Song Koi
Red Sea, *Afr./Asia*, 20 00N 38 00E 67
Red Tower Pass, *Rom.*, 46 30N 24 00E 46
Redcar, *tn.*, *Eng.*, 54 37N 1 04W 25
Redding, *tn.*, *Calif.*, *USA*, 49 35N 122 24W . . . 72
Redditch, *tn.*, *Eng.*, 52 19N 1 56W 27
Redruth, *tn.*, *Eng.*, 50 13N 5 14W 26
Ree, L., *Rep. Ire.*, 53 30N 8 00W 24
Regensburg, *tn.*, *W. Ger.*, 49 01N 12 07E 41
Reggio di Calabria, *tn.*, *It.*, 38 06N 15 39E . . . 45
Reggio Nell'Emilia, *tn.*, *It.*, 44 42N 10 37E . . . 45
Regina, *tn.*, *Sask.*, *Can.*, 50 30N 104 38W . . . 72
Reigate, *tn.*, *Eng.*, 51 14N 0 13W 27
Reims, *tn.*, *Fr.*, 49 15N 4 02E 44
Reindeer L., *Sask.*, *Can.*, 57 20N 102 20W . . . 71
Remscheid, *tn.*, *W. Ger.*, 51 10N 7 11E 39
Renfrew, *tn.*, *Ont.*, *Can.*, 45 28N 76 44W . . . 73
Renfrew Heights, *hs.*, *Scot.*, 55 51N 4 49W . . . 23
Rennell I., *Solomon Is.*, *Pac. Oc.*, 11 45S 160 15E . 63
Rennes, *tn.*, *Fr.*, 48 06N 1 40W 44
Reno, *tn.*, *Nev.*, *USA*, 39 32N 119 49W 72
Republican, R., *Kans./Nebr.*, *USA*,
40 10N 99 00W 72
Resistencia, *tn.*, *Arg.*, 27 28S 59 00W 77
Reşiţa, *tn.*, *Rom.*, 45 16N 21 55E 46
Resolute, *tn.*, *N.W. Terrs.*, *Can.*, 74 40N 95 00W . 80
Réunion, I., *Fr. terr.*, *Indian Oc.*, 22 00S 56 00E . 67
Reus, *tn.*, *Sp.*, 41 10N 1 06E 44
Reutlingen, *tn.*, *W. Ger.*, 48 30N 9 13E 41
Revda, *tn.*, *USSR*, 56 49N 59 58E 51
Revilla Gigedo Is., *Pac. Oc.*, 18 40N 112 00W . . 71
Reykjanes, *hdl.*, *Ice.*, 63 48N 22 40W 43
Reykjavik, *tn.*, *Ice.*, 64 09N 21 58W 43
Reynosa, *tn.*, *Mex.*, 26 05N 98 18W 72
Rēzekne, *tn.*, *USSR*, 56 30N 27 22E 42
Rheden, *tn.*, *Neth.*, 52 01N 6 02E 39
Rheine, *tn.*, *W. Ger.*, 52 17N 7 26E 39
Rheydt, *tn.*, *W. Ger.*, 51 10N 6 27E 39
Rhine, R., *Eur.*, 51 48N 6 18E 41
Rhine-Westphalia, *admin. reg.*, *W. Ger.*,
51 45N 8 00E 41
Rhineland, *admin. reg.*, *W. Ger.*, 50 50N 7 00E . 39
Rhineland-Palatinate, *admin. reg.*, *W. Ger.*,
50 50N 7 00E 41
Rhode Island, *admin. reg.*, *USA*, 41 38N 71 37W . 73
Rhodes, I. Gr., 36 15N 28 10E 47
Rhodes, *tn.*, *Gr.*, 36 26N 28 14E 47
Rhodesia, *U.K. terr.*, *Afr.*, 19 00S 29 00E 67
Rhodope Mts., *Bulg.*, 41 40N 24 20E 46
Rhódos see Rhodes
Rhondda, *tn.*, *Wales*, 51 40N 3 30W 26
Rhône, R., *Fr.*, 45 54N 5 55E 45
Rhône Delta, *Fr.*, 43 20N 4 55E 45
Rhuddlan, *tn.*, *Wales*, 53 18N 3 27W 26
Rhyl, *tn.*, *Wales*, 53 19N 3 29W 26
Rhymney, *tn.*, *Wales*, 51 46N 3 18W 26
Ribble, R., *Eng.*, 54 13N 2 20W 25
Ribeirão, Prêto, *tn.*, *Braz.*, 21 09S 47 48W . . . 77
Richards Bay, *tn.*, *Rep. S. Afr.*, 28 47S 32 05E . 67
Richmond, *tn.*, *Eng.*, 54 24N 1 44W 25
Richmond, *tn.*, *Va.*, *USA*, 37 34N 77 27W . . . 73
Riesa, *tn.*, *E. Ger.*, 51 18N 13 18E 41
Rif Mts., *Mor.*, 34 00N 4 20W 48
Rift Valley, *geog. reg.*, *Kenya*, 0 05S 28 00E . . . 67
Riga, *tn.*, *USSR*, 56 53N 24 08E 42
Riga, Gulf of, *USSR*, 57 40N 23 45E 42
Rijeka, *tn.*, *Yug.*, 45 20N 14 27E 46
Rimini, *tn.*, *It.*, 44 03N 12 34E 45
Ringuassøy, I., *Nor.*, 69 55N 19 10E 43
Ringwood, *tn.*, *Eng.*, 50 51N 1 47W 27
Rio Branco, *tn.*, *Braz.*, 9 59S 67 49W 77
Rio Bravo del Norte, R. *Mex.*, 29 15N 103 30W . 72
Rio de Janeiro, *admin. reg.*, *Braz.*, 22 50S 43 00W . 77
Rio de Janeiro, *tn.*, *Braz.*, 22 53S 43 17W . . . 77
Rio de Oro, *geog. reg.*, *Maur./Mor.*,
22 00N 13 00W 66
Rio Gallegos, *tn.*, *Arg.*, 51 35S 69 15 W 77
Rio Grande, *admin. reg.*, *Braz.*, 29 00S 53 00W . 77
Rio Grande, R., *USA*, 28 00N 100 00W 72
Rio Grande, *tn.*, *Braz.*, 32 03S 52 08W 77
Rio Grande do Norte, *admin. reg.*, *Braz.*,
5 32S 37 54W 77
Ripley, *tn.*, *Eng.*, 54 03N 1 34W 25
Ripon, *tn.*, *Eng.*, 54 08N 1 31W 25
Risca, *tn.*, *Wales*, 51 37N 3 07W 26
Riverside, *tn.*, *Calif.*, *USA*, 33 59N 117 22W . . 72
Riviera di Levante, *geog. reg.*, *It.*,
44 23N 9 15E 45
Riviera di Ponente, *geog. reg.*, *It.*,
43 50N 7 58E 45
Riyadh, *tn.*, *Si. Arab.*, 24 39N 46 46E 52
Rizaiyeh, *tn.*, *Iran*, 37 32N 45 02E 49
Rize, *tn.*, *Tur.*, 41 03N 40 31E 47
Roanne, *tn.*, *Fr.*, 46 04N 4 05E 44
Roanoke, *tn.*, *Va.*, *USA*, 37 15N 79 58W 73
Rochdale, *tn.*, *Eng.*, 53 38N 2 09W 25
Roche-sur-Yonne, La, *tn.*, *Fr.*, 46 40N 1 25W . . 44
Rochefort, *tn.*, *Fr.*, 45 57N 0 58W 44
Rochelle, La, *tn.*, *Fr.*, 46 10N 1 10W 44
Rochester, *tn.*, *Eng.*, 51 24N 0 30E 27
Rochester, *tn.*, *N.Y.*, *USA*, 43 12N 77 37W . . . 73
Rock Springs, *tn.*, *Mont.*, *USA*, 46 50N 106 13W . 72
Rockford, *tn.*, *Ill.*, *USA*, 42 16N 89 06W 73
Rockhampton, *tn.*, *Queensl.*, *Austr.*, 23 22S 150 32E . 63
Rocky Mts., *USA*, 46 00N 111 00W 72
Roermond, *tn.*, *Neth.*, 51 12N 6 00E 39

Roeselare, tn., Belg., 50 57N 3 08E 39
Roma see Rome
Roma, tn., Queensl., Austr., 26 32S 148 46E 63
Romania, Rep., Eur., 46 00N 25 00E 46
Rome, tn., It., 41 53N 12 30E 45
Romsey, tn., Eng., 50 59N 1 30W 27
Rona, I., Scot., 57 33N 6 00W 22
Ronay, I., Scot., 57 29N 7 11W 22
Rondane Mts., Nor., 61 66N 9 57E 42
Rondônia, admin. reg., Braz., 11 00S 63 00W . . . 77
Rønne, tn., Den., 55 07N 14 43E 42
Roosendaal, tn., Neth., 51 32N 4 28E 39
Roraima, admin. reg., Braz., 2 24N 62 02W 77
Roraima, mt., Guy., 5 14N 60 44W 77
Røros, tn., Nor., 62 35N 11 23E 42
Rosa, Mt., Switz./It., 45 57N 7 53E 45
Rosario, tn., Arg., 33 00S 60 04W 77
Roscommon, admin. reg., Rep. Ire., 55 38N 8 11W . . 24
Roscrea, tn., Rep., Ire., 52 57N 7 47W 24
Rosenheim, tn., W. Ger., 47 51N 12 09E 41
Rosetta, tn., Eg., 31 25N 30 25E 49
Roskilde, tn., Den., 55 39N 12 07E 42
Roslavl, tn., USSR, 53 55N 32 53E 50
Ross Ice Shelf, Ant., 82 00S 180 00W 80
Ross-on-Wye, tn., Eng., 51 55N 2 35W 26
Ross Sea, Ant., 75 00S 165 00W 80
Rosslare, tn., Rep. Ire., 52 17N 6 23W 26
Rossosh, tn., USSR, 50 15N 39 20E 50
Røssuatnet, L., Nor., 65 45N 14 00E 43
Rostock, tn., E. Ger., 54 06N 12 09E 41
Rostov na Donu, tn., USSR, 47 15N 39 45E 50
Roswell, tn., N. Mex., USA, 33 24N 104 33W 72
Rota, I., Pac. Oc., 14 10N 145 15E 63
Rota, tn., Sp., 36 37N 6 21W 44
Rothaargebirge, mts., W. Ger., 50 55N 8 13E . . . 39
Rotherham, tn., Eng., 53 26N 1 20W 25
Rothes, tn., Scot., 57 31N 3 13W 22
Rothesay, tn., Scot., 55 51N 5 03W 23
Rotorua, tn., N.Z., 38 07S 176 17E 63
Rotterdam, tn., Neth., 51 55N 4 29E 39
Rotuma I., Pac. Oc., 12 30S 177 05E 63
Roubaix, tn., Fr., 50 42N 3 10E 39
Rouen, tn., Fr., 49 26N 1 05E 39
Rousay, I., Scot., 59 10N 3 02W 22
Rouyn, tn., Que., Can., 48 15N 79 00W 73
Rovaniemi, tn., Fin., 66 29N 25 40E 43
Rovno, tn., USSR, 50 39N 26 10E 50
Roxas, tn., Phil., 11 36N 122 45E 55
Royal Canal, Rep. Ire., 53 29N 7 00W 24
Royal Leamington Spa, tn., Eng., 52 18N 1 31W . . 27
Royal Tunbridge Wells, tn., Eng., 51 08N 0 16E . . 27
Royston, tn., Eng., 52 03N 0 01W 27
Rtishchevo, tn., USSR, 52 16N 43 45E 50
Rub al Khali, des., Si. Arab., 21 00N 51 00E 52
Rudnyy, tn., USSR, 53 00N 65 03E 51
Rudolf, L. see Turkana, L.
Rugby, tn., Eng., 52 23N 1 15W 27
Rugeley, tn., Eng., 52 46N 1 55W 27
Rügen, I., E. Ger., 54 22N 13 25E 42
Ruhr, R., W. Ger., 51 25N 7 15E 39
Rum., I., Scot., 57 00N 6 20W 23
Runcorn, tn., Eng., 53 20N 2 44W 25
Ruse, tn., Bulg., 43 50N 25 59E 46
Rushden, tn., Eng., 52 17N 0 36W 27
Rüsselsheim, tn., W. Ger., 50 00N 8 25E 39
Russian Soviet Federated Socialist Republic,
admin. reg., USSR, 59 00N 61 00E 52
Rutherglen, tn., Scot., 55 50N 4 12W 23
Ruthin, tn., Wales, 53 07N 3 18W 26
Ruvuma, R., Tanz., 11 30S 36 00E. 67
Ruwenzori, Mt., Ugan., 0 30N 29 55E 67
Rwanda, Rep., Afr., 2 30S 30 00E 67
Ryazan, tn., USSR, 54 37N 39 43E 50
Rybachi Peninsula, USSR, 69 43N 32 00E 43
Rybinsk, tn., USSR, 58 01N 38 52E 50
Rybinsk Reservoir, USSR, 58 30N 38 00E 50
Rybnitsa, tn., USSR, 47 42N 29 00E 47
Ryde, tn., Eng., 50 44N 1 10W 27
Rye, tn., Eng., 50 57N 0 44E 27
Ryukyu Is., Jap., 26 00N 127 00E 57
Rzeszow, tn., Pol., 50 04N 22 00E 41
Rzhev, tn., USSR, 56 15N 34 18E 50

S

's-Hertogenbosch, tn., Neth., 51 41N 5 19E 39
Sá da Bandeira see Lubango
Saale, R., E. Ger., 51 25N 11 56E 41
Saar, R., W. Ger., 49 20N 6 45E 39
Saarbrücken, tn., W. Ger., 49 15N 6 58E 41
Saaremaa I., USSR, 58 30N 22 30E. 42
Saarland, admin. reg., W. Ger., 49 20N 6 45E . . . 39
Sabadell, tn., Sp., 41 33N 2 07E 44
Sabah, comm. nat., Malay., 5 30N 116 30E 55
Sabine, R., La./Tex., USA, 31 30N 94 00W 73
Sabrata, hist. site, Libya, 32 50N 12 24E. 48
Sabzawar, tn., Iran, 36 13N 57 38E 51
Sacramento, tn., Calif., USA, 38 33N 121 30W . . . 72
Sacramento Valley, Calif., USA, 39 00N 122 30W . . 72
Sado, I., Jap., 38 15N 138 30E 57

Saffron Walden, tn., Eng., 52 01N 0 15E 27
Safi, tn., Mor., 32 20N 9 17W 66
Safonovo, tn., USSR, 55 08N 33 16E. 50
Saga, tn., Jap., 33 16N 130 18E 57
Saginaw, tn., Mich., USA, 43 25N 83 54W 73
Sagunto, tn., Sp., 39 40N 0 17W. 44
Sahara, des., Afr., 23 00N 5 00W 48
Saida, tn., Lebanon. 33 32N 35 22E 49
Saigon see Ho Chi Minh
Saimaa Canal, Fin./USSR, 61 05N 28 25E 42
Saimaa, L., Fin., 61 33N 29 35E 43
St. Albans, tn., Eng., 51 46N 0 21W 27
St. Andrews, tn., Scot., 56 20N 2 48W 23
St. Austell, tn., Eng., 50 20N 4 48W 26
St. Blazey, tn., Eng., 50 22N 4 43W 26
St. Brides Bay, Wales, 51 50N 5 16W 26
St. Brieuc, tn., Fr., 48 31N 2 45W 44
St. Catherines, tn., Ont., Can., 43 10N 79 15W . . 73
St. Catherine's Point, hdl., Eng., 50 34N 1 18W . . 27
St. David's, tn., Wales, 51 54N 5 16W 26
St. David's Head, hdl., Wales, 51 55N 5 19W . . . 26
St. Denis, tn., Réunion, 20 52S 55 27E 67
St. Dizier, tn., Fr., 47 28N 6 58E 45
St. Étienne, tn., Fr., 45 26N 4 23E 45
St. Fergus, tn., Scot., 57 33N 1 51W 22
St. Gallen, tn., Switz., 47 25N 9 23E 45
St. George's Channel, str., Rep. Ire./Wales,
52 00N 6 00W 26
St. Gotthard Pass, Switz., 43 34N 8 31E 45
St. Helena, I., UK cr. colony, S. Atlan. Oc.,
15 55S 5 44W 66
St. Helens, tn., Eng., 53 28N 2 44W 25
St. Helier, tn., Jersey, Chan. Is., 49 12N 2 07W . . 27
St. Ives, tn., Eng., 52 20N 5 29W 26
St. Ives Bay, Eng., 50 15N 5 27W 26
Saint John, tn., N.B., Can., 45 16N 66 03W 71
St. John's, tn., Newf. & Lab., Can., 47 34N 52 41W . . 71
St. Lawrence, R., Can./USA, 45 00N 76 00W 71
St. Lawrence, Gulf of, Can., 48 25N 62 00W 71
St. Lawrence I., Bering Sea, 64 00N 170 00W . . . 70
Saint-Louis, tn., Maur., 16 01N 16 30W 66
St. Louis, tn., Mo., USA, 38 40N 90 15W 73
St. Lucia, assoc. st. of UK, W.I., 14 00N 60 50W . . 77
St. Magnus Bay, Scot., 60 25N 1 35W 22
St. Malo, tn., Fr., 48 39N 2 00W 44
St. Mary's, I., Eng., 49 55N 6 20W 26
St. Nazaire, tn., Fr., 47 17N 2 12W 44
St. Neots, tn., Eng., 52 14N 0 17W 27
St. Niklaas, tn., Belg., 51 10N 4 09E 39
St. Omer, tn., Fr., 40 45N 2 15E 39
St. Paul, tn., Minn., USA, 45 00N 93 10W 73
St. Peter & St. Paul Rocks, Is., Atlan. Oc.,
0 56N 29 22W 77
St. Peter Port, tn., Guernsey, Chan. Is.,
49 27N 2 32W 27
St. Petersburg, tn., Fla., USA, 27 45N 82 40W . . . 73
St. Pierre & Miquelon, Is., Atlan. Oc.,
43 07N 56 22W 71
St. Pölten, tn., Aust., 48 13N 15 37E 45
St. Quentin, tn., Fr., 49 51N 3 17E 39
St. Vincent, assoc. st. of UK, W.I.,
13 15N 61 12W 77
St. Vincent, C., hdl., Port., 37 01N 8 59W 44
Sainte Marie, C., hdl., Madag., 25 34S 45 10E . . 67
Saipan, I., Pac. Oc., 15 12N 145 43E 63
Sakarya, R., Tur., 40 05N 31 00E 47
Sakhalin, I., USSR, 51 00N 143 00E 53
Salado, R., Arg., 30 00S 61 42W 77
Salala, tn., Oman, 17 00N 54 04E 52
Salamanca, tn., Sp., 40 58N 5 40W 44
Salavat, tn., USSR, 53 22N 55 50E 51
Saldanha, tn., Rep. S. Afr., 33 00S 17 56E 67
Sale, tn., Eng., 53 26N 2 19W 25
Salé, tn., Mor., 34 04N 6 50W 48
Salem, tn., India, 11 38N 78 08E 54
Salem, tn., Oreg., USA, 44 57N 123 01W 72
Salerno, tn., It., 40 40N 14 46E 45
Salford, tn., Eng., 53 30N 2 16W 25
Salgótarján, tn., Hung., 48 05N 19 47E 41
Salihli, tn., Tur., 38 29N 28 08E 47
Salina, tn., Kans., USA, 38 53N 97 36W 72
Salinas, tn., Calif., USA, 36 39N 121 40W 72
Salisbury, tn., Eng., 51 05N 1 48W 27
Salisbury, tn., Rhod., 17 43S 31 05E 67
Salisbury Plain, geog. reg., Eng., 51 13N 2 00W . . 27
Salo, tn., Fin., 60 23N 23 10E 42
Salonica see Thessaloniki
Salop, admin. reg., Eng., 52 36N 1 39W 26
Salpausselkä, geog. reg., Fin., 60 50N 26 45E . . . 42
Salsk, tn., USSR, 46 30N 41 33E 51
Salt Lake City, tn., Utah, USA, 40 45N 111 55W . . 72
Salta, tn., Arg., 24 46S 65 28W 77
Saltash, tn., Eng., 50 24N 4 12W 26
Saltburn, tn., Eng., 54 35N 0 58W 25
Saltcoats, tn., Scot., 55 38N 4 47W 23
Saltillo, tn., Mex., 25 30N 101 00W 72
Salto, tn., Urug., 31 27S 57 50W 77
Salton Sea, L., Calif., USA, 33 20N 116 00W . . . 72
Salûm, tn., Eg., 31 31N 25 09E 49
Salvador, tn., Braz., 12 58S 38 29W 77
Salween, R., Burma, 24 00N 98 00E 55
(as Nu Kiang in China)
Salzburg, tn., Aust., 47 48N 13 03E 45
Salzgitter, tn., W. Ger., 52 02N 10 22E 41
Samar, I., Phil., 12 00N 125 00E 55
Samarinda, tn., Indon., 0 30S 117 09E 55
Samarkand, tn., USSR, 39 40N 66 57E 52
Sambre, R., Belg., 50 02N 4 15E 39
Sámos, I., Gr., 37 45N 26 50E 46
Samothrace, I., Gr., 40 27N 25 32E 46
Samsun, tn., Tur., 41 17N 36 22E 47

San Ambrosia I., Pac. Oc., 26 28S 79 53W 77
San Angelo, tn., Tex., USA, 31 28N 100 28W . . . 72
San Antonio, tn., Tex., USA, 29 25N 98 30W 72
San Bernardino, tn., Calif., USA, 34 07N 117 18W . . 72
San Carlos de Bariloche, tn., Arg., 41 11S 71 23W . . 77
San Cristobal, tn., Ven., 7 46N 72 15W 77
San Cristobal I., Solomon Is., Pac. Oc.,
10 30S 167 00E 63
San Diego, tn., Calif., USA, 32 45N 117 10W 72
San Felix I., Pac. Oc., 26 23S 80 05W 77
San Fernando, tn., Sp., 36 28N 6 12W 44
San Francisco, tn., Calif., USA, 37 45N 122 27W . . 72
San Joaquin Valley, Calif., USA, 37 00N 120 00W . . 72
San Jorge, Gulf of, Arg., 46 00S 66 00W 77
San Jose, tn., Calif., USA, 37 20N 121 55W 72
San José, tn., Costa Rica, 9 59N 84 04W 71
San Juan, R., Ariz./Utah, USA, 37 15N 109 30W . . 72
San Juan, tn., Arg., 31 33S 68 31W 77
San Juan, tn., P. Rico, 18 29N 66 08W 71
San Juan Mts., Colo./N. Mex., USA,
37 00N 106 30W 72
San Lucas, C., hdl., Mex., 22 50N 109 55W 71
San Luis, tn., Arg., 33 20S 66 23W 77
San Luis Obispo, tn., Calif., USA, 35 16N 120 40W . . 72
San Luis Potosí, tn., Mex., 22 10N 101 00W 71
San Marino, Rep., Eur., 43 56N 12 26E 45
San Mattias, Gulf of, Arg., 41 30S 64 00W 77
San Pablo, tn., Phil., 14 03N 121 19E 55
San Pedro Sula, tn., Hond., 15 26N 88 01W 71
San Remo, tn., It., 43 48N 7 46E 45
San Salvador, I., The Bahamas, 24 00N 74 32W . . 73
San Salvador, tn., El Salvador, 13 40N 89 10W . . 71
San Sebastián, tn., Sp., 43 19N 1 59W 44
San Severo, tn., It., 41 41N 15 23E 45
Sana, tn., Yemen, 15 23N 44 14E 52
Sanae, Rep. S. Afr. base, Ant., 71 00S 3 00W . . . 80
Sanakan, tn., Sabah, Malay., 5 52N 118 04E 55
Sancti-Spiritus, tn., Cuba, 21 55N 79 28W 73
Sand Hills, Nebr., USA, 42 00N 101 20W 72
Sanday, I., Scot., 57 03N 6 30W 22
Sandefjord, tn., Nor., 59 10N 10 15E 42
Sandnes, tn., Nor., 58 51N 5 45E 42
Sandnessjøen, tn., Nor., 66 01N 12 40E 43
Sandoy, I., Faeroe Is., 61 52N 7 01W 43
Sandray, I., Scot., 56 53N 7 31W 23
Sandviken, tn., Swed., 60 38N 16 50E 42
Sandwich, tn., Eng., 51 17N 1 20E 27
Sanlúcar de Barrameda, tn., Sp., 36 46N 6 21W . . 44
Sanmenhsia, tn., China, 34 46N 111 17E 56
Sansui, tn., China, 27 00N 108 30E 56
Santa Anna, tn., Calif., USA, 33 44N 117 54W . . . 72
Santa Barbara, tn., Calif., USA, 34 25N 119 41W . . 72
Santa Caterina, admin. reg., Braz., 27 25S 48 30W . . 77
Santa Clara, tn., Cuba, 22 25N 79 58W 73
Santa Cruz, tn., Bol., 17 45S 63 14W 77
Santa Cruz, tn., Can. Is., 28 28N 16 15W 66
Santa Cruz Is., Solomon Is., Pac. Oc.,
10 30S 166 00E 63
Santa Fe, tn., Arg., 31 38S 60 43W 77
Santa Fe, tn., N. Mex., USA, 35 41N 105 57W . . . 72
Santa Isabel I., Solomon Is., Pac. Oc.,
7 30S 159 00E 63
Santa Isabel, Maclas Nguemà I., see Malabo
Santa Maria, tn., Braz., 29 40S 53 47W 77
Santa Marta, tn., Col., 11 18N 74 10W 77
Santa Maura, I., Gr., 38 40N 20 43E 46
Santa Monica, tn., Calif., USA, 34 00N 118 25W . . 72
Santa Rosa, tn., Arg., 36 37S 64 17W 77
Santa Rosa, tn., Calif., USA, 38 26N 122 43W . . . 72
Santai, tn., China, 31 05N 105 02E 56
Santander, tn., Sp., 43 28N 3 48W 44
Santarém, tn., Braz., 2 26S 54 41W 77
Santarém, tn., Port., 39 14N 8 40W 44
Santiago, R., Mex., 22 00N 104 00W 71
Santiago, tn., Chile, 33 30S 70 40W 77
Santiago de Compostela, tn., Sp., 42 52N 8 33W . . 44
Santiago de Cuba, tn., Cuba, 20 00N 75 49W . . . 73
Santiago del Estero, tn., Arg., 27 48S 64 15W . . . 77
Santo Domingo, tn., Dom. Rep., 18 30N 69 57W . . 71
Santo Tomé de Guyana, tn., Ven., 9 26N 61 08W . . 77
Santos, tn., Braz., 23 56S 46 22W 77
Sanyuan, tn., China, 34 40N 108 56E 56
São Francisco, R., Braz., 15 05S 43 46W 77
São José, tn., Braz., 20 50S 49 20W 77
São Luis, tn., Braz., 2 34S 44 16W 77
São Paulo, admin. reg., Braz., 22 00S 49 00W . . . 77
São Paulo, tn., Braz., 23 33S 46 39W 77
São Roque, C., hdl., Braz., 5 28S 35 17W 77
São Tomé, I., G. of Guin., 0 25N 6 35E 67
São Tomé & Principe, Is., Rep., G. of Guin.,
0 25N 6 35E 67
Saône, R., Fr., 47 00N 4 55E 45
Sapporo, tn., Jap., 43 05N 141 21E 57
Saragossa see Zaragoza
Sarajevo, tn., Yug., 43 52N 18 26E 46
Saransk, tn., USSR, 54 12N 45 10E 50
Sarapul, tn., USSR, 56 29N 53 49E 51
Saratov, tn., USSR, 51 30N 45 55E 51
Sarawak, comm. nat., Malay., 2 00N 113 00E . . . 55
Sardinia, admin. reg., It., 40 00N 9 00E 45
Sardinia, I., It., 40 00N 9 00E 45
Sarek, geog. reg., Swed., 67 29N 17 40E 43
Sarh, tn., Chad, 9 08N 18 22E 67
Sari, tn., Iran, 36 33N 53 06E 52
Sariwon, tn., N. Kor., 38 30N 125 45E 57
Sark, I., Chan. Is., UK, 49 26N 2 22W 27
Särna, tn., Swed., 61 40N 13 10E 42
Sarnia, tn., Ont., Can., 42 57N 82 24W 73
Sarreguemines, tn., Fr., 49 06N 7 04E 39
Sarysu, R., USSR, 46 29N 67 14N 51
Sasebo, tn., Jap., 33 10N 129 42E 57

Saskatchewan, *admin. reg., Can.,* 55 40N 109 00W . . 71
Saskatchewan, *R., Sask., Can.,* 53 40N 107 00W . . . 71
Saskatoon, *tn., Sask., Can.,* 52 10N 106 40W 71
Sassari, *tn., Sard.,* 40 43N 8 34E 45
Sassnitz, *tn., E. Ger.,* 54 32N 13 40E 41
Satka, *tn., USSR,* 55 06N 58 59E 51
Satu-Mare, *tn., Rom.,* 47 48N 22 52E 46
Saudárkrókur, *tn., Ice.,* 64 45N 19 39W 43
Saudi Arabia, *Kingd., Asia,* 26 00N 44 00E 52
Sault Sainte Marie, *tn., Ont., Can.,*
46 32N 84 20W 73
Sava, *R., Yug.* 44 40N 19 50E 46
Savannah, *R., Ga./S.C., USA,* 34 00N 82 30W 73
Savannah, *tn., Ga., USA,* 32 04N 81 07W 73
Savannakhet, *tn., Laos,* 16 34N 104 45E 55
Savona, *tn., It.,* 44 18N 8 28E 45
Savonlinna, *tn., Fin.,* 61 54N 28 55E 43
Savoy, *geog. reg., Fr.,* 45 26N 6 35E 45
Sawbridgeworth, *tn., Eng.,* 51 50N 0 09E 27
Sawel, *mt., N. Ire.,* 54 49N 7 03W 23
Saxony, *admin. reg., E. Ger.,* 51 28N 13 06E 41
Sayan Ranges, *mts., USSR,* 51 50N 95 00E 53
Saynshand, *tn., Mong.,* 44 58N 110 10E 56
Scafell Pikes, *mt., Eng.,* 54 28N 3 12W 25
Scalpay, *I., Scot.,* 57 18N 6 00W 22
Scapa Flow, *anch., Scot.,* 58 52N 3 00W 22
Scarba, *I., Scot.,* 56 11N 5 42W 23
Scarborough, *tn., Eng.,* 54 17N 0 24W 25
Scarp, *I., Scot.,* 58 02N 7 07W 22
Scarpanto see Kárpathos
Schefferville, *tn., Que., Can.,* 54 50N 67 00W 71
Schelde, *R., Belg.,* 51 10N 4 20E 39
Schenectady, *tn., N.Y., USA,* 42 48N 73 57W 73
Schiedam, *tn., Neth.,* 51 55N 4 25E 39
Schiermonnikoog, *I., Neth.,* 53 30N 6 15E 39
Schleswig-Holstein, *admin. reg., W. Ger.,*
54 10N 9 40E 41
Schwedt, *tn., E. Ger.,* 53 04N 14 17E 41
Schwerin, *tn., E. Ger.,* 53 38N 11 25E 41
Scilly, Isles of, *Eng.,* 49 55N 6 15W 26
Scotland, *Kingd., UK,* 57 00N 4 00W 40
Scott I., *Ant.,* 67 00S 179 00E 80
Scott Station, *N.Z. base, Ant.,* 77 00S 168 00E . . . 80
Scranton, *tn., Pa., USA,* 41 25N 75 40W 73
Scunthorpe, *tn., Eng.,* 53 35N 0 39W 25
Seaford, *tn., Eng.,* 50 46N 0 06E 27
Seaham, *tn., Eng.,* 54 50N 1 20W 25
Seattle, *tn., Wash., USA,* 47 35N 122 20W 72
Sebha, *tn., Libya,* 27 04N 14 25E 48
Sedan, *tn., Fr.,* 49 42N 4 57E 39
Seg, L., *USSR,* 63 00N 33 10E 43
Segesta, *hist. site, Sicily,* 37 57N 12 51E 45
Segezha, *tn., USSR,* 63 42N 34 19E 43
Ségou, *tn., Mali,* 13 28N 6 18W 66
Segovia, *tn., Sp.,* 40 57N 4 07W 44
Seil, *I., Scot.,* 56 17N 5 37W 23
Seiland, *I., Nor.,* 70 25N 23 10E 43
Seinäjoki, *tn., Fin.,* 62 45N 22 55E 43
Seine, *R., Fr.,* 49 13N 1 52E 44
Sekondi-Takoradi, *tn., Ghana,* 4 59N 1 43W 66
Selby, *tn., Eng.,* 53 48N 1 04W 25
Selenga, *R., USSR,* 49 20N 101 00E 53
Selinunte, *hist. site, Sicily,* 37 35N 12 50E 45
Selkirk, *tn., Scot.,* 55 33N 2 50W 23
Selsey Bill, *hdl., Eng.,* 50 43N 0 48W 27
Selvas, *geog. reg., Braz.,* 6 30S 67 00W 77
Semarang, *tn., Indon.,* 6 58S 110 29E 55
Semipalatinsk, *tn., USSR,* 50 26N 80 16E 51
Semmering Pass, *Aust.,* 43 41N 15 45E 45
Sendai, *tn., Jap.,* 38 16N 140 52E 57
Senegal, *Rep., Afr.,* 14 30N 14 30W 66
Senegal, *R., Afr.,* 16 30N 15 30W 66
Senja, *I., Nor.,* 69 15N 17 20E 43
Senjavin Group, *Is., Pac. Oc.,* 6 00N 158 00E 63
Seoul, *tn., S. Kor.,* 37 30N 127 00E 57
Sept-Îles, *tn., Que., Can.,* 50 13N 66 22W 71
Serbia, *admin. reg., Yug.,* 43 30N 21 00E 46
Serengeti Nat. Park, *Kenya,* 2 30S 35 00E 67
Sergin, *tn., USSR,* 63 50N 65 00E 51
Sergipe, *admin. reg., Braz.,* 10 30S 37 20W 77
Serov, *tn., USSR,* 59 42N 60 32E 51
Serowe, *tn., Bots.,* 22 25S 26 44E 67
Serpukhov, *tn., USSR,* 54 53N 37 25E 50
Sérrai, *tn., Gr.,* 41 03N 23 33E 46
Sétif, *tn., Alg.,* 36 11N 5 24E 48
Settat, *tn., Mor.,* 33 04N 7 37W 48
Settle, *tn., Eng.,* 54 04N 2 16W 25
Setúbal, *tn., Port.,* 38 31N 8 54W 44
Sevan, *tn., USSR,* 40 33N 44 56E 51
Sevan, L., *USSR,* 40 20N 45 28E 49
Sevastopol, *tn., USSR,* 44 36N 33 31E 47
Sevenoaks, *tn., Eng.,* 51 16N 0 12E 27
Severn, *R., Eng./Wales,* 52 15N 2 13W 26
Severn, *R., Ont., Can.,* 56 50N 87 00W 71
Severnaya Zemlya, *USSR Arch., Arctic Oc.,*
79 00N 100 00E 53
Severo Kurilsk, *tn., USSR,* 50 40N 156 01E 53
Severodvinsk, *tn., USSR,* 64 35N 39 50E 50
Severomorsk, *tn., USSR,* 69 05N 33 30E 43
Sevilla see Seville
Seville, *tn., Sp.,* 37 24N 5 59W 44
Seward, *tn., Alaska, USA,* 60 05N 149 34W 70
Seychelles, *Rep., Indian Oc.,* 5 00S 56 00E 67
Seyhan, *R., Tur.,* 37 40N 35 50E 47
Sfax, *tn., Tun.,* 34 45N 10 43E 48
Shaba, *admin. reg., Zaire,* 10 00S 28 30E 67
Shackleton Ice Shelf, *Ant.,* 64 00S 100 00E 80
Shadrinsk, *tn., USSR,* 56 08N 63 32E 51
Shaftesbury, *tn., Eng.,* 51 01N 2 12W 27
Shahrud, *tn., Iran,* 36 30N 55 00E 51
Shahsien, *tn., China,* 26 27N 117 42E 56

Shakhty, *tn., USSR,* 47 43N 40 16E 50
Shakhunya, *tn., USSR,* 57 41N 46 46E 50
Shanghai, *admin. reg., China,* 31 15N 121 00E 57
Shanghai, *tn., China,* 31 13N 121 25E 57
Shanghsien, *tn., China,* 33 30N 109 58E 56
Shangkiu, *tn., China,* 34 28N 115 42E 56
Shangyashan, *tn., China,* 46 35N 131 15E 57
Shanhaikwan, *tn., China,* 39 59N 119 45E 57
Shanklin, *tn., Eng.,* 50 38N 1 10W 27
Shannon, *R., Rep. Ire.,* 53 10N 8 40W 40
Shansi, *admin. reg., China,* 38 20N 112 00E 56
Shantan, *tn., China,* 38 50N 101 08E 56
Shantung, *admin. reg., China,* 36 00N 117 30E 56
Shantung Peninsula, *China,* 37 00N 120 00E 56
Shaohing, *tn., China,* 30 02N 120 35E 57
Shaoyang, *tn., China,* 27 10N 111 25E 56
Shapinsay, *I., Scot.,* 59 03N 2 51W 22
Sharasume, *tn., China,* 47 30N 88 00E 52
Shasi, *tn., China,* 30 16N 112 20E 56
Shasta, Mt., *Calif., USA,* 41 25N 122 12W 72
Shatt al Arab, *R., Iran/Iraq,* 30 00N 48 31E 52
Sheelin, L., *Rep. Ire.,* 53 48N 7 20W 24
Sheerness, *tn., Eng.,* 51 27N 0 45E 27
Sheffield, *tn., Eng.,* 53 23N 1 30W 25
Shensi, *admin. reg., China,* 35 45N 109 30E 56
Shenyang, *tn., China,* 41 50N 123 26E 57
Sheppey, Isle of, *Eng.,* 51 25N 0 50E 27
Shepton Mallet, *tn., Eng.,* 51 12N 2 33W 26
Sherborne, *tn., Eng.,* 50 57N 2 31W 26
Sherbrooke, *tn., Que., Can.,* 45 24N 71 54W 73
Sheridan, *tn., Wyo., USA,* 44 48N 106 57W 72
Shetland, *admin. reg., Scot.,* 60 21N 1 30W 22
Shetland Is., *Scot.,* 60 30N 1 30W 22
Shevchenko, *tn., USSR,* 43 37N 51 11E 51
Shiant Isles, *Scot.,* 57 54N 6 30W 22
Shiel, L., *Scot.,* 57 00N 5 40W 23
Shigatse, *tn., Tibet,* 29 18N 88 50E 54
Shihkiachwang, *tn., China,* 38 04N 114 28E 56
Shihkwaikow, *tn., China,* 40 52N 110 14E 56
Shihping, *tn., China,* 23 43N 102 27E 56
Shikoku, *I., Jap.,* 33 30N 133 30E 57
Shilka, *R., USSR,* 52 50N 119 00E 53
Shimizu, *tn., Jap.,* 35 01N 138 29E 57
Shimonoseki, *tn., Jap.,* 33 59N 130 58E 57
Shin, L., *Scot.,* 58 07N 4 30W 22
Shioku, *I., Jap.,* 33 30N 133 30E 57
Ship Canal, *Eng.,* 53 25N 2 40W 25
Shipley, *tn., Eng.,* 53 50N 1 47W 25
Shiraz, *tn., Iran,* 29 38N 52 34E 52
Shiukwan, *tn., China,* 24 54N 113 33E 56
Shizuoka, *tn., Jap.,* 34 59N 138 24E 57
Shkodër, L., *Alb.,* 42 13N 10 40E 46
Shloder, *tn., Alb.,* 42 03N 19 01E 46
Sholapur, *tn., India,* 17 43N 75 56E 54
Showa, *Jap. base, Ant.,* 68 00S 40 00E 80
Showhsien, *tn., China,* 32 50N 117 00E 56
Shreveport, *tn., La., USA,* 32 30N 93 46W 73
Shrewsbury, *tn., Eng.,* 52 43N 2 45W 26
Shuicheng, *tn., China,* 27 00N 104 50E 56
Shuleh Ho, *R., China,* 41 00N 95 50E 56
Shumen, *tn., Bulg.,* 43 17N 26 55E 46
Shumerlya, *tn., USSR,* 55 30N 46 25E 50
Shuntak, *tn., China,* 22 54N 113 08E 56
Shuya, *tn., USSR,* 56 49N 41 23E 50
Shwangcheng, *tn., China,* 45 24N 126 14E 57
Shwangliao, *tn., China,* 43 30N 123 29E 57
Shwebo, *tn., Burma,* 22 35N 95 42E 56
Si Kiang, *R., China,* 23 00N 111 00E 56
Siakwan, *tn., China,* 25 33N 100 09E 56
Siam see Thailand
Siam, Gulf of, *Thai.,* 11 00N 101 00E 55
Sian, *tn., China,* 34 02N 109 00E 56
Siang Kiang, *R., China,* 27 10N 112 45E 56
Siangfan, *tn., China,* 32 15N 112 02E 56
Siangsiang, *tn., China,* 27 46N 112 26E 56
Siangtan, *tn., China,* 27 55N 112 47E 56
Siangyang, *tn., China,* 32 18N 111 00E 56
Siaokan, *tn., China,* 30 58N 113 57E 56
Šiaullai, *tn., USSR,* 55 51N 23 20E 42
Siberia, *geog. reg., USSR,* 60 00N 100 00E 53
Sibewik, *tn., Yug.,* 43 35N 15 55E 46
Sibiu, *tn., Rom.,* 45 46N 24 09E 46
Sibu, *tn., Sar., Malay.,* 2 18N 111 49E 55
Sichang, *tn., China,* 27 52N 102 16E 56
Sicily, *admin. reg., It.,* 37 30N 14 30E 45
Sicily, *I., It.,* 37 30N 14 00E 45
Sidi-bel-Abbès, *tn., Alg.,* 35 15N 0 39W 48
Sidlaw Hills, *Scot.,* 56 32N 3 10W 23
Sidley, Mt., *Ant.,* 77 12S 129 00W 80
Sidmouth, *tn., Eng.,* 50 41N 3 15W 26
Siedlce, *tn., Pol.,* 52 10N 22 18E 41
Siegen, *tn., W. Ger.,* 50 52N 8 02E 39
Siena, *tn., It.,* 43 19N 11 19E 45
Sienyang, *tn., China,* 34 22N 108 42E 56
Sierra de Gredos, *mts., Sp.,* 40 20N 5 00W 44
Sierra de Guadarrama, *mts., Sp.,* 41 00N 4 00W . . 44
Sierra Leone, *Rep., Afr.,* 9 00N 12 00W 66
Sierra Madre, Eastern, *geog. reg., Mex.,*
28 00N 103 30W 71
Sierra Madre, Southern, *geog. reg., Mex.,*
18 30N 102 30W 71
Sierra Madre, Western, *geog. reg., Mex.,*
31 00N 119 00W 71
Sierra Morena, *mts., Sp.,* 38 20N 4 00W 44
Sierra Nevada, *mts., Sp.,* 37 03N 3 15W 44
Sierra Nevada, *mts., USA,* 39 00N 120 30W 72
Sighişoara, *tn., Rom.,* 46 12N 24 48E 46
Siglufjördur, *tn., Ice.,* 66 09N 18 55E 43
Signy I., *UK base, Ant.,* 61 00S 46 00W 80
Sikhote Alin Range, *mts., USSR,* 46 00N 136 00E . . 57

Sikkim, *admin. reg., India,* 27 30N 87 00E 54
Silesia, *geog. reg., Pol.,* 50 48N 17 00E 41
Silistra, *tn., Bulg.,* 44 06N 27 17E 47
Siljan, L., *Swed.,* 60 55N 14 50E 42
Silsden, *tn., Eng.,* 53 55N 1 55W 25
Simav, *R., Tur.,* 38 40N 28 30E 47
Simferopol, *tn., USSR,* 44 57N 34 05E 47
Simplon Pass, *Switz.,* 46 15N 8 03E 45
Simpson Desert, *N. Terr., Austr.,* 25 00S 137 00E . . 63
Sinai Peninsula, *Eg.,* 29 00N 34 00E 49
Sinchang, *tn., N. Kor.,* 40 02N 128 50E 57
Sinelnikovo, *tn., USSR,* 48 19N 35 32E 47
Singapore, *Rep., comm. nat., Asia,* 1 17N 103 51E . . 55
Singaradja, *tn., Indon.,* 8 06S 115 07E 55
Singtai, *tn., China,* 37 08N 114 29E 56
Sinhailien, *tn., China,* 34 31N 119 00E 57
Sinhsien, *tn., China,* 38 25N 112 45E 56
Sining, *tn., China,* 36 35N 101 55E 56
Sinkiang Uighur, *admin. reg., China,* 42 00N 85 00E . . 52
Sinkin, *tn., China,* 39 30N 122 29E 57
Sinmin, *tn., China,* 42 02N 122 45E 57
Sinop, *tn., Tur.,* 42 02N 35 09E 47
Sinsiang, *tn., China,* 35 16N 113 51E 56
Sintai, *tn., China,* 35 56N 117 49E 57
Sinuiju, *tn., N. Kor.,* 40 04N 124 25E 57
Sinyang, *tn., China,* 32 10N 114 05E 56
Sioux City, *tn., Iowa, USA,* 42 30N 96 28W 72
Sioux Falls, *tn., S. Dak., USA,* 43 34N 96 42W . . . 72
Siple Station, *USA base, Ant.,* 75 30S 88 00W 80
Siracusa, *tn., Sicily,* 37 04N 15 18E 45
Siret, *R., Rom.,* 47 58N 26 05E 46
Sirte, *tn., Libya,* 31 10N 16 39E 48
Sirte, Gulf of, *Libya,* 32 00N 17 00E 48
Sisak, *tn., Yug.,* 45 30N 16 22E 46
Sittingbourne, *tn., Eng.,* 51 21N 0 44E 27
Sivash, L., *USSR,* 46 00N 34 00E 47
Siwa, *tn., Eg.,* 29 11N 25 31E 49
Skagen, *tn., Den.,* 57 44N 10 37E 42
Skagerrak, *chan., Den./Nor.,* 57 50N 9 00E 42
Skagway, *tn., Alaska, USA,* 59 23N 135 20W 71
Skara Brae, *hist. site, Scot.,* 59 03N 3 20W 22
Skegness, *tn., Eng.,* 53 10N 0 21E 27
Skellefteå, *tn., Swed.,* 64 45N 21 00E 43
Skellefteälven, *R., Swed.,* 65 25N 19 00E 43
Skelmersdale, *tn., Eng.,* 53 33N 2 48W 25
Skien, *tn., Nor.,* 59 14N 9 37E 42
Skikda, *tn., Alg.,* 36 53N 6 54E 48
Skipton, *tn., Eng.,* 53 58N 2 01W 25
Skokholm, *I., Wales,* 51 42N 5 16W 26
Skomer, *I., Wales,* 51 45N 5 18W 26
Skopje, *tn., Yug.,* 42 00N 21 28E 46
Skövde, *tn., Swed.,* 58 24N 13 52E 42
Skovorodino, *tn., USSR,* 54 00N 123 53E 53
Skye, *I., Scot.,* 57 15N 6 10W 22
Slaney, *R., Rep. Ire.,* 52 52N 6 45W 24
Slantsy, *tn., USSR,* 59 09N 28 09E 42
Slavonski Brod, *tn., Yug.,* 45 11N 18 00E 46
Slavyansk na Kubani, *tn., USSR,* 45 14N 38 08E . . . 47
Sleaford, *tn., Eng.,* 53 00N 0 24W 25
Sleat, *geog. reg., Scot.,* 57 01N 6 00W 23
Sleat, Sound of, *Scot.,* 57 05N 5 47W 23
Slieve Bloom Mts., *Rep. Ire.,* 53 04N 7 40W 24
Slieve Donard, *mt., N. Ire.,* 54 11N 5 55W 24
Sligo, *tn., Rep. Ire.,* 54 17N 8 27W 40
Sliven, *tn., Bulg.,* 42 40N 26 19E 46
Slonim, *tn., USSR,* 53 05N 25 21E 42
Slough, *tn., Eng.,* 51 31N 0 36W 27
Slovak Republic, *admin. reg., Cz.,* 48 25N 22 45E . . 41
Slovenia, *admin. reg., Yug.,* 45 58N 14 30E 46
Sluch, *R., USSR,* 51 10N 26 20E 42
Słupsk, *tn., Pol.,* 54 28N 17 00E 41
Slutsk, *tn., USSR,* 53 02N 27 31E 42
Smederevo, *tn., Yug.,* 44 40N 20 56E 46
Smøla, *I., Nor.,* 63 25N 8 00E 43
Smolensk, *tn., USSR,* 54 49N 32 04E 50
Smyrna see İzmir
Snaefell, *mt., Ice.,* 64 48N 15 34W 43
Snaefell, *mt., I.o.M.,* 54 16N 4 28W 24
Snaefellsjökull, *ice-cap, Ice.,* 64 48N 23 47W 43
Snake, *R., Idaho/Oreg., USA,* 44 30N 117 00W . . . 72
Snake River Plain, *geog. reg., Idaho, USA,*
43 13N 113 00W 72
Snizort, L., *Scot.,* 57 33N 6 28W 22
Snowdon, *mt., Wales,* 53 04N 4 05W 26
Soay, *I., Scot.,* 57 08N 6 14W 22
Sobral, *tn., Braz.,* 3 45S 40 20W 77
Soche, *tn., China,* 38 27N 77 16E 52
Sochi, *tn., USSR,* 43 35N 39 46E 47
Socotra, *I., S. Yemen,* 12 30N 54 00E 52
Södertälje, *tn., Swed.,* 59 11N 17 39E 42
Sofia, *tn., Bulg.,* 42 40N 23 18E 46
Sofiya see Sofia
Sognefjord, *fd., Nor.,* 61 10N 6 00E 42
Sohag, *tn., Eg.,* 26 33N 31 42E 49
Soissons, *tn., Fr.,* 49 23N 3 20E 39
Sokodé, *tn., Togo,* 8 59N 1 11E 66
Sokoto, *tn., Nig.,* 13 02N 5 15E 67
Solent, The, *chan., Eng.,* 50 45N 1 25W 27
Solikamsk, *tn., USSR,* 59 40N 56 45E 51
Solingen, *tn., W. Ger.,* 51 10N 7 05E 39
Sollefteå, *tn., Swed.,* 63 09N 17 15E 43
Solomon Is., *Pac. Oc.,* 8 00S 160 00E 63
Solomon Sea, *Pac. Oc.,* 9 00S 157 00E 63
Solway Firth, *Eng./Scot.,* 54 40N 3 30W 23
Somalia, *Rep., Afr.,* 7 00N 47 00E 67
Sombor, *tn., Yug.,* 45 46N 19 09E 46
Somerset, *admin. reg., Eng.,* 51 09N 3 00W 26
Somerset I., *N.W. Terrs., Can.,* 73 30N 92 30W . . . 71
Somme, *R., Fr.,* 50 12N 1 30E 39
Somport Pass, *Fr./Sp.,* 42 48N 0 31W 44
Söndre Strömfjord, *tn., Green.,* 67 00N 50 59W . . . 80

Song Bo, R., Viet., 22 00N 103 00E 56
Song Koi, R., Viet., 22 00N 104 00E 56
Songkhla, tn., Thai., 7 12N 100 35E 55
Soo Canals, Ont., Can., 46 30N 84 30W 73
Soochow, tn., China, 31 21N 120 40E 57
Soria, tn., Sp., 41 46N 2 28W 44
Sorocaba, tn., Braz., 23 30S 47 32W 77
Sorol, I., Pac. Oc., 8 09N 140 25E 63
Sørøya, I., Nor., 70 35N 22 30E 43
Sortavala, tn., USSR, 61 40N 30 40E 43
Sosnowiec, tn., Pol., 50 16N 19 07E 41
Sound, The, sd., Den., 55 45N 12 45E 41
Sousse, tn., Tun., 35 50N 10 38E 48
South Africa, Republic, Afr., 30 00S 25 00E . . 67
South Australia, admin. reg., Austr., 29 00N 134 00E . . 63
South Bend, tn., Ind., USA, 41 40N 86 15W 73
South Benfleet, tn., Eng., 51 33N 0 34E 27
South Carolina, admin. reg., USA, 33 45N 81 00E . . 73
South China Sea, 13 00N 115 00E 55
South Dakota, admin. reg., USA, 44 50N 100 00W . . 72
South Downs, hs., Eng., 50 53N 0 10W 27
South East Cape, hdl., Tas., Austr., 43 38S 146 48E . . 63
South Georgia, Falk. Is. dep., S. Atlan. Oc.,
54 30S 37 00W 80
South Glamorgan, admin. reg., Wales,
51 30N 3 25W 26
South Island, N.Z., 43 00S 170 00E 63
South Korea, Rep., Asia, 36 00N 128 00E 57
South Ockenden, tn., Eng., 51 32N 0 18E 27
South Orkney Is., Falk. Is. dep., S. Atlan. Oc.,
63 00S 45 00W 80
South Pole, Ant., 90 00S 0 00 80
South Ronaldsay, I., Scot., 58 47N 2 56W 22
South Sandwich Is., Falk. Is. dep., S. Atlan. Oc.,
57 00S 27 00W 80
South Saskatchewan, R., Sask., Can.,
49 50N 112 00W 72
South Shetland Is., S. Atlan. Oc., 62 00S 59 00W 80
South Shields, tn., Eng., 55 00N 1 25W 25
South Tyne, R., Eng., 54 46N 2 25W 25
South Uist, I., Scot., 57 10N 7 10W 22
South West Africa/Namibia, Rep., Afr.,
23 00S 17 30E 67
South Yemen, Rep., Asia, 15 00N 48 00E 52
South Yorkshire, admin. reg., 53 26N 1 34W . . . 25
Southampton, tn., Eng., 50 55N 1 25W 27
Southampton I., N.W. Terrs., Can., 64 30N 84 00W . . 71
Southend-on-Sea, tn., Eng., 51 33N 0 43E 27
Southern Alps, mts., N.Z., 43 41S 170 11E 63
Southern Uplands, hs., Scot., 55 25N 4 00W . . . 23
Southport, tn., Eng., 53 39N 3 01W 25
Southwold, tn., Eng., 52 20N 1 40E 27
Sovetsk, tn., USSR, 55 02N 21 50E 42
Sovetskaya Gavan, tn., USSR, 48 57N 140 16E . . 53
Sovietskaya, USSR base, Ant., 78 30S 80 00E . . 80
Soya Strait, Jap./USSR, 45 30N 142 30E 53
Spain, Kingd., Eur., 40 00N 5 00W 44
Spalding, tn., Eng., 52 47N 0 10W 27
Sparta, tn., Gr., 37 05N 22 25E 46
Spartivento, C., hdl., It., 37 56N 16 04E 45
Spassk Dalniy, tn., USSR, 44 37N 132 37E 57
Spencer Gulf, S. Austr., 34 30S 137 00E 63
Spennymoor, tn., Eng., 54 42N 1 35W 25
Sperrin Mts., N. Ire., 54 50N 7 00W 24
Spey, R., Scot., 57 26N 3 10W 22
Speyer, tn., W. Ger., 49 18N 8 26E 39
Spilsby, tn., Eng., 53 11N 0 05E 25
Split, tn., Yug., 43 31N 16 28E 46
Spokane, tn., Wash., USA, 47 40N 117 25W . . . 72
Springfield, tn., Ill., USA, 39 49N 89 39W 73
Springfield, tn., Mass., USA, 42 07N 72 35W . . . 73
Springfield, tn., Mo., USA, 37 11N 93 19W 73
Spurn Head, hdl., Eng., 53 36N 0 07W 25
Sri Lanka, Rep., comm. nat., Asia, 9 00N 81 00E . . 54
Srinagar, tn., Kashmir, 34 08N 74 50E 54
Stack Skerry, I., Scot., 59 05N 4 30W 22
Stade, tn., W. Ger., 53 36N 9 28E 39
Staffa, I., Scot., 56 26N 6 21W 23
Stafford, tn., Eng., 52 48N 2 07W 27
Staffordshire, admin. reg., Eng., 52 53N 2 10W . . 27
Staines, tn., Eng., 51 26N 0 31W 27
Stalingrad see Volgograd
Stalybridge, tn., Eng., 53 29N 2 04W 25
Stamford, tn., Eng., 52 39N 0 29W 27
Stanley, tn., Eng., 54 53N 1 42W 25
Stanley, tn., Falk. Is., 51 45S 57 56W 77
Stanley Falls see Boyoma Falls
Stanleyville see Kisangani
Stanovoy Range, mts., USSR, 55 00N 130 00E 53
Stara Zagora, tn., Bulg., 42 25N 25 37E 46
Staraya Russa, tn., USSR, 58 00N 31 22E 50
Start Point, hdl., Eng., 50 13N 3 38W 26
Staryy Oskol, tn., USSR, 51 20N 37 50E 50
Stavanger, tn., Nor., 58 58N 5 45E 42
Staveley, tn., Eng., 53 16N 1 20W 25
Stavropol, tn., USSR, 45 03N 41 59E 51
Steinkjer, tn., Nor., 64 00N 11 30E 43
Stepanakert, tn., USSR, 39 48N 46 45E 51
Sterlitamak, tn., USSR, 53 40N 55 59E 51
Stevenage, tn., Eng., 51 55N 0 14W 27
Stevenston, tn., Scot., 55 39N 4 45W 23
Stirling, tn., Scot., 56 07N 3 57W 23
Stockholm, tn., Swed., 59 20N 18 03E 42
Stockport, tn., Eng., 53 25N 2 10W 25
Stockton, tn., Calif., USA, 37 58N 121 20W . . . 72
Stockton-on-Tees, tn., Eng., 54 34N 1 19W 25
Stoer, Point of, hdl., Scot., 58 16N 5 23W 22
Stoke-on-Trent, tn., Eng., 53 00N 2 10W 27
Stone, tn., Eng., 52 54N 2 10W 27
Stonehaven, tn., Scot., 56 58N 2 13W 23
Stonehenge, hist. site, Eng., 51 11N 1 50W 27

Stonehouse, tn., Scot., 55 43N 4 00W 23
Stonington I., UK base, Ant., 67 55S 72 50W . . . 80
Stony Tunguska, R., USSR, 60 30N 98 00E 53
Storavan, L., Swed., 65 45N 18 10E 43
Storfjord, fd., Nor., 62 25N 6 20E 42
Storlien, tn., Swed., 63 20N 12 05E 43
Stornoway, tn., Scot., 58 13N 6 22W 22
Storsjön, L., Swed., 63 15N 14 22E 43
Storuman, L., Swed., 65 14N 16 50E 43
Stour, R., Eng., 52 07N 0 28E 27
Stourbridge, tn., Eng., 52 27N 2 09W 27
Stourport, tn., Eng., 52 21N 2 16W 27
Stowmarket, tn., Eng., 52 11N 1 00E 27
Strabane, tn., N. Ire., 54 49N 7 27W 24
Stralsund, tn., E. Ger., 54 18N 13 06E 41
Strangford L., N. Ire., 54 30N 5 35W 24
Stranraer, tn., Scot., 54 54N 5 02W 23
Strasbourg, tn., Fr., 48 35N 7 45E 45
Stratford-upon-Avon, tn., Eng., 52 12N 1 41W . . 27
Strath Dearn, val., Scot., 57 20N 4 00W 22
Strath Earn, val., Scot., 56 25N 4 10W 23
Strath Spey, val., Scot., 57 06N 3 53W 22
Strathbogie, val., Scot., 57 25N 2 45W 22
Strathclyde, admin. reg., Scot., 55 50N 5 50W . . 23
Strathmore, val., Scot., 56 30N 3 30W 23
Street, tn., Eng., 51 07N 2 43W 26
Streymoy, I., Faeroe Is., 62 10N 7 10W 43
Strimon, R., Gr., 41 00N 23 30E 46
Stromboli, I., vol., It., 38 48N 15 15E 45
Stromeferry, tn., Scot., 57 21N 5 34W 22
Stromness, tn., Scot., 58 57N 3 18W 22
Strömstad, tn., Swed., 58 56N 11 11E 42
Strömsund, tn., Swed., 63 51N 15 35E 43
Stronsay, I., Scot., 59 08N 2 38W 22
Stroud, tn., Eng., 51 45N 2 12W 27
Stuttgart, tn., W. Ger., 48 47N 9 12E 41
Styr, R., USSR, 51 20N 25 50E 42
Suanhwa, tn., China, 40 36N 115 01E 56
Subotica, tn., Yug., 46 04N 19 41E 46
Suceava, tn., Rom., 47 37N 26 18E 46
Suchow, tn., China, 34 17N 117 18E 57
Sucre, tn., Bol., 19 05S 65 15W 77
Sudan, Rep., Afr., 15 00N 30 00E 67
Sudbury, tn., Eng., 52 02N 0 44E 27
Sudbury, tn., Ont., Can., 46 30N 81 01W 73
Sudeten Mts., Cz./Pol., 50 20N 16 45E 41
Suduroy, I., Faeroe Is., 61 30N 7 02W 43
Suez, tn., Eg., 29 59N 32 33E 49
Suez Canal, Eg., 31 00N 32 20E 49
Suez, Gulf of, Eg., 28 40N 33 00E 49
Suffolk, admin. reg., Eng., 52 16N 1 00E 27
Suhsien, tn., China, 33 38N 117 02E 57
Suichung, tn., China, 40 19N 120 22E 57
Suihwa, tn., China, 46 40N 126 57E 57
Suining, tn., China, 30 31N 105 33E 56
Suir, R., Rep. Ire., 52 22N 7 40W 24
Sukhe Bator, tn., Mong., 50 00N 107 00E 53
Sukhoma, R., USSR, 60 30N 45 00E 50
Sukhumi, tn., USSR, 43 01N 41 01E 47
Sula Sgeir, I., Scot., 59 20N 6 08W 22
Sule Skerry, I., Scot., 59 05N 4 20W 22
Sulitjelma, Mt., Nor., 67 10N 16 24E 43
Sullom Voe, L., Scot., 60 27N 1 20W 22
Sulu Archipelago, Is., Phil., 6 00N 121 00E 55
Sulu Sea, Malay./Phil., 8 00N 120 00E 55
Sumatra, I., Indon., 1 00S 102 00E 55
Sumba, I., Indon., 10 45S 119 35E 55
Sumbawa, I., Indon., 9 00S 117 00E 55
Sumburgh Head, hdl., Scot., 59 51N 1 16W 22
Sumgait, tn., USSR, 40 35N 49 38E 51
Sumy, tn., USSR, 50 55N 34 49E 50
Sunchon, tn., S. Kor., 34 56N 127 28E 57
Sundarbans, geog. reg., Bangl./India,
22 00N 89 00E 54
Sunderland, tn., Eng., 54 55N 1 23W 25
Sundsvall, tn., Swed., 62 22N 17 20E 42
Sungari,, R., China, 47 00N 130 50E 57
Sunghua Kiang see Sungari R.
Suomenselkä, geog. reg., Fin., 63 50N 25 50E . . 43
Suoyarvi, tn., USSR, 62 02N 32 20E 43
Superior, tn., Wis., USA, 46 42N 92 05W 73
Superior L., Can./USA, 47 40N 87 00W 73
Surabaja, tn., Indon., 7 14S 112 45E 55
Surabaya see Surabaja
Surakarta, tn., Indon., 7 32S 110 50E 55
Surat, tn., India, 21 10N 72 54E 54
Surat Thani, tn., Thai., 9 09N 99 20E 55
Surinam, Rep., S. Amer., 4 00N 56 15W 77
Surman see Yüshu
Surrey, admin. reg., Eng., 51 16N 0 30W 27
Surtsey, I., Ice., 63 18N 20 37W 43
Susuman, tn., USSR, 62 47N 148 10E 53
Sutlej, R., Pak., 29 00N 71 00E 54
Sutton Coldfield, tn., Eng., 52 34N 1 48W 27
Sutton in Ashfield, tn., Eng., 53 08N 1 15W . . . 25
Suva, tn., Fiji, 18 08S 178 25E 63
Suya, R., USSR, 62 00N 32 30E 43
Suyung, tn., China, 28 17N 105 21E 56
Svalbard, Nor. Arch., Arctic Oc., 78 00N 17 00E . . 52
Svartisen, mt., Nor., 66 40N 13 56E 43
Svealand, geog. reg., Swed., 59 45N 15 00E . . . 42
Sveg, tn., Swed., 62 02N 14 20E 42
Sverdlovsk, tn., USSR, 56 50N 60 30E 51
Sverdrup Is., N.W. Terrs., Can., 78 00N 101 00W . . 71
Svobodnyy, tn., USSR, 51 24N 128 05E 53
Svolvaer, tn., Nor., 68 15N 14 40E 43
Swadlincote, tn., Eng., 52 47N 1 34W 27
Swaffham, tn., Eng., 52 39N 0 41E 27
Swakopmund, tn., S.W. Afr. (Nam.), 22 40S 14 34E . . 67
Swale, R., Eng., 54 18N 1 30W 25

Swaledale, val., Eng., 54 23N 1 55W 25
Swanage, tn., Eng., 50 37N 1 58W 27
Swansea, tn., Wales, 51 38N 3 57W 26
Swansea Bay, Wales, 51 34N 3 55W 26
Swatow, tn., China, 23 23N 116 39E 56
Swaziland, Kingd., Afr., 26 35S 31 30E 67
Sweden, Kingd., Eur., 62 00N 15 00E 42
Sweetwater, tn., Tex., USA, 32 27N 100 25W . . 72
Swift Current, tn., Sask., Can., 50 17N 107 49W . . 72
Swilly, L., Rep. Ire., 55 10N 7 32W 24
Swindon, tn., Eng., 51 34N 1 47W 27
Świnoujście, tn., Pol., 53 55N 14 18E 41
Swinton, tn., Eng., 53 31N 2 21W 25
Switzerland, Rep., Eur., 46 30N 8 50E 45
Swords, tn., Rep. Ire., 53 28N 6 13W 24
Sydney, tn., N.S., Can., 46 10N 60 10W 71
Sydney, tn., N.S.W., Austr., 33 55S 151 10E . . . 63
Syktyvkar, tn., USSR, 61 42N 50 45E 50
Syr Darya, R., USSR, 45 00N 65 00E 51
Syracuse, tn., N.Y., USA, 43 03N 76 10W 73
Syria, Rep., Asia, 34 55N 37 00E 49
Syrian Desert, Iraq, 31 30N 40 00E 49
Syzran, tn., USSR, 53 10N 48 29E 51
Szczecin, tn., Pol., 53 25N 14 32E 41
Szechwan, admin. reg., China, 30 10N 106 00E . . 56
Szeged, tn., Hung., 46 15N 20 09E 46
Székesfehérvár, tn., Hung., 47 11N 18 22E 46
Szemao, tn., China, 22 46N 101 03E 56
Szeping, tn., China, 43 15N 124 25E 57
Szolnok, tn., Hung., 47 10N 20 10E 46
Szombathely, tn., Hung., 47 14N 16 38E 46

T

Tabora, tn., Tanz., 5 02S 32 50E 67
Tabrïz, tn., Iran, 38 05N 46 18E 49
Tacloban, tn., Phil., 11 15N 125 01E 55
Tacna, tn., Peru, 18 00S 70 15W 77
Tacoma, tn., Wash., USA, 47 16N 122 30W . . . 72
Tadzhikistan S.S.R., admin. reg., USSR,
38 30N 70 00E 52
Taebaek Mts., S. Kor., 38 50N 127 50E 57
Taegu, tn., S. Kor., 35 52N 128 36E 57
Taejon, tn., S. Kor., 36 20N 127 26E 57
Taganrog, tn., USSR, 47 14N 38 55E 50
Tagus, R., Port./Sp., 39 00N 8 50W 44
Tahoua, tn., Niger, 14 57N 5 19E 67
Tahsien, tn., China, 31 20N 107 30E 56
Tahsueh Shan, mts., China, 29 00N 102 00E . . . 56
Tai, L., China, 31 10N 120 00E 57
Taian, tn., China, 36 15N 117 10E 57
Taichow, tn., China, 32 27N 119 56E 57
Taichung, tn., Taiwan, 24 09N 120 40E 57
Tainan (China) see Tsinan
Tainan, tn., Taiwan, 23 01N 120 14E 57
Taipei, tn., Taiwan, 25 05N 121 32E 57
Taitung, tn., Taiwan, 22 43N 121 10E 57
Taivalkoski, tn., Fin., 65 35N 28 20E 43
Taiwan, I., Asia, 23 30N 121 00E 57
Taiyuan, tn., China, 37 50N 112 30E 56
Tajamulco, Mt., vol., Guat., 15 30N 91 54W . . . 71
Takamatsu, tn., Jap., 34 20N 134 01E 57
Takaoka, tn., Jap., 36 47N 137 00E 57
Takla Makan, des., China, 38 40N 82 00E 52
Talavera de la Reina, tn., Sp., 39 58N 4 50W . . . 44
Talca, tn., Chile, 35 28S 71 40W 77
Talcahuano, tn., Chile, 36 40S 73 10W 77
Tallahassee, tn., Fla., USA, 30 16N 84 19W . . . 73
Tallinn, tn., USSR, 59 22N 24 48E 42
Tamale, tn., Ghana, 9 26N 0 49W 66
Tamanrasset, tn., Alg., 22 50N 5 28E 67
Tamar, R., Eng., 50 33N 4 15W 26
Tamatave, tn., Madag., 18 10S 49 23E 67
Tambacounda, tn., Sen., 13 45N 13 40W 66
Tambov, tn., USSR, 52 44N 41 28E 50
Tampa, tn., Fla., USA, 27 58N 82 38W 73
Tampere, tn., Fin., 61 32N 23 45E 42
Tampico, tn., Mex., 22 18N 97 52W 71
Tamworth, tn., Eng., 52 39N 1 40W 27
Tamworth, tn., N.S.W., Austr., 31 07S 150 57E . . 63
Tana, R., Fin./Nor., 69 50N 26 00E 43
Tana, L., Ethiopia, 13 05N 37 30E 67
Tanafjord, fd., Nor., 70 30N 28 20E 43
Tananarive, tn., Madag., 18 52S 47 30E 67
Tandil, tn., Arg., 37 18W 59 10W 77
Tandjungkarang, tn., Indon., 5 28S 105 16E . . . 55
Tang Pass, China, 32 59N 92 17E 56
Tanga, tn., Tanz., 5 07S 39 05E 67
Tanganyika, L., Afr., 7 00S 31 00E 67
Tangching Pass, China, 39 18N 94 30E 56
Tangier, tn., Mor., 35 48N 5 50W 48
Tangshan, tn., China, 39 37N 118 05E 57
Tanimbar Is., Indon., 8 30S 131 30E 55
Tanta, tn., Eg., 30 48N 31 00E 49
Tanzania, Rep., Afr., 5 00S 32 00E 67
Taonan, tn., China, 45 25N 122 46E 57
Tapa Shan, mts., China, 31 45N 109 30E 56
Tapajos, R., Braz., 4 30S 56 10W 77
Tapieh Shan, mts., China, 32 00N 114 00E 56

Tara, Hill of, *Rep. Ire.*, 53 35N 6 37W 24
Tarābulus see **Tripoli**
Taransay, *I., Scot.*, 57 54N 7 00W 22
Taranto, *tn., It.*, 40 28N 17 15E 45
Taranto, Gulf of, *It.*, 40 00N 17 15E 45
Tarawa, *I., Pac. Oc.*, 1 30N 173 00E 63
Tarbat Ness, *hdl., Scot.*, 57 52N 3 46W 22
Tarbert, *tn., Strathclyde, Scot.*, 55 52N 5 26W 23
Tarbert, *tn., W. Isles, Scot.*, 57 54N 6 49W 22
Tarbes, *tn., Fr.*, 43 14N 0 05E 44
Tarija, *tn., Bol.*, 21 33S 64 45W 77
Tarim, *R., China*, 41 00N 81 00E 52
Tarn, *R., Fr.*, 43 57N 2 25E 44
Tarnów, *tn., Pol.*, 50 01N 20 59E 41
Tarragona, *tn., Sp.*, 41 07N 1 15E 44
Tarrasa, *tn., Sp.*, 41 34N 2 00E 44
Tarsus, *tn., Tur.*, 36 58N 34 55E 47
Tartu, *tn., USSR*, 58 20N 26 44E 42
Tartus, *tn., Syria*, 34 55N 35 52E 49
Tashaus, *tn., USSR*, 41 49N 59 58E 51
Tashkent, *tn., USSR*, 41 16N 69 13E 52
Tasman Sea, *Pac. Oc.*, 38 30S 160 00E 63
Tasmania, *I., admin. reg., Austr.*, 42 30S 146 30E 63
Tatabánya, *tn., Hung.*, 47 31N 18 25E 46
Tatra Mts., *Cz./Pol.*, 49 20N 20 00E 41
Tatsaitan, *tn., China*, 37 55N 95 00E 56
Tatung, *tn., Anhwei, China*, 30 53N 117 40E 57
Tatung, *tn., Shansi, China*, 40 12N 113 12E 56
Taunggyi, *tn., Burma*, 20 55N 96 53E 56
Taunton, *tn., Eng.*, 51 01N 3 06W 26
Taunus, *mts., W. Ger.*, 50 15N 8 20E 41
Taurus Mts., *Tur.*, 37 00N 35 00E 47
Tavda, *R., USSR*, 59 30N 63 00E 51
Tavda, *tn., USSR*, 58 04N 65 12E 51
Tavistock, *tn., Eng.*, 50 33N 4 08W 26
Taw, *R., Eng.*, 50 58N 3 58W 26
Tay, *R., Scot.*, 56 37N 3 58W 23
Tay, Firth of, *Scot.*, 56 25N 3 08W 23
Tay, L., *Scot.*, 56 30N 4 10W 23
Taymyr Peninsula, *USSR*, 75 00N 100 00E 53
Tayside, *admin. reg., Scot.*, 56 37N 3 50W 23
Taza, *tn., Mor.*, 34 16N 4 01W 48
Tbilisi, *tn., USSR*, 41 43N 44 48E 51
Tczew, *tn., Pol.*, 54 05N 18 46E 41
Tébessa, *tn., Alg.*, 35 21N 8 06E 48
Tees, *R., Eng.*, 54 36N 1 58W 25
Teesdale, *val., Eng.*, 54 37N 2 10W 25
Tegucigalpa, *tn., Hond.*, 14 05N 87 14W 71
Tehchow, *tn., China*, 37 29N 116 11E 57
Tehran, *tn., Iran*, 35 40N 51 26E 52
Tehuantepec, Isthmus of, *Mex.*, 17 00N 95 30W 71
Teifi, *R., Wales*, 52 04N 4 14W 26
Teignmouth, *tn., Eng.*, 50 33N 3 30W 26
Tekirdağ, *tn., Tur.*, 40 59N 27 31E 47
Tel Aviv-Jaffa, *tn., Israel*, 32 05N 34 46E 49
Tel Aviv-Yafo see **Tel Aviv-Jaffa**
Telanaipura, *tn., Indon.*, 1 36S 103 39E 55
Telford, *tn., Eng.*, 52 42N 2 28W 26
Telukbetung see **Tandjungkarang**
Teme, *R., Eng.*, 52 33N 3 05W 26
Temirtau, *tn., USSR*, 50 06N 72 55E 51
Templemore, *tn., Rep. Ire.*, 52 48N 7 50W 24
Temuco, *tn., Chile*, 38 45S 72 40W 77
Tenasserim, *geog. reg., Burma*, 13 00N 99 00E 55
Tenby, *tn., Wales*, 51 41N 4 43W 26
Tengchung, *tn., China*, 25 02N 98 28E 56
Tenghiz, L., *USSR*, 50 30N 69 00E 51
Tengkow, *tn., China*, 39 45N 106 54E 56
Tennant Creek, *tn., N. Terr., Austr.*, 19 31S 134 15E . . 62
Tennessee, *admin. reg., USA*, 36 00N 87 30W 73
Tennessee, *R., USA*, 35 00N 87 30W 73
Tenterden, *tn., Eng.*, 51 05N 0 41E 27
Téofilo Otóni, *tn., Braz.*, 17 52S 41 31W 77
Teplice, *tn., Cz.*, 50 40N 13 50E 41
Teresina, *tn., Braz.*, 5 09S 42 46W 77
Ternate, *tn., Indon.*, 0 48N 127 23E 55
Terni, *tn., It.*, 42 34N 12 39E 45
Ternopol, *tn., USSR*, 49 35N 25 39E 50
Terre Haute, *tn., Ind., USA*, 39 27N 87 24W 73
Terschelling, *I. Neth.*, 53 25N 5 20E 39
Teruel, *tn., Sp.*, 40 21N 1 06W 44
Tete, *tn., Mozam.*, 16 10S 33 35E 67
Tetouan, *tn., Mor.*, 35 34N 5 22W 48
Tétuán see **Tetouan**
Teutoburger Wald, *hs., W. Ger.*, 52 15N 8 00E 39
Teviot, *R., Scot.*, 55 21N 2 51W 23
Teviotdale, *val., Scot.*, 55 25N 2 50W 23
Tewkesbury, *tn., Eng.*, 51 59N 2 09W 27
Texas, *admin. reg., USA*, 31 00N 97 50W 72
Texel, *I., Neth.*, 53 05N 4 50E 39
Thai Nguyen, *tn., Viet.*, 21 35N 105 46E 56
Thailand, *Kingd., Asia*, 16 00N 100 00E 55
Thakhek, *tn., Laos*, 17 25N 104 45E 56
Thames, *R., Eng.*, 51 24N 0 24W 27
Thanh Hoa, *tn., Viet.*, 19 49N 105 48E 56
Thar Desert, *India*, 28 00N 72 00E 54
Thásos, *I., Gr.*, 40 46N 24 42E 46
Thebes, *hist. site, Eg.*, 25 41N 32 40E 49
Theddlethorpe, *tn., Eng.*, 53 23N 0 20E 25
Thermai, Gulf of, *Gr.*, 40 15N 23 00E 46
Thermopylae, Pass of, *Gr.*, 38 50N 22 35E 46
Thessaloniki, *tn., Gr.*, 40 38N 22 58E 46
Thessaly, *geog. reg., Gr.*, 39 30N 22 00E 46
Thetford, *tn., Eng.*, 52 25N 0 45E 27
Thiés, *tn., Sen.*, 14 49N 16 52W 66
Thimbu, *tn., Bhutan*, 27 32N 89 43E 54
Thionville, *tn., Fr.*, 49 22N 6 11E 45
Thirsk, *tn., Eng.*, 54 14N 1 20W 25
Thon Buri, *tn., Thai.*, 13 43N 100 27E 55
Thorez, *tn., USSR*, 48 00N 38 38E 47
Thorne, *tn., Eng.*, 53 37N 0 58W 25

Thornton Clevelys, *tn., Eng.*, 53 52N 3 01W 25
Thrace, *geog. reg., Gr.*, 41 10N 26 00E 46
Thule, *tn., Green.*, 77 40N 69 00W 80
Thunder Bay, *tn., Ont., Can.*, 48 27N 89 12W 73
Thuringia, *admin. reg., E. Ger.*, 50 43N 10 43E 41
Thuringian Forest, *mts., E. Ger.*, 50 35N 11 00E 41
Thurles, *tn., Rep. Ire.*, 52 41N 7 49W 24
Thurso, *tn., Scot.*, 58 35N 3 32W 22
Tiaret, *tn., Alg.*, 35 20N 1 20E 48
Tiber, *R., It.*, 42 30N 12 20E 45
Tibesti, *geog. reg., Chad*, 21 00N 17 30E 67
Tibet, *admin. reg., China*, 33 00N 85 00E 52
Tibti, *geog. reg., Chad*, 21 00N 20 00E 48
Tiehli, *tn., China*, 46 57N 128 02E 57
Tieling, *tn., China*, 42 25N 123 51E 57
Tien Shan, *mts., China/USSR*, 43 00N 80 00E 52
Tienshui, *tn., China*, 34 25N 105 58E 56
Tientsin, *admin. reg., China*, 39 00N 117 15E 57
Tientsin, *tn., China*, 39 10N 117 00E 57
Tierra del Fuego, *I., Arg./Chile*, 54 00S 69 00W 77
Tifgu-Mureş, *tn., Rom.*, 46 33N 24 34E 46
Tigris, *R., Tur./Iraq*, 37 00N 42 30E 49
Tihua see **Wulumuchi**
Tijuana, *tn., Mex.*, 32 29N 117 10W 72
Tikhoretsk, *tn., USSR*, 45 52N 40 07E 51
Tiksi, *tn., USSR*, 71 40N 128 45E 53
Tilburg, *tn., Neth.*, 51 34N 5 05E 39
Tilbury, *tn., Eng.*, 51 28N 0 23E 27
Timaru, *tn., N.Z.*, 44 23S 171 14E 63
Timbuktu see **Tombouctou**
Timişoara, *tn., Rom.*, 45 45N 21 15E 46
Timmins, *tn., Ont., Can.*, 48 30N 81 20W 73
Timor, *I., Indon.*, 9 00S 125 00E 55
Timor Sea, *Austr./Indon.*, 10 30S 127 00E 55
Tindouf, *tn., Alg.*, 27 42N 8 10W 66
Tingsi, *tn., China*, 35 50N 104 17E 56
Tinian, *I., Pac. Oc.*, 14 58N 145 38E 63
Tinsukia, *tn., India*, 27 28N 95 20E 56
Tintagel Head, *hdl., Eng.*, 50 41N 4 46W 26
Tipperary, *admin. reg., Rep. Ire.*, 52 37N 7 55W 24
Tirana, *tn., Alb.*, 41 20N 19 49E 46
Tiranë see **Tirana**
Tiraspol, *tn., USSR*, 46 50N 29 38E 47
Tiree, *I., Scot.*, 56 31N 6 49W 23
Tîrgovişte, *tn., Rom.*, 44 56N 25 27E 46
Tîrgu-Jiu, *tn., Rom.*, 45 03N 23 18E 46
Tiruchirapalli, *tn., India*, 10 50N 78 43E 54
Tisza, *R., Hung.*, 47 38N 20 44E 46
Titicaca, L., *Bol./Peru*, 15 30S 69 30W 77
Titograd, *tn., Yug.*, 42 28N 19 17E 46
Titov Veles, *tn., Yug.*, 41 43N 21 49E 46
Tiverton, *tn., Eng.*, 50 55N 3 29W 26
Tizi Ouzou, *tn., Alg.*, 36 44N 4 05E 48
Tjirebon, *tn., Indon.*, 6 46S 108 33E 55
Tlemcen, *tn., Alg.*, 34 53N 1 21W 48
Tobermory, *tn., Scot.*, 56 37N 6 05W 23
Tobol, *R., USSR*, 55 00N 65 00E 51
Tobolsk, *tn., USSR*, 58 15N 68 12E 52
Tobruk, *tn., Libya*, 31 06N 23 56E 49
Tocatins, *R., Braz.*, 14 30S 49 00W 77
Tocopilla, *tn., Chile*, 22 05S 70 10W 77
Togliatti, *tn., USSR*, 53 32N 49 24E 51
Togo, *Rep., Afr.*, 6 15N 1 35E 66
Toishan, *tn., China*, 22 30N 112 50E 56
Tokaj, *tn., Hung.*, 48 08N 21 23E 46
Tokara Is., *Jap.*, 29 00N 129 00E 57
Tokat, *tn., Tur.*, 40 20N 36 35E 47
Tokelau Is., *Pac. Oc.*, 9 00S 172 00W 63
Tokmak, *tn., USSR*, 47 13N 35 43E 47
Tokyo, *tn., Jap.*, 35 40N 139 45E 57
Tolbukhin, *tn., Bulg.*, 43 34N 27 51E 47
Toledo, *tn., Ohio, USA*, 41 40N 83 35W 73
Toledo, *tn., Sp.*, 39 52N 4 02W 44
Tolima, Mt., *Col.*, 4 39N 75 22W 77
Tomakomai, *tn., Jap.*, 42 39N 141 33E 57
Tomaszów Mazowiecki, *tn., Pol.*, 51 33N 20 00E 41
Tombouctou, *tn., Mali*, 16 49N 2 59W 66
Tomelloso, *tn., Sp.*, 39 09N 3 01W 44
Tomsk, *tn., USSR*, 56 30N 85 05E 52
Tonbridge, *tn., Eng.*, 51 12N 0 16E 27
Tonga, *Is., Kingd., comm. nat., Pac. Oc.*,
  19 00S 175 00W 63
Tonga Trench, *Pac. Oc.*, 18 00S 175 00W 63
Tongatapu, *I., Tonga, Pac. Oc.*, 21 08S 175 16W 63
Tongue, *tn., Scot.*, 58 28N 4 25W 22
Tonkin, *admin. reg., Viet.*, 22 00N 105 00E 56
Tonkin, Gulf of, *Viet.*, 20 00N 108 00E 55
Tonle Sap, L., *Cambod.*, 13 00N 104 00E 56
Toowoomba, *tn., Queensl., Austr.*, 27 35S 151 54E 63
Top, L., *USSR*, 65 35N 32 00E 43
Topeka, *tn., Kans., USA*, 39 02N 95 41W 73
Torbay, *tn., Eng.*, 50 27N 3 32W 26
Torino see **Turin**
Torneälven, *R., Swed.*, 67 15N 23 00E 43
Torneträsk, L., *Swed.*, 68 14N 19 40E 43
Tornio, *tn., Fin.*, 65 52N 24 10E 43
Toronto, *tn., Ont., Can.*, 43 42N 79 25W 73
Tororo, *tn., Ugan.*, 0 42N 34 12E 67
Torquay, *tn., Eng.*, 50 28N 3 30W 26
Torrance, *tn., Calif., USA*, 33 50N 118 20W 72
Torre del Greco, *tn., It.*, 40 46N 14 22E 45
Torrelavega, *tn., Sp.*, 43 21N 4 03W 44
Torremolinos, *tn., Sp.*, 36 38N 4 30W 44
Torreón, *tn., Mex.*, 25 34N 103 25W 72
Torres Strait, *Queensl., Austr.*, 10 20S 142 00E 63
Torridge, *R., Eng.*, 50 57N 4 10W 26
Torridon, L., *Scot.*, 57 35N 5 50W 22
Tórshavn, *tn., Faeroe Is.*, 62 02N 6 47W 43
Tortosa, *tn., Sp.*, 40 49N 0 31E 44
Toruń, *tn., Pol.*, 53 01N 18 35E 41
Totnes, *tn., Eng.*, 50 25N 3 41W 26

Toubkal, Mt., *Mor.*, 31 03N 7 57W 48
Touggourt, *tn., Alg.*, 33 08N 6 04E 48
Toulon, *tn., Fr.*, 43 07N 5 55E 44
Toulouse, *tn., Fr.*, 43 33N 1 24E 44
Tourcoing, *tn., Fr.*, 50 44N 3 10E 39
Tournai, *tn., Belg.*, 50 36N 3 24E 39
Tours, *tn., Fr.*, 47 23N 0 42E 44
Townsville, *tn., Queensl., Austr.*, 19 13S 146 48E 63
Towy, *R., Wales*, 51 54N 4 00W 26
Toyama, *tn., Jap.*, 36 42N 137 14E 57
Toyohashi, *tn., Jap.*, 34 46N 137 22E 57
Trabzon, *tn., Tur.*, 41 00N 39 45E 47
Trafalgar, C., *hdl., Sp.*, 36 11N 6 02W 44
Trail, *tn., B.C., Can.*, 49 04N 117 39W 72
Tralee, *tn., Rep. Ire.*, 52 16N 9 42W 40
Transkei, *admin. reg., Rep. S. Afr.*, 32 15S 28 15E 67
Transvaal, *admin. reg., Rep. S. Afr.*, 25 00S 29 00E 67
Transylvanian Alps, *mts., Rom.*, 45 30N 25 00E 46
Trápani, *tn., Sicily*, 38 02N 12 32E 45
Trapezus see **Trabzon**
Trebizond see **Trabzon**
Tredegar, *tn., Wales*, 51 47N 3 16W 26
Trelleborg, *tn., Swed.*, 55 22N 13 10E 42
Tremadog Bay, *Wales*, 52 51N 4 18W 26
Trent, *R., Eng.*, 53 33N 0 44W 25
Trentino-Alto Adige, *admin. reg., It.*, 46 05N 11 00E 45
Trento, *tn., It.*, 46 04N 11 08E 45
Trenton, *tn., N.J., USA*, 40 15N 74 43W 73
Treviso, *tn., It.*, 45 40N 12 15E 45
Trier, *tn., W. Ger.*, 49 45N 6 39E 39
Trieste, *tn., It.*, 45 39N 13 47E 45
Trikkala, *tn., Gr.*, 39 33N 21 46E 46
Trim, *tn., Rep. Ire.*, 53 34N 6 47W 24
Trindade I., *Atlan. Oc.*, 20 42S 31 42W 77
Tring, *tn., Eng.*, 51 48N 0 40W 27
Trinidad, *tn., Bol.*, 14 46S 64 50W 77
Trinidad, *tn., Colo., USA*, 37 11N 104 31W 72
Trinidad & Tobago, *comm. nat., W. I.*, 10 30N 61 20W 77
Tripoli, *tn., Lebanon*, 34 27N 35 50E 49
Tripoli, *tn., Libya*, 32 58N 13 12E 48
Tripolis, *tn., Gr.*, 37 31N 22 22E 46
Tripolitania, *geog. reg., Libya*, 29 50N 14 50E 48
Trivandrum, *tn., India*, 8 30N 76 57E 54
Trnava, *tn., Cz.*, 48 23N 17 35E 41
Troisdorf, *tn., W. Ger.*, 50 49N 7 09E 39
Troitsk, *tn., USSR*, 54 08N 61 33E 51
Trois-Rivières, *tn., Que., Can.*, 46 21N 72 34W 73
Trollhätten, *tn., Swed.*, 58 17N 12 20E 42
Tromsø, *tn., Nor.*, 69 42N 19 00E 43
Trondheim, *tn., Nor.*, 63 36N 10 23E 43
Trondheimfjord, *fd., Nor.*, 63 40N 10 00E 43
Troon, *tn., Scot.*, 55 32N 4 40W 23
Trossachs, The, *geog. reg., Scot.*, 56 14N 4 24W 23
Trotternish, *geog. reg., Scot.*, 57 32N 6 15W 22
Trowbridge, *tn., Eng.*, 51 20N 2 13W 27
Troy, *hist. site, Tur.*, 39 55N 26 17E 46
Troy, *tn., N.Y., USA*, 42 43N 73 43W 73
Troyes, *tn., Fr.*, 48 18N 4 05E 44
Trujillo, *tn., Peru*, 8 06S 79 00W 77
Truk Is., *Pac. Oc.*, 8 00N 152 00E 63
Truro, *tn., Eng.*, 50 16N 5 03W 26
Tsaidam, *swamp, China*, 37 00N 95 00E 56
Tsamkong, *tn., China*, 21 10N 110 20E 56
Tsanghsien, *tn., China*, 38 19N 116 54E 57
Tsangpo, *R., Tibet*, 29 00N 92 00E 55
(*see also* **Brahmaputra, R.**)
Tsaochwang, *tn., China*, 34 53N 117 38E 57
Tsaratanana, Mt., *Madag.*, 12 40S 49 10E 67
Tsaring Nor, L., *China*, 35 00N 97 00E 56
Tselinograd, *tn., USSR*, 51 10N 71 28E 51
Tsiaotso, *tn., China*, 35 16N 113 30E 56
Tsimlyansk Reservoir, *USSR*, 48 00N 43 00E 51
Tsinan, *tn., China*, 36 41N 117 00E 57
Tsing Hai (L.) see **Koko Nor**
Tsinghai, *admin. reg., China*, 35 10N 96 00E 56
Tsingshih, *tn., China*, 29 43N 112 13E 56
Tsingtao, *tn., China*, 36 04N 120 22E 57
Tsining, *tn., China*, 40 58N 113 01E 56
Tsingkiang, *tn., Kiangsu, China*, 33 30N 119 02E 57
Tsinkiang, *tn., Kiangsi, China*, 27 50N 114 38E 56
Tsishih Shan, *mts., China*, 35 48N 102 25E 56
Tsitsihar, *tn., China*, 47 23N 124 00E 57
Tskhinvali, *tn., USSR*, 42 14N 43 58E 51
Tsu, *tn., Jap.*, 34 41N 136 30E 57
Tsugaru Channel, *Jap.*, 41 30N 140 30E 57
Tsunyi, *tn., China*, 27 41N 106 50E 56
Tsushima, *I., Jap.*, 34 20N 129 20E 57
Tsuyung, *tn., China*, 25 03N 101 33E 56
Tuapse, *tn., USSR*, 44 06N 39 05E 47
Tucson, *tn., Ariz., USA*, 32 15N 110 57W 72
Tucumán, *admin. reg., Arg.*, 26 50S 65 20W 77
Tula, *tn., USSR*, 54 11N 37 38E 50
Tulcea, *tn., Rom.*, 45 10N 28 50E 47
Tuléar, *tn., Madag.*, 23 20S 43 41E 67
Tullamore, *tn., Rep. Ire.*, 53 16N 7 30W 24
Tullow, *tn., Rep. Ire.*, 52 48N 6 44W 24
Tuloma, *R., USSR*, 68 37N 32 00E 43
Tulsa, *tn., Okla., USA*, 36 07N 95 58W 73
Tumbes, *tn., Peru*, 3 37S 80 27W 77
Tungchuan, *tn., China*, 35 09N 109 02E 56
Tunghwa, *tn., China*, 41 40N 125 52E 57
Tungjen, *tn., China*, 27 44N 109 10E 56
Tungkwan, *tn., China*, 34 36N 110 21E 56
Tungliao, *tn., China*, 43 37N 122 15E 57
Tungting, L., *China*, 29 00N 112 50E 56
Tunhwa, *tn., China*, 43 27N 128 16E 57
Tunhwang, *tn., China*, 40 05N 95 00E 56
Tunis, *tn., Tun.*, 36 50N 10 13E 48
Tunisia, *Rep., Afr.*, 33 30N 9 10E 48
Tura, *tn., USSR*, 64 20N 100 17E 53
Turda, *tn., Rom.*, 46 35N 23 50E 46

Turfan

Turfan, *tn., Sinkiang, China*, 42 55N 89 06E 56
Turfan Depression, *val., China*, 43 00N 88 00E 52
Turia, *R., Sp.*, 39 43N 1 00W 44
Turin, *tn., It.*, 45 04N 7 40E 45
Turkana, *L., Kenya*, 3 40N 30 20E 67
Turkey, *Rep., Eur.*, 39 00N 36 00E 47
Turkmenistan S.S.R., *admin. reg., USSR*,
39 00N 59 00E 51
Turku, *tn., Fin.*, 60 27N 22 15E 42
Turnhout, *tn., Belg.*, 51 19N 4 57E 39
Tůrnovo, *tn., Bulg.*, 43 05N 25 41E 46
Turnu-Severin, *tn., Rom.*, 44 36N 22 39E 46
Turriff, *tn., Scot.*, 57 32N 2 28W 22
Tuscaloosa, *tn., Ala., USA*, 33 12N 87 33W 73
Tuscany, *geog. reg., It.*, 43 28N 11 15E 45
Tuvalu, *Is., UK dep. terr., Pac. Oc.*, 8 00S 176 00E . . 63
Tuyun, *tn., China*, 26 16N 107 29E 56
Tuz, *L., Tur.*, 38 45N 33 30E 47
Tuzla, *tn., Yug.*, 44 33N 18 41E 46
Tweed, *R., Eng./Scot.*, 55 42N 2 10W 25
Tweedsmuir Hills, *Scot.*, 55 27N 3 30W 23
Tychy, *tn., Pol.*, 50 08N 18 56E 41
Tyler, *tn., Tex., USA*, 32 22N 95 18W 73
Tyne, *R., Eng.*, 54 58N 1 56W 25
Tyne and Wear, *admin. reg., Eng.*, 54 56N 1 17W . . 25
Tynemouth, *tn., Eng.*, 55 01N 1 24W 25
Tyrrhenian Sea, *It., Sicily*, 40 00N 12 30E 45
Tyumen, *tn., USSR*, 57 11N 65 29E 51
Tywyn, *tn., Wales*, 52 35N 4 05W 26
Tzehing, *tn., China*, 26 00N 113 00E 56
Tzekung, *tn., China*, 29 20N 104 42E 56
Tzepo, *tn., China*, 36 28N 117 58E 57
Tzeyang, *tn., China*, 35 44N 116 51E 57

U

Ubari, *tn., Libya*, 26 35N 12 47E 48
Ube, *tn., Jap.*, 33 57N 131 16E 57
Ubeda, *tn., Sp.*, 38 01N 3 22W 44
Uberaba, *tn., Braz.*, 19 47S 47 57W 77
Uberlândia, *tn., Braz.*, 18 57S 48 17W 77
Ubundi, *tn., Zaire*, 0 05S 25 50E 67
Ucayali, *R., Peru*, 8 00S 75 06W 77
Uddevalla, *tn., Swed.*, 58 20N 11 56E 42
Uddjaur, *L., Swed.*, 65 55N 17 50E 43
Udine, *tn., It.*, 46 04N 13 14E 45
Udjung Pandang, *tn., Indon.*, 5 09S 119 28E 55
Udon Thani, *tn., Thai.*, 17 29N 102 46E 56
Uele, *R., Zaire*, 3 50N 22 40E 67
Ufa, *tn., USSR*, 54 45N 55 58E 51
Uganda, *Rep., Afr.*, 2 00N 32 00E 67
Uig, *tn., Scot.*, 57 35N 6 22W 22
Uinta Mts., *Utah, USA*, 40 45N 110 30W 72
Uitenhage, *tn., Rep., S. Afr.*, 33 46S 25 25E 67
Ukhta, *tn., USSR*, 63 33N 54 44E 50
Ukrainian S.S.R., *admin. reg., USSR*, 48 00N 27 30E . . 50
Ulaanbaatar see Ulan Bator
Ulan Bator, *tn., Mong.*, 47 54N 106 52E 56
Ulan Ude, *tn., USSR*, 51 55N 107 40E 53
Ulanhot, *tn., China*, 46 02N 122 00E 57
Ulithi, *I., Pac. Oc.*, 10 00N 139 40E 63
Ullapool, *tn., Scot.*, 57 54N 5 10W 22
Ullswater, *L., Eng.*, 54 35N 2 55W 25
Ullung I., *S. Kor.*, 37 30N 130 30E 57
Ulm, *tn., W. Ger.*, 48 24N 10 00E 41
Ulsan, *tn., S. Kor.*, 35 32N 129 21E 57
Ulster, *geog. reg., N. Ire./Rep. Ire.*, 54 45N 7 50W . . 40
Ulugh Muztagh, Mt., *China*, 36 40N 87 30E 52
Ulverston, *tn., Eng.*, 54 12N 3 06W 25
Ulyanovsk, *tn., USSR*, 54 19N 48 22E 51
Uman, *tn., USSR*, 48 45N 30 10E 47
Umanak, *tn., Green.*, 70 40N 52 00W 71
Umbria, *geog. reg., It.*, 42 53N 12 30E 45
Umeå, *tn., Swed.*, 63 50N 20 15E 43
Umeälven, *R., Swed.*, 64 30N 18 45E 43
Umtali, *tn., Rhod.*, 19 00S 32 40E 67
Umtata, *tn., Rep. S. Afr.*, 31 35S 28 47E 67
Una, *R., Yug.*, 44 50N 16 15E 46
Unalaska I., *Aleutian Is.*, 52 30N 166 26W 70
Ungava Bay, *Que., Can.*, 59 30N 67 00W 71
Ungava Peninsula, *Que., Can.*, 60 00N 75 00W 71
Unimak I., *Aleutian Is.*, 55 00N 164 00W 70
Union of Soviet Socialist Republics, *Eur./Asia*,
54 00N 56 00E 52
United Arab Emirates, *Asia*, 24 40N 53 00E 52
United Kingdom, *Eur.*, 54 00N 2 00W 40
United States, *Rep., N. Amer.*, 37 30N 100 00W . . . 72
Unna, *tn., W. Ger.*, 51 32N 7 41E 39
Unst, *I., Scot.*, 60 45N 0 55W 22
Upernavik, *tn., Green.*, 72 40N 56 05W 71
Upington, *tn., Rep. S. Afr.*, 28 25S 21 14E 67
Upper Volta, *Rep., Afr.*, 12 20N 2 00W 66
Uppsala, *tn., Swed.*, 59 55N 17 38E 42
Ural, *R., USSR*, 49 00N 52 00E 51
Ural Mts., *USSR*, 60 00N 59 00E 51
Uralsk, *tn., USSR*, 51 19N 51 20E 51
Ure, *R., Eng.*, 54 20N 2 18W 25
Urfa, *tn., Tur.*, 37 08N 38 45E 49
Urga see Ulan Bator
Urgench, *tn., USSR*, 41 35N 60 41E 51

Urmia, *L., Iran*, 37 30N 45 30E 49
Uruguaiana, *tn., Arg.*, 29 45S 57 05W 77
Uruguay, *Rep., S. Amer.*, 30 30S 57 00W 77
Uruguay, *R., Braz./Urug.*, 28 00S 56 00W 77
Urumchi see Wulumuchi
Usak, *tn., Tur.*, 38 42N 29 25E 47
Ushuaia, *tn., Arg.*, 54 48S 68 19W 77
Usk, *R., Wales*, 51 37N 2 56W 26
Usk, *tn., Wales*, 51 43N 2 54W 26
Üsküdar, *tn., Tur.*, 41 01N 29 03E 47
Ussuri, *R., China/USSR*, 46 50N 134 00E 57
(see Wusuli Kiang)
Ussuriysk, *tn., USSR*, 43 48N 131 59E 57
Ust Kamchatsk, *tn., USSR*, 56 14N 162 28E 53
Ust Kut, *tn., USSR*, 56 48N 105 42E 53
Ust Labinsk, *tn., USSR*, 45 14N 39 41E 47
Ust-Urt, *plat., USSR*, 44 00N 55 00E 51
Usti nad Labem, *tn., Cz.*, 50 41N 14 00E 41
Utah, *admin. reg., USA*, 39 00N 112 00W 72
Utica, *hist. site, Tun.*, 37 30N 10 00E 48
Utica, *tn., N.Y., USA*, 43 06N 75 15W 73
Utrecht, *tn., Neth.*, 52 06N 5 07E 39
Utrera, *tn., Sp.*, 37 10N 5 47W 44
Utsunomiya, *tn., Jap.*, 36 33N 139 52E 57
Uttoxeter, *tn., Eng.*, 52 54N 1 51W 27
Uwajima, *tn., Jap.*, 33 13N 132 32E 57
Uzbekistan S.S.R., *admin. reg., USSR*,
41 58N 60 58E 51
Uzhgorod, *tn., USSR*, 48 38N 22 15E 50
Uzlovaya, *tn., USSR*, 53 55N 38 11E 50

V

Vaal, *R., Rep. S. Afr.*, 27 40S 25 30E 67
Vaasa, *tn., Fin.*, 63 06N 21 36E 43
Vadsø, *tn., Nor.*, 70 05N 29 47E 43
Vaduz, *tn., Liechtenstein*, 47 08N 9 32E 45
Vágar, *I., Faeroe Is.*, 62 00N 7 25W 43
Val d'Or, *tn., Que., Can.*, 48 07N 77 47W 73
Valdai Hills, *USSR*, 57 05N 32 14E 50
Valdez, *tn., Alaska, USA*, 61 07N 146 17W 70
Valdivia, *tn., Chile*, 39 46S 73 15W 77
Valdosta, *tn., Ga., USA*, 30 51N 83 51W 73
Valence, *tn., Fr.*, 44 56N 4 54E 45
Valencia, *geog. reg., Sp.*, 39 25N 0 45W 44
Valencia, *tn., Sp.*, 39 29N 0 24W 44
Valencia, *tn., Ven.*, 10 14N 67 59W 77
Valencia, Gulf of, *Sp.*, 39 30N 0 20E 44
Valenciennes, *tn., Fr.*, 50 22N 3 32E 39
Valga, *tn., USSR*, 57 44N 26 00E 42
Valladolid, *tn., Sp.*, 41 39N 4 45W 44
Valle d'Aosta, *admin. reg., It.*, 45 45N 7 22E 45
Valletta, *tn., Malta*, 35 54N 14 32E 48
Vallgrund, *I., Fin.*, 63 13N 21 19E 43
Valmiera, *tn., USSR*, 57 32N 25 29E 42
Valparaiso, *tn., Chile*, 33 05S 71 40W 77
Van, *tn., Tur.*, 38 30N 43 20E 49
Van, *L., Tur.*, 38 30N 43 20E 49
Vancouver, *tn., B.C., Can.*, 49 13N 123 06W 71
Vancouver Is., *B.C., Can.*, 49 50N 126 30W 71
Vänern, *L., Swed.*, 58 47N 13 50E 42
Vannes, *tn., Fr.*, 47 40N 2 44W 44
Vanua Levu, *I., Fiji, Pac. Oc.*, 16 30S 179 10E 63
Varanasi, *tn., India*, 25 20N 83 00E 54
Varanger Peninsula, *Nor.*, 70 22N 29 40E 43
Varangerfjord, *fd., Nor.*, 70 01N 29 00E 43
Varaždin, *tn., Yug.*, 46 18N 16 21E 46
Varberg, *tn., Swed.*, 57 06N 12 15E 42
Vardø, *tn., Nor.*, 70 22N 31 06E 43
Varese, *tn., It.*, 45 49N 8 49E 45
Varkaus, *tn., Fin.*, 62 20N 27 50E 43
Varna, *tn., Bulg.*, 43 12N 25 57E 47
Varsuga, *R., USSR*, 67 10N 36 00E 43
Vasa, *tn., Fin.*, 63 06N 21 36E 50
Västerås, *tn., Swed.*, 59 36N 16 32E 42
Västerdalälven, *R., Swed.*, 61 20N 13 10E 42
Västervik, *tn., Swed.*, 57 45N 16 40E 42
Vaternish, *geog. reg., Scot.*, 57 37N 6 39W 22
Vatersay, *I., Scot.*, 56 56N 7 32W 23
Vatican State, *city st., It.*, 41 54N 12 27E 45
Vatnajökull, *ice-cap, Ice.*, 64 30N 17 00W 43
Vättern, *L., Swed.*, 58 25N 14 30E 42
Vavau, *Is., Tonga, Pac. Oc.*, 18 30S 174 00W 63
Växjö, *tn., Swed.*, 56 52N 14 50E 42
Vega, *I., Nor.*, 65 38N 11 52E 43
Vejle, *tn., Den.*, 55 43N 9 33E 42
Velikiy Ustyug, *tn., USSR*, 60 47N 46 20E 50
Velikiya Luki, *tn., USSR*, 56 19N 30 31E 50
Velsk, *tn., USSR*, 61 05N 42 06E 50
Veluwe, *geog. reg., Neth.*, 52 25N 5 50E 39
Veneto, *geog. reg., It.*, 45 30N 12 00E 45
Venezia see Venice
Venezuela, *Rep., S. Amer.*, 0 00 65 00W 77
Venice, *tn., It.*, 45 26N 12 20E 45
Venice, Gulf of, *It.*, 45 20N 13 00E 45
Venlo, *tn., Neth.*, 51 22N 6 10E 39
Ventnor, *tn., Eng.*, 50 36N 1 11W 27
Ventspils, *tn., USSR*, 57 22N 21 31E 42
Veracruz, *tn., Mex.*, 19 11N 96 10W 71
Verde, *C., hdl., Sen.*, 14 43N 17 33W 66

Verdun-sur-Meuse, *tn., Fr.*, 49 10N 5 24E 39
Vereeniging, *tn., Rep. S. Afr.*, 26 41S 27 56E 67
Verkhoyansk, *tn., USSR*, 67 35N 133 25E 53
Verkhoyansk Range, *mts., USSR*, 66 00N 129 00E . . 53
Vermont, *admin. reg., USA*, 44 00N 72 30W 73
Verona, *tn., It.*, 45 26N 11 00E 45
Vérroia, *tn., Gr.*, 40 34N 22 18E 46
Versailles, *tn., Fr.*, 48 48N 2 08E 44
Verviers, *tn., Belg.*, 50 36N 5 52E 39
Vesterålen Is., *Nor.*, 69 00N 15 00E 43
Vestfirdir, *geog. reg., Ice.*, 65 40N 23 05W 43
Vestford, *fd., Nor.*, 68 00N 15 00E 43
Vestmannaeyjar, *tn., Ice.*, 63 25N 20 15W 43
Vesuvius, Mt., *It.*, 40 49N 14 26E 45
Vicenza, *tn., It.*, 45 33N 11 33E 45
Vichy, *tn., Fr.*, 46 08N 3 25E 44
Victoria, *admin. reg., Austr.*, 37 00S 144 00E 63
Victoria, *tn., Cam.*, 4 01N 9 12E 67
Victoria, *tn., China*, 22 16N 114 13E 56
Victoria, *tn., Seychelles*, 4 37S 55 27E 67
Victoria, *tn., Vancouver I., B.C., Can.*,
48 25N 123 22W 71
Victoria Falls, *w.f., Rhod.*, 17 55S 25 52E 67
Victoria Is., *N.W. Terrs., Can.*, 71 00N 110 00W . . . 71
Victoria, *L., Tanz.*, 1 00S 33 00E 67
Victoria Land, *Ant.*, 73 30S 165 00E 80
Viedma, *tn., Arg.*, 40 45S 63 00W 77
Vienna, *tn., Aust.*, 48 14N 16 22E 45
Vienne, *R., Fr.*, 47 05N 0 30E 44
Vientiane, *tn., Laos*, 17 59N 102 38E 55
Viersen, *tn., W. Ger.*, 51 16N 6 24E 39
Vietnam, *Rep., Asia*, 17 00N 107 00E 55
Vigevano, *tn., It.*, 45 19N 8 51E 45
Vigo, *tn., Sp.*, 42 15N 8 44W 44
Vijayawada, *tn., India*, 16 34N 80 40E 54
Vikna, *I., Nor.*, 64 55N 10 55E 43
Vila, *tn., New Hebrides, Pac. Oc.*, 17 45S 168 18E . . 63
Vila Nova de Gaia, *tn., Port.*, 41 04N 8 40W 44
Vila Serpa Pinto, *tn., Ang.*, 14 40S 17 41E 67
Vilhelmina, *tn., Swed.*, 64 38N 16 40E 43
Viliya, *R., USSR*, 54 25N 26 55E 42
Villach, *tn., Aust.*, 46 37N 13 51E 45
Villeurbanne, *tn., Fr.*, 45 46N 4 54E 45
Vilnius, *tn., USSR*, 54 40N 25 19E 42
Vilyuy, *R., USSR*, 63 30N 120 00E 53
Viña del Mar, *tn., Chile*, 33 02S 71 35W 77
Vindelälven, *R., Swed.*, 65 20N 18 15E 43
Vinh, *tn., Viet.*, 18 42N 105 41E 55
Vinnitsa, *tn., USSR*, 49 11N 28 30E 50
Vinson Massif, *mts., Ant.*, 78 02S 80 00W 80
Virginia, *admin. reg., USA*, 37 45N 78 00W 73
Visby, *tn., Swed.*, 57 37N 18 20E 42
Vishakhapatnam, *tn., India*, 17 42N 83 24E 54
Vistula, *R., Pol.*, 53 40N 18 45E 41
Vitebsk, *tn., USSR*, 55 10N 30 14E 50
Viterbo, *tn., It.*, 42 24N 12 06E 45
Viti Levu, *I., Fiji, Pac. Oc.*, 17 50S 177 50E 63
Vitória, *tn., Braz.*, 20 19S 40 21W 77
Vitoria, *tn., Sp.*, 42 51N 2 40W 44
Vittoria, *tn., Sicily*, 36 58N 14 32E 45
Vlaardingen, *tn., Neth.*, 51 55N 4 20E 39
Vladimir, *tn., USSR*, 56 08N 40 25E 50
Vladivostock, *tn., USSR*, 43 09N 131 53E 57
Vlieland, *I., Neth.*, 53 30N 4 55E 39
Vlorë, *tn., Alb.*, 40 29N 19 29E 46
Vltava, *R., Cz.*, 49 35N 14 10E 41
Vogelsberg, *mt., W. Ger.*, 50 41N 9 08E 39
Vojvodina, *geog. reg., Yug.*, 45 20N 20 00E 46
Volga, *R., USSR*, 47 30N 47 00E 51
Volgodonsk, *tn., USSR*, 47 35N 42 08E 51
Volgograd, *tn., USSR*, 48 45N 44 30E 51
Volgograd Reservoir, *USSR*, 49 39N 45 25E 51
Volkhov, *R., USSR*, 59 30N 32 00E 50
Volkhov, *tn., USSR*, 59 54N 32 47E 50
Vologda, *tn., USSR*, 59 10N 39 55E 50
Vólos, *tn., Gr.*, 39 22N 22 57E 46
Volsk, *tn., USSR*, 52 04N 47 22E 51
Volta, *R., Ghana*, 8 00N 0 10W 66
Volta Redonda, *tn., Braz.*, 22 31S 44 05W 77
Volzhskiy, *tn., USSR*, 48 48N 44 45E 51
Vopnafjord, *fd., Ice.*, 65 45N 14 45W 43
Vorkuta, *tn., USSR*, 67 27N 64 00E 52
Voronezh, *tn., USSR*, 51 23N 42 02E 50
Voronya, *R., USSR*, 68 30N 35 30E 43
Voroshilovgrad, *tn., USSR*, 51 10N 45 39E 50
Vosges, *mts., Fr.*, 48 20N 7 10E 45
Vostok, *USSR base, Ant.*, 78 27S 106 52E 80
Votkinsk, *tn., USSR*, 57 02N 53 59E 51
Vsevolozhskiy, *tn., USSR*, 60 03N 30 41E 42
Vulcano, *I., It.*, 38 25N 14 58E 45
Vuoksa, *R., USSR*, 61 04N 28 45E 42
Vyatka, *R., USSR*, 56 30N 51 00E 51
Vyborg, *tn., USSR*, 60 45N 28 41E 42
Vychegda, *R., USSR*, 61 50N 52 30E 50
Vyg, *L., USSR*, 63 30N 34 25E 43
Vyshniy Volochek, *tn., USSR*, 57 34N 34 23E 50

W

Waal, *R., Neth.*, 51 80N 5 00E 39
Wabash, *R., USA*, 39 10N 87 30W 73

Waco, tn., Tex., USA, 31 33N 97 10W 72
Wad Medani, tn., Sud., 14 24N 33 30E 67
Waddenzee, s., Neth., 53 13N 5 10E 39
Wadebridge, tn., Eng., 50 32N 4 50W 26
Wadi Halfa, tn., Sud., 21 46N 31 17E 49
Wagga Wagga, tn., N.S.W., Austr., 35 07S 147 24E 63
Wakayama, tn., Jap., 34 12N 135 10E 57
Wakkanai, tn., Jap., 45 26N 141 43E 57
Wakefield, tn., Eng., 53 42N 1 29W 25
Walbrzych, tn., Pol., 50 48N 16 19E 41
Wales, Principality, UK, 52 30N 3 30W 40
Walgett, tn., N.S.W., Austr., 30 03S 148 10E 63
Walla Walla, tn., Wash., USA, 46 05N 118 18W 72
Wallachia, geog. reg., Rom., 44 35N 25 00E 46
Wallasey, tn., Eng., 53 26N 3 03W 25
Wallingford, tn., Eng., 51 37N 1 08W 27
Wallis Is., Pac. Oc., 13 16S 176 15W 63
Wallsend, tn., Eng., 55 00N 1 31W 25
Walsall, tn., Eng., 52 35N 1 58W 27
Walton le Dale, tn., Eng., 53 45N 2 41W 25
Walvis Bay, tn., Rep. S. Afr., 22 59S 14 31E 67
Wanganui, tn., N.Z., 39 56S 175 02E 63
Wanhsien, tn., China, 30 54N 108 20E 56
Wankie, tn., Rhod., 18 20S 26 25E 67
Wantage, tn., Eng., 51 36N 1 25W 27
Warangal, tn., India, 18 00N 79 35E 54
Ware, tn., Eng., 51 49N 0 02W 27
Warley, tn., Eng., 52 30N 2 00W 27
Warminster, tn., Eng., 51 13N 2 12W 27
Warren, tn., Mich., USA, 42 31N 83 02W 73
Warrington, tn., Eng., 53 24N 2 37W 25
Warrnambool, tn., Vic., Austr., 38 23S 142 03E....63
Warsaw, tn., Pol., 52 15N 21 00E 41
Warta, R., Pol., 52 40N 16 10E 41
Warwick, tn., Eng., 52 17N 1 34W 27
Warwickshire, admin. reg., Eng., 52 15N 1 34W 27
Wasatch Range, mts., Utah, USA, 40 30N 116 30W 72
Wash, The, est., Eng., 52 58N 0 20W 27
Washington, admin. reg., USA, 47 45N 120 30W 72
Washington, tn., Dist. of Columbia, USA,
38 55N 77 00W 73
Washington, tn., Eng., 54 54N 1 31W 25
Washington, Mt., N.H., USA, 44 17N 71 19W 73
Watchet, tn., Eng., 51 12N 3 20W 26
Waterbury, tn., Conn., USA, 41 33N 73 03W 73
Waterford, tn., Rep. Ire., 52 15N 7 06W 40
Waterloo, tn., Iowa, USA, 42 30N 92 20W 73
Watford, tn., Eng., 51 40N 0 25W 27
Watling I. see San Salvador
Wau, tn., Sud., 7 40N 28 04E 67
Waukegan, tn., Ill., USA, 42 21N 87 52W 73
Waveney, R., Eng., 52 24N 1 20E 27
Weald, The, geog. reg., Eng., 51 07N 0 09E 27
Wear, R., Eng., 54 44N 1 58W 25
Weddell Sea, Ant., 68 30S 45 00W 80
Wei Ho, R., China, 35 45N 114 30E 56
Weifang, tn., China, 36 44N 119 10E 57
Weihai, tn., China, 37 30N 122 04E 57
Weimar, tn., E. Ger., 50 59N 11 20E 41
Weinan, tn., China, 34 30N 109 30E 56
Welkom, tn., Rep. S. Afr., 27 59S 26 44E 67
Welland, R., Eng., 52 43N 0 10W 27
Wellingborough, tn., Eng., 52 19N 0 42W 27
Wellington, tn., Eng., 50 59N 3 14W 26
Wellington, tn., N.Z., 41 17S 174 47E 63
Wells, tn., Eng., 51 13N 2 39W 26
Wels, tn., Aust., 48 10N 14 02E 45
Welshpool, tn., Wales, 52 40N 3 09W 26
Welwyn Garden City, tn., Eng., 51 48N 0 13W 27
Wenchow, tn., China, 28 02N 120 40E 57
Wensi, tn., China, 35 25N 111 07E 56
Wensleydale, val., Eng., 54 18N 2 00W 25
Werra, R., W. Ger., 51 24N 9 47E 39
Weser, R., W. Ger., 53 33N 8 30E 41
West Antarctica, geog. reg., Ant., 80 00S 105 00W ...80
West Bridgford, tn., Eng., 52 56N 1 08W 25
West Bromwich, tn., Eng., 52 31N 1 59W 27
West Burra, I., Scot., 60 05N 1 21W 22
West Dvina, R., USSR, 56 30N 24 00E 50
(see also Daugava, R.)
West Frisian Is., Neth., 53 30N 5 30E 39
West Germany, Rep., Eur., 51 00N 7 00E 41
West Glamorgan, admin. reg., Wales, 51 40N 4 00W ...26
West Ice Shelf, Ant., 65 00S 83 00E 80
West Indies, Arch., Caribbean Sea, 23 00N 76 00W ...71
West Irian, admin. reg., Indon., 3 00S 137 00E 55
West Midlands, admin. reg., Eng., 52 24N 1 50W 27
West Palm Beach, tn., Fla., USA, 26 42N 80 05W 73
West Siberian Plain, geog. reg., USSR, 63 00N 75 00E .52
West Spitsbergen, Arch., Arctic Oc., 79 00N 15 00E .52
West Sussex, admin. reg., Eng., 50 56N 0 30W 27
West Turkistan, geog. reg., USSR, 43 00N 70 00E ...52
West Virginia, admin. reg., USA, 38 00N 81 00W 73
West Yorkshire, admin. reg., Eng., 53 44N 1 20W ...25
Western Australia, admin. reg., Austr., 26 00S 121 00E .62
Western Ghats, mts., India, 15 00N 74 00E 54
Western Isles, admin. reg., Scot., 57 40N 7 15W 22
Western Samoa, Is., Comm. nat., Pac. Oc.,
14 00S 172 00W 63
Western Sierra Madre, mts., Mex., 26 00N 107 30W ...72
Westerwald, mts., W. Ger., 50 39N 8 00E 39
Westmeath, admin. reg., Rep. Ire., 53 25N 7 43W ...24
Weston-super-Mare, tn., Eng., 51 21N 2 59W 26
Westport, tn., N.Z., 41 46S 171 38E 63
Westray, I., Scot., 59 18N 2 59W 22
Westray Firth, Scot., 59 15N 3 00W 22
Wetherby, tn., Eng., 53 56N 1 23W 25
Wetzlar, tn., W. Ger., 50 33N 8 30E 39
Wewak, tn., Pap. New Guin., 3 35S 143 35E 63
Wexford, admin. reg., Rep. Ire., 52 25N 6 35W 26
Wexford, tn., Rep. Ire., 52 20N 6 27W 26

Wey, R., Eng., 51 19N 0 29W 27
Weybridge, tn., Eng., 51 23N 0 28W 27
Weymouth, tn., Eng., 50 36N 2 28W 26
Whalsay, I., Scot., 60 22N 0 59W 22
Whangarei, tn., N.Z., 35 43S 174 20E 63
Wharfe, R., Eng., 54 13N 2 00W 25
Wharfedale, val., Eng., 54 07N 2 04W 25
Wheeler Peak, mt., Nev., USA, 38 59N 114 19W 72
Whitby, tn., Eng., 53 16N 2 55W 25
Whitchurch, tn., Eng., 52 58N 2 41W 26
White Nile, R., Sud., 9 30N 31 40E 67
White Russian S.S.R., admin. reg., USSR,
53 30N 27 00E 50
White Sea, 65 30N 35 25E 50
Whitehaven, tn., Eng., 54 33N 3 35W 25
Whitehead, tn., N. Ire., 54 45N 5 43W 24
Whitehorse, tn., Yukon, Can., 60 41N 135 08W 71
Whitley Bay, tn., Eng., 55 03N 1 25W 25
Whitney, Mt., Calif., USA, 36 35N 118 17W 73
Whitstable, tn., Eng., 51 22N 1 02E 27
Whittlesey, tn., Eng., 52 34N 0 08W 27
Whyalla, tn., S. Austr., 33 04S 137 34E 63
Wiay, I., Scot., 57 24N 7 13W 22
Wichita, tn., Kans., USA, 37 43N 97 20W 72
Wichita Falls, tn., Tex., USA, 33 55N 98 30W 72
Wick, tn., Scot., 58 26N 3 06W 22
Wicklow, admin. reg., Rep. Ire., 53 02N 6 22W 24
Wicklow, tn., Rep. Ire., 52 59N 6 03W 24
Wicklow Mts., Rep. Ire., 53 00N 6 30W 24
Widnes, tn., Eng., 53 22N 2 44W 25
Wien see Vienna
Wiener Neustadt, tn., Aust., 47 49N 16 15E 45
Wiesbaden, tn., W. Ger., 50 05N 8 15E 39
Wigan, tn., Eng., 53 33N 2 38W 25
Wight, I. of, admin. reg., Eng., 50 40N 1 15W 27
Wigston, tn., Eng., 52 36N 1 05W 27
Wigton, tn., Eng., 54 49N 3 09W 25
Wigtown, tn., Scot., 54 52N 4 26W 23
Wigtown Bay, Scot., 54 46N 4 15W 23
Wilhelmshaven, tn., W. Ger., 53 32N 8 07E 39
Wilkes Barre, tn., Pa., USA, 41 15N 75 50W 73
Wilkes Land, geog. reg., Ant., 68 00S 120 00E 80
Wilkes Station, Austr./USA base, Ant., 66 15S 110 31E .80
Wilmington, tn., Del., USA, 39 46N 75 31W 73
Wilmington, tn., N.C., USA, 34 14N 77 55W 73
Wilmslow, tn., Eng., 53 20N 2 15W 25
Wilson, Mt., Colo., USA, 37 51N 107 59W 72
Wiltshire, admin. reg., Eng., 51 20N 2 12W 27
Wimborne Minster, tn., Eng., 50 48N 1 59W 27
Winchester, tn., Eng., 51 04N 1 19W 27
Windermere, tn., Eng., 54 23N 2 57W 25
Windhoek, tn., S.W. Afr. (Nam.), 22 34S 17 06E ...67
Windsor, tn., Eng., 51 29N 0 38W 27
Windsor, tn., Ont., Can., 42 18N 83 00W 73
Winnipeg, tn., Man., Can., 49 53N 97 10W 72
Winnipeg, L., Man., Can., 52 30N 98 00W 71
Winsford, tn., Eng., 53 11N 2 31W 25
Winston-Salem, tn., N.C., USA, 36 05N 80 18W 73
Winterthur, tn., Switz., 47 30N 8 45E 45
Wisbech, tn., Eng., 52 40N 0 10E 27
Wisconsin, admin. reg., USA, 44 50N 90 00W 73
Wishaw, tn., Scot., 55 47N 3 56W 23
Wisła see Vistula
Wismar, tn., E. Ger., 53 54N 11 28E 41
Witham, R., Eng., 53 03N 0 08W 25
Witham, tn., Eng., 51 48N 0 38E 27
Withernsea, tn., Eng., 53 44N 0 02E 25
Witney, tn., Eng., 51 48N 1 29W 27
Włocławek, tn., Pol., 52 39N 19 01E 41
Woking, tn., Eng., 51 20N 0 34W 27
Wokingham, tn., Eng., 51 25N 0 51W 27
Wolfsburg, tn., W. Ger., 52 27N 10 49E 41
Wollongong, tn., N.S.W., Austr., 34 25S 150 52E 63
Wolverhampton, tn., Eng., 52 36N 2 08W 27
Wonju, tn., S. Kor., 37 24N 127 52E 57
Wonsan, tn., N. Kor., 39 07N 127 26E 57
Woodbridge, tn., Eng., 52 06N 1 19E 27
Woodroffe, Mt., S. Austr., 26 20S 131 42E 62
Woods, L. of the, Can./USA, 49 30N 94 30W 73
Wooler, tn., Eng., 55 33N 2 01W 25
Woomera, tn., S. Austr., 31 11S 136 54E 63
Wootton Bassett, tn., Eng., 51 33N 1 54W 27
Worcester, tn., Eng., 52 11N 2 13W 27
Worcester, tn., Mass., USA, 42 17N 71 48W 73
Worcester, tn., Rep. S. Afr., 33 39S 19 26E 67
Workington, tn., Eng., 54 39N 3 33W 25
Worksop, tn., Eng., 53 18N 1 07W 25
Worms, tn., W. Ger., 49 38N 8 23E 39
Worms Head, hdl., Wales, 51 34N 4 20W 26
Worthing, tn., Eng., 50 48N 0 23W 27
Wotje, I., Pac. Oc., 9 30N 170 00E 63
Wrangel I., USSR, 72 00N 180 00E 53
Wrath, Cape, hdl., Scot., 58 37N 5 01W 22
Wrexham, tn., Wales, 53 03N 3 00W 26
Wrocław, tn., Pol., 51 05N 17 00E 41
Wu Kiang, R., China, 27 50N 108 00E 56
Wuchow, tn., China, 23 30N 111 21E 56
Wuchung, tn., China, 37 55N 106 11E 56
Wuhan, tn., China, 30 35N 114 19E 56
Wuhu, tn., China, 31 23N 118 25E 57
Wuliang Shan, mts., China, 25 30N 100 00E 56
Wulumuchi, tn., China, 43 43N 87 38E 52
Wuppertal, tn., W. Ger., 51 15N 7 10E 39
Würzburg, tn., W. Ger., 49 48N 9 57E 39
Wusih, tn., China, 31 35N 120 19E 57
Wusuli Kiang, R., China/USSR, 46 50N 134 00E 57
(see also Ussuri R.)
Wutai Shan, mts., China, 39 00N 113 00E 56
Wutu, tn., China, 33 27N 104 57E 56
Wutunghlia see Wutunghliao
Wutunghliao, tn., China, 29 21N 103 48E 56

Wuwei, tn., China, 38 00N 102 54E 56
Wuyi Shan, mts., China, 26 40N 116 30E 56
Wye, R., Eng./Wales, 52 00N 2 36W 26
Wymondham, tn., Eng., 52 34N 1 07E 27
Wyndham, tn., W. Austr., 15 30S 128 09E 62
Wyoming, admin. reg., USA, 43 30N 108 00W 72

X

Xánthi, tn., Gr., 41 07N 24 56E 46
Xiamen see Amoy
Xi'ang see Sian
Xingu, R., Braz., 2 25S 52 35W 77

Y

Yaan, tn., China, 30 00N 103 02E 56
Yablonovyy Range, mts., USSR, 54 00N 114 00E 53
Yaeyama Group, Is., Jap., 24 30N 123 40E 57
Yakima, tn., Wash., USA, 46 37N 120 30W 72
Yakutsk, tn., USSR, 62 10N 129 50E 53
Yallourn, tn., Vic., Austr., 38 09S 146 22E 63
Yalta, tn., USSR, 44 30N 34 09E 47
Yalu R., China/Kor., 41 30N 126 30E 57
Yalung Kiang, R., China, 32 00N 100 00E 56
Yamagata, tn., Jap., 38 16N 140 19E 57
Yamal Peninsula, USSR, 71 00N 70 00E 52
Yambol, tn., Bulg., 42 28N 26 30E 46
Yanbu, tn., Si. Arab., 24 07N 38 04E 49
Yangchow, tn., China, 32 22N 119 22E 57
Yangchuan, tn., China, 37 52N 113 29E 56
Yangtze Kiang, R., China, 26 00N 103 30E 56
Yannina, tn., Gr., 39 40N 20 51E 46
Yaondé, tn., Cam., 3 51N 11 31E 67
Yap Is., Pac. Oc., 9 30N 138 09E 63
Yaqui, R., Mex., 30 00N 109 15W 72
Yare, R., Eng., 52 36N 1 28E 27
Yarkand see Soche
Yarmouth, tn., Eng., 50 42N 1 29W 27
Yarmouth, tn., N.S., Can., 43 50N 66 08W 73
Yaroslavl, tn., USSR, 57 34N 39 52E 50
Yatsushiro, tn., Jap., 32 33N 130 35E 57
Yazoo, R., Miss., USA, 32 35N 90 50W 73
Yelets, tn., USSR, 52 36N 38 30E 50
Yell, I., Scot., 60 35N 1 05W 22
Yell Sound, Scot., 60 33N 1 15W 22
Yellow Sea, China, 35 00N 123 00E 57
Yellowknife, tn., N.W. Terrs., Can., 62 30N 114 29W ...71
Yellowstone, R., Mont., USA, 46 35N 107 00W 72
Yellowstone Falls, wf., Wyo., USA, 44 43N 110 30W ...72
Yellowstone National Park, Wyo., USA,
44 35N 111 00W 72
Yemen, Rep., Asia, 15 00N 44 00E 52
Yenan, tn., China, 36 40N 109 21E 56
Yenchang, tn., China, 36 40N 110 04E 56
Yencheng, tn., China, 33 23N 120 10E 57
Yenisey, R., USSR, 67 00N 86 00E 52
Yeniseysk, tn., USSR, 58 27N 92 13E 53
Yenki, tn., China, 42 45N 129 25E 57
Yentai, tn., China, 37 30N 121 22E 57
Yeovil, tn., Eng., 50 57N 2 39W 26
Yerevan, tn., USSR, 40 10N 44 31E 51
Yesil, R., Tur., 41 00N 36 40E 47
Yessentuki, tn., USSR, 44 03N 42 53E 51
Yeungkong, tn., China, 21 52N 111 52E 56
Yevpatoriya, tn., USSR, 45 12N 33 20E 47
Yeysk, tn., USSR, 46 43N 38 17E 50
Yezd, tn., Iran, 31 55N 54 22E 52
Yinchwan, tn., China, 38 30N 106 19E 56
Yingkow, tn., China, 40 40N 122 17E 57
Yirga Alam, tn., Ethiopia, 6 48N 38 22E 67
Yitu, tn., China, 36 40N 118 25E 57
Yiyang, tn., China, 28 39N 112 10E 56
Yli-Kitka, L., Fin., 66 05N 28 30E 43
Ylivieska, tn., Fin., 64 05N 24 30E 43
Yokohama, tn., Jap., 35 28N 139 38E 57
Yokosuka, tn., Jap., 35 18N 139 39E 57
Yonne, R., Fr., 48 12N 3 10E 44
York, tn., Eng., 53 58N 1 05W 25
York, Cape, hdl., Queensl., Austr., 10 42S 142 32E ...63
Yorkshire Moors, hs., Eng., 54 21N 1 08W 25
Yorkshire Wolds, hs., Eng., 53 57N 1 08W 25
Yosemite National Park, Calif., USA, 37 50N 119 30W ..72
Yoshkar Ola, tn., USSR, 56 38N 47 42E 50
Youngstown, tn., Ohio, USA, 41 05N 80 40W 73
Yoyang, tn., China, 29 23N 113 03E 56
Yozgat, tn., Tur., 39 50N 34 48E 47
Ystad, tn., Swed., 55 25N 13 50E 42
Yu Kiang, R., China, 23 00N 107 00E 56

Yuan Kiang, *R., China*, 28 00N 110 00E 56
Yuanli, *tn., Taiwan*, 24 29N 120 40E 57
Yuanling, *tn., China*, 28 30N 110 12E 56
Yubari, *tn., Jap.*, 43 04N 141 59E 57
Yucatán, *admin. reg., Mex.*, 19 30N 90 00W 71
Yucatán Channel, *G. of Mex.*, 22 00N 87 30W 71
Yugoslavia, *Rep., Eur.*, 44 00N 20 00E 46
Yuki, *tn., China*, 24 24N 102 29E 56
Yukon, *admin. reg., Can.*, 63 00N 138 00W 71
Yukon, *R., Alaska, USA*, 66 30N 143 00W 71
Yulin, *tn., Kwangsi, China*, 22 37N 110 08E 56
Yulin, *tn., Kwangtung, China*, 18 20N 109 31E 56
Yulin, *tn., Shensi, China*, 38 16N 109 29E 56
Yuma, *tn., Ariz., USA*, 32 40N 114 39W 72
Yumen, *tn., China*, 40 19N 97 43E 56
Yumenshih, *tn., China*, 39 54N 98 00E 56
Yuncheng, *tn., China*, 35 06N 111 02E 56
Yungan, *tn., China*, 25 52N 117 21E 56
Yunhsien, *tn., China*, 32 50N 110 50E 56
Yunlin, *mt., Taiwan*, 23 30N 121 00E 57
Yunling Shan, *mts., China*, 25 30N 99 30E 56
Yunnan, *admin. reg., China*, 25 00N 102 30E 56
Yushkozero, *tn., USSR*, 64 45N 32 03E 43
Yushu, *tn., Kirin, China*, 44 48N 126 31E 57
Yushu, *tn., Tsinghai, China*, 33 06N 96 48E 56
Yutze, *tn., China*, 37 40N 112 44E 56
Yuzhno Sakhalinsk, *tn., USSR*, 46 58N 142 45E 57

Z

Zaanstad, *tn., Neth.*, 52 27N 4 49E 39
Zabrze, *tn., Pol.*, 50 18N 18 47E 41
Zadar, *tn., Yug.*, 44 07N 15 14E 46
Zagazig, *tn., Eg.*, 30 35N 31 30E 49
Zagorsk, *tn., USSR*, 56 20N 38 10E 50
Zagreb, *tn., Yug.*, 45 48N 15 58E 46
Zagros Mts., *Iran*, 33 45N 47 00E 52
Zahidan, *tn., Iran*, 29 32N 60 54E 52
Zaire, *R., Zaire*, 2 00N 23 00E 67
(as Congo, R. in Congo)
Zaire, *Rep., Afr.*, 2 00S 19 50E 67
Zakopane, *tn., Pol.*, 49 17N 19 54E 41
Zambezi, *R., Afr.*, 16 30S 32 30E 67
Zambia, *Rep., Afr.*, 4 00S 24 00E 67
Zamboanga, *tn., Phil.*, 6 55N 122 05E 55
Zamora, *tn., Sp.*, 41 30N 5 45W 44
Zamość, *tn., Pol.*, 50 43N 23 15E 41
Záncara, *R., Sp.*, 39 20N 3 00W 44
Zante, *I., Gr.*, 37 45N 27 45E 46
Zanzibar, *tn., Zanzibar*, 6 10S 39 12E 67
Zapolyarnyy, *tn., USSR*, 69 21N 30 30E 43
Zaporozhye, *tn., USSR*, 47 50N 35 10E 50
Zaragoza, *tn., Sp.*, 41 39N 0 54W 44
Zárate, *tn., Arg.*, 34 07S 59 00W 77

Zaria, *tn., Nig.*, 11 01N 7 44E 67
Zarqa, *tn., Jordan*, 32 04N 36 06E 49
Zaysan, L., *USSR*, 48 00N 83 00E 52
Zealand, *I., Den.*, 55 30N 11 30E 42
Zeebrugge, *tn., Belg.*, 51 20N 3 13E 39
Zeist, *tn., Neth.*, 52 05N 5 15E 39
Zelenodolsk, *tn., USSR*, 55 50N 48 30E 51
Zenica, *tn., Yug.*, 44 11N 17 53E 46
Zetland see Shetland
Zhdanov, *tn., USSR*, 47 05N 37 34E 50
Zhigulevsk, *tn., USSR*, 53 26N 49 30E 51
Zhitomir, *tn., USSR*, 50 15N 28 40E 50
Ziatoust, *tn., USSR*, 55 16N 59 40E 51
Ziguinchor, *tn., Sen.*, 12 35N 16 20W 66
Zielona Góra, *tn., Pol.*, 51 57N 15 30E 41
Žilina, *tn., Cz.*, 49 14N 18 40E 41
Zimbabwe, *hist. site, Rhod.*, 20 16S 30 54E 67
Zinder, *tn., Niger*, 13 46N 8 58E 67
Zomba, *tn., Mal.*, 15 22S 35 22E 67
Zonguldak, *tn., Tur.*, 41 26N 31 47E 47
Zrenjanin, *tn., Yug.*, 45 22N 10 23E 46
Zuara, *tn., Libya*, 32 59N 12 40E 48
Zugspitze, *mt., W. Ger.*, 47 25N 11 00E 41
Zürich, *tn., Switz.*, 47 23N 8 33E 45
Zuwaitina, *tn., Libya*, 31 40N 20 10E 49
Zwickau, *tn., E. Ger.*, 50 43N 12 30E 41
Zwolle, *tn., Neth.*, 52 31N 6 06E 39

GEOGRAPHICAL GLOSSARY

A glossary is a special kind of dictionary, which explains words that are uncommon, archaic, or that have local significance.

An atlas glossary provides comparisons between different words used for essentially the same kinds of features shown on maps. For example, in the English language, a word often used to indicate *headland* is *Head* (as in St. David's Head); on other occasions the word *Cape* is used (as in Cape Wrath), or *Point* (as in Start Point), or *Ness* (as in Buchan Ness), or *Mull* (as in Mull of Oa), or *Naze* (as in The Naze), or *Butt* (as in Butt of Lewis), or *Bill* (as in Portland Bill). Other languages spell these words differently; thus in French *Cape* is spelt as *Cap* (as in Cap de la Hague), in Spanish as *Cabo* (as in Cabo Finisterre), and in Italian as *Capo* (as in Capo Spartivento).

Similar sets of interchangeable words exist in different languages for other features, such as lakes, rivers, woods, bays, islands, mountains, etc.

Names of human settlements also frequently include words that describe what the places are or were. Some of these words are so old that many people today have forgotten what the words originally meant. For example, the words *borough, brough,* and *burgh* (as in Peterborough, Middlesbrough, and Edinburgh) all mean a ''fortress'' or ''fortified place'', and date from periods when settlements were commonly walled or moated. In Europe, equivalent names are *borg* (as in Trelleborg — Sweden), *bourg* (as in Cherbourg — France), and *burg* (as in Hamburg — W. Germany).

Similar collections of interchangeable words exist in various languages for features such as houses, villages, towns, wells, thickets, fields, etc., and for other words that describe size (e.g., Grand, Grande, Gran, etc.) or colour (White, Blanc, Branco, etc.) incorporated in place-names. Two such names are Gran Chaco and Mt. Blanc.

All these kinds of names, and many others, are listed below alphabetically.

ABAD *(Persian, Hindi)* city.
See also BAD, CIUDAD, GRAD, PUR, STAD, STADT.
ABER *(Cymric),* confluence, or mouth of a river.
AFON *(Cymric),* a river.
See also ÄLV, AVON, BAHR, HO, JOKI, JOKKA, KIANG, RIO.
ALTO *(Italian, Portuguese, Spanish)* high.
See also ARD, ORD.
ÄLV *(Swedish),* river.
See also AFON, AVON, BAHR, HO, JOKI, JOKKA, KIANG, RIO.
ARD *(Celtic),* high, a height.
See also ALTO, ORD.
ATH *(Gaelic),* a ford.
AUCHTER *(Celtic),* upper.
See also ÖVRE, UPPER.
AVON *(Celtic),* a river.
See also AFON, ÄLV, BAHR, HO, JOKI, JOKKA, KIANG, RIO.
AY *(Scandinavian),* an island.
See also EY, HOLM, ILE, INCH, INISH, INNIS, INSEL, JIMA, O, Ö, OE, SAARI, SHIMA, TAO, YNYS.
BAB *(Arabic),* a gate.
BACH *(Welsh),* little.
See also PETIT.
BAD *(Persian, Hindi),* a city.
See also ABAD, CIUDAD, GRAD, PUR, STAD, STADT.
BAHR *(Arabic),* a river, sometimes a lake.
See also AFON, ÄLV, AVON, HO, JÄRVI, JOKI, JOKKA, KIANG, MERE, NOR, RIO.
BAIE *(French),* a gulf, or bay.
See also BAY, FLÖI, GOLFE, GOLFO, GULF, LAHTI, LUOKTA.
BARROW *(Anglo-Saxon),* a hill.
See also MÄKI, MON.
BAY *(Anglo-Saxon),* a gulf.
See also BAIE, FLÖI, GOLFE, GOLFO, GULF.
BECK *(Scandinavian),* a brook.
BEINN *(Gaelic),* a hill-top.
See also BEN.
BEL *(Gaelic),* a mouth or entrance; sometimes a ford.
BEN *(Gaelic),* a hill-top.
See also BEINN.
BERE *(Gaelic),* well, water, fountain.
See also BERVIE.
BERG *(German, Dutch),* mountain.
See also FELL, FJÄLL, JABAL, MONT, MONTE, PEN, SHAN, TJÅKKÅ, VARRA, YAMA.
BERVIE *(Gaelic),* well, water, fountain.
See also BERE.
BILL *(Anglo-Saxon),* a headland.
See also BUTT, CABO, CAP, CAPE, CAPO, HEAD, MULL, NAZE, NESS, NIEMI, POINT, POINTE, PUNTA.
BLANC *(French),* white.
See also BRANCO, GWYN.
BORG *(Danish, Swedish),* a fortress.
See also BOROUGH, BOURG, BROUGH, BURG, BURGH, DOR, DUN, WARK.
BOROUGH *(Anglo-Saxon),* a fortified town.
See also BORG, BOURG, BROUGH, BURG, BURGH, DOR, DUN, WARK.
BOURG *(French, Flemish),* a fortified town.
See also BORG, BOROUGH, BROUGH, BURG, BURGH, DOR, DUN, WARK.
BRANCO *(Portuguese),* white.
See also BLANC, GWYN.
BRE *(Norwegian),* glacier, ice-cap.
See also BROE.
BRO *(Danish, Swedish),* a bridge.
See also PONT.
BROE *(Danish),* glacier, ice-cap.
See also BRE.
BROUGH *(Anglo-Saxon),* a fortified town.
See also BORG, BOROUGH, BOURG, BURG, BURGH, DOR, DUN, WARK.
BUN *(Gaelic),* foot, or mouth.
BURG *(German),* a fortified town.
See also BORG, BOROUGH, BOURG, BROUGH, BURGH, DOR, DUN.
BURGH *(Teutonic),* a fortified town.
See also BORG, BOROUGH, BOURG, BROUGH, BURG, DOR, DUN.
BURN *(Gaelic),* a stream.
See also JOKK.
BURY *(Anglo-Saxon),* a fortified town.
See also BORG, BOROUGH, BOURG, BURG, BURGH, DOR, DUN.
BUTT *(Celtic),* a headland.
See also BILL, CABO, CAP, CAPE, CAPO, HEAD, MULL, NAZE, NESS, NIEMI, POINT, POINTE, PUNTA.
BWLCH *(Welsh),* a mountain pass.
BY *(Danish),* a town.
See also, HSIEN, KÖPING, TON.
BY *(Scandinavian),* a dwelling place (when used in Britain).
See also VILLE.
BY *(Swedish)* a village.
See also DORF, THORPE, TRE, VILA, VILLA, WICK.
CABO *(Spanish),* a headland.
See also BILL, BUTT, CAP, CAPE, CAPO, HEAD, MULL, NAZE, NESS, NIEMI, POINT, POINTE, PUNTA.
CAER *(Welsh),* a fortress.
See also CAR.
CAIRN *(Gaelic),* a heap of stones.
See also CARN.
CAM *(Celtic),* crooked.
CAMPO *(Spanish, Portuguese),* a field, moor.
See also FIELD, MOOR, MUIR.
CAP *(French),* a headland.
See also BILL, BUTT, CABO, CAPE, CAPO, HEAD, MULL, NAZE, NESS, NIEMI, POINT, POINTE, PUNTA.
CAPE *(Anglo-Saxon),* a headland.
See also BILL, BUTT, CABO, CAP, CAPO, HEAD, MULL, NAZE, NESS, NIEMI, POINT, POINTE, PUNTA.
CAPO *(Italian),* a headland.
See also BILL, BUTT, CABO, CAP, CAPE, HEAD, MULL, NAZE, NESS, NIEMI, POINT, POINTE, PUNTA.

CAR *(Gaelic)*, a fortress, crooked, bending.
See also CAER.
CARN *(Welsh)*, a heap of stones.
See also CAIRN.
CASTELO *(Portuguese)*, a castle.
See also CHÂTEAU.
CASTER *(Anglo-Saxon)*, a camp.
See also CHESTER.
CEFN *(Welsh)*, a ridge.
CHÂTEAU *(French)*, a castle.
See also CASTELO.
CHESTER *(Saxon)*, a camp.
See also CASTER.
CHIPPING *(Anglo-Saxon)*, a market.
CHOTT *(Arabic)*, salt-marsh.
CHUNTAO *(Chinese)*, archipelago.
See also RETTO.
CIUDAD *(Spanish)*, city.
See also ABAD, BAD, GRAD, PUR, STAD, STADT.
COED *(Celtic)*, a wood.
See also ROS.
COMBE *(Celto-Saxon)*, a bowl-shaped valley.
See also CUM, CWM.
CORDILLERA *(Spanish)*, mountain chain.
See also GEBIRGE, MONTAGNE, SIERRA.
CÔTE *(French)*, coast.
CRAIG *(Gaelic)*, a rock, rocky.
See also SCAR.
CRICK *(Gaelic)*, a crag.
CROFT *(Anglo-Saxon)*, an enclosed field.
CRUZ *(Spanish)*, cross.
CUM *(Celtic)* a bowl-shaped valley.
See also COMBE, CWM.
CWM *(Welsh)*, a bowl-shaped valley.
DAL *(Norwegian, Swedish)*, a valley.
See also DALE, DOL, DYFFRYN, GLEN, GLYN, NANT, TAL,
VAL, VALE, VALLE.
DALE *(Norse)*, a valley.
See also DAL, DOL, DYFFRYN, GLEN, GLYN, NANT, TAL, VAL,
VALE, VALLE.
DAR *(Arabic)*, house.
DARJA *(Persian)*, a river, sea.
See also HO, JOKKA, RIO.
DEN *(Anglo-Saxon)*, a wooded valley.
See also DENE.
DENE *(Anglo-Saxon)*, a wooded valley.
See also DEN.
DESERT *(Anglo-Saxon)*, a sandy or barren waste.
See also ERG, GOBI, KUM.
DOL *(Celtic)*, a dale, or field.
See also DAL, DALE, DYFFRYN, GLEN, GLYN, NANT, TAL,
VAL, VALE, VALLE.
DOR *(Celtic)*, a fort, or fortified place.
See also BORG, BOROUGH, BOURG, BROUGH, BURG, BURGH,
DUN, WARK.
DORF *(German)*, village.
See also BY, THORPE, TRE, VILA, VILLA, WICK.
DUN *(Celtic)*, a fort, or fortified town.
See also BORG, BOROUGH, BOURG, BROUGH, BURG,
BURGH, DOR, WARK.
DYFFRYN *(Welsh)*, a valley.
See also DAL, DALE, DOL, GLEN, GLYN, NANT, TAL, VAL,
VALE, VALLE.
ERG *(Arabic)*, a sandy desert.
See also DESERT, GOBI, KUM.
ESK *(Gaelic)*, water.
EY *(Icelandic)*, island.
See also AY, HOLM, ILE, INCH, INISH, INNIS, INSEL, JIMA,
O, Ö, OE, SAARI, SHIMA, TAO, YNYS.
FELL *(Scandinavian)*, a mountain.
See also BERG, FJÄLL, JABAL, MONT, MONTE, PEN, SHAN,
TJÅKKÅ, VAARA, YAMA.
FIELD *(Anglo-Saxon)*, a forest clearing where trees have
been felled.
See also CAMPO.
FIORD *(Icelandic, Norwegian)*, an estuary, or elongated
drowned valley.
See also FIRTH.
FIRTH *(Celtic)*, an estuary.

See also FIORD.
FJÄLL *(Swedish)*, a mountain.
See also BERG, FELL, JABAL, MONT, MONTE, PEN, SHAN,
TJÄKKÄ.
FLODDAL *(Swedish)*, a river valley.
See also WADI.
FLÓI *(Icelandic)*, a bay, or gulf.
See also BAIE, BAY, GOLFE, GOLFO, GULF, LAHTI, LUOKTA.
GEBIRGE *(German)*, a mountain chain.
See also CORDILLERA, MONTAGNE, SIERRA.
GILL *(Norse)*, a ravine.
GLEN *(Gaelic)*, a dale, or valley.
See also DAL, DALE, DOL, DYFFRYN, GLYN, NANT, TAL,
VAL, VALE, VALLE.
GLYN *(Welsh)*, a dale, or valley.
See also DAL, DALE, DOL, DYFFRYN, GLEN, NANT, TAL,
VAL, VALE, VALLE.
GOBI *(Mongolian)*, a desert.
See also DESERT, ERG, KUM.
GOLFE *(French)*, a gulf, or bay.
See also BAIE, BAY, FLÓI, GOLFO, GULF, LAHTI, LUOKTA.
GOLFO *(Spanish, Italian)*, a gulf, or bay.
See also BAIE, BAY, FLÓI, GOLFE, GULF, LAHTI, LUOKTA.
GRAD *(Slav.)*, a city.
See also ABAD, BAD, CIUDAD, GRAD, PUR, STAD, STADT.
GRAN *(Italian)*, great.
See also GRAND, GRANDE, GROSS, GROSSO, MORE.
GRAND *(Anglo-Saxon, French, Portuguese, Spanish)*, great.
See also GRAN, GRANDE, GROSS, GROSSO, MORE.
GRANDE *(French, Portuguese, Spanish)*, great.
See also GRAN, GRAND, GROSS, GROSSO, MORE.
GRANGE *(Scots)*, a corn farm, or granary.
GROSS *(German)*, great.
See also GRAN, GRAND, GRANDE, GROSSO, MORE.
GROSSO *(Portuguese)*, great.
See also GRAN, GRAND, GRANDE, GROSS, MORE.
GULF *(Anglo-Saxon)*, a bay.
See also BAIE, BAY, FLÓI, GOLFE, GOLFO, LAHTI, LUOKTA.
GWYN *(Welsh)*, white.
See also BLANC, BRANCO.
HAI *(Chinese)* sea, or lake.
See also BAHR, JÄRVI, LOCH, LOUGH, MER, MERE, NOR,
SEE, SJÖ, VATN, VESI, ZEE.
HAM *(Anglo-Saxon)*, an enclosure.
HAMN *(Swedish)* port, harbour.
See also HAVEN, HAVN, PORTH, PORTO, PUERTO.
HANTO *(Japanese)*, peninsula.
HASSI *(Arabic)*, well.
HAVEN *(German)*, port, harbour.
See also HAMN, HAVN, PORTH, PORTO, PUERTO.
HAVN *(Danish)*, port, harbour.
See also HAMN, HAVEN, PORTH, PORTO, PUERTO.
HEAD *(Anglo-Saxon)*, a headland.
See also BILL, BUTT, CABO, CAP, CAPE, CAPO, MULL, NAZE,
NESS, NIEMI, POINT, PUNTA.
HEATH *(Anglo-Saxon)*, shrub-covered wasteland.
HINTER *(German)*, further.
HITHE *(Anglo-Saxon)*, a wharf.
HO *(Chinese)*, river.
See also AFON, ÄLV, AVON, BAHR, DARJA, JOKI, JOKKA,
KIANG, RIO.
HOLM *(Scandinavian)*, an island, especially in a river.
See also AY, EY, ILE, INCH, INISH, INNIS, INSEL, JIMA, O,
Ö, OE, SAARI, SHIMA, TAO, YNYS.
HOLT *(Anglo-Saxon)*, a copse.
HRÁUN *(Icelandic)*, lava flow.
HSIEN *(Chinese)*, town.
See also BY, KÖPING, TON.
HU *(Chinese)*, lake.
See also BAHR, HAI, JÄRVI, LAC, LAGO, LOCH, LOUGH,
MERE, NOR, SJÖ.
HURST *(Anglo-Saxon)*, a thick wood.
ILE *(French)*, an island.
See also AY, EY, HOLM, INCH, INISH, INNIS, INSEL, JIMA, O,
Ö, OE, SAARI, SHIMA, TAO, YNYS.
INCH *(Celtic)*, an island.
See also AY, EY, HOLM, ILE, INISH, INNIS, INSEL, JIMA, O,
Ö, OE, SAARI, SHIMA, TAO, YNYS.
ING *(Scandinavian)*, family, tribe, meadow.

INISH *(Celtic),* an island.
See also AY, EY, HOLM, ILE, INCH, INNIS, INSEL, JIMA, O,
Ö, OE, SAARI, SHIMA, TAO, YNYS.
INNIS *(Celtic),* an island.
See also AY, EY, HOLM, ILE, INCH, INISH, INSEL, JIMA, O,
Ö, OE, SAARI, SHIMA, TAO, YNYS.
INSEL *(German),* an island.
See also AY, EY, HOLM, ILE, INCH, INISH, INNIS, JIMA, O,
Ö, OE, SAARI, SHIMA, TAO, YNYS.
INVER *(Gaelic),* mouth of a river.
JABAL *(Arabic),* mountain.
See also BERG, FELL, FJÄLL, MONT, MONTE, PEN, SHAN,
TJÅKKÅ, VAARA, YAMA.
JÄRVI *(Finnish),* lake.
See also BAHR, HAI, HU, LAC, LAGO, LOCH, LOUGH, MERE,
NOR, SJÖ, VATN, VESI.
JIMA *(Japanese),* an island, sandbank.
See also AY, EY, HOLM, ILE, INCH, INISH, INNIS, INSEL, O,
Ö, OE, SAARI, SHIMA, TAO, YNYS.
JOKI *(Finnish),* river.
See also AFON, ÄLV, AVON, BAHR, DARJA, HO, JOKKA,
KIANG, RIO.
JOKK *(Lapp),* stream.
See also BURN.
JOKKA *(Lapp),* river.
See also AFON, ÄLV, AVON, BAHR, DARJA, HO, JOKI, KIANG, RIO.
KAISE *(Lapp),* peak.
KEN *(Gaelic),* head, top.
See also KIN.
KERRY *(Gaelic),* cauldron, glen.
KIANG *(Chinese),* river.
See also AFON, ÄLV, AVON, BAHR, HO, JOKI, JOKKA, RIO.
KILL *(Gaelic),* church.
See also KIRK.
KIN *(Gaelic),* head, top.
See also KEN.
KIRK *(Scots),* church.
See also KILL.
KÖPING *(Swedish),* town.
See also BY, HSIEN, TON.
KOSKI *(Finnish),* rapids.
KUM *(Turkish),* desert.
See also ERG, GOBI.
LAC *(French),* lake.
See also BAHR, HAI, HU, JÄRVI, LAGO, LOCH, LOUGH, MERE,
NOR, SJÖ, VATN, VESI.
LAGO *(Italian, Portuguese, Spanish),* lake.
See also BAHR, HAI, HU, JÄRVI, LAC, LOCH, LOUGH, NOR,
SJÖ, VATN, VESI.
LAHTI *(Finnish),* gulf or bay.
See also BAIE, BAY, FLÓI, GOLFE, GOLFO, GULF, LUOKTA.
LAW *(Anglo-Saxon),* a mound.
See also LOW.
LEIGH *(Anglo-Saxon),* woodland clearing.
See also LEY.
LEY *(Anglo-Saxon),* clearing in a wood.
See also LEIGH.
LINN *(Celtic),* a deep pool.
See also LLYN.
LLANO *(Spanish),* plain.
LLYN *(Welsh),* a deep pool.
See also LINN.
LOCH *(Celtic),* lake, arm of the sea.
See also BAHR, HAI, HU, JÄRVI, LAC, LAGO, LOUGH, NOR,
SJÖ, VATN, VESI.
LOUGH *(Gaelic),* lake, arm of the sea.
See also BAHR, HAI, HU, JÄRVI, LAC, LAGO, LOCH, MERE, NOR,
SJÖ, VATN, VESI.
LOW *(Anglo-Saxon),* a mound.
See also LAW.
LUOKTA *(Lapp),* gulf or bay.
See also BAIE, BAY, FLÓI, GOLFE, GOLFO, GULF, LAHTI.
MÄKI *(Finnish),* a hill, or slope.
See also BARROW, MON.
MER *(French),* sea.
See also BAHR, HAI, SEE.
MERE *(Anglo-Saxon),* lake.
See also BAHR, HAI, HU, JÄRVI, LAC, LAGO, LOCH, LOUGH,
NOR, SJÖ, VATN, VESI.

MINSTER *(Anglo-Saxon),* monastery.
MON *(Gaelic),* a hill.
See also BARROW, MÄKI.
MONT *(French),* a mountain.
See also BERG, FELL, FJÄLL, JABAL, MONTE, PEN, SHAN,
TJÅKKÅ, VAARA, YAMA.
MONTAGNE *(French),* mountain range.
See also CORDILLERA, GEBIRGE, SIERRA.
MONTE *(Italian, Portuguese, Spanish),* mountain.
See also BERG, FELL, FJÄLL, JABAL, MONT, PEN, SHAN,
TJÅKKÅ, VAARA, YAMA.
MOOR *(Anglo-Saxon),* open waste ground.
See also CAMPO, MUIR.
MORE *(Celtic)* great.
See also GRAN, GRAND, GRANDE, GROSS, GROSSO.
MUIR *(Scots),* a moor.
See also CAMPO, MOOR.
MULL *(Gaelic),* a headland.
See also BILL, BUTT, CABO, CAP, CAPE, CAPO, HEAD, NAZE,
NESS, NIEMI, POINT, POINTE, PUNTA.
NANT *(Welsh),* a valley; sometimes a stream.
See also DAL, DALE, DOL, DYFFRYN, GLEN, GLYN, TAL, VAL,
VALE, VALLE.
NAZE *(Norse),* a headland.
See also BILL, BUTT, CABO, CAP, CAPE, CAPO, HEAD, MULL,
NESS, NIEMI, POINT, POINTE, PUNTA.
NESS *(Gaelic),* a headland.
See also BILL, BUTT, CABO, CAP, CAPE, CAPO, HEAD, MULL,
NAZE, NIEMI, POINT, POINTE, PUNTA.
NETHER *(Anglo-Saxon),* lower.
See also NIEDER.
NEU *(German),* new.
See also NEUF, NOVO.
NEUF *(French),* new.
See also NEU, NOVO.
NIEDER *(German),* lower.
See also NETHER.
NIEMI *(Finnish),* headland.
See also BILL, BUTT, CABO, CAP, CAPE, CAPO, HEAD, MULL,
NAZE, NESS, POINT, POINTE, PUNTA.
NOR *(Mongolian),* lake.
See also BAHR, HAI, HU, JÄRVI, LAC, LAGO, LOCH, LOUGH,
MERE, SJÖ, VATN, VESI.
NOVO *(Italian),* new.
See also NEU, NEUF.
O *(Danish, Norwegian)* island.
See also AY, EY, HOLM, ILE, INCH, INISH, INNIS, INSEL, JIMA,
Ö, OE, SAARI, SHIMA, TAO, YNYS.
Ö *(Swedish)* island.
See also AY, EY, HOLM, ILE, INCH, INISH, INNIS, INSEL, JIMA,
O, OE, SAARI, SHIMA, TAO, YNYS.
OBER *(German),* upper.
OCCIDENTAL *(French, Spanish),* western.
OE *(Norse),* an island.
See also AY, EY, HOLM, ILE, INCH, INISH, INNIS, INSEL, JIMA,
O, Ö, SAARI, SHIMA, TAO, YNYS.
OR *(Anglo-Saxon),* a shore, or bank.
See also OVER.
ORD *(Gaelic),* high, a height.
See also ALTO, ARD.
ORIENTAL *(French, Spanish),* eastern.
OVER *(Anglo-Saxon),* a shore.
See also OR.
ÖVRE *(Swedish),* upper.
See also AUCHTER, UPPER.
PAS *(French),* sound, straits.
See also SUND.
PEN *(Welsh),* mountain.
See also BERG, FELL, FJÄLL, JABAL, MONT, MONTE, SHAN,
TJÅKKÅ, VAARA, YAMA.
PETIT *(French),* little.
See also BACH.
PIC *(French),* a peak.
See also PICO, PIK, SPITZE, TJOKKO.
PICO *(Spanish),* peak.
See also PIC, PIK, SPITZE, TJOKKO.
PIK *(Russian),* peak.
See also PIC, PICO, SPITZE, TJOKKO.
POINT *(Anglo-Saxon),* a headland.

See also BILL, BUTT, CABO, CAP, CAPE, CAPO, HEAD, MULL, NAZE, NESS, NIEMI, POINTE, PUNTA.
POINTE *(French)*, a headland.
See also BILL, BUTT, CABO, CAP, CAPE, CAPO, HEAD, MULL, NAZE, NESS, NIEMI, POINT, PUNTA.
PONT *(Welsh)*, a bridge.
See also BRO.
PORTH *(Welsh)*, a port.
See also HAMN, HAVEN, HAVN, PORTO, PUERTO.
PORTO *(Italian, Portuguese, Spanish)*, port, harbour.
See also HAMN, HAVEN, HAVN, PORTH, PUERTO.
PUEBLA *(Spanish)*, town, or village.
See also PUEBLO.
PUEBLO *(Spanish)*, town, or village.
See also PUEBLA.
PUERTO *(Spanish)*, port, harbour, pass.
See also HAMN, HAVEN, HAVN, PORTH, PORTO.
PUNTA *(Italian, Spanish)*, headland.
See also BILL, BUTT, CABO, CAP, CAPE, CAPO, HEAD, MULL, NAZE, NESS, NIEMI, POINT, POINTE.
PUR *(Hindi, Urdu)*, city.
See also ABAD, BAD, CIUDAD, GRAD, STAD, STADT.
RETTO *(Japanese)*, archipelago.
See also CHUNTAO.
RIO *(Portuguese, Spanish)*, river.
See also AFON, ÄLV, AVON, BAHR, DARJA, HO, JOKI, JOKKA, KIANG.
ROS *(Celtic)*, a wood, sometimes a promontory or headland.
See also COED.
ROUGE *(French)*, red.
See also ULAN.
SAARI *(Finnish)*, island.
See also AY, EY, HOLM, ILE, INCH, INISH, INNIS, INSEL, JIMA, O, Ö, OE, SHIMA, TAO, YNYS.
SAN *(Italian)*, saint (male).
See also SANTO, SÃO.
SANTA *(Italian, Portuguese, Spanish)*, saint (female).
SANTO *(Spanish)*, saint (male).
See also SAN, SÃO.
SÃO *(Portuguese)*, saint (male).
See also SAN, SANTO.
SCAR *(Norse)*, a rock.
See also CRAIG.
SEE *(German)*, sea or lake.
See also BAHR, HAI, JÄRVI, LAC, LOUGH, MER, NOR, ZEE.
SHAN *(Chinese)*, mountain.
See also BERG, FELL, FJÄLL, JABAL, MONT, MONTE, PEN, TJÅKKÅ, VAARA, YAMA.
SHIMA *(Japanese)*, island.
See also AY, EY, HOLM, ILE, INCH, INISH, INNIS, INSEL, JIMA, O, Ö, OE, SAARI, TAO, YNYS.
SHOTO *(Japanese)*, islands.
SIERRA *(Spanish)*, mountain range.
See also CORDILLERA, GEBIRGE, MONTAGNE.
SJÖ *(Swedish)*, lake.
See also BAHR, HAI, HU, JÄRVI, LAC, LAGO, LOCH, LOUGH, MERE, NOR, VATN, VESI.
SPITZE *(German)*, peak.
See also PIC, PICO, PIK, TJOKKO.
STAD *(Swedish)*, city town.
See also BAD, CIUDAD, GRAD, PUR, STADT.
STADT *(German)*, city, town.
See also ABAD, BAD, CIUDAD, GRAD, PUR, STAD.
STAN *(Norse)*, a stone.
See also STEN.
STEN *(Icelandic)*, a stone.
See also STAN.
STOKE *(Anglo-Saxon)*, a stockaded place.
See also STOW.
STOUR *(Anglo-Saxon)*, water.
STOW *(Anglo-Saxon)*, a stockaded place.
See also STOKE.
STRATH *(Gaelic)*, wide valley.
SUND *(Danish, Swedish)*, sound, channel, strait.
See also PAS.
TAL *(German)*, valley.
See also DAL, DALE, DOL, DYFFRYN, GLEN, GLYN, NANT, VAL, VALE, VALLE.
TAO *(Chinese)*, island.

See also AY, EY, HOLM, ILE, INCH, INISH, INNIS, INSEL, JIMA, O, Ö, OE, SAARI, SHIMA, YNYS.
TARN *(Norse)*, small mountain lake.
TERRE *(French)*, land
See also TIERRA, ZEMLJA.
THORPE *(Danish)*, a village.
See also BY, DORF, TRE, VILA, VILLA, WICK.
THWAITE *(Norse)*, a forest clearing.
TIERRA *(Spanish)*, land.
See also TERRE, ZEMLJA.
TIPPER *(Erse)*, a spring.
See also TOBER.
TJOKKO *(Lapp)*, a peak.
See also PIC, PICO, PIK, SPITZE.
TJÅKKÅ *(Lapp)*, mountain.
See also BERG, FELL, FJÄLL, JABAL, MONT, MONTE, PEN, SHAN, VARRA, YAMA.
TOBER *(Gaelic)*, a spring.
See also TIPPER.
TON *(Anglo-Saxon)*, a town, or village.
See also BY, HSIEN, KÖPING.
TOR, *(Celtic)*, a rock pinnacle.
TRÄSK *(Swedish)*, a marshy lake.
TRE *(Cymric)*, a village.
See also BY, DORF, THORPE, VILA, VILLA, WICK.
ULAN *(Mongolian)*, red.
See also ROUGE.
UPPER *(English)*, upper.
See also AUCHTER, ÖVRE.
VAARA *(Finnish)*, a mountain.
See also BERG, FELL, FJÄLL, JABAL, MONT, MONTE, PEN, SHAN, TJÅKKÅ, YAMA.
VAL *(Italian)*, a valley.
See also DAL, DALE, DOL, DYFFRYN, GLEN, GLYN, NANT, TAL, VALE, VALLE.
VALE *(Anglo-Saxon)*, a valley.
See also DAL, DALE, DOL, DYFFRYN, GLEN, GLYN, NANT, TAL, VAL, VALLE.
VALLE *(Spanish)*, valley.
See also DAL, DALE, DOL, DYFFRYN, GLEN, GLYN, NANT, TAL, VAL, VALE.
VATN *(Norwegian)*, lake.
See also BAHR, HAI, HU, LAC, LAGO, LOCH, LOUGH, MERE, NOR, SJÖ, VESI.
VESI *(Finnish)*, a lake.
See also BAHR, HAI, HU, JÄRVI, LAC, LAGO, LOCH, LOUGH, MERE, NOR, SJÖ, VATN.
VIK *(Swedish)*, small bay, or inlet.
See also VOE.
VILA *(Portuguese)* village; small town.
See also BY, DORF, THORPE, TRE, VILLA, WICK.
VILLA *(Spanish)*, a town, or village.
See also BY, DORF, THORPE, TRE, VILA, WICK.
VILLE *(French)*, an abode.
See also BY.
VOE *(Norse)*, a small bay, or inlet.
See also VIK.
WADI *(Arabic)*, a river valley.
See also FLODDAL.
WALD *(German)*, a forest.
See also WOLD.
WARK *(Norse)*, a fortress.
See also BORG, BOROUGH, BOURG, BROUGH, BURG, BURGH, DOR, DUN.
WEALD *(Anglo-Saxon)*, woodland.
WICK *(Anglo-Saxon)*, a village.
See also BY, DORF, THORPE, TRE, VILA, VILLA.
WOLD *(Anglo-Saxon)*, a forest.
See also WALD.
YAMA *(Japanese)*, a mountain.
See also BERG, FELL, FJÄLL, JABAL, MONT, MONTE, PEN, SHAN, TJÅKKÅ, VAARA.
YNYS *(Welsh)*, an island.
See also AY, EY, HOLM, ILE, INCH, INISH, INNIS, INSEL, JIMA, O, Ö, OE, SAARI, SHIMA, TAO.
ZEE *(Dutch)*, sea.
See also HAI, SEE.
ZEMLJA *(Russian)*, land.
See also TERRE, TIERRA.

DISTANCES, AIR ROUTES

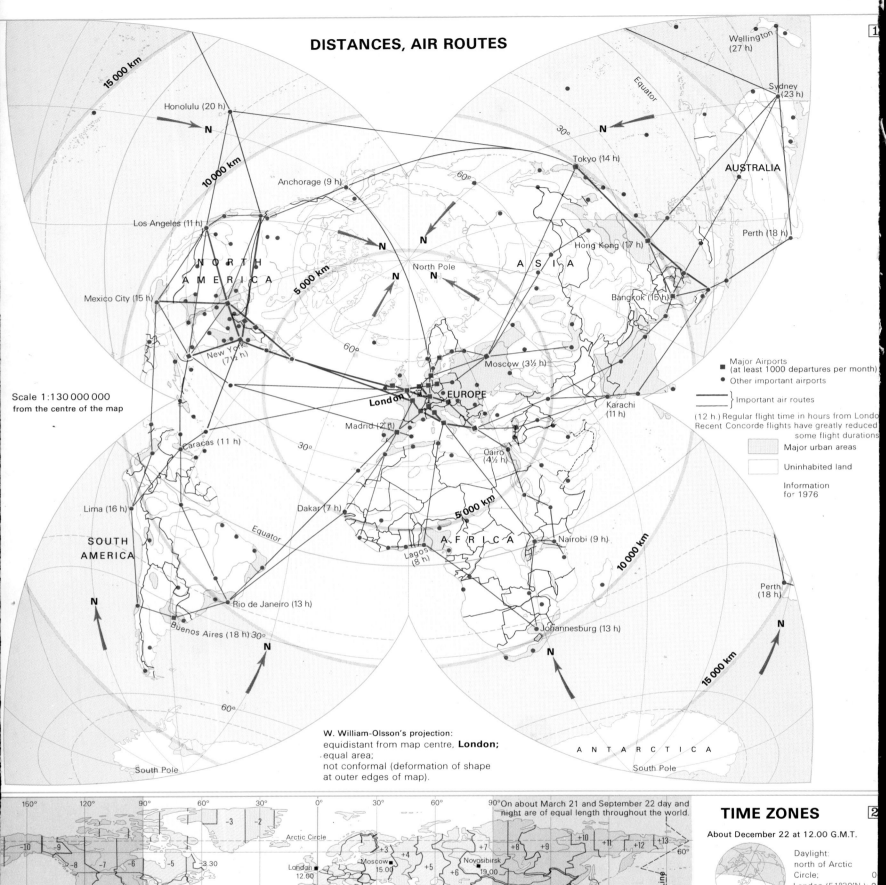

W. William-Olsson's projection:
equidistant from map centre, **London;**
equal area;
not conformal (deformation of shape
at outer edges of map).

Scale 1:130 000 000
from the centre of the map

Major Airports
(at least 1000 departures per month)
● Other important airports
} Important air routes
(12 h.) Regular flight time in hours from London
Recent Concorde flights have greatly reduced
some flight durations
Major urban areas
Uninhabited land
Information
for 1976

Selected labels: Wellington (27 h), Sydney (23 h), Honolulu (20 h), Anchorage (9 h), Tokyo (14 h), Perth (18 h), Los Angeles (11 h), Hong Kong (17 h), Mexico City (15 h), Bangkok (15 h), New York (7½ h), Moscow (3½ h), London, Madrid (2 h), Karachi (11 h), Caracas (11 h), Cairo (4½ h), Lima (16 h), Dakar (7 h), Nairobi (9 h), Rio de Janeiro (13 h), Lagos (8 h), Buenos Aires (18 h), Johannesburg (13 h)

North Pole · South Pole · NORTH AMERICA · SOUTH AMERICA · EUROPE · ASIA · AFRICA · AUSTRALIA · ANTARCTICA · Equator

Distance rings: 5 000 km, 10 000 km, 15 000 km

TIME ZONES

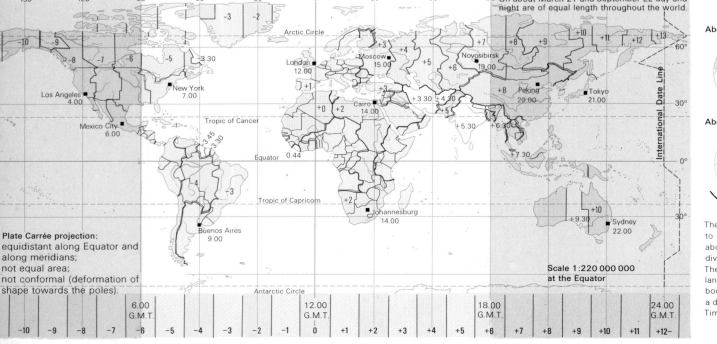

Plate Carrée projection:
equidistant along Equator and
along meridians;
not equal area;
not conformal (deformation of
shape towards the poles).

90° On about March 21 and September 22 day and
night are of equal length throughout the world.

Scale 1:220 000 000
at the Equator

City local times: Los Angeles 4.00, Mexico City 6.00, New York 7.00, Buenos Aires 9.00, London 12.00, Cairo 14.00, Johannesburg 14.00, Moscow 15.00, Novosibirsk 19.00, Peking 20.00, Tokyo 21.00, Sydney 22.00

About December 22 at 12.00 G.M.T.
Daylight:
north of Arctic
Circle;   0
London (51°30'N.); 8
at the Equator   12

About June 21 at 12.00 G.M.T.
Daylight:
north of Arctic
Circle;   24
London (51°30'N.); 17
at the Equator   12

→ direction of Earth's rotation

The Earth rotates on its axis from west
to east and completes one rotation in
about 24 hours. The Earth has been
divided into 24 Standard Time Zones.
The lines separating these Zones on
land mostly follow country or province
boundaries. Many countries however use
a different standard, eg. British Summer
Time.